Please accept this book, freely given as a

Gift of Love

from

Wisdom Master Maticintin

INITIATION

It is a story of honesty, spiritual courage, and divine love.

The Wisdom Master hopes that you will enjoy it, and share it with others.

♥

If you have any questions, or would like to write to Wisdom Master Maticintin, you can do so by e-mailing her at: office@HUMUH.org.

Higher Consciousness Books

2005

INITIATION

International Copyright © 2005 HUMUH
Printed in the United States of America

All rights reserved. No part of this book may be reproduced or transmitted, in any form or by any means now known or to be invented, electronic or mechanical, including photocopying, recording, or by any information storage or retrieval system whatsoever, without written permission from the author or publisher, except for inclusion of brief quotation in a review.

ISBN# 0-932927-20-3

Rose drawing on back cover by Larry Mishler

HÜMÜH™
TRANSCENDENTAL AWARENESS
The Jeweled Path of Transcendental Wisdom™

♦

P.O. Box 2700, Oroville, WA 98844 USA
or P.O. Box 701, Osoyoos, B.C. V0H 1V0 Canada
Phone/fax (250) 446-2022 / Phone Orders (800) 336-6015
E-mail: office@HUMUH.org   Web Site: http://www.HUMUH.org

To my beloved Teacher, Wisdom Master Maticintin, who guides me every step of the way. She is the handrail on this rickety bridge I am crossing. And to Ryan and Rachael, may you discover the road that leads you to your true destiny.

Table of Contents

	Preface	7
Prologue	When the Student Is Ready	9
Chapter 1	Meeting My Teacher	13
Chapter 2	Initiations and Journeys	22
Chapter 3	Preparing to Visit Eastcliffe	31
Chapter 4	Eastcliffe	46
Chapter 5	The Medicine Walk	64
Chapter 6	A Foot in Each World	76
Chapter 7	A Painful Lesson on Impermanence	91
Chapter 8	The First Empowerment	101
Chapter 9	Expanding Horizons	113
Chapter 10	Unanticipated Disturbances	126
Chapter 11	An Opportunity to Serve	135
Chapter 12	Living in the Moment	149
Chapter 13	A Big Lesson	169
Chapter 14	Expectations Uncovered	180
Chapter 15	Box Mentality	186
Chapter 16	The Teacher Begins to Reel Me In	196
Chapter 17	The Value of Life	214
Chapter 18	The Divine Consciousness Moves Quickly	240
Chapter 19	Attachments Threaten My Apprenticeship	253
Chapter 20	Endings and Beginnings	267
Chapter 21	Embracing My Destiny	278
Chapter 22	The Bodhisattva Vow	293
Chapter 23	Being With the Nature of the Enlightened Mind	306
Chapter 24	Expansion	319

Chapter 25	Feedom from Limitations	341
Chapter 26	Freedom Lives without Limitations	344
Chapter 27	Everything All at Once	366
Chapter 28	My Teacher Is a Buddha	380
Chapter 29	Ordination Day	397
Chapter 30	The Fall	401
Chapter 31	Satiety with Life	411
Epilogue	The Pieces Fall into Place	422

"The prize of enlightenment is not easily won, it is all-consuming. Instead of clasping it as a prize, one must yield to it."

Wisdom Master Maticintin
-- Preface, page 7

Preface

Sakyamuni and Padmasambhava, both of whom were buddhas and great teachers of the transhistorical consciousness, touched the lives of a multitude of people through their tremendous capacity to love. Their love was heartfelt, selfless, and spontaneous, and because of this, was able to penetrate the dark clouds that bonded the human minds of their time. This is not to say that the influence wielded by these buddhas has waned any, quite the contrary. Their influence has cultivated and inspired the minds and consciousness of modern spiritual teachers, those who were their students long ago, in those ancient lifetimes. Thus is the thread of spiritual lineage as it weaves through time and space.

Initiation is a true account of the relationship of a student and her spiritual teacher. It tells the actual story of an initiate's transformational experiences and her courageous struggles to transcend the limitations of her ordinary/habitual mind into an enlightened consciousness. She learns that the prize of enlightenment is not easily won; that it is all-consuming; that, instead of clasping it as a prize, she must yield to it. For Sharon Shier it is a continuing story, with a sequel already in the making.

Wisdom Master Maticintin

PROLOGUE
When the Student Is Ready

February 24, 1992

It was a bitter-cold, gray, blustery winter day, typical of Michigan in February. Normally it was not I who walked to our mailbox to retrieve the day's mail. Between my husband Walter and my son Terry there had always been a friendly competition to see who could get to the mailbox first, so I never concerned myself with it. Besides, it usually contained loads of junk mail and many bills, which at that time in our lives, we were always hard put to pay.

This day, however, Walter was away at a business conference and Terry had returned to finish his last semester at college. I saw the mail truck pull up and the postman open our box. Reluctantly, I put on my winter coat and boots and walked down the long driveway. There was the anticipated stack of magazines, bills, catalogues and advertisements.

As I absently sorted through the mail, intending to place most of it on Walter's desk, a postcard fell out on the dining room table and caught my eye. On it was a painting of a stunning woman who looked like a shaman or medicine woman, fierce and commanding.

At that time I was in an artistic phase, teaching myself to draw by using a technique of upside-down copying. I had picked up a well-known book, *Drawing from the Right Side of the Brain,* while on a trip to Carmel, and it taught me that by drawing upside down, I could disengage the part of my brain that controlled my perceptions as to how things looked. Oddly, it proposed that how I perceived things was not how they really were.

It was fascinating to see the transformation that drawing upside down had made on my otherwise elementary artistic abilities. As long as I turned a picture upside down, I could draw a pretty decent replica of most anything, including people, the idea being that my brain no longer had an idea of what it was that I was drawing, and therefore, would not distort through misperception.

Anyway, this picture on the postcard fascinated me. The presence of this woman was so powerful that I couldn't stop gazing at her. Quickly glancing at the reverse side of the postcard, I noted that it was announcing the availability of a book titled *'Woman Between the Wind.'* The author was unfamiliar to me, but I found the title of the book intriguing. After a short debate, I decided that I wouldn't purchase the book since I didn't recognize the author, but I would keep the picture to draw later. So, placing the post card in my special drawing drawer for future use, the whole incident promptly slipped my mind.

July 1992

Six months later, as I was cleaning out that drawer, the postcard once again presented itself to me. This time, I ordered the book. I figured the author had excellent taste in paintings, so perhaps her writing would also be of that quality.

At this point in my life, I had been remarried for four years and was working two jobs, one as a therapist in private practice and the other as a school social worker for a large, inner city school district. Walter had two teen-age children at the time we married, a son Rex and daughter Michelle, both of whom I felt blessed to have in my life. At various times they had lived with us along with my sons Kevin and Terry. Now, we only had Kevin, who had just begun his first year in law school, with us full time, and the others were off at college, but home on vacations and during the summers. My elderly parents (now in their early eighties) visited us during the summer and stayed anywhere from three to five months. So my physical life was full. My spiritual life had taken wings a few years prior to receiving the postcard with the beautiful woman on it, but was teacher-less.

For about three years prior to this experience, I had been meeting with a group of a dozen or so local men and women for the purpose of studying spiritual material together. We were an odd lot of characters from all different walks of life and circumstances, but there was a common bond among us. We were all disenfranchised from organized religion, yet we had strong spiritual yearnings without means of fulfilling them.

The other thing we had in common was a belief that we could be self-taught; and therefore, we were a self-directed group. Between us, we had studied many different paths, attended workshops, and adapted our own style to what we learned. At the point I received the postcard, we were practicing various shamanic and meditative techniques mostly by trial and error.

Enthusiasm and sincerity of purpose had carried us along for quite a while, but at the time I received that postcard, the truth was that we were floundering, stuck in our own egos, spinning, not knowing how to take the next step. Deep down I knew it, but denied it vehemently up front. After all, we were a self-directed group. It was painful to admit that no one could figure out what we should do next, especially me.

When it happened serendipitously that I cleaned out that catch-all drawer and once again ran into the postcard, there was no denying it was time for a change. Perhaps this author would have some new ideas for us to delve into. I knew there were no accidents in life, and here she was showing up in my life at a time when I was really stuck.

The book arrived a few days later. I began reading it immediately, and became so totally engrossed that I couldn't put it down.

Having finished it late the same night, to my surprise and delight, I noticed at the end of the book a letter inviting me (the reader) to request an application if I was interested in becoming an apprentice. Wow, was I ever interested! After reading this book, I knew beyond a doubt that I wanted to become a shaman and I wanted the author, whose power name was Winged Wolf, to be my Teacher. I wrote a letter right then asking for an application and telling her a bit about myself, then waited eagerly for a response.

As I waited, I worried. Surely she would be too expensive, or she would find me unacceptable as a student, or there would be some assignment I had to complete to prove myself worthy, or, or, or. It couldn't be this easy. It couldn't be happening to *me*. This was the stuff you read about in other people's books about their lives. Gone was any memory of the thought that I didn't need a teacher. Suddenly, I wanted this more than

I had ever wanted anything, and I didn't even know why. This book was going to change my destiny; I could feel it.

August 1992

Every day for the next ten days I dashed home from work and hurried to check the mail. Never had I taken such an active interest in what was coming to us. On the tenth day, Walter met me at the door. *"You've got something from her,"* he grinned, knowing how anxiously I had been waiting.

The envelope was on the dining room table, all by itself. The name and address were handwritten and I wondered if that was her handwriting. Before opening it, I said a prayer *'please let her accept me,'* feeling that she would because it seemed so right, yet not really knowing her or what she might expect. My heart was racing as I opened the envelope and tried to brace myself for whatever answer it might contain.

Her response was brief but potent; the envelope contained a letter that said, *"Thank you for your very sincere letter and application......Initiation Journey 1 is enclosed. It will take you over the threshold. Please read it over carefully aloud to yourself."* And here was the treasured Journey about which I knew nothing except it felt sacred and life-altering and filled with secret Teachings.

My heart was singing; she had accepted my application. *"Take me over the threshold,"* I repeated the words aloud, heart thumping in my chest. Those words carried such power. I didn't know exactly what she meant, but I knew the bottom line was I had taken the first step toward becoming a shaman. My apprenticeship had begun.

The joy I experienced when the Teacher accepted me as her apprentice will forever be imprinted in my memory. First of all, it confirmed my sense that I was destined to be with her. And, to my great surprise and relief, her fees were so reasonable that any suspicions I might have had that she was teaching for the money were extinguished. Also this meant I could afford to be a long-term apprentice. All the built-up anxiety of receiving that first response completely evaporated.

Chapter 1
Meeting My Teacher

November, 1992

Here I was, standing in the Arizona desert face to face with my Teacher for the first time and shaking in my shoes. My husband, in contrast, was the picture of confidence and anticipation; at least it seemed that way to me. She had sent him off to explore the river that flowed through the back of her property and turned to face me. Her penetrating blue eyes pierced me and I felt naked and exposed, and terribly inadequate. Here I stood, at the gateway to all I had dreamed for myself, and I could only cry, shiver and shake.

"What are you crying about?" she asked, seeming genuinely interested.

"I'm afraid," I said in a wavering voice.

"Of what?" Again she gazed steadily at me, holding my eyes for a moment. I looked away. My Teacher was an unusual looking person. She had clear, dark blue eyes which, when she fixed them on me, carried the power to see through me to my core. She was physically solid, about 5'6", with striking features. There was nothing fragile at all in her appearance. Her body was not heavy, but it was full and muscular. Her hair was pure white and flowed freely to her shoulders. When she walked, there was a solidness of total purpose and foundation, each step planted firmly on the ground headed in a particular direction. She was a force to be reckoned with.

By contrast, I saw myself as tentative and lacking the courage to trust myself. While we were the same height, I was not so solid on my feet and felt unsure of myself, especially in unfamiliar situations. While I had worked hard to become an assertive, self-confident woman, independent and self-reliant, if one scratched the surface, underneath there still lived the fear of being inadequate. I still believed the answers lived outside of myself. *"I'm afraid I'm not up to the task."* Now I was really sniffling. Hearing the words out loud, I realized how true this statement was. Barely at the beginning of my apprenticeship and already I wanted to run as far as I could to escape the feelings that were flooding me in waves as this powerful woman continued to gaze at me.

'She must think me a coward and a wimp,' I flashed, as in my peripheral vision I could see my husband, who had also become an apprentice, leaping happily over the rocks in the freezing cold river. I knew it was cold because earlier we had all taken a walk down to the water's edge and put our feet in. It was probably a hundred feet across, crystal-clear and cold. Mountains on the other side framed it, and Winged Wolf had told us that in the evenings with a full moon, the mountains turned a brilliant, shimmering white. She said it was a magical sight and perhaps we would one day see it, maybe even climb it. I shivered at the thought of what might be lurking in those mountains.

"Of what are you afraid?" she asked again, and I realized I had wandered off in my mind, hoping to find a hiding place from that gaze. But when I looked up at her, there was still that patient look, kind, but there was fierceness to it, and I thought of the eagle circling its prey, and shivered again. Once again I could feel myself leave this moment, as I remembered a time not so long ago when I was not an apprentice, a time when I thought I didn't need a teacher.

"That I won't be able to do this," I finally admitted, lowering my eyes. I felt my cheeks redden as I continued, *"and I'm not sure I want to be 100% responsible for my thoughts and actions."* What a dumb thing to say. I couldn't even look at her. My Teacher had recently sent me a new Initiation Journey, and in it she posed the question: *"Pause and ask yourself, are you willing to be TOTALLY responsible for yourself?"* And when I read this, I froze with fear and every fiber of my being screamed 'NO!' I told her this, and immediately I felt better. It was out in the open. I could go home now, if she agreed with me, and my little adventure into apprenticeship would be complete. Already this was more than I had bargained for and nothing had even happened, at least nothing I could put a finger on.

"Of course you can do it," she said, dismissing my fear matter-of-factly.

"And you're forgetting the best part. It is only through total responsibility that you can achieve total freedom, and you do want total freedom, don't you?" And that was that, as far as she was concerned.

We began to walk, my mind racing. She had trapped me and I knew it, because I did desperately want freedom. Even though I couldn't have said exactly what freedom was, I wanted it more than I wanted to run. The way she spoke the word 'freedom' created such energy around my heart that I thought it would burst. This person really believed in me, like I had never believed in myself. She took me seriously, and because she did, I did.

But as would often happen in my experience with her, there was a dual effect: on the one hand, there was an awareness of the heights I could attain if I kept my attention on where I was going; on the other, I could feel the grip of responsibility tighten on me just a bit. I knew she was already beginning to reel me in, and my little-self balked. *'This isn't the first time. This has happened before,'* flashed through my mind quickly, so quickly I couldn't grab hold of it, and then it was gone.

Winged Wolf had been talking as we walked. I realized because of all my mind chatter I had missed some of what she was saying. With great effort I returned my attention to what was being said.

What I heard was, *"Don't look at what you **cannot** do. Instead, look at what you **can** do. The little-self, which is personality, sees the job at hand and says, 'I can't' or 'it's too difficult.' Divine self sees the big picture and knows It can do anything It wants to, and those are not just words. If you stick around long enough, you will come to know I am speaking the truth. But you have to stay long enough to test it out."*

The afternoon ended, and we headed back to Los Abrigados, where Walt and I had been staying in the beautiful town of Sedona. We had discovered Sedona too late, really. It was congested, touristy and full of new-age seekers, but I could picture what it must have looked like to the original settlers. The pristine beauty of Oak Creek and the West Fork, the spectacular red rock formations were breathtakingly beautiful, and our Teacher had been there before it was discovered, so we had the privilege of seeing it through her eyes, too.

As we headed back to our hotel, I might just as well have been on another planet; somehow the encounter had shaken me to my core, and thus I was silent as we drove back. What had just happened? Nothing really. It was only a simple interaction with the Teacher. Why was I feeling this way? Walter didn't seem affected like this. He was exuberant from the adventure, but unscathed by the encounter with the most powerful being I had ever known in my lifetime. So I barely heard him when he said, *"She suggested we meet to go to the West Fork of Oak Creek Canyon for a walk tomorrow or the next day."*

Involuntarily I shuddered. Could I withstand another confrontation such as the one encountered today? If my identity were starting to break apart after one interaction, what would happen if I spent even more time with her? Secretly I longed to pack up and fly home to my totally safe, suburban existence, where I could study the Teachings at a distance. But something inside me stood firm and insisted I stay and walk my talk. Just because I felt like a wimp didn't mean I had to act like one.

The next morning our phone rang and I answered, thinking the front desk was calling about our jeep tour.

"Hello, Sharon." I instantly recognized her penetrating voice and my hands began to shake. *"Would this afternoon be a good time for you and Walter to meet me for a walk?"*

I heard my voice agree that it would.

"I'll be there to pick you and Walter up about 1:30."

Walter was delighted. I was nervous, irritable and restless. Time dragged, and I found myself glancing repeatedly at the clock, both wanting time to stand still and wanting to get it over with.

Winged Wolf pulled up a few minutes early, one of her trademarks, I would come to learn, and of course, I wasn't ready, since one of mine was to always be late. She and Walter chatted outside as I ran around trying to decide what to take with me. Winged Wolf had her dog Yoda, a darling little Cairn terrier, and Sioux, her white wolf. Meeting Sioux for the first time the day before at Eastcliffe had been an unsettling experience for me. It was the first time I had ever known someone with a wolf, and since she looked like a dog at first glance, I started to approach her as she came down the steps.

Winged Wolf had said sharply, *"Don't look at her; cast your eyes down."*

I quickly looked away.

She told me, *"Sioux is a wolf and she's shy. Don't ever look her straight in the eye, until she accepts you completely. And when you speak, keep your voice gentle. Let her approach you when she's ready. And don't push. Just be natural."*

To Walter she said, *"Whatever you do, don't try to push yourself on her; she's particularly shy with men."*

We piled into her big white Suburban and headed for the Canyon. I greeted Yoda as I joined him in the back seat and noted that Sioux was crouched in the farthest corner of the rear of the vehicle, as though if she could, she would back herself right out of the car. Winged Wolf didn't seem concerned about her, so I shrugged and settled into my seat. She and Walter were already engaged in conversation and continued their chat. I sat quietly, feeling on the outside, too uncomfortable to express myself for fear she would disapprove. How to interact with this Teacher who was so different from anyone I'd ever known, became a question I could not yet answer.

Most initial relationships were a little stiff for me because I was shy and often tentative about expressing myself in the face of the unknown. Most comfortable for me was to observe a situation for a while before entering into it. Many of my friends were also therapists and other helping professionals, so we had a common language and identity. Otherwise I was with clients or my family where there was such a long history with each other, that there really was no discomfort. We were like old shoes.

With Winged Wolf I had no idea what to talk about and none of the usual rules for establishing a relationship applied here, so I kept still and listened. This was so totally different from our written communications that had a natural flow back and forth. Winged Wolf was enthusiastic about the West Fork of Oak Creek; she told us of her frequent walks through it, sometimes for days at a time, camping out under the stars at night, and how much she loved being in the forest.

The closest I had ever been to camping in the forest was in a pop-up trailer in a trailer park with indoor showers and toilets. Being in an unknown forest, sleeping out under the stars, and eating who knows what, with wild animals lurking in the shadows, sounded dangerous to me. Silently I prayed I would never have to do it.

After walking for some time, traversing the creek that flowed through the canyon and hiking up and down over the rocks, I began to relax and enjoy myself. The intense fear had dropped into the background. She hadn't said anything to me of any consequence, so more and more I surrendered to the walk. As I got to know her better, I came to realize that this ability to disarm me prior to moving in for the sting was one of her talents as a Teacher.

At a certain point we stopped and gazed at a beautiful section of water that was so still you could scarcely determine what was reflection and what was real. I said something about it reminding me of the lakes down in Michigan, and Walter made a correction, saying, *"up in Michigan."*

"What do you mean?"

"Michigan is not down from here, geographically it is up."

Immediately I took exception to his comment, feeling my hackles rise as they so often did in those days when I felt criticized or corrected on something I said.

Winged Wolf looked at me directly and asked, *"You're upset with him, aren't you?"*

I wasn't used to being confronted so directly and didn't much like it. *"Not at all,"* I asserted.

"Yes, you are," she said. *"The energy just shifted."* She paused a moment and when I failed to respond, she went on, *"He was just making a correction, and he was right. It is important to be aware of the words you use and to be precise in what you say."* Right then I decided she was clearly taking his side over mine and he was to be the favored student. She probably liked men better than women anyway.

The rest of the walk was vigorous; we crossed over the river so many times I lost count and it took all my attention to keep balanced and not fall in. There was no time to feel sorry for myself or irritated with my Teacher while all my attention was focused on what we were doing; the experience was invigorating, charged. By the time we returned to the

Meeting My Teacher

hotel, I was exhausted, but Winged Wolf still seemed to be going full steam. In fact, there were some cyclists passing by our room on these unusual three-wheeled bicycles you peddled with your hands, and she asked if they would show her how to ride one. They were delighted, and off she went full speed down the hill, laughing gaily as she gained momentum. *"Where does she get all that energy?"* I wondered aloud.

Hearing my comment, Walter shrugged, *"Must be all that divine energy flowing through her."*

As we said our good-byes, Winged Wolf casually asked, *"When do you think you can come for a visit to Eastcliffe?"* Eastcliffe was the name she had given her ranch, and she only allowed apprentice visits after an apprentice had reached a certain level of study. I was unprepared for the question and stalled in my response.

"Oh, not until the summer when school is out," I finally responded, thinking that would give me a few months to strengthen my foundation by studying my Initiation Journeys a little longer.

"That will be fine," she said. *"Let me know as soon as you have the dates so I can reserve a space for you. Then once your flight is arranged, I'll tell you how to catch the shuttle to Cottonwood, and I'll pick you up at the shuttle's drop-off point."*

Turning to Walter she said, *"I'd like the two of you to have separate visits, at least in the beginning."*

My stomach sank as I thought, *'She's interested in my husband.'* Quickly I banished the thought from my mind. It was too awful to even contemplate.

Winged Wolf must have been hearing my thoughts because she said, *"You know, I really have no interest in any personal relationship with my students."* I could feel my face turning red and looked away. Walter seemed oblivious to any nuances in the conversation.

Life-Altering Experiences

After that experience, I was relieved and happy to return to our normal vacation behavior. In fact, we spent the next few days eating at wonderful restaurants and looking at real estate, things I had a sense of control over. We headed home with several brochures and an idea of bringing some friends together and making an offer on a parcel of property we had seen in Sedona. I put my experience with the Teacher on the back burner for the time being, although she was never too far from my thoughts after that.

Once home, all our friends wanted to get together to hear about our meeting with the Teacher. Before we left for the vacation, I had assured everyone we would not be calling Winged Wolf. I had felt it would be intrusive and bold, but once there, Walter had insisted that we at least call to say hello and see if she might meet with us. I had been truly amazed when she seemed happy to hear from him and said, *"Of course, I would like to meet you."*

Back at home, we set a date for the weekend to 'share all' with our friends. By then, my fear had faded and an excitement stirred deep within me as I remembered the effect being with her had on me. How after each experience of being in her presence, my life force surged with an aliveness I had never before experienced.

There were eleven of us in the core group and several already had become apprentices; the others were interested in knowing our reaction to meeting with the Teacher. Our group met that Friday evening, and everyone had a million questions. Each question brought forth more excitement and reduced my fear quotient exponentially. Even those who still held to the *'I don't need a teacher'* viewpoint were stirred.

When that evening was over, the six who were already apprentices decided to write Winged Wolf and try to arrange for our first visit together, in two groupings: some with me, and some with Walter who would go right after my trip. I felt better knowing that some of my friends would be visiting with me; at least that part would be familiar.

Also, two more of the group who had read Winged Wolf's book *Woman Between the Wind* while we were away had written to apply for apprenticeship.

By then I had purchased and read the second book in the series, *Flight of Winged Wolf,* and was eagerly awaiting the release of the third book in the trilogy. Winged Wolf had told us it would complete the circle of

Meeting My Teacher

her apprenticeship with her Teacher Alana Spirit Changer, and, of course, I was fantasizing over the prospect of meeting Alana at some point.

Our group's evening ended on a joyful note. Individually and as a group, we had struck a course and there was a good feeling about having a Teacher to guide and direct us. Those who hadn't already done so, I was convinced, would want to become apprentices once they read Winged Wolf's books and saw how their friends' lives were changing. Life was good and I was high on it. My spiritual transformation had begun.

Chapter 2
Initiations and Journeys

The way in which Winged Wolf taught her apprentices was multi-faceted and multi-dimensional: there were personal encounters, phone calls, letters, and one of the primary means was via Initiations, which were written Teachings called Initiation Journeys given on an individual basis for each apprentice to experience as we showed a readiness to receive them. Also, she told us that often she met us in other dimensions where she also worked with us and taught others. I can attest to this through my own sleep time dream experiences with the Teacher.

For the most part, apprentices lived at quite a distance from Winged Wolf; they received lessons and corresponded with her by mail. So, for example, after Winged Wolf sent a letter accepting me as her apprentice, to my great joy and relief, she also sent the first of a series of these lessons, called Journeys, and each of these Journeys was an Initiation to the next level of study.

An apprentice's progress on the Initiation Journeys was evaluated by the Teacher after the apprentice submitted a written report to her; and if Winged Wolf's perception was that we had grasped the Teachings presented in whatever Initiation Journey we were working on, she would send us the next level Initiation Journey.

The trek toward living our divinity was broken into four segments of one hundred 'miles' each. Winged Wolf told us the final hundred miles were in the form of oral transmissions, given one-on-one, from Teacher to apprentice. It seemed she had designed a road map to take us all the way to our destination of enlightenment. That fact alone was astounding. She said the final hundred miles were particularly significant to us as apprentices because once we crossed a certain line in our awareness, we became what Winged Wolf referred to as Thunderbeings.

She told me early in my apprenticeship, *"A Thunderbeing is someone who has reached the first stage of enlightenment or self-realization, referred to as 'The Irreversible Way'; and it is a highly unusual place to be. Perhaps only one person in three million attains this level of consciousness. It requires tremendous perseverance, and the reason it is referred to as The Irreversible Way is because, once truly there, you can never go back to who you previously were."*

"Is that what is meant by the divine consciousness?" I had asked her.

"No, it is not," she replied firmly. *"The divine consciousness is Buddha or Christ Consciousness; a Thunderbeing is not that. They have passed through the doorway, or crossed a line that we refer to as The Irreversible Way. It is the beginning of the spiritual trek toward becoming That. Remember, until you reach the consciousness of Thunderbeing, it is all preparation.*

"To pass The Irreversible Way, you have relinquished all attachments, and that is a tremendously free state to experience. You are that open that you are no longer encumbered by the karma that you once allowed to hold you back. From that point on you will be constantly learning, evolving, exploring, and expanding. But whether or not you can fully awaken to yourself as divine consciousness in the same lifetime is up to you and how your karma lines up."

Her statement brought up a host of other questions, but Winged Wolf silenced me.

"Other than feeding your curiosity, it doesn't serve you for me to tell you any more than what I have already said," she told me. And that ended the conversation.

Once an apprentice received the first Initiation Journey in the mail, their studies began. These Initiations contained special spiritual Teachings for us to study and integrate into our lives, and they included experiential assignments to assist us with this. After we worked with these Initiation Journeys for a period of time, then we were to write Winged Wolf with our Journey reports, after which we anxiously awaited a response.

It didn't take long to realize that if a white 6" x 9" envelope arrived in the return mail, it contained our next Journey; we had satisfied the requirements of the Journey we had been working on and we were moving on to the next level of Initiation Journey. But, if the mail contained a standard-size envelope, we had more work to do on the current Journey. In the beginning, I didn't know any of this.

Also, it was difficult not to take it as a failure, from a little-self perspective, when those smaller envelopes arrived in the return mail, even though the most important lessons were usually contained in them. That is to say, my ego got involved when I saw that the Teacher had held me back from moving on to a new Initiation Journey, because she saw that there were still some areas that required further exploration. Winged Wolf told me she was usually gentle with apprentices for the first few Journeys, moving us along with words of encouragement. We needed to get some of the Journeys under our belts before we could even begin to talk intelligently about them.

Later, as we delved into the higher Initiation Journeys, frequently there were several small envelopes before the big one arrived moving us on. The encouragement then was to dig into the lesson, develop and expand with it prior to moving along. The foundation had to be solid before the greater awareness could develop. Sometimes I would read a Journey or even a letter from the Teacher and then later go back and reread it. I was astonished at the difference in my ability to perceive what was said. It was often like night and day. Walter used to laughingly say, *"How did she manage to rewrite this between the time I first read it and now?"*

That first Journey was like gold to me, and I couldn't wait to curl up in my favorite chair and read it. She had told me to read it aloud. In fact, I read it aloud three times, feeling the magic of her words penetrate my being and carry me into a state of heightened awareness. This was real and it was happening to me, in my life, right now! My joy overflowed. I had found a route to my destiny; now all I had to do was learn how to live it. What a relief it was to stop seeking and begin working. I spent days reading and rereading that first Journey, trying to absorb every pearl.

Gradually, I discovered that the secret Teachings and practices contained in the Initiation Journeys Winged Wolf sends to her apprentices are designed to guide the student/apprentice toward their own awakening, self-realization, called enlightenment, or realization of the God-self, or awakened consciousness. So whether it is called Shamanism, Buddhism or Christianity, all of which are based on Primordial Teachings, the result is an awakened consciousness. Again, in the beginning, I didn't really understand or care about what all this meant. Deep within me was simply a burning desire to have THAT, and I trusted that desire as worthwhile, fulfilling my life's purpose.

This Teacher was actually promising that, if I studied the Teachings as she presented them, fully integrated them into my life, and developed a strong relationship with her, patiently persevering, then one day, I would achieve enlightenment.

In fact, she said it is every sentient being's birthright to realize themselves as divine consciousness, if not in this lifetime, at least in some lifetime. That is the divine plan. This was so much bigger than anything I had anticipated when I applied to become an apprentice.

The Primordial Teachings are called 'secret' for many reasons, but the one I see as most important is that the Teacher can guide the student through the great mysteries or veils of spirituality at the most propitious time for the student to receive them. Prior to that, they could easily be misused, for personal gain only, or misunderstood.

Winged Wolf said, *"It is dangerous to give power to people who are not prepared to handle it. If the mind-passions are still intact, power will naturally be abused and the student will be karmically devastated."* Also, she said, *"Without a Teacher, there is no possibility of achieving an awakened consciousness, because people are so caught in their own personal stories, their viewpoint is colored by them. No matter how much someone reads and how committed they are to living impeccably, they are blinded by their hypnotized consciousness."*

Further, Winged Wolf said, *"It is true that many so-called secret Teachings are being revealed in books and tapes by those calling themselves 'teachers.' We are being inundated with material to read, workshops to attend, and information is thrown at us helter-skelter."*

She continued, *"People attend workshops without any prior preparation where they are taken out of their bodies and travel to other dimensions and realms, then the workshop leader moves on to another city or another workshop, and the previous participants are left reeling from the impact of 'too much given out of context,' trying to fit the pieces of an incomplete puzzle together without a proper foundation."*

"Why is it that people are so drawn to that type of thing?" I once asked her.

"The westernized consciousness demands quick fixes," she answered, "but there is no easy way to awaken consciousness. While the truths are simple, the implementation requires a willingness to live them, to integrate them into one's life, and usually that is not an easy thing to do.

"On the physical plane, it is similar to a musician tuning his instrument. If it is a stringed instrument, the string must be at just the proper level of tension to produce a clear note. If it is off just a little bit, the sound will be flat or screechy.

"With an apprentice, it is much the same way. They must be fine- tuned so that they do not become overwhelmed and imbalanced. After a time, their vibrations become finely tuned to the spiritual energy that the Teacher imparts.

"A Teacher is always watching their apprentices to see what result is produced as they squeeze a student into refinement. If it is too much, the Teacher will back off until the student is ready. But if it is not enough, nothing will happen, and the student will become flat and lifeless. Then the Teacher has to increase the tension or the squeeze to bring the student forward in their awareness."

Winged Wolf suggested that we, her apprentices, observe her, test her to see if she was absolutely impeccable in both her teaching and her life. By living right on the property where we visited, she opened her personal life-space to us so we could observe her. In this way, we could gradually develop trust in her personal impeccability as well as trust in the Teachings she gave us, which are really the same in an awakened consciousness. Winged Wolf told us of shocking experiences several of her apprentices had with other teachers, making it difficult for them to trust any teacher. It was pretty amazing to learn of the things that were done to people under the guise of teaching them, including sexual misbehavior.

Because the beginning Teachings were so powerful in themselves, when practiced regularly, they produced amazing results; they gave me an immediate sense of purpose and happiness greater than I had ever known. Also, it was like all my life I had been watching a two-dimensional movie, when suddenly, a new set of eyes arrived and now everything was playing in 3-D or 4-D.

The more advanced Teachings, I knew, would require greater effort, but by then, I figured I would have developed the tenacity to persevere. My attitude toward life had always been positive, and I was a highly energetic person, always on the go; but there was a frenzied quality to my life, a running from this thing to that thing, always looking to find satisfaction for a deep inner restlessness. This connection with the Teacher and the Teachings brought me peace of mind.

Developing a Relationship with the Teacher

The first Initiation Journey I received gave me the divine perspective and an overview of the work I would be doing with my Teacher. It began to lay the groundwork to shift my viewpoint on life from ordinary consciousness to one of heightened awareness. And, best of all, the results were immediate. I had a prophetic dream the night I received the first Journey and watched myself cross over the threshold. Subsequent to that, I could feel changes taking place on a deep, cellular level each time I studied it. After working with it for a while, I submitted a report and counted the days, waiting for the Teacher's response.

It was exactly a ten-day turnaround for the reply. This was pretty fast, better than I had hoped for. It was another large envelope! This time I understood what it meant. I ripped it open and saw that Initiation Journey #2 was enclosed along with a letter from Winged Wolf. The letter was encouraging and excited me. She was happy with me, but in that first response to me as an apprentice, she also dropped a hint of something for me to be wary of, and that was my over-reliance on the analytical mind.

She said, *"Your report was very clear and very clean and I appreciate you for it. You have showed that you are a worthy apprentice and that you will do your work from your heart."* Then she gave me instructions: *"Initiation Journey 2 has nothing to do with the analytical mind. It is meant to show you why you live a certain way. Look at what is there and quickly move on. What you gain will ground you for Initiation Journey 3 which begins your life on the mountain top."*

I read and reread her message, wanting to extract every sip of nectar from it. What really grabbed me was the part where she said that after this, I would be living on the mountaintop. There was no mistaking the symbolism of that statement. *'Oh my gosh!* She said, *"on the mountaintop." It will begin my life on the mountaintop.'* Every fiber of my being wanted to be on that mountaintop; I could feel the strings of energy from her consciousness pulling my awareness up there with her. I could even see the mountaintop, and feel it under my feet. I wanted to share it with everyone in my world, *"I'm going to be on top of the mountain, and you will want to join me, I'm sure."* But Winged Wolf cautioned me early on that these Initiation Journeys and her letters were private, for my eyes only, and could not be shared even with my husband, so I had to contain my excitement and be content with knowing where I was headed.

Well, it was a good thing I was flying high from her encouraging letter to me, because this next Initiation Journey was geared toward ripping apart my sense of identity, my personality; and plunging into it, I was horrified to learn that there wasn't much to me other than a bunch of programs and conditioned responses. It was quite devastating at the time, and I wrote to her to comment on it, but really, as a cry for reassurance. It was pretty scary to discover there's no one authentically present. *"There is no me,"* I complained to her in my report. *"All I am is a bunch of conditioned responses."*

Her response surprised and delighted me. It said, *"When you began to see yourself separate from the personality, you assumed the position of divinity. Remember this separation/attitude in Initiation Journey 3. It will be very helpful to you. You are ready to begin to live from Third Eye Consciousness."* And then, *"Learn about life on that mountain top."*

"She thinks I'm ready to move on, and here I thought there was something wrong with me." At that time, I couldn't see how those two possibilities could co-exist.

Oddly, it had been that next Initiation Journey, the trip to the mountaintop, that had me crying and shaking in my shoes when I had met her the first time. The DO of the work was in being able to sustain life on the mountaintop, which meant *looking out* at life (Third Eye Vision). The tools she provided in the Initiation Journey to take me to the mountaintop were easy enough to learn, but oh, so difficult to discipline myself to sustain. That was where the real work came in. The Teacher couldn't do it for me; and I soon discovered that my ability to sustain it was about five seconds on a good day. This was hard work and required a level of self-discipline that I sure didn't have. I was just beginning to understand what Winged Wolf meant when she told me that awakening *'is simple but not necessarily easy.'* My forehead hurt from the effort of keeping my attention at the Third Eye.

About then, as I was discovering the work involved in shifting my attention from ordinary reality to living from the Third Eye Viewpoint, I was reading *Flight of Winged Wolf.* Her experiences seemed so far out of reach that I wrote to her in awe and despair: awe that someone could do what she had done; despair that I would ever be able to do as she had done. My head hurt daily just from trying to keep my attention at the Third Eye. How could I ever expect to do the amazing things she had done?

She responded with great compassion, *"The trouble with books like 'Flight of Winged Wolf' is they make everything seem so extraordinary. I am an ordinary person who dared to squeeze through the eye of the needle. Why? Because, like you, I wanted to break loose, to be free. Someday you will look back and laugh for the joy of discovering what you never dreamed imaginable. Be patient, enjoy the journey, wonderful experiences await you."*

What good fortune that I had found such a loving and compassionate Teacher, so down-to-earth and real, but fierce at times, too. Not that these feelings changed after my first face-to-face encounter with her, but meeting her did give me a slightly broader perspective as to who she was in the physical as well as the spiritual realms. There was a congruency to her spirituality and her physical being.

Over the next weeks and months, I worked enthusiastically through several Journeys, and out of this work, I felt an inner core of strength begin to build in me. A solid foundation was developing that gave me a natural confidence in myself and a sense of higher purpose. My life-force was stronger. It took a lot of the frenzy out of my life and pointed me in a particular direction. My spiritual essence was coming to the forefront. I knew where I was headed, and it felt right. There was nothing in me pulling in another direction, although it was definitely challenging and painful to my sense of identity. There was this solid sense of knowing it was the right direction.

Finally, I had discovered my life's purpose, what I had been looking so many years for, an awareness of what my life was about. Here was a choice for ultimate happiness that was not defined by circumstances unfolding before me. Awareness of my spiritual or divine essence transcended the mundane aspects of my life in its ability to empower and uplift. This essence, which Winged Wolf refers to as divine self, is based on realization of Oneness with all life, and translates into unconditional love, compassion, and total acceptance of what is. It is directly transmitted from Teacher to student. These were the spiritual truths I was learning about from my Teacher, not just intellectually, but experientially where it counted. But I also learned it wasn't easy and smooth-flowing all the time as it had been in the beginning when I was so high on the promise and glimmers of awakening.

When I complained that I wasn't making enough progress with keeping my attention at the Third Eye and that I kept reacting to things and only seeing afterwards what I had done, she responded quickly and with kindness.

"Sharon, be patient with yourself on this. You will become IT. A fine steady rain is always better than a deluge that quickly saturates. The latter creates mud. You are doing a really good job, and I am happy to work with you."

A few weeks after returning from that first brief visit to Arizona, I could honestly send in a Journey report accepting that responsibility for myself. Her reply to me said, *"I feel your impeccable intent in your journey with me. You honor divinity in yourself and its oneness with all. Now, you are a true apprentice. You were right to hesitate in Initiation Journey 3. You knew you would never be the same and you certainly aren't."*

'It doesn't get any better than this,' I told myself, clutching her letter to my heart. Somehow hearing her acknowledge my hesitation on Initiation Journey 3 made me feel better; it validated my gut feeling that this was a huge commitment to step into and not one to be taken lightly. It was certainly a huge commitment on the Teacher's part.

Chapter 3
Preparing to Visit Eastcliffe

The winter months flew by as I focused my attention on my Journeys and my relationship with the Teacher. Usually I dreaded the long, cold, dreary winter days with the early darkness. My spirits would sag as days dragged by, but not so this winter. I greeted each day with a sense of adventure and anticipation. Everything that happened was part of my spiritual unfoldment. Ordinary events took on mysterious qualities. Nothing had changed, and yet my perception of life was completely different.

We had a series of correspondences during that winter that gradually began to reshape my identity in gentle but definite ways. Winged Wolf had a way of reframing what I said to her in a manner that caused a paradigm shift, or what she referred to as 'shifts in my assemblage point.' These were confrontations of my way of perceiving and believing about life. Each time I received a letter from the Teacher, I would end up scratching my head, realizing something had shifted but at first not realizing what. There was a feeling of being 'had,' but not really, because the result was always more freedom. Still, I knew there was a trick to the way she responded to me. She was outsmarting me, tricking me into becoming bigger than I was, and I knew it. But it is said that 'old habits die hard,' and I am living proof of the truth of this adage. I wrote her again about the current identity crisis I was having.

She answered, *"You are not really in an identity crisis. You are merely recognizing that you are everyone you loved and admired, and everyone you resisted and found distasteful. Now that you are aware, the qualities that you no longer want will be leaving you, becoming their opposite polarity as you reclaim your energies from the situations that created them. This reclaiming process begins actively in a later Journey. Be patient. You have interesting work to do between now and then....Your* destiny is unfolding. Love yourself and that great impeccable _be_ing you are becoming.

"As you are becoming truly aware, no person is an island unto themselves. While you have your own identity, you will also one day realize that we are truly ONE."

This was the second time she had gently referred to my tendency to be critical, both of self and others. By talking to me as though I was already dropping it, she bypassed any discussion and elevated my consciousness to see what I had been doing. I had written her wanting to discuss what I saw, and she had responded as though it was a done deal. That was how she outsmarted me and refused to play at my level. It kept me off-balance and ever-so-attentive. I couldn't take my eyes off her, and therefore, the Path. But I had been this way habitually for a long time and it wasn't as easy to let go as one might think. It was a continual shaping and reshaping process, surrendering a little, taking it back, giving it up, pulling it back. Overall, she was winning, and for that I was grateful, but sometimes I wondered whose team I was playing on.

It seemed as though there were two me's – the one who was aligned with the Teacher and heading toward my destiny of spiritual awakening, and the other me who wanted to cling to old habitual ways of living and relating. The divine part of me wanted to be in companion energy with the Teacher. In my mind that was the 'winning' team. The 'losing' team was my little-self and its self-sabotaging ideas and behaviors. My fear was that the losing team might win.

The Power of Resistance

From my side, I had been attempting indirectly to convince the Teacher on a couple issues. For fear of her response, I didn't approach them directly, but I couldn't let them go either. One, I was a therapist and proud of it, while Winged Wolf suggested there were few therapists who knew a bean about actually helping people. And two, I valued the analytical mind and its abilities, especially in my work, while she said the analytical mind was mostly a nuisance that interfered with the awakening process and limited divine expression.

In a rather puffed-up letter, I wrote to her espousing what I thought was true about such things as instincts, the value of mind, and the need to discipline and program it. This was one of those times I was quite pleased with myself for my presentation, and of course, the response was unsettling. When would I learn there was no way to argue her out of what she saw?

She replied at some length, *"When we are thirsty, our instincts tell us to drink water. When we are hungry, they tell us to eat. When danger is pursuing us, they tell us to run or get out of the way.*

"The mind, on the other hand, analyzes how much water and food to take, the nature of the danger pursuing us. If we were running from a tiger, the mind might suddenly say something foolish or embellish on the danger, depending on the programming it had already received. The center of the stick *is the balance point or place of divinity. From there, we go about our business, using our instincts, or using our minds as tools to carry on. A burning desire to grab the other end of the stick is just that — emotion from mental programming that finds synchronicity in some incident or event.

"If one is functioning from divinity, the mind falls into order, just as water seeks its own level; it becomes balanced. Even when it is not, when emotional buttons are being pushed, all one needs to do is return the attention to the seat of divinity. From there, the activity can be safely watched, and/or expressed, without being consumed in the passion of the moment. So, you see, it is divinity that is in charge of the mind. In this way, the mind becomes a power tool, electrified for maximum usage. If the mind is in control, it nitpicks everything to death, slowly reducing it to uselessness.

"So you see, the mind in itself, even a well-programmed mind, is limited by its own programming. Whereas, the divine self is part of God, or the Void, unlimited, using the limited (mind, instincts) as tools. Because the mind is merely a tool (though it may be a powerful tool) it cannot in itself find solutions outside of its programming.

"As a therapist, to lead someone out of a maze, you either require experience with that maze, have finely tuned instincts or wander about — the blind leading the blind. Operating from divinity, however, you are tapped into the unlimited knowledge, you fall into knowledge belts, so

---

*This is a reference to a metaphor Winged Wolf's Teacher Alana Spirit Changer used to demonstrate the ways in which one runs from their seat of power. She spoke of the midpoint of a stick as being the balance point and representing one's seat of power.

to speak; the Oneness and the direction are provided in a way that heals the mind or damaged brain. (The brain actually becomes damaged by strong, sustained emotions.) A sudden trauma bruises the brain, making a temporary quirk in the nerve endings to create a specific reaction. Some people have greater damage through sustained emotion, but this too can be healed. This is what a shaman does. She/he heals by being divine, communicating as divinity."

Once again, she ended with encouraging me to *"Be patient with yourself on this."*

As gently as this letter was written, it was still upsetting to me on all those issues I held dear, and I felt as though my job was at stake since she had as much as said it was useless. How could I continue working at a profession that my Teacher valued so little? And if I didn't work, how would I live? It was all I knew how to do. So I did what I always did when I didn't know what to do; I stewed and stalled. And I added a prayer, *'If there is something else I am meant to do, please let it show up soon.'*

Old Patterns Get Confronted

Our spiritual discussion group of about a dozen continued to meet weekly. There were so many phases and stages we had gone through, and depending on what we were working on, different people would join us for a while. At this time, we were working on dream interpretation and guided meditation. It was easy enough to pick up guided meditation techniques from the myriad of books written on the subject, and the same was true for dream interpretation.

In my meditations, an enormous white owl was appearing, and I realized that, for me, this symbolized the Teachings, literally a higher perspective. I would merge with the owl and we would soar together over mountains and valleys, sometimes looking for food, but always I would disengage from the experience at that point. So I wrote Winged Wolf about what I was experiencing in my meditations, and she wrote back,

Hello Sharon, White Eagle,

A white owl (night eagle) symbolizes a great transformation in consciousness, a willingness to expose the darkness within

one's self to the light of divinity. It is a role of great courage, of steadfastness/perseverance and a consuming, burning desire for high altitude. The higher you fly, the more white your feathers become, bleached by the blinding, all-seeing (knowing) light of divine consciousness. A good beginning. Remain as divine consciousness to travel higher.

This was the first time she had ever called me anything but my street name and I was thrilled by the reference and the interpretation she provided. The idea of flying had always fascinated me. Many times I had longed to become a bird that could rise above all of life's little pettiness to see the overview, rather than being enmeshed in the mundane story of life.

The second time she wrote to me in this way was in the same month, April, in response to an Initiation Journey report I had submitted. It was an extension of the previous letter with an added twist. In it she said,

"Your report was all about transformation, shifting to freedom from stuck situations. Such is the nature of the phantom eagle. The phantom is unseen but felt. You are very much like the phantom being you described but try to keep hidden. The interesting part is that you are ashamed of this being, not to me, because that part of you likes and admires me, and it knows I can see it, and doesn't care. It knows I won't judge."

The part she had written about freedom and shifting from stuck places was really appealing, but the part about hiding and being ashamed made me squirm. And because I didn't like it, I understood it struck a chord, but I couldn't get past my analytical mind to allow the meaning of her words to penetrate my defenses. It made me really uncomfortable to realize she saw parts of me that were so hidden I couldn't see them myself even when she pointed them out. I mustered up the courage to call her and ask about this.

"Well," she said, *"do you remember when you told me your father liked to sweep things under the rug, literally?"*

"Yes, I do." She was referring to an incident I had shared with her earlier, *"but what does that have to do with me?"*

"It has everything to do with you," she said. *"You told me he was your idol and you always tried to be like him. You thought he was impeccable, but when he showed you how to sweep the dirt under the rug, you immediately were dismayed at his deceitful behavior, but pretended it was okay because you so strongly identified with him and wanted to believe in his impeccability. It caused a split in you that said you had to deny what you knew was impeccable in order to continue admiring your father."*

On some level, I could sense the connection of what she was saying, but it was elusive. I'd get a glimmer, and then lose it. He was still my idol.

"Are you saying that I deny what I know for the sake of maintaining my father's image?"

"Something like that," she agreed. *"There's more to it than that, though. Why don't you be with it for a while; see what you come up with, and we can talk more about it later. Meanwhile, just recognize the part of you that sees; observe that part without judging it. Get to know that part of yourself. That's the part where your power lives."*

"All right," I agreed skeptically, thinking I would need a great deal more help with this one if I were to grasp it. After that, there were no further references in her letters to the phantom being, and I went into hiding for a few weeks. Something was stirred up inside me though, bubbling deep down, but I wasn't ready to look any further. Vaguely I thought, *'It must be my dark side that I don't want to see.'*

Walking My Talk

The closer the time came to the dates I had scheduled for a visit with my Teacher, the more ambivalence I felt. It was one thing to study and practice from afar and write about the magnificent experiences I was having; but I hadn't gotten over the effects of that last letter and the fear that I had a dark side lurking just under the surface. Also, I remembered what it was like to have those intense blue eyes fix me with their gaze, and how totally exposed I had felt. It was scary to think about doing it again, and this time I understood more. The divine consciousness would mirror and magnify the dirt that I had been covering. It would come bubbling up whether I wanted it to or not. Physical distance provided a comfortable buffer.

One day in early May, I arrived home from work to find a letter with the Teacher's now-so-familiar and beloved handwriting waiting for me on the dining room table. Her handwriting was as unique as she was. She was left-handed, but that did not account for the distinct impression the energy of her writing made. The nature of the handwriting was bold, definitive, and it carried the power of the intent behind the words. Sometimes it was a dance of love and great joy, and other times it was fierce or stern. Looking at the envelope, the essence of the energy of her message was contained in the way my name and address were written. Before I even looked inside, there was a vibration set up inside of me in response to that energy.

It was a large envelope so I knew it contained my next Journey, but when I opened it, instantly I noted it was unusual because her letter to me was typed. In fact, I had never before received a typed letter from Winged Wolf. Immediately, I was put on alert. I quickly scanned the letter, and noted the last line, which said, *"I would very much like for you to arrive a few days early, ahead of the others, if that is possible."*

'Uh, oh,' I thought as my heart started pounding, *'something out of whack here.'* Quickly I re-read the letter and realized that it was written in response to a communication I had recently sent her expressing confusion and inner conflict about some of the Teachings. At the time, I had been working on a particularly challenging Journey that focused on reclaiming stuck energy from the past. I was trying to sort out cause and effect and get to the core of some of my issues.

Prior to meeting Winged Wolf, our group had been studying alternate forms of healing and energy movement. We explored and experimented with many avenues of healing, including channeling and Reiki. Winged Wolf had cautioned us that this type of energy work was dangerous to our health and mental well-being. Specifically, she told us we could pick up another's karmic baggage by becoming involved in this type of work; and finally, she ordered us to quit doing it, telling us it was literally dangerous to our bodies. At the time of my writing to her, several people in the group were having a variety of mishaps and illnesses that I felt might be related somehow to our giving up our previous ways of doing things. My overt issue was concern for their well-being.

On the surface, we had complied with the Teacher's directives, but vestiges of desire to continue with what we had been doing remained. Some people were still attached to the old ways, which had brought them a certain sense of personal power. Plus, those who were still non-apprentices had to go along with the group decision to do as the Teacher asked; so there were undercurrents. I knew Winged Wolf perceived me as the 'ringleader of the pack' and in essence, my communication had questioned her on some of these areas she had cautioned us about. I was caught between the energies of those wanting to continue the old ways and those of us committed to doing as the Teacher requested. Of course, I wouldn't have been caught there if a part of me hadn't also been clinging to the old ways. I communicated this, albeit again indirectly, in the form of many questions. She responded strongly.

An additional part of her response addressed the threat to my ego that her leadership represented. Since I had been the informal group leader, or perhaps the catalyst for our group's being together, rather than its leader, Winged Wolf, who had become the Teacher for most of us, was now replacing me; she challenged me to take a look at this. So my dark side was rearing up again from a slightly different angle, but while I couldn't see it when I wrote the letter to her, I sure could see it from her response.

Her letter said, *"The idea is to live in the present moment, which is AS divine consciousness, where your energy stays intact, or at least you have the presence to reclaim the energy as you 'feel' it escaping into various situations.*

"Your dream about feeling badly after your Teacher told you that you were not in Third Eye Vision says that you are afraid of failure, or that you won't be able to 'measure up,' so to speak. When this happens, you tend to gather up the energies of those in your group to protect you or insulate you from your fear. Their reassurance gives you a feeling of being in control. However, now that is somewhat threatened. Suppose they succeed and you don't? Thus, a feeling of competition begins. Inattention is a part of this, because instead of living centered in the present moment, it is living in the 'suppose this happens...or that,' wondering if you will measure up."

I could feel the life force draining out of me as I read her words. She was plunging the stake into me, gently in a sense, but powerfully. That was all I could read for the moment, so I put the letter away until I could catch my breath. Later, maybe after a long walk, I could come back to it. That evening I had the house to myself. Steeling myself for what might come next, I pulled the letter out and continued reading.

"*Inattention to the moment breeds accidents and stress. Of course, when you are DOing something new, there are uncertainties. The only way out of uncertainties is to test them out AS divine consciousness; that is from the Third Eye center. As divine consciousness, one perceives energy and makes choices. Is your Teacher setting you up on a negative path? Is your life in forward or backward motion? Are you happier?*"

She continued, "*The personal myth that you carry is built around insecurity. Once you acknowledge this, you can keep the good that you created out of the myth, and no longer be controlled by insecurity.*" Then she gave me reassurance, "*You, Sharon, have the potential to go all the way in this work as I already told you.*

"*So you see, there is no room for insecurity. Can you see where we are headed with this? Here is an incident to TRULY recall your energy. There is no forward motion in getting caught up in group personalities, competitiveness and pettiness.*

"*When I speak of you in this way, it means it is time for you to release and reclaim your energy. Competitiveness drains and distorts. And please don't be heavy on yourself, I do not judge you or anyone, and there is no reason for you to do so. Laughter heals.*"

And then, at the very bottom, came the request for me to arrive several days early.

In typical Winged Wolf fashion, she had tuned in to the energy of my communication to her and went directly to the source of it, my insecurity and fear of being dethroned, removed from my protective group and made vulnerable in my aloneness; and this had triggered resistance, fear of failure, and had resulted in my questioning her authority. I had been flying high until now, but here I was faced with the reality of what apprenticeship would mean to me personally. This was not someone who could be manipulated, or who was interested in compromise or understanding more about my thoughts on how things should be done. Why would she be? I was still stuck in the muck and the mire, stamping my feet and wanting her to do it my way.

Now she was sending for me. She was holding up a mirror for me to look into, the mirror of true and honest reflection in which I could see only what was looking back at me. It made me squirmy, uncomfortable and embarrassed to be so naked in front of someone, even if they did love me unconditionally. I really didn't even know what that meant. Plus, it forced me to look honestly at myself. *'This is really painful,'* I thought as I read and reread her words and felt their impact.

Since I had already purchased the plane tickets for my scheduled visit to Eastcliffe later in the month, I surely didn't want to change my ticket now; it would be a great expense, and besides, I was feeling especially vulnerable.

My Teacher had ripped me open and gotten to the core of my essential neurosis as a personality. I was insecure, competitive and controlling, not to mention I used my friends as a security blanket. Just reading her letter pushed my panic button.

After stewing on it for a few days, I knew I must do what she requested if I was truly committed to my apprenticeship, so I called and changed my ticket, at quite an extra expense as I had anticipated. To myself I grumbled, *'Doesn't she realize this is costing me a lot of money?'* Deep down, I knew Winged Wolf was operating on an entirely different set of principles than I. She operated on what the energies of the moment called for, not what was practical or convenient for me.

Up until my crisis of identity struck, I had been enjoying some advice she gave me early in my apprenticeship when she had told me that if there was anything she could do over again, it would be to *'relax and enjoy the Journey to power. It is sweeter than you now know. Life really is so much fun.'* I had taken this jewel to be true and tried my best to live it from that viewpoint.

Fun was a good buzzword for me; it was right up my alley. A spiritual path that was fun, how fortunate could one get? Of course, she also knew 'fun' was one of my buzzwords. *'Okay, so it's not always going to be fun,'* I told myself; after all, *'if it was really all fun, everyone would be here doing it. And, besides, this is fun of a different sort; it's the fun of learning to fly.'*

As a result of my Teacher's encouragement and timely interventions, I had worked diligently on my Journeys, moving from one to the next, with peaks and valleys along the way. I walked, talked, lived and breathed the Teachings to the best of my ability. I had never been so completely at peace with any decision in my life as this one, even in the rough times, and it felt wonderful to know at last where I was headed. It felt so right.

But when I began the lesson on reclaiming my stuck energy, there was a much deeper sense of really 'rolling up my sleeves and working on some heavy stuff, my shadow side.' I shed many tears working through this Journey, looking at memories that were deeply buried, and trying to remember to laugh from time to time; but no matter how much I laughed, that much more did I cry. Winged Wolf had tried to prepare me for this one by cautioning me about not getting caught up in the emotions attached to the energy these memories contained. But even without getting caught up in the drama of each scenario, the deeper work created a kind of 'tension-release, tension-release' effect, and the release side was often teary.

It was a Journey to be reckoned with and it demanded my full attention to work through, and it was definitely not a lot of fun. It put me face to face with every karmic encounter I had ever had in my life, and there were literally thousands of them, often terribly painful to look at honestly.

The plus side of this work was a great sense of freedom as the energy from these situations was reclaimed and restored to its natural integrity. So this letter from the Teacher arrived at a time when I was feeling raw and vulnerable, which always triggered defenses because I didn't want to be seen. I was edgy and critical.

It is difficult to capture in words the energy that a letter sent from the Teacher encapsulated. It held the power of alchemy; a letter or phone call transformed my ordinary reality to something vital and alive, but sometimes devastated me in the process. Mail time took on a whole new meaning after my apprenticeship began. Any day might bring that familiar, beloved handwriting with some jewels in it for me, even though in the moment they could be quite disruptive to my self-image.
Prior to receiving Winged Wolf's letter requesting my early arrival, I had spent some time preparing myself physically as well as spiritually for the trip to Eastcliffe. Since I had decided to make the trip piggyback with one of Winged Wolf's medicine walks, physical preparation was important. These medicine walks were experiences in nature, hiking

trips that she led into the West Fork of Oak Creek Canyon, opportunities to meet ourselves in the silence of that pristine environment, sacred journeys both real and symbolic of everyone's inner search for the meaning in life, the search to discover our authentic selves. We would be hiking over rugged terrain, carrying heavy backpacks and walking several miles in a day.

The plan was for me and several other Michigan apprentices to stay with the Teacher for several days prior to the medicine walk; then leave from Eastcliffe to participate in the medicine walk for another three days, departing for home right after the walk.

Since Walter and I were not permitted to visit simultaneously, he would come in for the medicine walk and stay afterwards for his visit, thus honoring Winged Wolf's request that we have separate visits. Now, in light of this request, I would be traveling alone, carrying my own weight.

In those days, I was ambivalent with anything new or different, and so it was with the medicine walk. Winged Wolf said we would be sleeping out in the forest, eating lightly, and hiking several miles carrying backpacks and sleeping bags. I had never carried a backpack and didn't really want to. While I was in good physical shape, it was due to walking our local nature trails and exercising at the Fitness Center, not wandering around for miles in the wilderness and probably eating food I didn't like. *'Why am I doing this?'* I would ask myself repeatedly, like a petulant child. *'Do you want to be a shaman or not?'* would come the silent reply.

In contrast, Walter was terribly excited. He bought all new, special lightweight clothes, hiking boots, even a water bottle that could be carried over the shoulder and had a long straw so he could just turn his head and drink. I was fascinated with his preparations and finally relented to his insistence that we practice on some local trails to see if our new hiking shoes were comfortable, and to discover how heavy a load we could carry and so forth. So off we went with me grumbling all the way, but secretly, I was grateful to be having this practice lesson. I just couldn't admit it to him. By the time we finished, at least I knew how to load up a backpack, attach the sleeping bag and hoist it up on my shoulders. The change of plans had me carrying all my own gear, so it worked out well that I had practiced for it. I had become accustomed to Walter taking care of me in many ways, especially those requiring physical strength or mechanical ability, so this trip was a big deal for me.

Preparing to Visit Eastcliffe

While I was deeply engrossed in the spiritual adventure of my life, the physical world I lived and worked in carried on. There seemed to be room for both to peacefully co-exist.

Looking back in the history book, this was a wonderfully happy time for me. The ups and downs of apprenticeship, family life, marriage and work were all experienced under the umbrella of an internal grin that nothing could erase. I was going to be a shaman; no matter what it involved, I knew where I was headed, and it put a song in my heart even during the toughest of times.

At that time, nothing made me happier than having my entire family together under the same roof, and that summer it all came together that way. In May, a month or so before my departure for Eastcliffe, my aging parents drove in from Florida to spend the summer with us and avoid the Florida heat. Both my adult children and my stepdaughter Michelle had also come home from college at about the same time. In addition, we had my oldest son's fiancée living with us. She was a wonderful addition to the family and my son's love for her made her a positive influence on him.

Everyone was working, so our home had a swinging door, people coming and going all the time. Meanwhile, my mother insisted on cooking dinner for us every night, then worried about everything: the food getting cold, the kids going hungry, whether the cat was in, trying to keep everyone's schedule straight, and waiting up until we were all in so she and dad could lock the doors. They acted like we were all kids and they were taking care of us. It was humorous in a way, but mixing three generations like that sometimes frayed people's nerves.

My biggest concern was for my parents' safety and well-being. With dad's dementia progressing and mom's heart problems and high blood pressure, it fell to me to keep the energy flowing as smoothly as possible. We hid keys to the house outdoors under the rocks by the porch and at the back door so when mom and dad locked up for the night, the adult children would be able to get in the house without waking everyone up. This lesson was learned the hard way after the second time someone had to bang on the bedroom window to wake up dad to let them in. This created lots of grumbling and lectures from him about people coming in on time, and of course awakened my mother, who had difficulty sleeping anyway. So, after our second experience with the mid-night awakenings, we figured out the key system. Of course, then there were always times when the last one to use the key forgot to replace it and so the next one who needed it couldn't find it. That was why we ended up with multiple key hiding places. That seemed to work for everyone.

Then we had Max, the cat, who by virtue of my mother's spoiling him terribly, insisted on coming in and going out every five minutes. Whenever he was inside, he cried and badgered her for treats, which she naturally could not refuse to give him.

The adult children had the least tolerance for the grandparents. Although they loved them dearly, their 'rules' impinged on the freedom to come and go as they pleased without being accountable for meals and such. My parents also had rules for sitting at the table that included not wearing hats, and always wearing shirts. They were simple rules, not unreasonable, but the boys in particular were in the habit of wearing a hat whenever their hair was either uncombed or unwashed. Now, not only was my mother insisting they sit down to eat, but she wouldn't tolerate the wearing of hats.

Needless to say, no one was thrilled to learn that Walt and I would be away for ten days. I dreaded telling them, but was also relieved to be heading out of all that energy for a while. Even though I loved them all, it was a bit much.

Of our local spiritual group, all but two were now apprentices, causing a slight schism in the energy, although we didn't confront it. The two holdouts were pretty well dug in for various reasons, so we tried to continue as we previously had, being self-directed, and making use of spirit guides to coach us and make suggestions. We met faithfully every Saturday evening and did everything from guided meditations to healings, to past-life regressions and long, silent meditations.
Outsiders sent us their dreams via friends in the group, and people came to us for many types of help. It was a hodgepodge, in a sense, but the primary goals were spiritual self-development and helping others. What was seen but not spoken was that the group became dysfunctional for a while, and it pointed out a bigger lesson: *it drains the energy of any situation to have people pulling against each other.*

A split situation like that can only continue for so long before it breaks apart. And eventually our group did break apart as we became more and more committed to the Teacher and the Teachings she presented for us,

Preparing to Visit Eastcliffe

giving up old ways to make room for the new learning that was taking place. A Wisdom Circle of Winged Wolf's design ultimately replaced the informal meetings we had been having and allowed a natural ending of the split energy.

Chapter 4
Eastcliffe

When I arrived at the airport to leave for my visit with Winged Wolf, it seemed I had just about everything I owned with me, plus my sleeping bag and camping equipment. After landing in Phoenix, I managed to gather my entire luggage and find the shuttle that would take me to a drop-off point where Winged Wolf would pick me up.

By now I had the jitters, especially since I was without the protection of my friends. I would be there at Eastcliffe with other apprentices whom I had not met before and the Teacher, whom I dearly loved but whose presence made me so uncomfortable, especially since she had felt it important to see me in advance of the others. Being with her was like looking into a still pond and seeing your face so clearly that you could see every line and wrinkle you had been pretending wasn't there. I knew from what Winged Wolf had told me that reality was beautiful, but getting to it seemed a rocky road.

This was the boldest and most adventurous thing I had ever done in my life. A part of me felt unreal, dreamlike, as though it was happening to someone else or in a sleep dream. In my mind, the story of my life had already been written; therefore, not only was this track not one of the chapters, but this was not even the same book. It was as though I had been following a map to one destination, when suddenly, someone took the map away.

Of course I knew intellectually this was all a fantasy of my own creation for my own comfort, because I had clearly chosen to pursue this path of awakening. But it had the split feeling of schizophrenia that Winged Wolf talked about in her books. I literally pinched myself in these early days of my apprenticeship to make sure I was awake!

Eastcliffe

Sure enough, as the shuttle pulled up to the drop-off point, I saw the big white Suburban, and Winged Wolf was standing next to it, all dressed in white herself. This was the third time I had seen her and every time she was dressed in all white. I wondered what the symbology of that was and whether she expected her apprentices to dress like that. Immediately, my mind said, 'No way, I look terrible in white!'

"Hello there," she greeted me with a big smile, seeming genuinely happy to see me. *"Here, let me help with your bags."* Immediately I was embarrassed because I knew I was grossly over-packed. But she just kept grinning and grabbed my bags. She hoisted them into the rear of the car effortlessly and motioned me into the front passenger seat. "So how was your flight?" she asked, making some small talk. She must have sensed my anxiety because she was so kind and gentle with me.

"Smooth," I managed to whisper.

As we drove the short distance to Eastcliffe, Winged Wolf told me about the little town of Cottonwood and how she had almost not found this ranch. It had shown up as the last place the realtor had to show her, and it was perfect for the work she wanted to do. She said she knew it immediately. I could feel myself relaxing in the seat listening to her, and the tension eased out of me. This was not the scary person I remembered, but more like a friend who was happy to see me.

"This is it," she said as we pulled up into the driveway of her home. I saw someone out in front pulling weeds from the flowerbed. Someone else was riding on a tractor mower cutting the grass. It was so hot. I was dripping wet, and wondered about these people out working in the heat of the day. It must have been over a hundred. My contact lenses were already beginning to stick to my eyes from the dryness of the heat.

The house itself had a southwestern flavor, flat-roofed and rambling. The exterior was the color of clay. We stepped inside the front door and I felt the cooler air wash over my body. It was either air-conditioned or very well insulated. Also, there were no windows at the front of the house, so none of the sun's heat could directly penetrate. I noticed there were terra cotta tiled floors throughout the area I could see.

"How does it stay so cool in here? I don't see any air vents." I asked, curious.

"It uses a swamp cooler," she informed me. Seeing my look of puzzlement, she went on, *"It's a cooling system that is only effective in hot, dry climates because it uses water, which evaporates and in the process cools the air. It's perfect for this climate."*

We were standing in a long hallway. Looking to the left, several doorways were visible that turned out to lead into bedrooms and a bath for apprentices. To my right I could see part of a large room with a dining table in it. Winged Wolf turned to the left and motioned for me to follow her.

She showed me the three small sleeping rooms, then led me back to the first room, which was attractive in a southwestern motif. It contained a single bed, desk and chair; another doorway led to a shared bath. *"This will be your room during your stay here this time,"* she commented.

Then she faced me squarely, *"Whatever you do, don't leave anything to eat in your suitcases, because Siouxy (her white wolf) will look through everything you have."* I thought about closing the door, but she was tuned in to my thoughts because she said, *"The door doesn't close completely; the latch won't hold, and Sioux has no difficulty pushing it open. She's very smart and she is crafty. If you have something in there, she will find it."*

Something in her attitude shifted; I thought, *"The honeymoon is over."* She stopped at the door, fixed me directly with her eyes and asked, *"Did you bring something to journal with, because I want you to write down everything that happens, everything! And I'll be reading your Journal, so I expect you to keep up with it."*

This was said with a great seriousness that put me on edge. Fortunately I had remembered to bring a notebook and several pens, so, with her looking on, I rummaged around in the suitcase and found the notepad and kind of waved it at her. She nodded once as if satisfied, turned and left.

There was a long moment when I just stood there looking at the place where she had stood. Her energy was so powerful; it left a residue, such that I kept expecting her to magically reappear. Eventually I tore my gaze away from the spot where her energy imprint remained, and sat down on the edge of the bed to begin writing copious notes. She wasn't going to find me unprepared.

A few moments later she was back. *"If you're ready, I want to show you around the house and introduce you to the other apprentices who are here."*

Grabbing my notebook and pen, I quickly followed. At the end of the hall beyond the bedrooms, there were steps leading down to a large, beautifully tiled room that obviously served as Winged Wolf's office. Stacks of books were everywhere, and a large desk dominated the left corner; it had a burl wood top that was stunning.

I commented on it.

"That piece was from the Redwood trees at Big Sur," she said, *"and when I found it, I knew it would make a perfect desk. Believe me, it wasn't easy to get it home,"* she laughed, remembering. *"It was just as you see it, other than the finish I put on to preserve the wood."*

Then a slight motion on the other side of the room caught my attention; I glanced in that direction. There was a box containing a beautiful, multi-colored cat; from inside the box, I could hear the mewing sound of kittens.

"Ichinen is protective of them," she told me. *"It makes her nervous if anyone gets too close to her babies. They're only a few days old."*

"Ichinen is an interesting name for a cat," I mused.

"In Japanese, it means chi, or life force. I named her that because of her enormous life force. I found her when she was only a baby herself," Winged Wolf went on, *"and it was on my birthday so I knew she was meant to be mine. Sioux thought she was her baby and carried her everywhere in her mouth. She used to wash her so much I thought she might hurt her, but she never did. Ichinen's scrappy; she has a big spirit and isn't afraid of anything."*

The idea of a wolf nurturing a kitten was intriguing, and I would have liked to talk more about it but Winged Wolf was ready to move on. *"My office is off-limits unless I give you permission to be in it. Do you understand?"* I nodded.

"There may be times when I ask you in; then it is all right to enter. Otherwise, do not go in there."

Initiation

I noticed she was clear and direct in explaining the guidelines, without personality. I couldn't help but compare her style with my own, which would have been ingratiating, 'please do this, please don't do that,' always speaking in a way to be liked. It was refreshing to be spoken to in this manner, uplifting. She headed up the steps and back down the hall toward the dining room with me trotting after. She did everything so quickly; I was continuously hurrying to keep up.

We entered the dining area, and I could see this end of the house was where the living took place. This end of the house had a dramatic, southwestern look. It was light and open; all the windows of the house faced out the back toward the east. There was a large, functional kitchen off the dining room and beyond the dining room was a step-down living room.

Southwestern-looking rugs hung from the walls in the living room that soared to probably twenty feet, and a huge floor-to-ceiling fireplace dominated the north wall. Above, and to the left, was a balcony.

Winged Wolf pointed toward the balcony, *"That area is off limits; it is my private space, and so is my sacred space over there."* She now pointed to an alcove area in the kitchen that had a bay window and was filled with items that looked like they might be sacred; there were feathers and crystals and what looked like a meditation cushion. *"No one is ever allowed to go into my sacred space."* She didn't need to worry about my violating the rules. I was still much too afraid of her to even consider violating a rule. But I was soon to receive my first lesson on 'there are always exceptions to rules.'

About then, a woman came through the back door and announced to Winged Wolf that she had finished mowing the lawn. As she approached, I could see she was dripping with sweat, and her face was flushed from the heat. She appeared to be in her early 40's, and Winged Wolf introduced her to me as Marla. She said Marla would be in charge of work assignments and would show me what needed to be done outdoors.

Winged Wolf suggested I might like to spend some time with Marla since she had already been here over four weeks and was familiar with how Winged Wolf wanted certain things done, and she left the room, saying there was work she needed to do and we would meet again later. I breathed deeply and relaxed my shoulders, feeling the tension begin to drain out of me a bit.

It wasn't at all clear what the rules were about eating and drinking. It felt awkward being in the Teacher's home, tentative; but Marla seemed perfectly comfortable. She took a glass from the cupboard, filled it with ice and water, motioning to me to help myself.

"Whenever you want something, just help yourself. I need a minute to cool down, then we can talk."

I couldn't wait. *"Did you do the entire lawn yourself? In this heat?"*

"It really isn't that bad," she said. *"I'm from the south, and it's the humidity there that affects me. It's so dry here, you don't really notice the heat."*

I thought she looked like her body noticed it but kept my thoughts to myself. For sure, I didn't think it was healthy to work so hard outdoors in the middle of the day in 100-degree weather. I was soon to learn my opinion of things didn't matter much. Mostly, when I listened to what I had to say, it was full of attitudes and opinions that were robotic, the result of years of adapting to or rebelling against somebody else's viewpoint.

Winged Wolf was absolutely clear with us that she was the Teacher and we were the students. We had not earned the privilege or the clarity or the trust required to express our viewpoints on how things were to be run at Eastcliffe. The 'reality' of the impact of shifting from a world where I was top dog in most areas of my life to one where I was an acquiescent follower was beginning to sink in. Already I could see that I didn't approve of some of her ways. What she said to us was, *"Until you reach the level of Thunderbeing, your little-self is still in charge, and the little-self can never be fully trusted."*

She used the term 'Thunderbeing' to describe an apprentice who had reached such a level of purity, meaning freedom from mind passions (anger, lust, greed, vanity and attachment), and clarity of vision that they were no longer controlled by their emotions. She told us since that was the first stage of enlightenment, at that point we would be trustworthy because the ego would be tamed or dissolved. I wasn't sure which, but it would no longer be in charge.

From where I stood at that moment, reaching the level of Thunderbeing was a long, long way off, because enlightenment seemed a long way off. I figured it would be at least three years, maybe more. That turned out to be a gross miscalculation.

That first day is somewhat of a blur. I remember sitting outside on the back porch writing in my notebook and watching the sunset. It was difficult to write honestly what I was experiencing in the way I would normally write it, because I knew at any moment Winged Wolf would take the notebook and read it. This meant I had to phrase everything from a Third Eye or objective viewpoint.

"What do you mean by the 'Third Eye perspective'?" I had asked her.

"It is the viewpoint of divine consciousness," she explained. *"When your attention is placed on that spot in the center of the forehead above the eyebrows, all mind chatter is clipped off, and you can see forever. It gives you an objective perspective of what you are looking at. You are pure consciousness looking out through the physical eyes. You realize yourself as a part of God and you no longer identify with your physical vehicle or body as who you are. You no longer operate from the mind passions."*

"What are considered to be the mind passions?"

"The mind passions are anger, lust, greed, vanity and attachment, and the greatest of these is attachment, although there is always fear at the bottom of any mind passion."

"So this means I am to let go of all my self-centered responses?" I asked trying to imagine what that might be like.

"It means to live as a fully conscious human being, awake and aware. It means you live in the moment, right now, and there really is only one moment," she added, *"and this tells you that the past, present and future are really only one segmented moment of now."*

Without full grasp of the meaning of all this, it didn't take much brainpower to realize there would be no complaints in my writing, because that would not be a Third Eye perspective. The rest of what she told me I decided would go into my journal for later study. It scrambled my brain to think about it. In fact, Winged Wolf told me not to think, instead to absorb what she was telling me. *"Don't try to analyze what I tell you, or you won't be able to grasp it."*

I was never so grateful to fall into bed as I was that first night, although even in the privacy of 'my' room there was some anxiety; I was fearful I would never sleep. Another thing Winged Wolf had told me before leaving for the night was that she could hear my thoughts, and if I had a lot of mind chatter, it would keep her awake and she hoped that wouldn't happen.

Then she said, *"And if I don't sleep well, especially for more than a day or two, it makes me crabby."*

Once in bed, I prayed my mind would be still. I don't remember falling asleep, but the next thing I knew the sunlight was shining through my open window and the day's heat was beginning to arise.

There was a morning ritual already established at Eastcliffe, which was to gather in the living room, notebook in hand, at about 8:00 a.m. There, we would sit in a circle with the Teacher, and sing the HÜM, a sound something like the OM sound, but a higher vibration. According to Winged Wolf, the HÜM is the original sound, or the sound of the VOID. After HÜMing for a while to bring the energies into alignment, there was an open forum that lasted for an hour or so where we could ask any questions and receive oral Teachings from Winged Wolf.

That first morning I was partially numb with sleep and jet lag, but mostly paralyzed with fear that I would say something wrong. It's hard to describe why I would feel this way because Winged Wolf really hadn't done anything to me that would warrant my reaction; but she was so direct and outspoken, honest, and sharp in her responses, that I felt intimidated. No one had ever talked to me in such a way before. I was used to the polite lies people tell each other out in the world, and while a part of me abhorred that phoniness, I also could see how comfortable I had become with it. It was so predictable and safe.

Fortunately, Marla didn't seem a bit concerned by all the things I found so frightening; and she had many questions about the workings of the Shaman Consciousness so our time was occupied until Winged Wolf declared we should eat breakfast and then busy ourselves in the garden. Afterward, she had some book mailings we were to help her with. One thing I noticed during this interactive time was that Winged Wolf didn't pull any punches with Marla. If there was something off-base, she confronted it directly; but contrary to my overly sensitive nature,

Marla didn't seem remotely troubled by these confronting experiences. She took it more like a debate.

"Life is a dream," Winged Wolf taught us, *"a succession of images passing through the mind. If you can begin to understand what this means, you can take control of your lives."*

By the way she said it, I understood this was important, so I wrote it down for future study. When the morning session ended, I had barely spoken, although I took copious notes and tried to look intelligent. I felt like an alien watching a strange movie. I longed for the day when my friends from Michigan would arrive, and I would feel some sense of normalcy again surrounded by their familiar faces and ways. This was going to be really intense.

During my first full day at Eastcliffe, we did things I had never done before, simple things on the surface, but so different from my typical day. I learned how to pack books in boxes without damaging their bindings, weigh them for postage, secure the boxes properly and sort and label by zip code. I'd never known an author before and assumed they just wrote books and someone else took care of publishing, marketing and shipping. But this was a one-person show. Winged Wolf did it all herself, including having her own publishing company. I was in awe of her independence, while simultaneously complaining in my head about the tedium of the work. Why didn't she let someone else take care of all these details?

After we boxed up all we could and loaded the car, Winged Wolf announced we were leaving for the post office and town, and to 'hurry up.' I still wasn't allowed to look directly at Siouxy and was self-conscious about whether she would ever accept me. If she didn't, I felt Winged Wolf might take that as a black mark against me, and maybe I wouldn't be allowed to stay. Certainly this was another irrational fear I assured myself, but it seemed Siouxy had great importance to her. She had been given to Winged Wolf by people Alana Spirit Changer knew, who were also Sioux.

"It was a gift to help me get in touch with my wolf nature," she told us. I could see she and the wolf were very close and she valued her as a dear friend and something deeper than that, but I wasn't sure exactly what. Thus, Sioux's approval of me was important.

Meanwhile, Winged Wolf was in the car, motor running, as I dashed out of the house clutching a purse and my notebook. Marla was sitting in the front seat passenger side, so I got in the back, relieved to be as far in the background as I could. Maybe this was how Siouxy felt when she was in the car crouching as far to the back as she could. Perhaps she, too, wanted to be invisible. I hoped Winged Wolf wouldn't notice I was tongue-tied and overwhelmed. It seemed she and Marla had an ease of communication that amazed me. How could Marla be so relaxed with this Teacher who frightened me speechless?

And all the while, a part of me was saying, *'This is just like in the books when she wrote about her apprenticeship with her Teacher Alana Spirit Changer. It's real, and I'm here doing it too!'* And again I literally pinched myself to make sure this wasn't a dream. Later, I came to realize that all life is a dream; the only difference being that a conscious being presents their own dream, but it was just words to me then.

For some reason, I had a difficult time staying all the way in my body. This whole scene was so foreign to my life at home. Winged Wolf said this was because I wasn't used to staying in the present moment. When I was little, everything frightened me and I clung to my mother for support. I controlled situations by leaving my body when I became uncomfortable. Here, I had no place to run and no place to hide, so whenever Winged Wolf's attention wasn't fully on me, I automatically jumped out of my skin, halfway.

Somehow it helped if I thought about my friends, or my grown children, or my dog, or some activity I had planned for the future. Then I remembered my life as normal and comfortable. There was an identity to it that gave me a sense of security. I said to myself, *'You can do anything for a week. Then it will be over, and you can go home.'* As long as I looked at it this way, I could survive my visit.

Winged Wolf must have heard my mind chatter, because she said, *"While you're here, I want you to live as though you are staying forever, as if there is no other place. Be totally focused in this moment, because there really isn't anything but now. Don't think about home or family or friends. Be totally here each moment."*

'She's taking away my security anchors,' I thought, as I tried to do what she asked. Surprisingly, I felt better for a little while. The paradox was that if I didn't put any attention on home, I became relaxed and

Initiation

comfortable where I was. Yet, as soon as I relaxed and became comfortable, something out of the ordinary would occur and I would become frightened. To relieve my anxiety, my thoughts would return to home. What a vicious circle! The observer part of me was curious about these habitual patterns that were surfacing for me to witness.

Cottonwood, from what I could see of it, was a tiny town, a couple blocks long at the most. It took about ten minutes to drive to the post office, and most of that was getting off the dirt road that led to Eastcliffe. There was a health food store, a feed store that supplied needed items for the horses, a restaurant, bank, and two or three antique stores. Oh, and there was a movie theatre that was so old and rickety that it was quaint.

Winged Wolf parked in front of the post office and Marla quickly got out of the car; she and Winged Wolf started hauling in boxes. I joined in and followed everything Marla did. She exuded a level of confidence that felt comfortable for me to follow, like a big sister.

After putting the boxes to be mailed on the counter, Marla took the keys for the post office box and I followed her to the mailbox, where she retrieved the mail and returned to Winged Wolf, handing it to her. I felt like a little puppy dog in a human body.

Winged Wolf was standing at the counter talking to the clerk about weights and postage. *"She likes to have it all ready for them,"* Marla whispered.

What a surprise that one could have such a degree of control over their own mail. Winged Wolf weighed it, stamped it, sorted it by zip code and told them at what rate to ship it. She did just about everything short of delivering it herself. It was interesting to watch someone who was so in command of situations. Even though the postal clerk was theoretically in command, I could see that was not the case. Winged Wolf was definitely orchestrating, albeit in a kind and friendly manner. *'Imagine treating every situation you encounter as this important, even going to the post office,'* I thought to myself. I could almost hear her voice respond, *'It is.'*

Mail time was apparently a big deal because she didn't wait to get home to go through it. Instead, she animatedly flipped through it in the car as soon as Marla handed it to her, appearing curious about every piece, and occasionally commenting on something she received. Her favorite mail seemed to be letters from apprentices, which she separated from the rest of the mail and quickly opened and skimmed. At times, she would talk to the person writing as though they were present. I watched in fascination.

Once she said, *"Shush,"* to me, and I realized I had been mentally speculating as to the content of a letter she was reading.

We sat in the car until Winged Wolf had finished opening all the apprentice letters and cursorily reading them. Then she put them back in the pile and we took off. I was going to have a tour of the town, which was very small and looked old. The area wasn't pleasing to my eyes because it was so dry and brown, but I tried to look with new eyes since she was so enthusiastic about the area. Perhaps I would come to like it if I could see it as she did.

After that, the days gained momentum and began to pass quickly. It was like a snowball effect; the week had begun with every minute seeming to take a week, then suddenly, days were passing so quickly. It was only because of my journaling that I could make any distinctions about them. I began to see that time and space were really only illusions we had created to help distinguish one thing from another. Tomorrow my Michigan friends would be arriving.

With delight, I realized it no longer mattered. Even though I was still sometimes uncomfortable in Winged Wolf's presence, I was no longer waiting to have protection or planning an escape. I was beginning to appreciate being in the presence of the Teacher.

It mattered little whether or not I voluntarily stuck my neck out by speaking. One of the natural effects of the spiritualized consciousness is that it acts like a magnet or vacuum, drawing people's gook, their stored-up, negative mind stuff, to the surface, like a vacuum cleaner does on the carpet. The closer you get to the vacuum, the more likely it is that the dirt will come up. Winged Wolf referred to the mind gook that became visible as 'handles.'

She would say, *"That handle was sticking so far out, I just had to grab it."* Then she'd open her eyes wide, and grin. But I could see it was painful for her, too, at least until she had grabbed the handle. Our pain became her pain because of the strings of energy between us.

One day, as we were riding in the Suburban, a dark mood descended upon me as though a storm cloud had just moved in and settled into my being. I didn't know exactly why it came and I couldn't shake it off, so I tried to hide it, but that was futile.

Winged Wolf asked, *"What just happened with your energy?"*

"I honestly don't know," I responded. *"This horrible, dark mood just came over me and I can't shake it."*

By now we had turned off the main road to drive up a steep hill. She stopped the car.

"Get out," she said. I just looked at her.

"Get out of the car," she repeated, looking directly at me without any expression on her face. So I did.

"Shut the door." I did, my insides churning.

"Now run," she ordered, and began to move the car.

I ran, jogged really, up the hill, breathing heavily, a mixture of thoughts running through my mind. *"I can't believe this is happening,"* I thought. *"Is she going to take off and leave me?"*

She continued driving slowly up the hill, until pretty soon there were no more thoughts. When she stopped the car to allow me back in, I was breathing heavily from the exertion, but my mood had totally shifted.

The darkness was gone and I felt light and buoyant, almost giddy. Where had it gone? Nothing had changed that I could see. *'What happened?'* My analytical mind demanded an explanation.

Certainly in the past I had used physical exercise to influence my moods, and I understood all about endorphins and their effects. But this happened in only a few minutes, and besides the mood shift, it was as if the cellular memory of the incident had also been erased. And that was not a result of exercise! I felt completely at ease and light-hearted. *'If a feeling can be this easily transmuted,'* I pondered, *'what is a feeling really? And what does the Shaman Consciousness DO to enable that to happen?'*

"What just happened, Winged Wolf?" I asked.

"The negative energy was transmuted. That's the DO of shamanism, the transmutation of negative energy through action and interaction with the Consciousness."

That made sense in a way, but I still didn't understand what the Consciousness did to transmute the negative energy, or what caused it in the first place. So this was one of the big puzzlements I wrote about in answer to my question *'What have I learned during my stay at Eastcliffe?'*

I couldn't pull together an intelligent response, because, while I could see what happened, I didn't understand it. The impact was therapeutic, and I saw that the Teacher was a catalyst for change, but the result was not typical of therapy where one might spend weeks or months working through a feeling. This happened instantaneously and didn't require knowing the cause.

This is why most of what Winged Wolf did, I didn't understand. I kept trying to fit it into some system or theory that was familiar to me. As a practicing psychotherapist, that part of me kept trying to understand the techniques, but they didn't fit any pattern I could see, other than to use motion of some sort to transmute energy. I didn't believe in magic, but something was going on behind the scenes to make it look like that.

And it produced rapid shifts that resulted in a sense of well-being and contentment. And not just in me. It was obvious in the other apprentices, and I even saw it in the post office. The clerk would talk to Winged Wolf and suddenly the clerk's face would light up or she would start dropping things. Or, the Visa machine wouldn't work, or the lights would go off.

There were certain unusual environmental responses like shifts in weather patterns, but I couldn't make sense of them. It kept me continuously off-balance, not having any idea what to expect, but in a way, I was having a great time and felt totally alive and on my toes. Maybe this was what she meant by 'releasing karmic baggage.'

I had spent years as a therapist working with clients without producing such effective results as Winged Wolf was able to produce in a few moments. I was really hoping to gain some experiences that I could take back to my therapy practice, but my brain kept going on tilt. I was happy, but I sure didn't feel as smart as I did before my visit. Whatever was transpiring to produce these changes was not based on any technique that I could see. There was something much deeper occurring here.

Months later, as I would reflect on the 'jogging incident,' some pieces would come together. A talk at Winged Wolf's would awaken something in me and stimulate the reflection. She would tell us to, *"Wake up! You spend lifetimes going in circles, repeating the same patterns, producing the same results. The only way to wake up is through awareness of the images that are passing through your minds."*

I would realize that at the time I had been so caught up in the excitement of the incident that I failed to consider the broader implications of it in my life. I would remember the image that had triggered the mood of despondency, and realize that very image in many disguises was still controlling me, sending me into deep despair, causing me to repeat self-destructive behavior patterns. Mindlessly going in circles, that's what I had been doing when she interrupted my mood in the car. But that realization came later.

Now, near the end of my visit, Winged Wolf came into my room one night and said, *"I'd like to read your journal."*

Handing it to her, my hands began to tremble. What would she say about what I had written? Did I sound as dumb as I felt? Surely she would see how spiritually ignorant I was, resistant and judgmental in my thoughts, because even though I was having many high spots and learning a great deal, old patterns still continued to haunt me.

I found myself automatically judging and assessing everything: the way she dressed, the way she talked, the way she had us work long hours in the heat. It didn't seem to matter what was going on, my mind always compared what she did with what I thought was right. Sometimes Winged Wolf came out on top, and then I was her adoring student; other times I came out on top, and then I was her judge and jury. It was constant flip-flopping.

The next morning after she took my journal, Winged Wolf handed it back to me without a word. I couldn't read her expression at all. Later, I noticed there were some notes here and there in red ink where she had asked a probing question, or made a comment, but nothing critical was said. When I had some time to study the comments, I saw they were geared toward expanding or deepening my understanding of something. They led me to another level of awareness about something previously unseen. Her mind was sharp; it picked out the gaps and zoomed in on them.

There had been some relief for me when my two Michigan friends arrived, since it took some of Winged Wolf's attention off of me and put it on them. Or at least that was my perception. By then, I was tuned in enough to know when someone said something she was going to pounce on, and I would hold my breath waiting. It always made me uncomfortable and squirmy, whether it was someone else or myself. To an extent, it all felt like me, but secretly, it was a relief to be off the hot seat for a while.

A couple mornings after they arrived, my one friend pulled me aside and whispered to me, *"She came to my room in the middle of the night."*

"She did?" I could feel my eyes widen. *"What did she say?"*

"She told me to get dressed, we were going for a walk."

"What?" I was astounded.

"Yes, it was because of my mind chatter. I was giving her a headache."

"Well, what happened?" I was enormously curious.

"I don't know exactly, but after we took a walk and talked, she said her headache was gone and for me to go back to sleep."

This was an amazing thing to me, a Teacher who wakes you up in the night and accuses you of giving her a headache. I found it difficult to believe that anyone could give another person a headache in their sleep. But my friend seemed to accept it, so maybe there was something to this. What a strange idea!

One day I was sitting on the back porch writing in my journal when, out of the blue, Winged Wolf came out and said, *"Do you see that cottonwood tree over there?"*

"Yes," I said squinting in the bright light.

"I'd like you to dig a hole about 4-feet wide and 3-feet deep right over there under it. Then sit in the hole until I tell you to get out." Pausing as if I'd asked a question, she replied, *"I'll talk to you more about it later."*

'What brought this on?' I wondered, as I dug the hole and sat there for at least a couple hours. *'I wonder what I am supposed to learn from this experience, or what I did to cause it?'* After a while, it didn't matter. I relaxed and watched the day roll by, grinning to myself at the strange experiences I was collecting. Surely they would serve some purpose in my work and in my life.

Eventually, Winged Wolf came and motioned me out of the hole, and without a word, turned her back and went into the house. The incident was never mentioned again, although I waited in anticipation for her to tell me more.

Months later it dawned on me that she needed a break from my constant mind chatter. Back then it was still beyond my imagination that one being could hear another's thoughts. But the bigger lesson for me was that by distracting me from my ordinary ways, it quieted my mind and made me look more deeply into other things. It actually created an opening for learning to take place.

There was a moment during that first visit when I recognized that some of the Teaching was actually being integrated into my being. It was a small triumph, but something tangible. I was walking in the pasture with my dear friend, who had just arrived, and I had been describing to her some of the work we would be doing in the next few days. Actually, I was enthused about it, as we would be chopping bamboo to be used as walking sticks on the medicine walk.

My friend looked at me skeptically and said, *"I didn't come here to do all this work,"* and I responded, *"The physical work is part of how Winged Wolf teaches us, part of the DO of shamanism. You'll be amazed what realizations you have during your stay here, and the physical work is an important part of it."* I was so startled to hear myself say this. I really had learned something without any conscious awareness of having learned it!

The end of my stay was nearing, and again I asked myself the question, *"What have I learned from being here?"* On the inside of me, there were major shifts occurring. It felt like I was getting an oil change and a tune-up. My breath no longer caught when Winged Wolf looked at me, although I was still cautious in my speaking.

Whatever one of us said, there was something off-balance about it, and Winged Wolf swooped in on us so quickly, it was stunning. Like a snake strike, so fast you don't even see it coming and you are only left with the sting of the bite. Depending on the degree of our imbalance, the resultant sting could be major or minor. I was not ready to stick my neck out and have it bitten any more than I already had, which really wasn't very much, but my ego couldn't take much confrontation at that time.

Chapter 5
The Medicine Walk

Preparations were now fully underway for the medicine walk. This meant we went to the store and bought things that could be cooked simply over a fire for about twenty or so people. Winged Wolf was so quick in everything she did. No time was wasted; every moment was used purposefully. Even when she played, and Winged Wolf loved to play, there was always a sense of purpose to it.

"The divine consciousness never acts without a purpose, never speaks without a purpose," she used to say to us. *"Even laughter has a purpose; often it is a healing purpose."*

We walked up and down the aisles of the grocery store, the three of us apprentices following along behind her like baby ducklings following their mama. We watched as she bought dried beans, instant potatoes, peanut butter, bread, cheese crackers, some dried fruit, and some baggies to package them in.

Next, we went to WalMart and hustled up and down the aisles getting supplies for the medicine walk: flashlights, batteries, and plastic in case it rained. There was no pausing to look around at all the displays that usually caught my attention and sidetracked me.

At one point, Winged Wolf stopped abruptly to look at some blouses on a rack in front of her. Pulling one colorfully patterned shirt from the rack, she held it out to me and said, *"Sharon, I think you would look really good in this shirt, don't you?"*

Startled, I wasn't sure how to respond. I didn't need a shirt, but it wasn't really sounding like a 'yes-no' question, more a rhetorical statement, so I half-nodded, and to my surprise, she handed it to me. I guess she expected me to buy it, so I did.

Later, as I wrote about the experience in my journal, it came to me that this was one of the ways Winged Wolf had of gluing my attention to her, that is, always doing the unexpected with me, keeping me slightly off-balance, which resulted in my attention always being glued to her. *'She is always challenging my habitual ways of being.'* I chuckled with the realization.

A big part of this lesson was to keep my attention so focused on Winged Wolf that nothing would distract me, and there would be no space for mind chatter since, in order to keep up, it took 100% concentration. More and more, I realized how easily my mind was distracted and tended to wander about as a form of self-entertainment. Early in my training, I learned there was no room for this type of wandering off on my own if I wanted the Shaman Consciousness.

This time, I worried that if I started lagging behind while we were shopping she might leave me there. It wasn't that anything was said, but there was an amazing non-verbal communication that accompanied any of Winged Wolf's conversations, that so underscored the meaning of what she was saying that the entire picture became clear.

So, if she said, *"It's your job to keep up with me when we're in the store; I don't like to waste any time; I like to go in, get what is needed, and be on our way,"* the message was clear: there would be no dilly-dallying around. Winged Wolf would not be standing around waiting for me, and if she did have to wait, there would be consequences, that is to say, she would hold me accountable for not listening and following through with her instructions. Even though I didn't really know what the consequences would be, I didn't want to find out.

Follow-through was becoming an important lesson to grasp. I was expected to pay attention to what was being said and remember it. I couldn't do my usual 'listen and fluff it off,' because she was like a mirror reflecting back my behavior and it was a most uncomfortable reflection when I wasn't being impeccable.

Later, Winged Wolf told me, *"The reason my words have such impact is that every fiber of my being is 100% involved in what I am communicating, and because of this, the energy of words carries great power. I live totally in the present moment and my communication reflects this.*

"The ordinary consciousness is usually so caught up in thoughts of the past or fantasies of the future, it is rare when someone puts their total attention on what they are communicating. All of my speech and actions are completely in line with my intent. This is why it is so important that you learn to live in the moment. All true power comes from this understanding."

Mentally, I searched my mind for evidence of this and realized she was speaking the truth. The only person in my life who I felt spoke clearly and directly was my father, whom I adored and idolized. He was my hero and role model, but he allowed my mother to overshadow and dominate him. Our relationship was in the background and generally focused on her needs. Because of this, while my father was straightforward, honest and had a wonderful sense of humor, he was in the background. This was especially true after his retirement.

For the most part, I was unused to this type of communication; it made me work hard to focus my attention on what was said, and kept a healthy respect present in my attitude toward our relationship. Not only did Winged Wolf speak with authority, she meant exactly what she said and expected the same from me.

I flashed on all the times in my life that I had complained I wasn't being heard. Now I could understand why that was. I had never learned to communicate with such power behind my words in the way Winged Wolf did, and so no one listened. I really didn't intend to be heard. It was easier to complain.

Back at Eastcliffe, we began making sandwiches and other preparations for an early departure the following morning. Since I was still really attached to my comforts, I was worried whether I could make the long hike carrying a heavy backpack, so mostly I chatted away in my head about that and got little pleasure in the preparations.

Marla had already done a medicine walk with Winged Wolf earlier in the summer, so she would take care of the animals and the house. She had also done a vision quest, which made her really special in my eyes.

An image of an evening prior to the others' arrival popped into my mind. Winged Wolf had not been around, and I was so curious about Marla's experiences during the four weeks she had been at Eastcliffe that I couldn't refrain from plying her with questions.

She had answered my questions patiently, and then I had tried to pry some information from her on the nature of a vision quest she had mentioned. At that point in my spiritual development, it was way beyond me why anyone would want to sit out in the forest by themselves, deprived of food and stimulation; but I was, oh, so curious. Marla had told me there was only one part she could talk about. It happened on her second day out.

In an incredulous voice, she had told me this part of her experience. *"I was sitting in my circle, trying to be still and focused at the Third Eye when a bee began circling. I've always been terrified of a bee sting, so I began to panic. Then I remembered to put my attention on the Third Eye and call for Winged Wolf. Instantly I became calm. Pretty soon there were more bees, a lot of them; a few of them landed on my arm."*

She had continued on, *"I stayed totally still and watched. Pretty soon there were maybe forty of them all over my body. I could feel them walking up and down my arms and face. It must have gone on like this for a couple hours, and I stayed focused the whole time. Suddenly, for no apparent reason, they all flew off in a swarm. I hadn't been bitten once."*

As she had told me this story, she relived it and I could see it all unfold through her eyes. What an amazing experience of living the power of the Teachings, keeping her attention on the Third Eye. Her fear of bees had been completely erased. It made my concerns about carrying a backpack look so silly to me. It didn't quiet them, but caused me to admire Marla's courage all the more.

There were about twenty people participating in the medicine walk, including several more friends from Michigan, so I began to feel relaxed and comfortable with my support system intact. Plus, I had just spent a week with the Teacher and they hadn't; so at least I had some experience on that score.

Winged Wolf told me that a really motivated student imitates the Teacher's every move, their walk, their talk and their facial expressions. I remembered her saying, *"To become like someone you admire, you must imitate them, but that doesn't mean you imitate their limp."*

Since I wasn't sure I'd recognize a limp at this point, I just decided to imitate everything she did. To do so, I wanted to be in number one position behind her and was unusually assertive about it, not at all my usual behavior. I stuck to Winged Wolf like we were tied together, like she was a great ship and I was riding in her wake. That's how intense my intention was. I wanted what she had, and what I saw was a power and fierceness of commitment that I had never experienced before and I didn't care if anyone knew it.

Some time afterwards, I learned from one friend how obnoxious she found my behavior to be on that trip, but for once in my life, I honestly didn't care what anyone thought. There were times when I knew my friend wanted to be in the first slot behind the Teacher, and she shot me a few looks to let me know how she felt about my refusal to relinquish my position, but it just didn't matter.

During the walk, I learned many valuable lessons from being so focused on my Teacher: things about following, and about being part of a whole yet being individual. I also observed my Teacher. Her style of movement was different from mine. Whereas I tended to be tentative, watching every step, she was a starburst, surefooted and fast. She would move rapidly for several hundred feet until she was out ahead of the group, and then pause to catch her breath and wait for us to catch up. This allowed no time to think or for any uncertainty. While she was waiting for the others to catch up, she would scan ahead, looking for gateways, or openings for us to proceed through in our trek toward the evening's campsite. We were constantly crisscrossing the creek, and I learned the hard way that if I hesitated or got distracted instead of following in her footsteps, I fell in.

Several times she stopped and made comments to people, clearly either reading their minds or sensing the energy of the group. We had one person in particular in the group who was in terrible physical condition and lagged behind. One time Winged Wolf stopped abruptly, turned and spoke firmly to the person behind me who was a strong hiker. *"She's your sister,"* she said quietly in a compassionate tone of voice. I understood immediately that this person had been mentally criticizing the slower person, perceiving her as holding us back, and was being reminded by the Teacher to have compassion.

After we walked about six miles into the forest, Winged Wolf began looking for a spot to camp for the night, and I lightened up. This wasn't so difficult after all. How much mental energy I had wasted with my foolish concerns!

We found an open area, spread out our gear, and with a bright sunny afternoon ahead, some of us took off walking up-stream. The air was so fresh and clean, I felt high on life. We found a secluded spot, stripped, and jumped into the cold, clear water, swimming, splashing, laughing and just playing around. It was the most pristine beauty I'd ever seen captured in one place and totally ours. What luxury!

Finishing our water play, we let the sun dry us off, dressed, and headed back to the campsite. Those who had stayed at the site were also relaxing, lounging around in small groups or individually, soaking up the pristine environment and letting the wear and tear of all life's stresses fall away. Winged Wolf seemed totally relaxed and happy, although she kept herself a little separated from the group, building castles from the rocks she found by the river.

That evening, we cooked the dried beans and instant potatoes, and it tasted like a gourmet meal. As darkness descended, we made drumming music and rocked our bodies to and fro, letting the rhythm of the drumbeats carry our bodies in a gentle back-and-forth motion.

Earlier in the day, Winged Wolf gave a lesson on distinguishing between dead rocks and living rocks, and she demonstrated the different sounds so we could hear and feel the difference.

She said, *"In order to tell if a rock is still alive, listen to the sound it makes when you tap it against something. It's easiest if you tap together two rocks that are about the same size.*

"A rock that is dead will not resonate; the sound will be flat, with no reverberation, like a dull clunk. The feeling is one of dullness, like you've just stopped the energy from flowing. Whereas, a living rock, when tapped against another rock, vibrates with energy, and the sound is pleasant to the ear. It feels alive and there is a sense of movement of energy."

We all scurried about tapping rocks together until we found pairs of living rocks that made fine-sounding, ready-made drumming instruments. What fun to be so spontaneous and improvisational. That evening a healing took place. As we lit the torches in a semi-circle and swayed to the rhythm of the drums, I watched people's faces transform. I felt hearts open and love pouring out of people, not toward anyone in particular, just loving life and freedom and feeling good and *being* together.

Winged Wolf leaned over toward me and asked, *"Did you ever see her look so totally open and wholehearted in what she is doing?"* I looked in the direction of her gaze and saw my long-time friend swaying to the music, completely relaxed and open.

"No, I never have, Winged Wolf. It's quite amazing the power of divine love."

Occasionally I saw her glance at Walter with a peculiar look, and I tried to speculate on what she might be seeing. Earlier in the day she had made a few comments to him that caught my attention.

Her first interaction had been to comment on his attire. *"Walter,"* she said, *"you look like you're wearing army fatigues."*

When I took a good look at him, it did appear he had dressed with a military look.

He had seemed nonplussed by her comment, and just nodded and smiled, perhaps thinking it was a compliment.

After a pause, she had pressed him, *"Why do you want to look like you're in the military?"*

I could see the light go on. *"Oh,"* he said, *"I didn't realize I looked like the military. Let me change that look."* He had brought a second outfit with him and quickly changed his attire.

Then, later in the walk, she had commented, *"Walter, what is that thing you've got around your neck?"*

"It's a water bottle with a tube attached that comes right up to my mouth," he said proudly showing it to her.

This time she had said nothing further, giving him another of those sideways looks that I read as a message un-received. Did she think this was more of the military attire? I had wondered. Or was it a comment about his attachment to comforts?

As darkness descended and we settled in for the night, I discovered that sleeping wasn't too great, since our sleeping bags were on an angle, and Walt and I kept sliding down the side of the rock; then we'd have to pull ourselves back up and try to sleep again. I was just as glad when morning arrived, but still happy because it was the first time ever I had spent a night out under the stars. There were no bugs! If this had been Michigan, we'd have been eaten alive by mosquitoes.

In the morning after breakfast, we packed up our gear and began the hike back out of the forest. Partway back, Winged Wolf stopped us at a special place and had each of us pass through it, one at a time, and pause to notice what we felt.

As I passed through, I paused to feel the energy shift. There was a definite pressure point where the energy shifted noticeably from the pristine, peaceful, vibrant energy we had been experiencing, which was so powerful, to something different, more condensed, thicker.

After we had each passed through, she told us, *"This place is special because of how the energy forms here."* I looked around at the rock formations and noted that physically there was an indentation, a grotto in the rocks.

"The energy hovers here," she continued, *"because of the shape of the rock; it is shaped like a cove. It is like a vacuum that picks up the sensations of the energies that come through. And because of the way it is shaped, the energy doubles back on itself and you can feel the energy of the area magnified. This makes it a power spot."*

Then, looking directly at me, she said quietly, *"I want you to become more aware of the energies around you, Sharon. This will become most important as you progress on your Journeys."* And in response to my unspoken 'why?' she said, *"There is no point in telling you more now. You couldn't make use of the information; just begin to pay attention to what is happening to the energy in your environment. Be aware that there are many power spots where energy can be used in various ways, but you must first become aware of them. Train yourself to be present in each moment, keep your awareness on that 360-degree viewpoint which sees everything that each moment contains."*

"That sounds impossible to me," I responded trying to imagine being aware of everything all at once.

"It's not impossible at all. That is the way I live life. You just need focused concentration, and to have that, you must get your little-self,

with all its thoughts and beliefs and opinions, out of the way."

I didn't know what to say after that, so I said nothing, but my mind was sure chattering. I simply couldn't imagine there was nothing going on in her mind and she could still be aware and respond to situations.

"Your analytical mind is much too strong," she said. *"If you don't learn to discipline it you will never attain Shaman Consciousness."* And with that, she turned and continued the forward trek out of the forest. *'Oh boy,'* I thought, *'there she goes on my analytical mind again.'*

As we walked, I remembered the sensation of walking through that power spot. How many times in my life had I absently walked through energy and been impacted by it without any awareness of what was happening? Surely I would not have noticed it on the way in as preoccupied as I was with whether I could make the walk.

After a day of being in the energy of that power spot, I had relaxed and let go of enough mind chatter to notice the difference, and even then, it had to be pointed out to me. But, once noticed, the difference was no longer subtle at all; it was dramatic and obvious. I could tell from the little Winged Wolf had said and from reading her books that a Shaman made use of power spots. Hadn't she and Alana used the energy of the sun's rays to move back and forth between Colorado and California?

Although I had asked her to tell me about that experience during one of our morning talks, she had said, *"What purpose would it serve? If it would serve you, I would tell you about it."*

Winged Wolf interrupted my reverie to comment quietly, *"I see you have your sunglasses on."* I understood her meaning. I had been deliberately training myself to give up the dark glasses after Winged Wolf made some statements to us that wearing dark glasses blocked our ability to relate, since the eyes are the seat of divine expression. By covering them, in essence I covered myself. She had noticed that I walked into the forest without sunglasses, with my heart open, and instinctively I had put them back on to walk out and face the world; I would be going back to Michigan the next morning.

Also, she had told me that in many ways it is more difficult to walk the Path as a married person than one who is unattached. Although many saw having a spouse on the Path as a blessing, I had some glimpses that it would bring challenges the others, who were single, would not have to face.

While I held my marriage out as something to be valued, an asset, I also knew it brought out all my insecurities. I was glad Walter and I had come separately so I could have the experience of being myself with Winged Wolf, without the added complication of a spouse.

At this point in my apprenticeship, Winged Wolf was treading lightly on marital issues, but I knew she was observing us individually and as a couple. She had caught me a few times with jealous thoughts, so she was already aware of one of my great weaknesses. And Walter loved to flirt, so together we had a dynamic that caused friction.

'She was smart to separate us,' I thought to myself. *'Otherwise we would always be aware of each other and not able to focus solely on the Path.'*

During the rest of our exit walk, I tried to stay totally focused on the present moment, to clear my mind of all thought and just *be*. I listened to the 'crunch, crunch, crunch' of our footsteps as we walked in companion energy with the Teacher. As she lifted her foot, I lifted mine, no thought, only synchronized motion.

We became a whole, not many individuals separate from each other, but one whole, like a snake with Winged Wolf as the head and eyes and the rest of us as the body. Mark (a deaf male apprentice that she trusted) was the tail. We did this because of our common goal and our agreement to follow the Teacher both physically and spiritually.

If one person refused to accept these conditions, the oneness would break down, as it did briefly in those instances when Winged Wolf had to correct someone's mental attitude or behavior. When this happened, I saw how our bodies were affected.

As I mentioned, Winged Wolf was naturally agile, quick and competent, as solid on her feet as any mountain goat, but when the group energy got weird, when someone was tired, complaining in his or her mind, or lagging behind, Winged Wolf literally would be thrown off her feet at times, often from a rock into the water. At first when I observed this happen, my mind denied that it was possible; the ramifications were awesome. I decided it was coincidence, knowing full well there are no coincidences. But when it happened repeatedly at the precise point that one of us got out of balance, I could no longer deny it.

Awareness dawned in me of how powerful group energy is and how subtle it can be, and I realized some of the broader implications for my life and the broader community. My gosh, the minute we make a connection with someone, we become influenced by their energy and vice-versa, because of the agreement we have between us. Even when there is no agreement, we would still be impacted by energy that is out there in the environment, although to a lesser degree, and it would be worse if we were unaware of it. Right there, I saw one reason for me to become aware of the energy around me.

Winged Wolf had taught us about something she called *'strings of energy'* that are literally made up of collections of molecules and atoms that form between people and objects, and between people and entities that have translated. She said that by putting our attention strongly, with feeling, on something or someone, we connect ourselves to them by our intent. And not just in a mental or psychic sense, but literally, through the power of our attention to direct those atoms and molecules.

This was seeing the Teachings in action. Whenever I was totally in sync with Winged Wolf's steps on the trail, I could feel the connection of our feet. As her foot lifted, mine was pulled forward too, like the wheels of a train all moving together, pulled forward by the first wheel. When the person behind me got out of step, I felt a tiny, but noticeable, pull against me until the person had completely broken stride, then the experience changed. The jolt actually came in the pulling away.

The awareness of ramifications of this understanding were so great to look at in that moment, I decided to tuck it away for the time being. It would force me to relook at all my relationships, all my agreements; maybe even force me to change my thinking that I was a separate, independent being, and alter my definition of what responsible action really meant. Every time I tried to put it down though, it came at me from another angle. *'Oh, look at this; oh, look at that.'* Amazing how quickly I could go from a silent mind to all this mental chatter. It was such a long-standing habit.

In no time, we were back near the main road, and Winged Wolf pointed to the blackberry bushes, *"Look at the feast that is waiting for us,"* and she began to eat the blackberries that were fully ripened on the bushes.

Naturally, we all stopped to join her and feast on the most delicious berries. We all turned blue and purple as we crammed these sweet, juicy berries into our mouths as fast as we could. This was manna from heaven. Soon I had forgotten all about strings of energy in the sheer pleasure of that explosion of flavor as the berries burst open in my mouth — what a simple but powerful moment to bring our healing walk to its conclusion.

We said our good-byes right there on the road, and those of us going with Winged Wolf headed back to Eastcliffe, three of us to pack up and leave in the morning and the other three to stay for their week. We were pretty much exhausted on the ride back, so there was a comfortable quiet in the car.

After showers and a light supper, we all sat out on the back porch and watched darkness descend. One by one, the stars popped out as the sky darkened and turned black.

It was a brilliant night, full moon shining, and we could see the magic mountain across the river turn white and shimmering. What a phenomenal sight for my last evening. I wished it would go on forever, all of us together, sitting there enjoying the same sight, feeling at One with each other and the night.

Finally, Winged Wolf rose and announced, *"It's getting late and we've got an early morning. Let's everyone get a good night's sleep. I'll see you in the morning."* It was a beautiful ending for my visit, and I felt full and satisfied. There was nothing I needed to make me happy. I was already there.

Chapter 6
A Foot in Each World

After returning from my visit to Eastcliffe, I experienced myself living a double existence. It was the oddest sensation. Everything was exactly the same on the surface. I still did all the things I had always done, but there was a tiny capsule of the Teacher's consciousness living within me. I carried her around with me always, and it was expanding, something like a beginning romance that makes the heart sing, but is too personal to speak about. I could talk about the Teachings, but my relationship with Winged Wolf was still pretty private.

With my children and my parents, I downplayed my spiritual studies. My mother had already decided I was in a cult and freely told anyone who would listen, *"My daughter's lost her mind. Do you know what she's doing? Why she's joined a cult."* Even when my friends were over, she would say to them, *"You're not in that same cult that Sharon is, are you? I thought you had better sense."* There was no reasoning with her brand of logic, so I finally just let it be. I was disappointed though. I anticipated she would be more supportive.

This sense of being split or having split attention occurred whenever my inner truth was not expressed through my DO. In other words, inside, I knew I was different; I was living with new understanding of what my life was about, but outside, I was still driven by a desire to please so I adapted to what others expected of me. I wasn't willing to walk my talk. It was more comfortable for me to allow others to think nothing had changed. *'This way there will be no disruption in our relationship,'* was the lie I told myself to justify the behavior.

After this, I began to observe myself. I noticed there were two types of behavioral response to difficult situations that I found most comfortable. Depending on how I perceived a situation, when a challenge to my integrity arose that demanded I conform to someone else's standards, I both rebelled angrily and distanced myself or I adapted on the surface and did my own thing privately. Either way, I was being untrue to myself; both were ways of adapting to others' expectations. I wasn't *'aligning my actions with my dreams,'* as Winged Wolf taught us to do.

This adapting to please others or rebelling against them were really flip sides of the same coin; both denied the truth. This was a pattern that became one of the major challenges of my apprenticeship, because it was so deeply ingrained. The most I could do at the time was to observe what a stranglehold it had on me and try not to be too hard on myself. In a way, I was choosing to use this tendency to adapt as a way to find my own inner core. By choosing the Teacher to align with, I was choosing to bring forth those higher qualities in me that I had been seeking to uncover. But in order to do this, I had to adapt to doing things her way. So it was taking my weakness and putting it to a higher purpose until I had the strength to stand on my own.

My adult sons were right there on my mother's bandwagon, so I decided to camouflage myself from them also. Since my divorce from their father, my oldest son felt duty bound to protect me.

Anytime the subject came up of my apprenticeship, he couldn't resist responding, *"Mom, why can't you think for yourself? You don't need somebody to tell you what to do. Don't be a sheep. Use your own mind."*

At first, I would try to reason with him, but he had a lawyer's mind that loved to argue, and it didn't change anything. In his mind, his logic was airtight. Other times, I would take the bait and become defensive, trying to 'prove' my Teacher was guileless and genuinely wanted to teach me something important to my well-being. But no matter what I said, the opposition continued to believe their own viewpoints, until I simply zipped my lips. I had been judged foolish. It stung, and I suffered over their demeaning attitudes toward me; but they, too, had the right to their own perceptions.

For whatever reason, it was threatening to my family to have me develop spiritually. Perhaps they saw it as just another crazy thing I was getting into, since I had made many questionable decisions as a single parent raising two boys. Maybe this fit right in with their impression of my being easily misled by people with ulterior motives.

In addition, I stepped on my own feet and continued to use poor judgment early in my apprenticeship in the things I selected to speak about. Because I was excited, I led with my heart instead of using some wisdom to screen my communications. I told my family things I thought would impress them positively, things out of context, especially some the extraordinary things Winged Wolf had talked about in her books, beginning with *Woman Between the Wind,* that were part of her apprenticeship with her Teacher, Alana Spirit Changer.

In the beginning, my attention focused on the phenomena of her experience. Later, I realized that if the information had been presented to me initially in a way similar to what I presented to my family, it is likely I would have reacted in a like manner. Wisdom came to me much later; unfortunately, the 'evidence' already had been accumulated and the damage was done. At that time, what I had was enthusiasm, commitment and the inner knowing that I was on the right path without the discernment to know what was wise to say and what was not.

Winged Wolf subsequently talked with me about how one learns wisdom and incorporates it into their life, and she included in this talk the way I used my energy unwisely. *"You must acquire wisdom. It is not something that comes automatically. It means to be quiet when there is nothing to say. It means to contain your energy; don't let it spill out all over everyone you meet. You pollute the environment. Even though you are well intended in your enthusiasm, you still impact the environment."*

"But I am containing my energy," I'd assert. *"I'm just enthusiastic."*

"What you are calling enthusiasm is more like excitement bordering on agitation. Your energy becomes excited and it emits a buzzing type vibration. It impacts the environment and those living in it. You have no right to spill it all over the place. It's intrusive. And, more importantly, it lacks wisdom."

This was a really difficult lesson for me to grasp, and it cost me in many ways. My resistance arose from a reluctance to realize that enthusiasm is intrusive rather than infectious, because enthusiasm felt good. So I would be fine for a while, then I'd slip.

"You can never be around large animals like Spirit and Pepe (her Lipizzaner stallion and burro) if you cannot contain your energy. Animals are very sensitive to energy."

A Foot in Each World

The first time Winged Wolf had taken me with her into the corral where Spirit and Pepe lived, she had talked to me outside their gate. *"Hold your energy in,"* she said sternly. *"These animals are responsive to energy and if you are not contained, their energy will get out of balance. Accidents can happen this way. Stay next to me and do exactly what I tell you. Never raise your voice. Speak gently. They love the attention; but you must always remember their size."*

By the time she had finished speaking, I was terrified and stuck to her like glue. Finally, she had told me, *"You can say hello to them and stroke Spirit's muzzle."* It didn't take a minute to figure out that Pepe, the burro, was a pistol, and I did my best to keep Winged Wolf between us. She said *"He's full of mischief,"* but it looked pretty scary to one who had never been close to a burro before. He had this way of looking at me and lowering his ears that seemed like he'd enjoy taking a bite out of me.

Other times she would say, *"You are giving me a headache with your energy. It feels like you are buzzing."*

There was a noticeable pattern to my 'buzzing.' It occurred when I became nervous or excited; then my mind would race and the energy from it oozed out. I had thought that because I wasn't speaking, my Teacher couldn't feel it. And if I was excited, it felt so alive on the inside that I thought it would have to feel good to others outside of me to be a part of that.

Finally she told me, *"It's not that enthusiasm or excitement are inherently good or bad, it's that you do not contain your emotions. All energy must be contained; otherwise, it oozes out into the environment and adds to the confusion that is already present. Then it sticks to others who are in your environment and for the most part they aren't aware how it is affecting them. Suddenly, someone has a headache and they have no idea that it is caused by your leaking energy."*

It took years for me to integrate this lesson, not because I am such a slow learner, although in that area I was, but because I was so unconscious of when it was occurring. Most people didn't give me feedback as directly as the Teacher in a way I could receive and integrate into my being.

About this time, I had turned the corner in my Journeywork, moving from the thirteenth Initiation to the fourteenth. This meant I had become an Elder apprentice. My attention, previously directed toward self and self-awareness, was now directed outward, toward others, the environment, the big picture and how it all fit together.

Once past this point, we were considered to have developed enough self-awareness that we no longer needed to focus so much attention on ourselves, but could now begin to see how life worked and how, through our mental images, our particular life came to be the way it was. I began to look at underlying causes and results, natural law. Who was I as part of the Oneness and how could I be a healthy, wholesome, well-balanced presenter of life as I wanted it to be? Ultimately, the answer was *'by becoming a spiritualized consciousness,'* but along the way there were many lessons to be learned.

Turning this corner was a big stretch for me. I had been comfortable with the self-centered focus of the first hundred miles that represented the walk of the first circle of Initiations. The shift in focus away from self into a more scientific study of self-in-environment, or self-in-motion, was disruptive to my comfort zone. Plus, it carried more responsibility with it.

Winged Wolf's communications to me confronted some deeper issues that I carried, and was symbolic of this shift in expectation. So the tone had been set for my next 100 miles of Journeying around the Medicine Wheel. I was no longer a "baby" apprentice. All right. I would quit grumbling and move on. Certain privileges were granted at this juncture, the biggest of which was that I was given Winged Wolf's private phone number and told, *"You can now call me any time, except on Wednesday nights."* That was the night for those who hadn't reached the level of Elder, who were allowed to call on another phone line.

Her only acknowledgement of my difficulty in turning the corner to become an Elder apprentice was a brief comment, *"And isn't it interesting that while you were procrastinating with the end of your first 100 miles, a tad bit frightened to move forward, you entered the vortex in spite of yourself."*

Shortly after I turned the corner, Winged Wolf announced that she would like those of us who were Elders to develop study groups in our home areas to expose the public to the Teachings. We could use her books and articles as our study guides.

"You should not present yourselves as teachers, but rather as facilitators. There should be no need for interpretation; the Teachings are literal," Winged Wolf had cautioned us repeatedly. *"None of you are ready to teach. Once you are Thunderbeings, then you may teach. Until then, you are Elders being given the privilege to facilitate a group."*

She said, *"Just share your experiences with the Teacher and the Teachings and encourage others to share theirs. And do not turn it into a therapy group. It is not that."* She was looking right at me when she spoke these last words emphatically.

Winged Wolf spoke with us at length about how to share the Teachings with others who might be of like mind; and the directive was that we were to open our hearts and speak from our own experience; allow other people to have their own experiences. We were to draw no conclusions. It was not our role to draw conclusions for the participants. I felt really comfortable and protected in the role of facilitator; since I didn't have to know everything, it would be a great learning experience.

Walter and I had the good fortune to be in Cottonwood when the first study group ever was held at a local bookstore. Actually, the bookstore was in Sedona, and the study group was to be facilitated by Winged Wolf's lead apprentice in that area. We were able to attend and participate in the group and left with a feel for how to begin.

With the Teacher's approval, we would facilitate a six-week session on Shamanism titled, *Third Eye Vision: Living at the Third Eye.* Each meeting would include one or more principles that were essential to the mastery of Shamanism, starting with Third Eye Vision and companion energy. Then we would have an experiential section to help anchor the concepts.

It was enlivening to work out our material with each other and with Winged Wolf. It brought a new dimension to our marriage, a common purpose, and we worked well together in companion energy with the Teacher to the best of our ability at the time.

Once we had the outline together, we set about presenting it to anyone who would listen. We went to heads of night school programs, community resources, and privately found a large meeting room that was used by a yoga group during the day and had a wonderful, clean energy to it.

After consulting with the editors of a local spiritual publication, we chose a weekday evening for our meetings and placed an ad in their paper. They were so helpful and supportive of us, genuinely excited about what we wanted to do. They helped us find the room at the yoga center and offered to print an article by Winged Wolf in the next month's publication.

This was a big deal to us. Their paper had a large following throughout Michigan and Ohio, and they always included articles by well-known authors on the spiritual scene. After all the preparatory work had been completed, including selection of an article titled *Earth Changes,* that Winged Wolf had written for one of the newsletters, we were on pins and needles waiting for the publication with our ad and Winged Wolf's article to be printed and distributed.

When the opening night came for our first meeting at the yoga center, we were nervous, excited, and ready. That is to say, I was nervous. I kept arranging and rearranging the chairs. *"I wonder if anyone will show up?"* I'd say to Walt, checking the time.

"Of course," he always replied, confidently.

To our absolute delight, a total of eight people arrived for the first meeting. It was a lively evening, and we had worked up some exercises to enliven each of the spiritual principles presented, so the energy flowed pretty smoothly. I sure could tell I was a novice though once we paused for discussion and the questions began.

Questions from the group really helped us identify areas where we needed to deepen our understanding of the Teachings, and it gave us viewpoints on how different minds look at things.

Many of our attendees were coming into the group without any prior exposure to Winged Wolf's books and Teachings, so they needed more details before accepting what was said at face value. Mostly, for us it was about developing skills in managing group energy and dynamics and learning to give people just enough to whet their appetites but not so much that they went away feeling too full. I didn't know anything about that then, so I tried to give them everything all at once.

The first evening was exhilarating and exhausting. When it was over, I couldn't wait to get home and write Winged Wolf all about it. In the beginning, I always called or wrote her after every meeting. She was so patient with me. I described each attendee in detail and if I could reach her by phone immediately afterwards, she'd listen as I rattled on and on. I became attached to each participant, and if they missed a time or two, I would worry about them.

At that time in my apprenticeship, I was moving along pretty smoothly, still talking to everyone I encountered about The Path, and my enthusiasm was infectious. And it was authentic. Prior to finding the Path, I had given up on ever really discovering what my life's purpose was, and to find it after having given it up, made me incredibly happy. Every day I awoke with deep appreciation and gratitude to have at last found my way.

By now, all but one of our original spiritual study group had become apprentices, so we met together often for any excuse to discuss the Teachings. Those were such innocent and exciting times. We really didn't have to change a thing in our outer existences, so there was little pain and lots of gain. We still saw ourselves as a group, even though apprenticeship was individual. Oddly though, for the first several months, none of this group participated in the study groups, which were named Wisdom Circles.

Our new Wisdom Circle completed the six-week course we had outlined and wanted to learn more!! We didn't know what to do after that. We didn't have 'more,' so we invited them to attend the next 6-week scheduled course, which would be a repeat, except with a new group. Most of them stayed, and so it came to pass that we ultimately retired the original outline and launched a more spontaneous format. Our discussions of the Teachings deepened as we looked at how people's lives were being affected by their spiritual practice of living from the Third Eye Center and dug into such statements as, *"a Shaman never manipulates."*

A good, solid core group evolved out of this, and while some came a time or two and left, many came and stayed. Pretty soon, one by one, they started writing Winged Wolf asking to become apprentices, and as a result, the commitment level deepened. In fact, one day I looked around and realized the group was entirely comprised of apprentices. And finally, the apprentices from our original study group began attending Wisdom Circles. Soon they were able to facilitate the group themselves.

We all learned, through trial and error, about some of the tendencies and pitfalls of group dynamics. Participants began sharing their personal problems in the group, then other participants would give them solutions based on their experiences. Someone would say, *"I've got a problem with my teenage son,"* and suddenly everyone who had a teenager was interviewing the person and giving advice.

There was a fine line here that we were crossing, becoming more of a therapy group than a Wisdom Circle. At first, I didn't understand what was happening, but in a conversation with Winged Wolf, I said, *"The group has been flat for the past few meetings. I don't quite know what the issue is, but I'm finding myself bored during parts of the meeting."*

"Tell me about it, what's being said when it begins to go flat?" she responded.

"Usually it's when someone brings up a personal issue they are trying to confront using Third Eye Vision." As I described in more detail what was occurring when I felt bored, she interrupted, *"You're turning it into a therapy group. Stop that! The Teachings cannot be interpreted, and people aren't there to give each other advice. It's one thing to share an experience they have had using Third Eye Vision, but they are just trying to 'fix' someone. You'll have to turn it around right away or you'll lose them."*

She gave specific guidelines for how to disrupt the patterns that were developing and basically reclaim the reins from the group. It sounded simple, but when the next week came, I was nervous. This meant a confrontation of sorts, so I waited until the discussion developed, and at the point where it began to turn, I followed her directions.

"We're not a therapy group here," I told people. *"This is not the place to come for advice, but the place to come and learn spiritual principles. It's great to share your experiences with the Teachings with each other, but we're not about 'fixing' each other."*

The energy shifted immediately. There was a startled silence; then there was a tug as some people tried to pull it back. This was something to observe, this push-pull that occurred just after the confrontation.

"I don't understand what you mean by a therapy group? Why can't we give each other advice? It's just trying to help."

"Because this group is about learning spiritual principles and how to take them into our lives. The idea is to take a principle and practice it until it becomes integrated into your life. Share your experiences along the way with the group if you like, but remember, it is your experience. If someone else gets involved, then they are not only interfering with your experience, but they begin to take on your karma. Who needs that? We all have enough karma of our own to work through."

After that, things seemed to relax and we were able to continue, revitalized. It still took monitoring because people tended to slip into familiar, habitual ways of relating to each other, but at least the parameters were established, and it was now easy to redirect if people got off-track.

This was a powerful learning experience – there is a huge difference between a therapy group and a spiritual studies group. Pointing people to specific Teachings to use in resolving their conflicts fostered self-reliance, not dependency on another person.

It was fascinating to watch what would happen the moment one member would begin a sentence with, *"I had that problem, too, and you know what I did………"* In about thirty seconds the room went flat and people began to fidget. Winged Wolf said this was because it was not in keeping with the original intent, the intent to present and study the Primordial Teachings and learn to integrate them into our lives.

One time I wrote to Winged Wolf about a problem situation with a particular group member. Basically, by complaining about the person's behavior in the group, I was looking for Winged Wolf's sympathy. I told her all the ways this person was annoying.

Here is what I learned from that incident. Guideline number 1: Never try to hook the Teacher into seeing things from your little-self perspective. She is not going to be sympathetic to how the little-self views things. Guideline number 2: The idea is to learn to see things from the Teacher's viewpoint, which is the Higher Consciousness Viewpoint, and transmute the energy of an uncomfortable situation.

Winged Wolf told me, *"I never relate to anyone's little-self (meaning personality). I always relate as divine self from the Third Eye viewpoint. This brings forth the divine self in others."* Then emphatically, **"Never relate as a personality."**

This may sound strange if someone believes, as I did, that they are their personality. She went on, *"Once refined, the personality is merely a tool for divine consciousness to express Itself, the two become merged. Prior to this, however, the personality is driven by ego. This is not who we are, only the persona or mask we have developed to live life with.*

"Realizing this simply cuts away all the crap, and brings out the absolute best in both of you. If you relate only as divine consciousness, you bring out the divine self in the one you relate to; it's inevitable. It doesn't matter if it's a person, an animal, bird or insect. But it isn't always easy to do; it takes practice and training to know the difference."

So, under Winged Wolf's tutelage, we began to train our group participants to take the Teachings into their lives and share their experiences. It turned the group around, because it created an opening to continue our spiritual evolution.

During this time, a different type of difficult situation arose in our Wisdom Circle. One of our most faithful group attendees wrote Winged Wolf and requested to become an apprentice, and she was turned down. She was stunned and so were we. This had never happened before in our group. It was traumatic for everyone.

She came to the meeting despondent, and I didn't know what to say to her. But as we began talking about what had happened, we learned Winged Wolf had said she wasn't ready *yet* to become an apprentice, because she was in therapy and she would be analyzing the Teachings with her therapist. Winged Wolf had told her, *"When you complete your relationship with your therapist, then you may reapply to become an apprentice with me."*

What a relief to put a proper perspective on what had occurred, and to look at the situation from the Teacher's viewpoint. It wasn't actually a rejection of this person as being an acceptable apprentice, but a recognition that, in this case, one relationship needed to be completed before the other could begin. Otherwise, it could be a set-up for failure because the student was not yet ready to become an apprentice.

We all encouraged her to continue studying the Teachings and attending the group, and eventually she did. A year or so later, after completing her therapeutic work, she re-applied and was accepted as an apprentice. We all cheered. To me, this was another indicator of the impeccability of our Teacher and her commitment to serve us, not as our little-selves demanded, but as appropriate to the situation.

I received a letter from an old friend and in it she had said some things that troubled me. I wrote to Winged Wolf about the letter and she responded, "*It's best to not mull things over, that is a habit with a bear trap! Relax, laugh, go out and have some fun, and while having it, practice your Journey. Walk the miles as part of your life. If a letter from the past stirs you emotionally, there is some stuck energy for you to reclaim. Use the techniques you've been given, and let it go. I hear many things but I listen only to that which I choose.*"

"*I listen only to that which I choose,*" what power, what freedom in that statement. Reading her response, I was uplifted back into balance. There was compassion, but never did she fall into sympathy with me or get involved in my life's little soap operas. As soon as I saw it from her viewpoint, the hold it had on me dissolved. This became an excellent focal point for our group to discuss, both the distinction between hearing and listening, and the conscious choosing of what we listened to was quite revolutionary.

"*Why can't I see life naturally from divine consciousness without you pointing it out?* " I complained to her.

"*Because you are not able to hold the consciousness yourself yet. When I put my attention on you, I allow you to borrow my consciousness to look at whatever we are discussing. Then when my attention turns to something else, you are back to looking from your own level of awareness, except that a little bit of my consciousness has been added to yours. That is the part you keep as your own. Bit by bit, it will continue to grow until one day your consciousness will merge with the divine and you will be able to sustain it on your own.*"

When I was looking at a situation from her eyes, everything was amazingly clear and decisions were obvious. All the confusion I usually experienced during a struggle dissolved into the illusionary world it came from and my mind was clear as a bell.

"How I long to be in the state of divine consciousness," I told her, wishing she could magically put me there permanently.

"When one longs to be in the Void, they are the mind looking at a feeling memory of the Void, remembering That, when they were in the here and now. They were one with it (Void). All you have to do to reclaim that position is to set your attention at the Third Eye, which brings you to the present moment. The Void lives here. It is nothing and yet it is everything. It (Void) contains. It is a container both empty and full. When you are one with It, you are one with the power of God."

"I don't feel that I am grasping the material as clearly as I should be. When you talk to me about it, I feel I understand, but then when I walk away and try to put it into practice, all the pieces don't fit together."

She said, *"This feeling of 'getting it and not getting it' means that as divine consciousness the information is enlivened in you, although you think you don't intellectually understand it. But, actually, it is there for you to use, without mentalizing or internalizing. This is what is meant by 'looking out.'"*

Changing the subject, she said, *"I'd like you to write an article for the next newsletter, if you're agreeable, that is."*

"Sure," I agreed, *"on what?"*

"Why not talk about your relationship with your spiritual Teacher, especially the nature of resistance and how it binds you to the Teacher."

"Oh, well, I'll give it a try," I said feeling myself pull back. Why does she persist in referring to me as resistant? I don't see myself as resistant.

"I'm sure you'll do just fine," she encouraged me.

This was an uncomfortable subject and one we had been going around on for the past few weeks.

"You are learning through resistance," she had told me, *"and it is the most difficult way to learn. I know I did it, but I don't recommend it."*

"I don't see myself as resistant," I responded defensively. *"What do I do that's resistant?"*

"Just like now," she said, *"you demand explanations from me, and you like to argue. Even if you don't argue out loud, you argue with me in your head. Do you think I don't hear you?"*

"How can I understand what you are telling me without asking any questions?"

Silence.

She had given me a couple of assignments to help me work through my resistance, one of which was compiling quotes from her books describing her apprenticeship with Alana Spirit Changer, and I had been loving the work. It was so uplifting. But I always reacted when she accused me of being resistant. *"A sure sign that you are that,"* she had told me.

So I wrote the article and was quite proud of it. Once again, I had called upon my experiences as a therapist to compare my relationships with my clients to my relationship with the Teacher. It was only a slightly camouflaged attempt to bolster my ego. Her response was gentle, but shattering. Basically, she told me the article was inauthentic and pretentious. She asked if I would like her help in *'healing'* the article.

My first response was to tear it up and give it up, since she couldn't appreciate a good article when it was presented. After I calmed down and looked at what she had said and reread the article, it was crystal clear to me that she was correct. So, putting my ego aside, I followed her suggestions in rewriting the article.

After receiving the revised article, she wrote to me, *"A truly spiritual person can be recognized by their authenticity. They are quite natural and open about themselves. This is what you experienced in 'healing your article.' By accepting who you are, and where you are, you empowered yourself, and you will empower your readers as well."*

Deeply grateful, I wrote back, *"If only there comes a time when I don't react so, perhaps then, my resistance to my Teacher will have dissolved. I pray that time will be soon. Thank you for your unfailing support and relentless honesty. Even when I complain and resist, I know you are doing it because you love me and want to see me evolve in spite of myself."*

Chapter 7
A Painful Lesson on Impermanence

One night in February, I called Winged Wolf to talk. I had just received a delightful letter from her, one that left my heart singing. She had been pleased with my Initiation Journey report. She wrote me, *"I'm enjoying your report enough that I've taken it outside to answer. There are 1001 blackbirds in a tree near the deck and their chirping could be mistaken for spring."*

In my report, I had talked to her about the incredible aliveness I was experiencing as my heart opened and unconditional love flowed into and out from me. She responded, *"The open heart produces aliveness in us, and when it closes, it makes us feel dull, dead-like. The secret to keeping the heart open: Releasing <u>gives</u> (opens); tension <u>takes</u> (closes). Whenever resistance presents itself—release. It is very subtle sometimes and it occurs on many levels, but you will gain in your perceptions of this in time. The more you pick something up the more you see it. Much makes more principle.*

"When I shocked you a few weeks back, I opened you or threw light on an area that was once dark to you (referring to the incident with the article that needed healing).

"Isn't it interesting to be so alive! So you see, life is a very great gift indeed."

And then in response to a question I had about the symbology of the circle.

"The real <u>POWER</u> of the circle is that it has no end; circle meaning no entrance, no exit. To enter the circle, you must enliven your intent. Ah, riddles and more riddles."

Still on a high from this round of communications and the opening they created as my resistance was released, I didn't even remember what I wanted to talk about, except perhaps to prolong the ecstasy through hearing her voice. I sat by the phone for two hours dialing and redialing, only to hear the beep, beep, beep of a busy signal. This should have been a message to me, but I ignored it. It was a work night and I was tired, the three-hour time difference made it late to stay up and continue calling, but I was determined to get through.

At last, I heard the wonderful sound of a phone ringing, and she picked up.

"Hello, Winged Wolf," I said cheerfully, happy to hear her voice, assuming she would be happy to hear mine. *"I'm so glad I was finally able to reach you."*

"Do you know what time it is?" she asked sharply.

I glanced at the clock on my desk, and with a sinking feeling said, *"It's two minutes after eleven."* (That was two minutes past eight where I was and that was the cutoff point for us to call.)

"I'm going to have to change my number if apprentices don't respect the time limits," she said.

"I'm so sorry," I gasped, feeling hurt, embarrassed, and surprised at the intensity of her response. *"Do you want me to hang up and call tomorrow?"*

"You've got me now, might as well tell me what it is you want," she said.

Briefly I told her what was on my mind, which earlier seemed so important and now seemed so trivial. Then, after a brief silence, I clumsily said, *"That's all I needed to ask about. I'm sorry to have disturbed you."*

Never before had I experienced my Teacher in a mood like this. I wanted to get off the phone, it was so uncomfortable, but I had to wait until she dismissed me. It wasn't long after this that she did. Obsessing over the call, it was a long time before sleep descended on that night. What had I done to cause such a sharp response? The conversation kept repeating over and over in my mind, *"Why hadn't I just given up when the*

A Painful Lesson on Impermanence

line was busy? Why hadn't I looked at the clock? Why was she so disturbed?" Finally I drifted off into a restless sleep, and awoke feeling heavy and disturbed.

Shortly after that night's phone call, rumors began circulating among the apprentice body: Alana Spirit Changer had translated (died). I was stunned. It couldn't be true! Winged Wolf had never mentioned her being old, or ill, or near death, or anything. Surely she would have said something about it.

Selfishly, I had anticipated meeting Alana Spirit Changer one day. After all, she was the catalyst for my meeting my Teacher. It seemed impossible that she was gone. Then a memory struck me: the night I called and reached Winged Wolf after hours, the night she sounded so tired and crabby, could that have been near the time Alana had translated? NO, that couldn't be! I clung to the hope that this was nothing more than a rumor that was circulating among the apprentice body.

To further support my wish that the rumor was mistaken, I received another letter from Winged Wolf toward the end of March that sounded 'normal' to me. Certainly, if something had happened to Alana Spirit Changer, my Teacher would not be sounding like this. Of course my viewpoint on this was completely colored by my projection of how I would be reacting if someone I loved dearly had translated. It was not possible for me at my level of awareness to perceive from the eyes of the divine consciousness, that her commitment to her students would go on uninterrupted, regardless of any personal pain she might experience.

A letter arrived in the mail. It was dated April. This is a day that will forever be imprinted in my memory. It was another of those rare times I was bringing in the mail when I noticed an envelope with Winged Wolf's handwriting on it. Actually, there were two letters, one for Walter and another for me. Quickly I tore it open, eager, as always, to be touched by her. My heart sank as I read the letter. It was dated March 28, and it read:

"To All Apprentices,"

"In the early morning of February 24th, the postman knocked at my door with a package from Alana Spirit Changer.

There was no mystery to it, like there was the first time, which I wrote about in 'Circle Of Power.' On this occasion as well, Alana was presenting me the eagle stick she had given me years ago. I had returned my stick to her early last December as a way of telling her that I needed her to stay in the world to assist me, after she had announced that she was going to translate (die). This time the stick signaled me to her side......"

The letter went on to say some personal things, but the essence of the message cut through all my fantasies. The news was now confirmed. There would be no meetings with Alana Spirit Changer. She was gone.

Winged Wolf said she would say more about what had transpired in her soon-to-be released book, *The Shamanic Journey of Living as Soul*, and she asked us to wait until that time with our questions. It was obviously a painful time for our Teacher.

I wept for the loss of someone I had only known through my Teacher's eyes, but the love of the student for the Teacher had been so strong, I felt somehow connected to it, also.

It was several days before I could bring myself to call Winged Wolf again, and when I did, I needed to say something. I couldn't pretend nothing had happened, so I said, *"I received your letter about Alana translating."* After saying that I didn't know what more to say, but Winged Wolf helped me out by taking charge of the conversation.

"Yes," she said, *"that's true."* Then, she put closure on the subject by saying, *"You'll be able to read more about it in my next book, 'Shamanic Journey of Living as Soul.' It will be published soon."*

This seemed to close the circle for the time being, and it was a long time before she spoke to me of Alana Spirit Changer after that. When the book was released, I read it hungrily, looking for some picture of what had happened between the Teacher and the student, how their love had completed itself on this physical plane. Of course I was projecting myself into the scenario, imagining my relationship with Winged Wolf and what it would be like if this happened to me.
It was satisfying somehow to learn the circumstances of Alana's translation, the power of it, the choice, and to feel the intimacy of their relationship as it had developed to this point of unity. I still cried for the loss of Alana and the pain it caused my Teacher, but it was such a

beautiful gift to be able to merge totally with the Teacher like they did, so empowering. This understanding brought it full circle again at another level and allowed me to accept the loss as my Teacher had accepted it, as seen through her eyes.

Several weeks passed before our next communication. Finally, I wrote to her and shared some experiences I was having related to my Journey work. Her response intrigued me. She said, *"By your nature, you walk between the worlds—between day and night, between light and darkness, between forces. You are discovering there are gates between forces, and like a woman between the wind, you move between the energies, and you find the way. And this is the way of a Shaman, and the way is on-going, never-ending.*

"It won't be long when you will visit me without visiting me. It is a very thin, fine line that keeps you from it now. It will be natural, and seemingly ordinary. In the meantime, it may be useful to take the trip once or twice. When are you coming?"

This was a really juicy carrot for me. It was the most definitive statement the Teacher had ever made about me, the first time she had spoken of my 'nature' in a positive way, not to identify some ego projection that needed transmuting. I was beginning to have a shape! Not an expression, but at least a shape. It felt good. And she seemed to be happy. I had been worried about how Alana's death would impact her; again, my own projection, but the energy of this letter felt solid. And she sent me a new Journey to work on. What a mind-expander this Journey turned out to be. It dealt with what Winged Wolf called 'pivots and hinges,' and opened doorways in my normal way of viewing life to seeing a much broader picture.

Looking at life from the viewpoint of pivots and hinges turned everything I saw into a grand mystery to be understood. The opening of a closet door, the tying of a shoelace, the passing of a cloud overhead, starting the car; all could be seen in a framework of pivots and hinges. What the understanding of this revealed could be as mundane as something to hold my shoe on so I can walk down the street, to an alternative way of seeing how energy worked, or a realization of 'how atoms and molecules relate to magnetic forces.' I was beginning to understand how the universe operated and with this understanding came power. I could look at something and know how it came to be.

Meanwhile, Winged Wolf had announced the first annual gathering of her apprentices, to be held in Sedona, Arizona. She wrote us a letter saying we would be having an Empowerment, a gathering of apprentices in honor of her Teacher Alana Spirit Changer. The subject would be *Healing in the Dreamtime*.

My response to the letter was, *'Oh no, not me. I don't like large groups. I'm not going.'* It seemed overwhelming to spend a whole week with a large number of people, most of whom I didn't know. My shyness of being in large groups surfaced and I dug in my heels. Walter could go, but I would rather see the Teacher in a small group where there was plenty of individual attention. And of course, Walter wouldn't miss it for anything. I communicated with Winged Wolf that I wasn't planning to attend and made arrangements to visit Eastcliffe later in the summer.

Names Change

Arriving home from work one day, I found an envelope waiting on the kitchen table for me with the now-so-familiar handwriting of my dear Teacher. Hurriedly, I dropped my briefcase on the floor and ripped open the envelope.

The letter opened, *"Hello Sharon, Wings of Change."* I could read no further for staring at the phrase *'Wings of Change.'* What did it mean? Why was she referring to me in this way? This was the first reference to a name other than my 'street' name since the few times she had referred to me as White Eagle early in my apprenticeship. Wings of Change wasn't nearly as glamorous a name or as powerful sounding as White Eagle.

As I read on, I relaxed. She went on to say, *"You have the daring capacity of touch that changes and transforms. In the past you have done this with yourself but now you lightly touch the lives of others as well and serve as a transformer for those you touch. You can blend with many, which makes you a multi-colored butterfly."*

"Oh," I said aloud, *"it's because of the butterfly."*

Recently, we had moved to a new home, one a little more in the country, much newer, with a lake across the street, and there had been a couple of really good omens that occurred right after the move. The first was on

A Painful Lesson on Impermanence

the day of our move when a large mother turtle trekked up our walkway from the lake and laid her eggs in our front yard, while everyone watched astounded as she dug, seemingly oblivious to all the spectators around her.

The second omen was an incident that occurred a week or two after our arrival. While I was out on the front porch washing windows, a gorgeous yellow and blue butterfly circled me a few times and then landed directly on the tip of my nose. The butterfly's circling several times got my attention; then, as I paused in my cleaning to watch it, it deliberately landed right on my nose. We stood there looking at each other. An unusually large species, it was only an inch or two from my eyes. I could see its consciousness looking out at my consciousness, just as I was looking at its consciousness. Consciousness recognizing itself. That told me in no uncertain terms that all sentient life is made of the same divine stuff.

It was such a profound experience that, after a time, I could no longer contain my excitement at this discovery. I wanted to share the experience with someone; so I carefully raised my hand and tapped on the window to attract the family's attention. As they looked my way, the butterfly lifted gently off my nose and flew away. Clearly, this was meant to be my experience alone.

Since I had written Winged Wolf about these incidents, thinking them good welcoming omens to our new home, I concluded aloud, *"This is what Winged Wolf is referring to, the butterfly incident. This is what prompted her referring to me as 'Wings of Change'."* And that was what I concluded for a long time to come.

Reading her letter brought a sense of fullness for the many blessings I had received. Never did I perceive it meant anything more than that. After all, much earlier in my apprenticeship she had written to me as White Eagle, again based on certain experiences I had written to her about, and while I found that name much more exotic and to my liking than Wings of Change, naturally one's power name was the Teacher's choice. *'Don't resist. Let it unfold,'* I assured myself, repeating her words.

We were settling into our new home and adjusting to having my parents arrive once again for the summer. They were both eighty-eight by now, and my father had insisted on making the three-day drive from Florida unassisted. I spent the time pacing and worrying about them. His dementia was progressing so he often forgot where he was and where he was going. My mother, on the other hand, was sharp as could be, but her vision was poor. When they arrived, both were exhausted.

Meanwhile, we had my son Kevin and his wife Tracy living in the finished basement; they were on pins and needles waiting for the results of Kevin's law bar exam. Son Terry, and daughter Michelle were out of college for the summer and also living with us. They were all adults by now, uncomfortable at still needing to live at home when they wanted to be out on their own, so each was edgy in their own way and it showed up as a tension between and among them. No one had the finances to make a move out on their own, nor did they yet have the maturity to appreciate they had a roof over their heads while preparing to move out.

The only way I could find any privacy at all during this time was to go to the library or drive around in the car. In fact, that summer my communication with Winged Wolf often originated from the parking lot of the corner grocery store using my cell phone. About the second time I called her from the parking lot and described my situation, she became adamant, *"I want you to find some place in that house and claim it as yours."*

"But there isn't any place," I told her in despair. *"Every corner is occupied or used by people and their things."*

It was comic in a way, but I was feeling pretty desperate for some privacy. We had purchased a larger home so there would be more space and had immediately expanded into it so it felt crowded again.

"There must be a place for you," she insisted. *"It is unacceptable for you not to have a place to set up your altar and meditation space. How can you possibly progress on the Path or even keep your sanity if there is no place for you to be still other than the car and the public library? It doesn't have to be a large area, just private."*

As she talked, an image formed in my mind. *"The laundry room,"* I said. "There's a tiny laundry room that we're currently using for storage, upstairs between the bedrooms. I can clean that out and use it."
"Do it," she said. *"Go home and do it right away. I want you to promise me you will do that."*

A Painful Lesson on Impermanence

"I'm on my way," I agreed feeling a weight lift. I had become submerged in all the energy from the people occupying the house. It had overwhelmed me, and it was so overpowering I couldn't see my way out. She lifted my karma enough that I could see clearly what had happened, and in so doing, I could reclaim my life force because my balance was restored. Now what was needed was to act, move forward, set some boundaries for myself, and claim some space. That little meditation room along with the library and the parking lot conversations with Winged Wolf were my salvation for the summer of '94.

Winged Wolf wrote to me saying, *"It is a time to recoup energy to begin anew. So remember to relax! Laugh! H.A.!* (H.A. being her code for reminding me to stay focused at the Third Eye in a place of Heightened Awareness)

She went on to tell me, *"Enlightenment occurs when the mind comes under control. The dream still goes on around you but you know it is a dream and you consciously play a part,* **as you choose to do it.**

"Divine consciousness is meant to be the operator of the mind, just as we operate our computer. We (divine consciousness) turn on the power switch, call up the programming we want to use, and also access data from it. We are a part of the Void or God and have the ability via awareness to access information or knowledge from The Source."

She was responding to my writing that *"My mother and I are so different; I feel like I'm always vying with her for a sense of acceptance for who I am, and no matter what, she continually tells me and everyone else that I am 'just like her.' I don't want to be like her, I want to be myself."*

Her advice surprised me initially. *"You will be more comfortable with your mother if you look at your similarities, rather than your differences. Enjoy yourself with her in this way and learn <u>from</u> it. You will be surprised what comes to you in a universal way through your acceptance. This is 'fixing' something rather than changing it. A good riddle for you."* She had drawn a big heart underneath these words.

'Fixing something rather than changing it,' I mused. 'What in the world does that mean? And how do I look at the similarities when I want to look at the differences?' I contemplated these riddles for several days during my meditation time. At first it was just a glimmer of understanding on an intuitive level. I noticed a softening of my attitude toward my mother and began to release the defensive stance I assumed in her presence, always prepared for the next jab. I saw how much I was like her in my own relationships with the people I loved. It was just hard for my mother to see me as a separate person from herself. And, of course, as divine consciousness, I wasn't separate. And the more I softened, the more I could love her freely and unconditionally, and the less I needed to defend myself.

'So that's what the Teacher meant by 'fixing' something. She was telling me to correct my viewpoint, not to try to change my mother to fit my expectations.'

Chapter 8
The First Empowerment

It was approaching the time of the first annual Empowerment of the Eagle Tribe, the name Winged Wolf had given our Spiritual Order in honor of her Teacher, Alana Spirit Changer.

While I was on the phone with Winged Wolf one afternoon, she casually mentioned, *"I know you're not planning to attend the Empowerment, but if you should change your mind, please let me know right away because there is something I want you to do."*

Okay, she had my attention. *"What's that, Winged Wolf?"* I asked curiously.

"Well," she said animatedly, *"as you may recall, a group of apprentices got together here at Eastcliffe to do some brainstorming about the best way to structure the Empowerment, and they recommended we do something similar to what I wrote about in my book 'The Awakening Stone.'"*

An image of Winged Wolf's trilogy, entitled *'The Awakening Stone'* popped into my mind. Throughout the three books, the main character is a young woman named Deetra who is embarking on a spiritual journey to self-realization. She lives in a village where the Elders, who are evolving spiritual beings, help to maintain the spiritual integrity of the village and set the tone for the awakening that is about to occur. I didn't quite see how to make a connection between the book and our Empowerment. *"How do we do that, Winged Wolf?"*

"We'll have a village, or tribe, made up of apprentices, and the senior apprentices will be the Elders, just as they were in 'Through the Crystal' (the first book in *'The Awakening Stone'* trilogy*). Of course, we'll need a village chief, too, and I would like you to be chief of the tribe. You would be perfect in that role."*

"What does a chief do?" I asked cautiously, thinking it sounded rather silly, but inviting, too.

"Oh, they oversee the tribe, for one thing, and take care of myriad other matters. If you decide to come, we'll talk about it further. Otherwise, I'll have to pick someone else," she paused, *"but I really do want you to be chief,"* she said. *"Why don't you give it some consideration and let me know, but I need to know soon."*

By the time we said good-bye I was hooked. She knew all the right things to say to pique my curiosity, and yes, hook my ego. Being chief sounded like an honor and a huge responsibility, although at the time I assumed there would be several chiefs, not just one.

As the time neared for the event, apprehension surfaced. How had I allowed myself to agree to this? I had been flattered and won over in that way. Now I was chief. Whatever that meant, I was nervous about it. No matter what questions I posed to Winged Wolf, she kept saying, *"Just relax, and let it unfold. You'll be fine."*

She was all excited about the event and kept feeding me news of the plans that were being made. Everyone would have a name different from his or her street name. *'What will my name be?'* I wondered.

My cynical, city mind objected to all this silly game-playing anyway, giving people odd-sounding names and pretending we lived somewhere we didn't. I couldn't see why Winged Wolf found it so much fun, and I still didn't understand what my job would be. I'd never met anyone who was so skilled in evading questions. Winged Wolf simply ignored my questions and distracted my attention from them.

Walt had a role and a title in the Empowerment, too. He was to be the sound coordinator as well as MC for the program. The whole thing sounded like great fun to him and that irritated me even further. I was beginning to see a pretty consistent theme in my personality. I was threatened by anything that I couldn't control, terrified really of any kind of change, and my knee-jerk responses were resistance, criticism and anger. It was then I wondered if Winged Wolf had given me the name Wings of Change as a learning tool. I certainly was one who needed to learn to yield to change.

The First Empowerment

Six of us from Michigan had booked plane reservations together to Phoenix, and then we rented two cars to drive up to Sedona. I insisted we stop and get something to eat, making us late for registration.

Winged Wolf swooped down on us the moment we arrived, *"Where have you been? We needed you here early. You're the chief."* Walter flashed me a look, which I ignored. His look said, *'I knew we should be here, and I let you talk me out of it.'* And I did know it, too, I just ignored what I knew was right in favor of staying in my comfort zone a little while longer.

Instantly we were swept up in Winged Wolf's stream of endless energy as she sent this one to do one thing and that one to do another. Already she wanted me to go talk to the park managers about some things we needed from them; and it sounded confrontational to me.

Since I abhorred confrontation, I didn't want to go, but it didn't seem like 'no' was an option. I was being introduced into the role of the chief, and it didn't look glamorous to me at all.

The campground was buzzing by now; and people were arriving in droves. There were these funny-sounding names that were given to people based on mini conversations they had with Elder apprentices who had been assigned the task of name designation. The instructions were to *'stay in the moment'* and *'only use these names; don't talk about your life outside of this village.'*

One of the apprentices told me, *"The idea is for us to create the actual feel of living totally in the present moment, with no past and no future,"* so I marched off to Winged Wolf to determine why all this was necessary.

"Why, so you can fully enjoy being present at the Empowerment," she replied. *"How can people be fully present here if their thoughts are wandering in all different directions, if they are wondering what's happening at home or what will happen when they get home? I want everyone to have a full experience of living in the present moment."*

That made sense to me as I thought about it, *"But why are you giving us different names?"* That seemed really silly to me, and made me feel self-conscious.

"Because it is an additional way of helping people detach from their ordinary lives and have an experience of the extraordinary. The names people receive will enlighten them to an aspect of themselves that sits near the surface but has not yet fulfilled itself.

"In other words, it will empower them to become more of their divine self. That's why it is called a 'power name,' and that is why we are called the Village of the Present Moment."

Well, I certainly couldn't disagree with that concept, so I just decided to let go of my resistance to this unusual way of doing things.

My nametag said *'Wings of Change,'* so that question was answered. I decided I could live with that name for a while, until I had earned a more exotic one. It never dawned on me that ten years later this would still be my name or that it would come to symbolize so much of my evolution on the Path.

Having just returned from my first interaction with the managers of the park, which had been moderately successful, I was about to relax a bit when someone hailed me over.

"Wings of Change, we have a situation for the chief to handle. That person over there doesn't like their name assignment. What do we do?"

I couldn't believe it. I'd only been there twenty minutes and already we had problems. How was I supposed to know what to do? It wasn't my game. And what could it possibly matter what their name was for a few days?

"Let me talk to her," that would be a beginning point. After that, I'd wing it. The apprentice who alerted me to the upset led me over to the disgruntled apprentice. After we had talked for a while and the apprentice had assured me the person who had given her the name had completely missed the point, I understood exactly why she had been given the name *'Goes with the Flow,'* but there was going to be difficulty if she wasn't given the name she had chosen for herself that had the word Eagle in it.

"What would the Teacher do in this situation?" I asked myself. *"Uh, oh,"* I gulped, *"she might tell the person to keep the name."*

The First Empowerment

That would mean another confrontation. I opted for the middle road and led her to a different name-giver. *"See if you can give her a name she can accept, but don't give her the one she has chosen for herself."* And I walked away.

Already I was ready to pass the chief's job along to someone better qualified. Certainly Walter could have done it. He was comfortable and confident in managing people. I was uncomfortable in positions of authority even though I enjoyed being a leader: I wanted to make everyone happy, and this position, while it appealed to my ego's wanting to be seen as someone important, also made me squirm with all the decision-making responsibility and potential for having people upset with me.

When there was finally a lull in activity, I took a moment to look around. I saw some people who looked even more frightened than I felt, and for some reason this made me feel better. At least having a role in this fantasy town gave me something to focus my attention on other than myself.

There were some perks that went with my new position. Winged Wolf insisted I stay in a cabin that backed right up to the creek where the sound of the water rushing past was soothing; and she also insisted that I sleep on the only double bed. There was literally nothing in the cabins except beds; the bathhouses were a hike up the hill, as was the dining hall.

Earlier, it had been decided that because there were so many beds in each cabin, men and women would sleep separately even if they were married. That way there would not be the discomfort of having single people in cabins with married people nor would married couples be sharing cabins. So, Walt was assigned to the men's cabin. I didn't like that either, but Winged Wolf had a good point. It would be awkward for the other women in a cabin if there was a man present. It turned out none of the men wanted to sleep in the same cabin after the first night, so most of them took their mattresses outside to sleep under the stars.

None of us had seen the program prior to registration, and I simply assumed that Winged Wolf would be doing all the talks and we apprentices would make announcements and such. To my great surprise, upon opening the program, I discovered my name listed as giving one of the talks, and the subject was "The Dreamtime."

Not only did I not want to give a talk in front of all these unfamiliar people, who, in my mind, had instantly become my critics, but I had no clue what this dreamtime topic was really about. It was too general for my mind to put any definition to it and at that point in my life, definition was pretty important.

When I voiced my concern to the Teacher, Winged Wolf merely said, *"Don't worry, the part I want you to talk about is covered in your next Journey and I'm going to give it to you today so you can have some time to study it and prepare for your talk."* This meant I had two days before it was my turn on the program!

As I scanned the program further, I saw her general strategy. During the day, apprentices were giving talks on selected topics that corresponded to material in our various Initiation/Journeys, and each evening Winged Wolf was giving a talk on some aspect of healing. After all, healing was the overall theme for this Empowerment in honor of Alana Spirit Changer.

'People aren't going to want to hear the apprentices talk,' I grumbled to myself. *'They've come here to hear Winged Wolf.'*

All around I could hear the buzzing as apprentices opened their programs and gasped as they saw their names listed under the 'talk' section. Some faces turned stark white as the realization struck, *"I'm expected to give a talk. I'm not good at public speaking."*

There were so many things claiming my attention. I didn't even know where to begin. My job, as it turned out, was primarily to be a troubleshooter. Everyone who had a complaint, question or concern about anything was sent to me, including the people who managed the campground.

It was truly amazing how many issues people had during the first two or three days. In the beginning, there were issues with the kitchen, issues with room assignments, names, noise, the management of the children.

After a few days, we settled in and became a cohesive unit; the energy of Samadhi (a Buddhist word meaning deep inner silence) began to envelop us. There was a quote at the end of our program that spoke to the power of a group sitting in Samadhi. It read:

The First Empowerment

"IF A GROUP OF ONE HUNDRED WOULD SIT IN SAMADHI, OR COMPLETE SILENCE, THAT INFLUENCE CREATED WOULD SUFFICE FOR THOUSANDS. THEREFORE, THOUSANDS WOULD BE ELEVATED TO A GREATER ENLIGHTENMENT BY THAT ONE HUNDRED. And this is the true purpose of The Empowerment."

Winged Wolf

What power there was in that profoundly simple statement. Each time I read it, it gave me chills and inspiration. Although we had come a long way in a few days, there was still so much to learn on the spot. We were babies at this, learning as we went, moment to moment. During this time, the issues we faced were more internal, such as how to keep our focus turned outward so those of us who were Elders could serve the group. We really didn't know much about service, so each morning Winged Wolf met with us to set the tone for the day, and she taught us about service.

More than 100 adults were present. Winged Wolf had promised us Samadhi, and as we began to taste it, a sweet peace came over most people.

But, at first I had to deal with all sorts of questions that I didn't have answers to; and what compounded the challenges was the fact that I identified and agreed with many of the challengers. *"Why are there children here? We were told there were no children allowed. I had to find a sitter for my children."* And, *"Why are there dogs here? We were told there were no dogs allowed; I had to leave my dog at home."*

Then there were bathroom issues: the women's bathroom always had a long line-up, whereas the men's line was fewer and faster. Finally, we decided to give the men's room to the women during certain hours. Fortunately, the guys were easier in many ways than the women were to deal with, and they had no problem giving up their bathroom for certain periods of the day. As long as they didn't have to sleep in the same cabin, pretty much everything else was okay.

The children present were having a great time, but they got on people's nerves, and there were complaints. *"Why can't you ask her to keep that child quiet?"* And so on. That was the difficult part for me because I really didn't have any answers for people in many of the situations since it was just the way things were.

Our choices were to accept certain circumstances and move on or to focus on them and be miserable. So to my great relief and fascination, by the end of the third day, we had moved forward; happiness and good humor prevailed, although there were still raised eyebrows from time to time. It was incredible that people could find so many things to complain about.

The week was punctuated by pronounced highs and lows as we went through our stuff. Time and space didn't exist here as we entered the flow of the Village of the Present Moment. We were like a new orchestra with everyone playing their own instrument, and Winged Wolf was the orchestrator, conductor, musical director and writer of the script. She was tireless; she was everywhere.

Winged Wolf met with the Elders every morning at 7 a.m. to set the tone for the day. It was a time when Winged Wolf talked to us about what she saw was working, and what was not, sometimes chastising us for being spiritually asleep, meaning we didn't see something important that needed to be dealt with, sometimes praising us for an act of kindness or job well done. It was an important time for us, a chance to pull together and focus our attention on the day ahead, to remember to look out from the Third Eye and not get caught up in our own petty concerns. Inexperienced though we were, our roles were to be of service to the Teacher and the participants. She was constantly teaching us, stretching our limits.

Meantime, rumors spread that Terra Lenda (Alana Spirit Changer's friend) was present. Whispers of, *"Have you seen her?"* and *"I think so-and-so saw her,"* and we all looked. I never did ask Winged Wolf if Terra was really there. It added another dimension, a sense of mystery to the event and we all loved it, especially since most of us had so looked forward to the day we would meet Alana. With Alana gone, Terra Lenda somehow represented a connection to someone who was forever lost to us (physically, that is). Winged Wolf had told us when Alana died that she and Alana had literally merged consciousness, so there really was no Alana anymore. The two of them had become One.

The week flew by, developing a rhythm of its own, the tone and direction set and closely managed by Winged Wolf. Still, we were a rowdy bunch, untrained, jewels in the rough, and we were really rough, but a strong love bond developed between all of us. And most of all, we loved Winged Wolf. Her intent, her unconditional love, her vision of all of us in Samadhi;

The First Empowerment

this was the glue that kept the forward momentum going. And the marvelous, mysterious Teachings she shared with us each evening. The air was electric with the energy and aliveness that this brought forth in everyone.

Winged Wolf was like a locomotive that just kept rolling, and we were the cars that kept moving behind her, not of our own volition, but through our attention on her. It was a time of experiencing spiritual power at work as we all stretched into the images she had of us, capable of doing anything she asked. And of course, she only asked us to do what she knew we were capable of.

During the day we apprentices gave our talks. Winged Wolf sat in a chair on the side of the stage, smiling, encouraging, assisting. When we stumbled, or got off-base, she would gently interrupt and step in to clarify, expand and redirect. It was all done spontaneously.

She told us not to use notes, because we needed to have an experience of living in the moment, trusting what came out of our mouths. The secret, according to Winged Wolf, was to *"Keep your attention focused at the Third Eye; then anything you say will be coming from your divine self. It is not your divine consciousness or my divine consciousness, but divine consciousness. There is no separation, we are all one, different only by our karma."* Repeatedly she told us, *"I am no different from any of you; I am simply awake."* We all did our best, and it was quite remarkable how well everyone did. It was a lesson in trust.

Each evening we got out our drums and sat in a large circle pounding out rhythms, sometimes dancing to the beat, relaxed and happy in the Village of the Present Moment. Winged Wolf joined us for the drumming and after a while, a natural silence would occur. We simply stopped drumming. Then she talked, and we all sat in rapt silence. Her talks were so potent; it was really all we could take in. And there was such an aura of mystery to the evenings as we watched the sun setting behind the mountain, and felt darkness descend.

As Winged Wolf spoke to us, she naturally shape-shifted from one image to another. '*That was Alana,*' we whispered to ourselves, or '*that was an eagle.*' So we listened, and we watched intently for the magic we knew was there, and we became One. During that week, we came to experience Samadhi and a sense of the Oneness of all life, the song of ourselves and all of life as it is interwoven inextricably together.

Initiation

It was awe-inspiring, the magic that was occurring before my eyes; I was unable to deny what my eyes perceived. This was a Teacher of extraordinary power, not because she could shape-shift, I understood this was a power that others had as well, but because of the miracles I watched over the week as her shower of unconditional love opened hearts and minds to the divine beings that we all are. It was her incredible dedication to service, to uplifting all sentient life, and her continuous outflow of unconditional love that made her so extraordinary. Plus, she had a life force that naturally took command and directed.

On the final morning of our Empowerment, Winged Wolf stood before the group and announced, *"It is time for us to find a new spiritual home, one where I can work with my apprentices one-on-one. We need a place with more privacy and some acreage. The work that needs to be done cannot be done here at Eastcliffe* (the name of her ranch in Cottonwood). *There is not enough space between the neighboring ranches and us for me to have the privacy necessary to do my work with you.*

"I'm going to begin looking immediately, and I'm asking for all of you to help. If anyone has any ideas about places to move, I'd like to hear from you. It needs to be totally private and remote."

Totally unprepared for this announcement, I flashed on the Eastcliffe ranch that had already become my sacred place with the Teacher. It had seemed absolutely perfect. Why did she want to interrupt a good thing? *'Oh well,'* I thought, *'perhaps it is just the excitement of the moment and her interest will pass soon.'* That shows how little I really knew my Teacher at the time. I was used to people saying many things but meaning few of them. After some further discussion on the move, Winged Wolf talked to us about how to exit our gathering place properly, leaving it exactly as we found it or better.

"It should be one smooth move," she said, *"no ripples, no wake, no evidence we have ever been here, and further, all of you should re-enter your lives in the same way after you leave here, no waves, no ripples, one smooth move. Don't go home and start talking about your experiences here. They won't know what you are talking about, and they'll think you are weird. Just keep the gift of love you have received and let that emanate from your heart to others. That is all they want to see from you."*

And with that, she disappeared, and we began to pack up. We did as she asked, in one smooth move. Not a gum wrapper was left behind. There was great joy and great sadness that day; many of the participants were teary as they prepared to return to lives that caused them suffering, lives they had come here to escape and find freedom from. Now they had to face the reality of their situations and do something about them. And, while I didn't consider myself to be in a desperate situation by any means, the lessons learned during this Empowerment took months for me to integrate, and some of them took many years.

The final moments of preparation before departing from the Empowerment were also a time of great joy, and a few people were so high from the unconditional love they had experienced during the week, perhaps for the first time in their lives, I worried they literally might not be safe to drive. But we didn't hear of any accidents or injuries, and to my knowledge, everyone arrived home safely.

This was another lesson about the level of responsibility taken on by the divine consciousness that was embodied in our Teacher; and there was no doubt in my mind that she was the embodiment of divine consciousness.

Winged Wolf told me her job was not complete until each and every person arrived home safely, including the cooks, who were not apprentices. I didn't see how she could be responsible for what people did after they left, but she assured me, *"They are under the umbrella of the divine consciousness until they complete the trip. After that, they are on their own."*

The Teacher Is Omnipresent

Still aglow from the experience of the week in Sedona, and with Winged Wolf's words burning in our minds, we decided to take my parents and drive up to our northern Michigan cottage for a few weeks. It would give everyone a welcome break from each other, meaning the young adults and the grandparents.

The cottage sat fronting an aqua blue, crystal clear lake, about four hours drive 'up north' from where we were living. Behind it were hundreds of acres of state and county land. We settled in to enjoy some relaxation and good swimming (for me anyway). The water was a bit icy for the others.

One day, I was taking my typical afternoon walk through the pine forest, deep into the parkland. There wasn't another soul around as I sat down and leaned my back against a tall pine. This was a magical forest; I'd never seen anyone else enter it, and it was a place to meditate without being disturbed.

As I got deeper into my meditation, an image appeared of Winged Wolf on our last day at the Empowerment, and I remembered her words, *"If anyone has any ideas about places to move, I'd like to hear from you."* I had wanted it to be a passing fancy at the time, but now, an idea flashed. I stood up and excitedly began surveying the land. Aware that there was some adjoining property for sale, at least fifty acres, I became convinced this was the place for us to relocate.

Suddenly a shiver ran down my spine, and I felt the tingling of energy approaching. Turning quickly toward the feeling, down the sandy lane I saw my Teacher striding quickly toward me. She looked purposeful, but not happy. And immediately I saw the land through her eyes. *"It's not private enough,"* I said aloud, really taking an objective look at the area. And the moment I saw this clearly, her image began to shimmer, and gradually it dissolved, leaving me staring at the empty space where her figure had appeared.

When I called her later to tell her of my experience, she said, *"It was beautiful, but it wasn't private enough."* Almost the exact words I had said when she showed me the scene from her all-seeing eyes.

Chapter 9
Expanding Horizons

Winged Wolf's third book of the trilogy describing her apprenticeship with Alana Spirit Changer was titled *Circle of Power*. A few of us were with her at Eastcliffe busily helping to prepare a huge mailing of the publication. I had finished re-reading the book a few days prior to my visit. It was uplifting to be able to follow Winged Wolf in her apprenticeship with Alana; I found courage to proceed vicariously through the courage she had expressed. And this book completed the circle of her apprenticeship. She had made it through the eye of the needle!

During the first week of my visit, the phone rang, and after taking the call, Winged Wolf called me to her office. *"How would you like to do a book review on 'Circle of Power'?"* she asked. *"That call was from a book store in Sacramento. They want a book review immediately to run in their newsletter, and we don't have one available* yet."

Winged Wolf had given me a great teaching early in my apprenticeship, *"If you don't take that window of opportunity when it is open, it may be a long time before it opens again, maybe even another lifetime, depending on your karma."*

"I'd love to do that, Winged Wolf, although I don't have any experience with it." My heart was pounding in my ears.

"You said you wanted to be a writer," she said. *"Here is an opportunity. I know you can do it. Just keep your attention at the Third Eye, keep your heart open, and don't think. Write what comes to you.* Pausing to see if I was following her, she added, *"I need it right away, at least by tomorrow."*

This was such an incredible gift for me, and in her presence I never doubted for a moment that I could do it. Had I been at home, it might have been a struggle, but now it was a challenge that ignited my life force.

That evening I scanned the book, but it was still so fresh in my mind I found it was effortless to draft a rough outline of what I wanted to say. The next morning, I wrote and refined the review and handed it to Winged Wolf to critique. I must admit my anxiety raised some while I waited for her to read it. I had been in the magical power of her belief in me up until that point, one with her energy, but now, it was as if we had just separated and I stood alone, waiting.

She said, *"This is perfect. I knew you would do a fine review. Your love and enthusiasm for the book are infectious. Let's fax it off to them."*

A big sigh escaped my lips as I realized I had been holding my breath. It meant so much to me to have been given the opportunity; and even more so, the unexpected experience of becoming one with Winged Wolf's consciousness for that time, showed me the power of companion energy to move a lesser consciousness into becoming a greater consciousness, temporarily.

Because I had no resistance, I was enveloped in Winged Wolf's consciousness for that twenty-four hours; and from that experience, I learned I could be so much bigger than my personal identity led me to be. By simply suspending thought, judgment and mental imagery, then focusing my attention wholeheartedly 100% on what I was intending to accomplish and asking for the Teacher's companion energy, I wrote a book review that satisfied the Teacher. The greatest or most significant of these attitudes is **'asking for the Teacher's companion energy,'** for no matter had I all the other qualities, it was the pristine state of the Teacher's consciousness that brought forth a new state of awareness in me. And I learned something else: this state of higher consciousness was borrowed. I hadn't sufficiently refined myself to maintain that place of awareness, and gradually it faded, to be further developed over time and work with the Teacher.

It felt like magic, yet I knew it wasn't because it was now a part of my experience and my memory to be that; and I knew that was where I was heading and someday I would be able to live in that place myself. Winged Wolf had told me, *"a miracle is a changed consciousness,"* so for me, this was a miracle, but it was also scientific, because I could identify the elements that allowed it to occur, which meant I could replicate the experience. The possibilities from this realization were as unlimited as the divine consciousness.

This is also a wonderful example of how Winged Wolf supported all her apprentices in accomplishing their goals. I had privately told her that my secret dream was to write, but had never had the opportunity or direction to do so. I didn't even know if there was any ability there, but at least I wanted to try. She remembered what I had shared with her and gave me every possible opening, with her companion energy, to write. And it was like this with all her apprentices. If the goal was toward our spiritual evolution, she was behind us one- hundred-percent.

Vision Quests

It was during the first few days of this visit that I began hearing more about vision quests. There were several apprentices present I had not previously spent time with, and they seemed to know many things that were new to me. I sensed they had a different, maybe closer, relationship with Winged Wolf than I had. They were California folks, and had a 'hip' air about them. I felt a bit like a country bumpkin, although I didn't see that they felt that way about me.

And so it turned out to be my good fortune to arrive early and be privy to many talks and discussions I would have otherwise missed. One of the fellows in particular had a probing way about him and asked these really deep questions about aspects of subjects I had never even considered. It gave me some insight as to how others' minds worked, how they perceived themselves in relation to the Teacher and the Path.

This fellow was curious about reincarnation and auric fields, how the chakra systems worked and what was different about the shaman from the ordinary human. Winged Wolf was quite personable with him; although I noted she often redirected or reframed his questions with an answer she wanted us to have rather than the answer he was looking for. She was so skilled in reframing and redirecting that I almost didn't notice it was happening. And it was kinder than simply saying, *"You are out of line with that question."* Although when he pressed, she would say, *"If there was any need for you to have an answer to that question, I would give it to you, but there is not. It would just be food for your mind to chatter about. Be patient, it will all come to you in its right moment."*

In those days, Winged Wolf wouldn't talk with us about reincarnation, astral bodies, doubling, or most of the veiled subjects we all wanted to know about. As near as I could gather, she wanted us to focus totally and wholeheartedly on the present moment of this physical plane, and trust that all other questions would be answered in their time or out of our studies. So she was continually bringing us back into that focus; like the person taking pictures is forever adjusting the lenses to capture a true picture. I could feel she was relentlessly fine-tuning and redirecting us, although it was probably "rough-tuning" in those days, fine-tuning came much later. Nevertheless, we all tried in our own way to eke out as much of the mysterious stuff as we could.

One evening, this same apprentice from California brought up the subject of vision quests for the second or third time. He was pressing, eager to go on a vision quest himself. I was all-ears, my curiosity piqued. While I had heard Marla's tale of her unusual experience on a vision quest, other than that, I really had only an idea of what was involved. She hadn't given me any specifics. A friend of mine once told me her husband had done a vision quest and there was no food or water allowed. He was taken to a place in an isolated setting, bare-naked except for a buffalo skin as covering. I couldn't imagine Winged Wolf would want us to wear a buffalo skin, or to go without water for several days.

The idea of fasting for a period of time didn't concern me; I had experimented with fasting on several occasions and rather enjoyed the lightness of body and mind that it produced. But the idea of being alone in this vast Arizona wilderness, which we had already been told was ripe with rattlesnakes and large wild animals, sent shivers up my spine. It seemed that this fellow's wife, also an apprentice but not present, had flatly refused to do any vision questing because of the fasting required, but he was eager to do one and wanted to know when that would be possible.

"What is the purpose of a vision quest, Winged Wolf?" I finally spoke up.

"When I was apprenticing with Alana Spirit Changer, I must have done thirty of them. Alana felt they were important, and during that time I also felt it was important for me to spend a great deal of time alone. Alana told me that four days is the right amount of time. Any less than that and the benefits are not fully received. She said that the third day is

when everyone feels like they are done, but it isn't so. It is the fourth day when the vision quest is realized."

Further, Winged Wolf said *"While four days is the ideal amount of time for a vision quest, if you have never done one before this, in order to prepare adequately, you will first be required to do a two-day vision quest. Once you have that under your belts, then we'll see about scheduling a four-day."*

At this point, a two-day vision quest sounded fine with me. I knew I could survive for that long. There were so many elements to embrace all at once. Not only would we be without food and living alone with all the wild animals, we would be confined to a circle the length of our outstretched arms and that was just the physical plane! I had no idea what to expect from the dimensions I couldn't see, including my own inner depths. That sent shivers down my spine!

"But I still don't understand what is supposed to happen or what I should be doing during those two days." My mind was searching for some type of direction, but it was not to be.

"That is for you to determine. It is part of your vision quest. I cannot tell you what to do, except to say 'keep your attention focused at the Third Eye and let it unfold.' Don't try to plan it in advance, then you won't be living in the moment."

After that evening, Winged Wolf decided to let those of us, she felt were ready go out on the two-day vision quest. Several of the Michigan apprentices were arriving in a couple days. After giving them a day to adjust, the plan was to head out to the forest service land; and those of us Winged Wolf felt were ready to go on a vision quest would be assigned spaces. The others would stay with her at the base camp. She agreed that I could go on a two-day quest.

"Remember, just keep your attention on the Third Eye and no harm will come to you," she instructed me for the umpteenth time, sensing my anxiety. *"As long as you keep your attention there you will be safe, but if your attention is not at the Third Eye, I cannot promise your safety, so you must do the DO of it yourself."*

"But that's the scary part," I responded instantly, seeing the difficulty. *"You already know how to focus at the Third Eye for long periods, but*

I'm on-again off-again."

"*I can't do it for you,*" she replied seriously, gazing at me sideways. Then she lightened things up by saying *"but I have every confidence that you can do it."*

For the next two days we prepared for the vision quest; mostly for what would be needed at base camp, since during the vision quest we could only have water and personal necessities. The others arrived to a flurry of activity and the teams were quickly lined up.

Three others would be allowed to join us on the two-day vision quest, making a total of six, although not everyone would go out on the same day. One of my Michigan buddies was declined, much to her disappointment, although she would stay with Winged Wolf in her tent at base camp, which sounded like quite a privilege to me. I certainly understood her desire to participate in the vision quest. Later she told me Winged Wolf said she spent too much time alone, and was too comfortable with it; so, for her, it would be more challenging to stay in relationship with the Teacher.

Finally, we were ready and the car was loaded. It took two trips to haul all the supplies and people to the site of our base camp. Three of us remained at the site as Winged Wolf returned to Eastcliffe for the others and more supplies. There was big-time excitement in the air, and some anxiety, too. It was a step into the unknown.

We all gathered around Winged Wolf as she talked to us about how to be on a vision quest and what we might experience from the environment. The rules were simple: we could make a circle of stones no wider than the length of our bodies with arms outstretched; and we must stay within the boundaries of that circle at all times. Yes, even latrine needs required us to keep our feet in the circle. This circle was our protected, sacred space.

Winged Wolf picked out the general location for each apprentice, but we could select our own spot and secure it with rocks found in the area. Once the circle was formed, with us inside it, we were sealed in, and as long as we stayed within the boundaries we would be safe. In addition, we were also to keep our attention at the Third Eye and our awareness on the Teacher at all times. Again, I wondered what might happen during those times when my attention wandered.

Everyone was allowed one gallon of water per day, our personal necessities and a journal to write in. That was it. We could expect to hear coyotes at night, and perhaps see wild boar and rattlesnakes. If that happened, we should immediately quiet our minds by putting our attention at the Third Eye (assuming it had wandered) and sit motionlessly, calling to the Teacher silently in our minds.

There was one person who was going out for four days, since she had previously completed her two-day vision quest, so Winged Wolf selected a location for her and immediately took her to it. This woman had become my immediate idol upon her arrival at Eastcliffe. She had an air of sophistication and confidence about her that fascinated me, not to mention that she was comedic in nature and kept us all in stitches with her witty comments.

Winged Wolf found spots for the other two slated to begin that morning and then decided the rest of us should have a lesson on finding 'gateways.' *"Gateways are natural openings that call to you as you move through life. They can be nudges from your divine self, and if you go through them, there will be other openings you couldn't see without going through the initial gateway. Right now we are looking for physical plane gateways, there are others, but for now we will concentrate on discovering gateways in nature."* And she headed out up the side of a hill full of scrub brush and small trees. As we walked, she talked.

"Now you see here is a natural opening that calls to me," and she turned quickly to move through it.

"How do you know it calls to you?" I asked, not feeling called more to it than to the several other openings I saw around us.

"It is a feeling, an actual physical tugging at the solar plexus," she replied, *"and when you allow yourself to move through it, it will lead you to the next gateway, which you may not be able to see until you move through the first one. To do this,"* she continued, *"you must focus at the Third Eye and clip off all mind chatter. This does not involve thinking, or planning. We are simply moving with forward momentum. Don't pause to analyze where you want to go and why."*

Each time we moved through an opening, I thought she had picked one that dead-ended, but I was amazed to see another opening appear that was not immediately apparent before we moved, and so we followed as she moved effortlessly through the maze, until Winged Wolf decided we had at least experienced a sense or glimmer of what she was teaching us. Then we headed back to base camp with instructions to *"practice this on your own until you are comfortable with it."*

One of the local apprentices arrived at base camp while Winged Wolf was busy setting up camp. She lived nearby and knew we were going out, so decided to stop by for a visit. She called me aside and quietly told me about a spot she had been in during her recent vision quest and what a fabulous view it had. She described the location to me and said, *"Winged Wolf knows the spot. Be sure and ask her to take you there. It's a long walk, but the view is spectacular. It's well worth the effort to get there."*

As I set up my tent in the vicinity of Winged Wolf's and waited for her to return, I pondered how to approach her about this 'fabulous' site. I was hooked and couldn't imagine being any place else for my vision quest.

Off in the distance I could see one of the apprentices at her site. She was from California and had told me this was the first time she had ever been with Winged Wolf. She was quite a character, delightful, but a non-stop talker. As I looked in her direction, I saw her waving wildly at me, like spotting an old buddy you haven't seen for a long time.

I giggled as I tried to decide whether to respond. It was such unseemly vision quest behavior, yet so guileless. I pictured her out there, feeling isolated and desperately wanting to connect with someone, but decided I had best go about my business rather than feeding her little-self need to be connected, as well as my own. Perhaps Winged Wolf had realized this about her and placed her in view of base camp for this reason. I noted that no one else had been placed in this close proximity.

We had a fine time at base camp for the next couple days. It was a happy time together before trekking out to my isolated spot. It gave me time to become accustomed to that eerie sound of the coyotes howling as they cornered their prey, and all the other unfamiliar night sounds. We talked with Winged Wolf, listened as she told stories to us about her apprenticeship with Alana Spirit Changer, some of which made the hair on my neck stand up. These were not stories she told in her books. Told in person, we could see the relationship that existed between student and Teacher, how the student had called forth the Teacher's response and how perfect the response was under those circumstances.

But in writing, they might have been startling to the reader and left a misimpression.

Each evening, as darkness descended, Winged Wolf's Cairn Terrier Yoda would start to whimper and she would say, *"He's not very brave. When it gets dark he feels safer in the car."* And off she would go to put Yoda in the car for the night.

Our meals were pretty interesting those two days; we dined on peanut butter and jelly, cold spaghetti eaten right out of the pot, and protein bars. For a toilet, we dug a pit. The second night, once dusk began to descend at base camp, the coyotes started howling and they carried on for hours. As I finally drifted into a light sleep, one of the fellows hollered and leapt up. We were all awake by then and dashed over to see what had happened.

A giant rat had fallen from the tree under which he lay (after the Teacher had specifically cautioned us about not sleeping under trees for that very reason). Ironically, the rat had fallen directly on his Third Eye at cannonball speed and left an actual bruise. After that, he moved his sleeping bag into the open. Then, after we were all settled in again, we were awakened when a wild boar, being chased by a coyote, ran through the center of our camp.

What sounds they emitted! I felt for that huge boar with the big horn protruding from its nose, and wondered at the nerve of the coyote chasing that big pig. Winged Wolf told us it was this coyote's job to chase the boar into the open where the pack of coyotes could attack it. Ugh. She said not to make a big deal of it; this is how nature works. Still, I couldn't help saying a prayer that the pig found a way to safety. For me, this was right out of the movies, and way out of my prior experiences. The remainder of the night was uneventful.

Those who were on the first vision quest returned at dawn, except the apprentice who was out for four days, and were quickly given a protein drink to strengthen them. As my chatty friend came down to base camp, she immediately began talking about her experiences, and Winged Wolf said sternly, *"Be quiet. Do not speak of your experiences to anyone but me, or you dissipate their impact. This is how you give away your power."* They were instructed to remain totally silent until Winged Wolf had taken the remaining three of us to our spots.

When Winged Wolf got around to choosing a spot for me, I asked if I could have the same place that the other apprentice had recommended. For some reason, she was uncomfortable with my staying there, saying it was too far away, but I pressed a bit, insisting I would be fine, and she relented. I knew it was not my place to interfere with what she saw for me, yet the spot sounded so incredible. It was the only place that would satisfy me.

After walking for quite some distance, Winged Wolf pointed ahead and said, *"That's the area over there. You can select your spot anywhere in that general area. If you can find a place with a tree, I recommend you do so. I'll be back for you in two days. Remember, once it is sealed, do not leave your circle for any reason, or you are not protected."* And with that she turned on her heels and left me alone with my two jugs of water. I guessed she was annoyed with me for being so self-centered.

There had to be a perfect spot for this experience. I knew the tree should be large enough in height and foliage that it would give me a little shade. The days easily climbed to 105f and the sun beat down steadily in nearly cloudless skies, and my complexion is fair. Some shade was a necessity.

Plenty of scrub trees grew all around but not much of what could be called a real tree. Frustrated, I had just about given up, when I came over a small crest, and oh my goodness, there was the spot! There was a large mesquite tree that stood overlooking a huge expanse of valley below, and beyond that was part of the stunning red rock formations that surrounded Sedona. The view was breathtaking. And, there was plenty of flat ground in front of the tree for me to build my circle. I stood gaping at the view, awed by the beauty. I could understand why so many old western movies had been filmed in this area. It was a perfect wild-west setting.

Suddenly a shiver went down my spine, as I realized it had been a long time since my Teacher had dropped me off. What could happen to me without the protection of my circle wasn't clear, but neither was it something I wanted to find out. Swiftly I set to work gathering rocks; it seemed urgent that I form my circle and seal it off. There was no apparent danger, but then it was still daylight and the coyotes hadn't started howling yet. But that shiver said to me, *'You're stretching the window of protection; don't ask why, just get busy and make your circle.'*

Given all the events of the previous two evenings, I was acutely aware that the desert was alive with unknown, unseen and frightening creatures, and I took seriously my instructions to seal myself in and keep my attention at the Third Eye. I trusted Winged Wolf when she said this would keep me safe, but I still didn't completely trust myself to stay focused.

Surprisingly, it began raining sometime during my first night out, and I fished around in my backpack to find the plastic cover I had brought just in case. It took a while to tie it up to the tree in a way that kept me dry, but once secure, I actually slept off and on the rest of the night. I must confess I was grateful to see the beginning light of dawn. Somehow it was reassuring to see that time had not stood still, nor had wild animals attacked me; and I promptly fell sound asleep, awakening at some time later as I felt the warmth of the sun creeping in under my makeshift awning and warming me.

What a fabulous day I awoke to! One of my most profound experiences of the two-day vision quest was the discovery that I really did enjoy being alone and could sit gazing out at the vast expanse of beautiful scenes for hours. I felt like an eavesdropper in time and space: slipping into another era, envisioning what life must have been like thousands of years ago before the two-legged beings arrived and began to dominate things. All types of prehistoric creatures flowed past my vision, and for a while I was really there, a visitor from the future, watching a movie of the past.

Along about dusk on my second day, I was startled out of my reverie by the appearance of Winged Wolf, who said I had completed my assignment and it was time to return to base camp.

My senses were on guard. *"Is anything wrong?"* I asked, concerned.

"Not at all," she responded too cheerfully, *"everything's just fine."* And she quickly began gathering my things. I would have liked to conclude that my time there had been so spectacular that she determined there was no need to stay longer, but it somehow didn't feel right. There was something she wasn't telling me.

At base camp, one of the apprentices whispered to me that there was a fellow on a motorcycle who had arrived suddenly and was riding all around, heading in my general direction. Apparently he had a look to him that made Winged Wolf uncomfortable about leaving me out there. I didn't see any problem with it, but at least I now understood what had prompted my sudden removal from that heavenly place.

More and more, I came to understand that my Teacher took no chances with her apprentices, and while she seemed overprotective by my standards, I must admit she kept us all safe, and I admired her for her commitment to us regardless of how we might feel about it. If there was going to be an error, it would be on the side of safety. At least now I felt confident about going on the four-day. That night, once again I was in base camp with those who were not questing. I was both relieved and disappointed. It had been a good experience.

The next morning Winged Wolf went to get the others before dawn, carrying the signature protein drink. They came marching in from all directions looking disheveled and tired. Walter was weak and dizzy; he said he'd been sick the whole time and had a difficult experience. In fact, he told me that he had declared to Winged Wolf, *"If this is what vision questing is like, I'm not doing it again."* Winged Wolf spent some private time working with him so he was able to see that this was all part of the vision quest, part of the experience he had presented for himself to learn from.

There was plenty of help this time from other local apprentices who had arrived to be with us, so it only took one trip to get everything back to Eastcliffe. It was amusing how weak everyone felt after just a couple days of fasting. We were pretty well attached to our comforts back in those days, and anything that was a little strenuous or out of the ordinary disturbed us.

That evening we had a wonderful meal of fresh vegetables, brown rice, and green salad. I savored every mouthful as though I hadn't eaten in weeks, and then we sat around the table relaxed and happy. Winged Wolf again reminded us not to talk about our experiences on the vision quest, as it would take away from their power.

In fact, she said, *"Never talk about your acts of power, never."* I think we were all curious about each other's experiences, but we didn't ask. I wanted to know more about what was an act of power and whether I had had one, but the timing didn't seem right to ask.

The next day she talked with each one of us individually about what we had experienced. She looked at my journal, skimmed it quickly, and declared I had done a fine job. What she told the others might have been the identical thing or not, I don't know. I asked to return later that summer to do my four-day vision quest and she agreed. After his private session with her, Walter decided he would return and do a four-day as well. How quickly things changed. We set a tentative date for early September.

Chapter 10
Unanticipated Disturbances

The phone rang in the middle of the night. Walter's sister-in-law Teri was on the line. I answered the phone and, half asleep, could barely make out her words as she said something about Walt's brother David. I had to ask her to repeat herself. *"I think Dave was on that plane that crashed,"* she said.

"What plane crashed?" I asked stupidly.

"The one that crashed over Pittsburgh," she answered. *"He was supposed to be on the 6:30 flight, but they have no record of him being on it. I think he got to the airport early and caught the flight that crashed."*

Fully awake now, I mouthed the words to Walter, *"David's plane crashed."* It was such a shock to grasp the enormity of it, *"Teri, how can you be sure?"* I asked.

"I'm not," she said, *"but I can feel there's something wrong; he would have called by now if he was all right. He would have called."* Then she said, *"I'm going to hang up now and leave the phone open. I've called the airlines and they promised to get back to me as soon as they know something. I'll call you back."*

We were dazed, waiting for the phone to ring again. It wasn't real. People you *know* don't die in plane crashes; people you *don't* know die in plane crashes. He wasn't even supposed to be on that plane; but why else wouldn't he have called? David would never be so irresponsible as to let people worry about him. Round and round we went trying to digest what this meant. Walter, I could see, was in total shock. He knew, really, before the phone ever rang again.

Unanticipated Disturbances

About 6:30 that morning, three long sleepless hours after the first phone call, the phone rang again. Walt picked it up, and I saw the color drain from his face as he listened to the voice on the other end.

Hanging up the phone he said, *"He must have arrived early at the airport, in time for the 5:30 flight. That was the one that went down. They still don't know what happened. One moment the pilot had called in to the tower for landing clearance, and the next moment, they were crashing. No one knows exactly what happened."*

"Were there any survivors?" I asked hopefully, knowing the answer.

"None. The plane is totally destroyed. They're out there now going through the wreckage for the black box. We're supposed to be contacted soon by the airlines to make arrangements to fly to Maryland to be with the family."

"You'd better call Winged Wolf," I said.

He nodded. *"I will, just as soon as we hear from the airlines, and it's only 3:30 in the morning in Arizona, I can at least wait until she's up."*

Walter was on remote control, speaking in a monotone, all business; it was too horrible to take in. Thankfully, the phone rang again. It was a representative of the airlines. They had made arrangements to fly us to Maryland that afternoon. Actually, we would fly to Pittsburgh and drive to Maryland; there was no easy way to get to the remote area in which his brother had lived.

Walt talked with Winged Wolf before we left. On the way to the airport, he relayed a part of their conversation to me. *"She told me I will be fine as long as I don't get caught up in the drama of it,"* he related.

"What does that mean?" I queried, puzzled.

"It means not to get caught up in emotions from the past, like looking at pictures of David and recalling times together from an emotional perspective."

What was Winged Wolf's view of mourning, I wondered. Did she not think it important to grieve a loss? And how else did one grieve unless they dredged up memories of their life experience with the person or situation that was lost? Okay, now was not the time for this conversation either in my head or out loud. But some day I wanted to talk with her about it.

We flew to Pittsburgh, accompanied at all times by an airlines representative who was solicitous of our every need. They were trained to talk with families of victims of airline crashes, and we were relieved to have someone to talk with, just to keep our attention looking out.

After landing, we rented a car and drove the three hours to the remote area where Walter's now-deceased brother and wife lived. It was a dream-like experience from the moment we received the call. I had never known anyone else who had been killed on a plane crash. The devastation that occurs around it is unbearable. The staff at the airline was despondent; they could barely function. A crisis team had been assigned to each of the families affected, and they were with us every step of the way, but it was also tearing them apart. In fact, the airlines people assigned to us were so distraught, it was heart-wrenching to feel their pain.

The next few days passed as in a dream; the family gathered together and showed their best faces in the wake of this tragedy. I saw clearly the beauty and oneness of purpose that crisis brings out in people. One of the worst parts of this accident was that the phone began ringing off the hook with reporters angling for a story. What a difficult job those people had chosen, to feed off others' tragedies. The family was united in their disinterest, and they assigned a close family friend to ward off the vultures and screen the calls. Walter's conversation with Winged Wolf assisted him greatly in maintaining composure and not collapsing in on himself. I know it was one of the reasons everything flowed so lovingly and smoothly, that and having Winged Wolf's companion energy with us the whole time.

After we had been with the family for several days and had the memorial service, Walt announced that he still intended to do the four-day vision quest as planned. He would fly directly from the family home to Arizona.

Looking back, I'm sure he was in shock and felt that being with Winged Wolf would be the best place for him, which really did make sense. But I needed to unwind some before heading to Arizona, so I flew home for a couple days, regrouped, and then headed to Eastcliffe.

"Winged Wolf has been exceptionally kind and supportive," he told me. *"She has even traveled to the accident site to determine David's experience with dying. She was able to reassure me that David had died swiftly and without pain."* Hearing this was so comforting and cut through all the terrible images of what might have occurred during those last few moments of life.

He went on, *"She also said that everyone on that plane had the agreement to die or it wouldn't have happened."*

"You mean to tell me they all came together on that plane to die?"

"Something like that, if I understood her correctly."

This was a different perspective, and a tough one for my mind to accept. But I had to admit that as the family had recounted their experiences with David during the weeks prior to this trip, it seemed he had been doing much unusual preparation, as if he knew something was going to happen. No one had placed much attention on it prior to the accident though. Afterwards, the pieces began to fit together. He set in motion the preparations for major changes: a new will, an insurance policy, company reorganization. Could what Winged Wolf said be true, I wondered? All of them? That meant the pilots and stewards and stewardesses as well. What an extraordinary idea!

Walter later told me that besides the advice Winged Wolf had given him during their initial call after David's death, she had also cautioned, *"Whatever happens, don't get stuck in the emotionalism of going back into the past, and don't get caught up in projecting into the future. Stay in the present moment."* She told him, *"You can make a huge difference in how the family handles this death by holding your focus at the Third Eye and living in the present moment."*

He had been concerned about one family member in particular and had told her that this person was prone to depression and emotional volatility in the best of situations. If she got off to a bad start, it could have thrown everyone into despair. For Walter, Winged Wolf's guidance and invisible presence were a great source of inner strength and had allowed him to be present during those days in a loving, supportive way. The family had pulled together; they mourned together, and found comfort in each other, but there had been no chaos or hysterics.

Since I had arrived at Eastcliffe later than previously scheduled, there was no time to settle in before going on the vision quest. Everyone was ready to leave the morning after my arrival. They were in full-swing. Walter seemed surprisingly intact.

After a short night's sleep, we loaded up the Suburban and headed out. Six of us were going out this time, some for two days and others for four. I was ready for four days of solitude after the stress of the last couple weeks.

On this trip there was an apprentice going on her second four-day vision quest, and I learned from her that, after the first four-day, the rules change. There was no strict confinement to a small circle. Instead, there was a general area that one occupied, much larger than the length of the body, and it was permissible to bring spiritual reading material. Somehow this was encouraging to me, a carrot perhaps. This person already had the ability to communicate with Winged Wolf telepathically. I don't think Winged Wolf had intended to tell me this, but it happened that someone spoke to her at a time she was gazing intently off in the distance. She snapped a response, *"Be still, can't you see I'm having a conversation with someone!"*

The intensity of her response took me aback, and even though it wasn't me who had interrupted her, I could still feel the impact of the sting. Curious, I could hardly wait for an opening to question her. Obviously, she hadn't been in conversation with any of us, and this apprentice was the only one out at the time, so the natural conclusion was that she was having a telepathic conversation. This was like magic as far as I was concerned.

When Winged Wolf re-entered the space we were in, she said nothing, and I could sense it was not the time to bombard her with my curiosity-driven questions.

Soon it was my time to have a spot selected for my vision quest, and this time I had learned my lesson. I had experienced the results of my impetuousness in contradicting the Teacher's sense of how things should be. If I had accepted her wisdom about where I should be placed, most likely I would have been able to complete my two days and reap the full benefits. I was learning to trust my Teacher's wisdom over my own 'feelings' about how things should be. My strong feelings were ego-driven and brought distorted results.

My rational mind would argue that it could have happened to anyone wherever they were, and it was simply coincidence that it happened to me, but deep down, I knew it wasn't true. There is no coincidence when it comes to the divine consciousness. That was demonstrated to me so consistently during my apprenticeship that it bore no denial, even though I stubbornly tested it pretty regularly.

Winged Wolf found a dandy spot for me, a little plateau up on a small incline, complete with tree, and said, *'I'll see you in four days, unless you run into difficulties; then just call for me from your heart and I'll hear you. You may experience some nausea and weakness, but that's normal, don't worry about it. It is part of your body's response to being deprived of food. And don't try to come down on your own on the fourth morning. I'll be up here with a protein drink, which you'll need. So wait here for me."*

That first night I felt pretty lonely. The coyotes were howling off and on for hours and they sounded so close I thought for sure they were coming right to me. And there was a rustling in the bushes nearby. Four days seemed a long time to be out. My initial excitement faded into anxiety.

I completely forgot about *'the Teacher is always with us if we keep our attention on her,'* and *'if we place our attention on the Third Eye and look out, all mind chatter is clipped off,'* which means No Fear! I gasped, suddenly realizing how completely I was collapsing in on myself or *'staring at myself,'* as Winged Wolf put it. Okay, time to get up and move around the circle, get some energy flowing, because I also flashed on her saying, *"The only time you are vulnerable is when you do not have your attention on the Third Eye."* What a motivator that was!

This helped me to quickly refocus my attention, and I sat down to make some notes in my journal, holding the flashlight in my teeth; and the next thing I knew, the light of dawn was in my eyes. After that first night passed, time seemed to roll from one moment to the next. I became fascinated with the movement of the sun across the sky and the shadows that were produced by its different angles. I watched as the moon presented itself some time in the afternoon so that sun and moon were simultaneously visible. And I watched as the first star twinkled in the sky as darkness settled in. Soon the sky was brightly lit with moon and stars. What luxury to be able to observe every moment evolve into the next. How often in life does an opportunity such as that present itself?

To watch life evolve on a moment-to-moment basis was fascinating. Each moment at first seemed the same as the previous moment, but upon closer inspection, there were subtle variations. For instance, the tiniest of breezes would come up gently, seemingly from nowhere, and then pass into total stillness. Then a bird would sing, or an ant would crawl by carrying some treasure, almost bigger than it was, back to the anthill. It was sort of like watching an animated cartoon in slow motion; I was in it, yet not of it.

On the third day, I had become involved in writing a children's story, based loosely on my experiences on the vision quest, when I heard a rustling and looked up to see Winged Wolf approaching. I must admit my attitude was less than welcoming as a flood of thoughts passed through my mind, *'What happened this time?'* and, *'Don't tell me she's going to pull me out again.'*

Well, she sat down just outside my circle, *"How are you doing?"* she asked, gazing at me with that sideways look.

"Fine, I'm working on a children's story." I could feel myself puffing up a little, believing it to be a creative story and imagining myself a popular writer of children's books.

Winged Wolf didn't seem too interested, and I didn't sense that she wanted anything in particular. I was a little annoyed at being interrupted, thinking perhaps she was checking up on me as though I needed some help. Soon she left saying she would see me in the morning. I wondered briefly what had really brought her up the hill, but quickly forgot about it and went back to my work.

The next morning barely at dawn, Winged Wolf was at my site, with the protein jar in hand, telling me to *"drink it all."* And just briefly, as if in passing, she said, *"You were annoyed at my interrupting you yesterday."* I started to deny it.

She went on, *"You should never be annoyed at the presence of the Teacher, no matter what you are doing. You missed an opportunity to see me in my light body, because you were so annoyed at being interrupted."* And with that she said, *"Get your things, I'll help you carry them down."*

Stunned by her words, I hurried after her down the hill, with my mind chattering wildly. What did she mean by her 'light body?' Was she saying she was doubling and I didn't even notice? She seemed real enough. But then, I didn't touch her. Perhaps she only looked real. Why hadn't I been paying attention instead of grumbling inside my head? Questions flew by. What were the signs? How would I know if she was in her light body?

It was clear she was in no mood to talk about anything with me, and I would be left to the agonizing process of digesting this giant faux pas, living with the knowledge I had blown my chance to learn something in favor of indulging an attitude. Darn my self-centeredness! I would have to file the questions away to be asked when, or if, a propitious moment arose, because I surely did want to know the answers. I made the error of assuming there would be another opening.

Once again, we gathered at base camp and began loading up the vehicles. It was a pretty funky group. The conversation turned to showers and how wonderful it was going to feel to wash our dirty, dusty bodies. I participated in the banter, but internally I was stewing over my missed opportunity.

For months prior to this, we had all whispered these same questions among ourselves, questions about how to double, and to transport ourselves through time and space. We were always prodding her to tell us more. Her response was to say, *"I'm not a performer, and I'm not about to perform for you. When the time is right, you'll understand."* Yet here she had given me a demonstration of the very thing I had been salivating to learn about, and I hadn't even noticed it. I knew I didn't dare tell the others. They would think me incredibly stupid, as I would have them if the situation were reversed. And, if it got back to Winged Wolf, she'd have my hide. So I couldn't even tell anyone about it.

That evening Winged Wolf called us all in one at a time, just as she had previously done for the two-day vision quest, and she reviewed our journals with us. When it was my turn, I could tell there were still ripples from my earlier inattention and snappy attitude.

She had read my story and commented: *"You must have been pretty far out there."* Otherwise she had little else to say to me. I was just beginning to get a glimmer of understanding that often when I felt 'high' about something, I was really off-balance; it was my ego showing off.

The subject of my attitude did not arise again for a long time, but eventually it did. Winged Wolf never forgot an incident, especially if there was a missed lesson, and she never let loose of a lesson until it had come full circle and was thoroughly understood. She was infinitely patient and tenacious; all she had to do was bide her time until the moment was ripe when, with snakelike movement, she would strike to make the point again and again and again.

Chapter 11
An Opportunity to Serve

Days at home flew by quickly. School was back in session, and so I was working full-time there and in private practice in the evenings. One day melted into another. My parents left for their Florida home, the adult children returned to college, and Walt and I were once again alone, except for Dallas and Max, the dog and cat. Our Wisdom Circle was meeting every week at that time, and the local apprentices usually got together one night a week as well; any excuse to meet was our motto. Life was happy and busy and filled with adventure.

One evening in October, I had called to chat with Winged Wolf, when she casually mentioned she had just returned from a mini-vacation, property-scouting trip. Then, just as casually she said, *"I think I've found the right property. It's in the San Juan island chain so the climate is moderate year round; it's a beautiful place and it's accessible by an hour-long ferryboat ride."*

"The San Juan Islands?" I said, imagining something in the Caribbean. *"Where are they?"* I asked.

"Why, they're in Washington," she said as if everyone knew that. *"Near Vancouver,"* she added, as I remained silent.

Then I remembered something. My cousin Jane had moved suddenly from northern California to a town called Bellingham in northern Washington. She had wanted me to visit her, had mentioned some islands off the Pacific Coast called the San Juans that were of moderate climate because they caught the Japanese trade currents. She kept trying to entice me out for a visit, telling me about the lush terrain and beautiful mountains that surrounded the area. It had sounded intriguing but our schedules never lined up and I had put it on the back burner.

Another light went on, *"Do you mean there's no bridge to the island?"* I was used to the island my parents lived on in Florida that had a bridge over the intercoastal waterway. This island sounded pretty far away and not readily accessible. *"Doesn't it rain all the time in Washington?"* I asked, suddenly uncomfortable about the prospects.

"Oh, not on the San Juan Islands. They say it only rains half as much as it does on the mainland. And it's beautiful there. I've never seen so many shades of green. I'm sure you will love it, and it's perfect for the work I want to do. We wouldn't want it to have a bridge; this way we can maintain our privacy."

"Are you sure you bought it?" I asked.

"There's still some paper work to sign and some inspections, but it should go through. I've got it set for a February closing."

Winged Wolf went on telling me some details about getting her Eastcliffe place on the market and about finding a way to transport the horses and such; and that was that. I forgot entirely what I had called her about. It shocked me that she wanted to move to Washington. From what I knew of her, she was a sunshine, warm-weather person. I had spent some time looking for property with her driving around the White Mountains in Arizona, a beautiful area, plenty remote, and I assumed we would eventually find something there.

Once she had said, *"Who knows, the next move may be to Canada,"* and we all had laughed with her. Now, we would be almost there. My entire life had been lived in Michigan, in different houses but always within a few minutes of each other. My parents were born and raised there, too. I'd had the same jobs for over twenty years. Stability was the key value. My mind was rattled somehow by Winged Wolf's lack of an apparent rootedness, which I equated with stability and reliability, trustworthiness and so forth. How could I depend on someone who wouldn't stay still? She sure was able to keep my attention riveted on her, though. I'd never met anyone quite like her.

Some weeks later, I was talking with my 'idol' apprentice from Pennsylvania, the one who claimed the telepathic abilities. She was an idol to me because she seemed to be so spiritually awake and devoted to the Teacher, always quoting the Teachings; I wanted to be more like that. Also there was a strong connection on my side because she could

An Opportunity to Serve

have been a twin of my ex-sister-in-law and best friend in my younger years. So, we were frequently in touch. That evening she was telling me how badly she felt at not being able to help Winged Wolf with the upcoming move.

I asked, *"Why do you think she needs help? She's a shaman."* In my naiveté, being shaman had some magic quality to it that meant Winged Wolf didn't need anything from anyone.

The apprentice said, *"Do you realize how much work is involved in moving and then unpacking and getting set up in a new place? She will need all the help she can get, and I can't go because of the kids."*

Then she paused and said coyly, *"Why don't you go? It would make me feel so much better to know you were there."*

"Do you really think she needs help?" I asked.

"Yes, dummy, I really do. She is human you know." She sounded big-sisterly.

I thought about it. There was no reason I couldn't take my February break from school and fly out to help with the move. The dates coordinated perfectly. *"All right, I'll call her and make the offer, but I bet she'll say she doesn't need any help."*

Convinced Winged Wolf would decline my offer, I still called to make it, and she accepted readily. So much for what I knew about being a shaman. Because my school break was exactly at the time Winged Wolf would be arriving on the island, I could fly in, rent a car, and meet her and the others who were driving with her in time to help with the unpacking.

And there it was. I was going to Orcas Island, Washington, to help my Teacher unpack at our new spiritual home, as she now referred to it. She planned on driving up in caravan fashion with two other apprentices who would drive the U-haul trucks with her following.

"It will be a grueling drive," she told me. *"I have to take both cats, plus Sioux and Yoda. Peaches will be terrified, and Sioux will not urinate along the road unless I can find a perfect spot with no noise and no one else around. It's terrible traveling with her. We'll just load up the*

vehicles and drive as far as we can. We have to make it in three days. Sioux will be miserable and suffering the entire time."

Another lesson in the differences between the nature of wolves and dogs; they look similar, but it pretty much ends there. Sioux was high-maintenance.

There was really no direct way to get to this island. After picking up a rental car in Seattle, there was still a two-hour drive to the ferry landing and then, depending on the ferry schedule, there might be a several-hour wait for the next ferry, which took over an hour-and-a-half to get to the island, again, depending on how many stops it made. Navigating through this seemed overwhelming until I remembered Winged Wolf would have been driving for three days straight with a dog and a wolf in the car, along with two cats. That helped to put my trip in proper perspective. Suddenly gratitude flooded me, for by comparison, my trip was a piece of cake.

Expansion

Everyone arrived at approximately the same time, tired, but oh-so-grateful to be there. The caravan of travelers had apparently just rolled onto the last ferry of the day within minutes of its sailing off without them. I had taken an earlier ferry to the island and had time to do some shopping prior to their arrival, so I was only a few minutes ahead of them.

Winged Wolf and the caravan arrived shortly thereafter, and the first item on the agenda was Sioux. Let her out of the vehicle, tell her this is her new home and stand back. She was so happy to be there that her eyes sparkled and she did a little dance. It lifted my spirits immediately.

The property itself was unique, I discovered, as I joined the other two drivers, also apprentices, and took a look around. The acreage was visually and physically contained in the shape of a bowl, so although there were only twenty-one acres, no adjoining property could be seen anywhere, giving the impression of spaciousness and a sense of privacy.

The main house was a small cabin, rustic, cozy, and ideal for one person. It was probably sixty-years-old; the roof looked brand new though.

That was about all that looked new, and the place had a *'diamond in the rough, but recently neglected'* look to it.

At about mid-point inside the tiny living area, was a wood-burning stove set on a platform. Beyond it, was a step-down dining area surrounded by windows, and off to the left was a good-sized kitchen, cute, with country-style wood cabinets. Just before the kitchen and dissecting the living area, cutting down its available space even further, was a steep set of stairs that led to the loft. The stairs were so steep that you almost crawled up and slid down them.

The loft was large, but there was only one section of it where I could stand at full height; otherwise, it was a *'stoop down to walk'* type of loft. This was where I and the other female apprentice would sleep. It was cold and damp inside the cabin, maybe colder than it was outside. I couldn't see any signs of insulation. Nor did I see a furnace or any other type of heating than the wood stove. Having no idea what to expect from Winged Wolf's description of 'rustic,' to my relief, there was indoor plumbing, hot water, and an old-fashioned, free-standing tub, no shower. All right, it was definitely cute in a primitive sort of way and with some work it might be quite livable.

The cabin stood on a little hill about in the center of the property (we thought), and it overlooked the future barn and pasture, which was the concave part of the bowl. That area was green even in February, suggesting heavy rain had fallen.

Next to the cabin on the same hill, was a two-story structure that perhaps had been intended as guest quarters and was newer than the cabin. It was cedar-sided. On the main level were several undefined rooms, including a two-car garage, and a full bathroom with shower. That was a relief. I envisioned long, hot showers away from the flow of traffic. Then I noted there was no heater anywhere in the bathroom, and the window didn't even close fully. Above the first floor was a lovely, large room with windows on all sides and an elevated purple bathtub set in a window alcove. That area was to be Winged Wolf's private office. It also contained another bathroom and a storage area off it. This was definitely the coolest spot I'd seen thus far and hot baths under the stars sounded so romantic, but Winged Wolf said the tub was to be covered with plywood and used as a bed for Sioux whenever Winged Wolf was working up there. She certainly treated her animals well. Clearly, she had different priorities than I did. Loftier.

This tour took place after Winged Wolf had been upstairs for a while, setting up her computer and whatever else she probably did to bring the energies into alignment. When she came downstairs, she seemed refreshed and had gathered us all around to share with us part of her vision for the land, the cabin, the office; and with her usual contagious enthusiasm, she led us from place to place designing the future, which she said, already lived in her mind in the present.

The horses would get that lower central area, and we would need to immediately fence it off and build a makeshift barn to get them through the winter protected from the rains. Next, simultaneously really, we needed to get cabins built right away so apprentices could begin to schedule their visits to the property. There could be no down-time spiritually.

Winged Wolf said, *"We will have three to four visiting apprentices at any one time, no more. Plus, I've asked Mark, now named Skywolf, to bring his trailer up from Arizona and set it up on the back side of the property. He will be the maintenance person and all-around handy man."* She went on, *"I've asked Standing Turtle* (an apprentice from Arizona) *to consider coming here to live. She will be the office staff and can live down here,"* she was pointing to the undefined area beneath her office.

In all then, there would be up to six apprentices, including the live-ins, at any one time on the property. It was beginning to sink in with me that my Teacher was not going to operate in the same manner as her Teacher had. Meaning she was not going to have only one or two apprentices at any given time, instead she would be working with numbers of apprentices. A twinge of jealousy for the future competition for her attention passed through me. I tried to brush it aside quickly because I knew she could hear my thoughts if I allowed them to linger with any intensity.

We continued our walk through the lower level of the office and Winged Wolf showed us a small, empty room in the back that could be used as a kitchen, and I mean, it was really small. Another room could be a live-in staff bedroom, and all apprentices would share the bathroom with the shower.

There was no heat at all in the lower level, and when I pointed this out, saying to her that we would need a heater, Winged Wolf responded,

"That will mean people won't be lingering in the bathroom for too long." And she grinned sideways at me, rolling her eyes.

I was shocked by her attitude, but kept my mouth shut, thinking, *'No way am I coming to stay here with no heat! At least not in the winter.'* That was only one of a hundred or so times I was to eat my words during the course of my apprenticeship.

That first evening we unpacked just enough so that everyone had a place to sleep and a bedroll. We ordered a pizza from town, which we had to pick up as there was no delivery to our area. It turned out to be awesome pizza, a real plus in my mind for the island.

Winged Wolf built a great fire in the wood stove, and after a long time, amazingly, it warmed the tiny cabin, transforming it from a cold, damp roof over our heads to a warm and welcoming, cozy, if not very comfortable, home.

The female apprentice, who had driven one of the trucks for Winged Wolf, brought up the subject of sleeping and mentioned that from their two nights on the road, she learned that Skywolf snored loudly. Since he is deaf, she was able to communicate this to Winged Wolf without his hearing her, not wanting to hurt his feelings, but Winged Wolf promptly said, *"Well, it's because he sleeps on his back. Let's ask him to sleep on his side."* It wasn't clear who was supposed to do this so I ventured to ask. *"Oh,"* she said, *"would you prefer I do it?"* That was a unanimous *'yes.'* So up she went to him and said, *"Skywolf, will you sleep on your side tonight? That way you won't snore and keep people up."*

He looked at her, comprehension dawning, and nodded agreeably. I thought to myself, *'sure.'* But in fact he did as he said he would, and we all had a good night's sleep, at least I did. Simple, direct, non-judgmental communication.

Winged Wolf said, *"If you speak from your heart, it will not arouse anger or defense in others because of its genuineness. But, it must be genuine; if it's a thinly disguised way of criticizing or poking at another from one's little-self, there will definitely be a reaction. The mirror doesn't lie."*

The next few days all rolled together in a flurry of unpacking. Winged Wolf was determined to have no break in her work schedule, so every morning we were up at the crack of dawn; we rebuilt the fire and went about unpacking boxes for the house.

By this time, Winged Wolf had established a large e-mail correspondence with apprentices who were eagerly forsaking 'snail mail' for the much faster e-mail method. She would never tell us exactly how many apprentices there were, and if anyone asked, the standard response was *'only one,'* meaning the person who asked the question, and because there is only One divine consciousness.

Few apprentices hand-wrote their reports any more. Even I had succumbed to the seduction of a laptop computer; and the motivation for learning how to use it was so I could keep more closely in touch with Winged Wolf. Walter was a primary source of support and education for me in becoming computer literate. He had been after me for a long while to at least try out a computer before judging it. He would spend hours sitting at the computer doing I knew not what. He told me he could not have run his business without one, but I suspected he was fascinated with them and determined to need one. So I still had a bit of an attitude about them. Seemed to me our whole society was going machine-mad and creating a dependence on them that was making us lazy and impatient.

Up until the point when Winged Wolf told me she couldn't imagine anyone in this day and age being without a computer, I had repeatedly refused to consider using one. Her comment carried enormous weight with me, and as I saw that other apprentices were e-mailing journey reports and getting rapid responses, I began to feel like a dinosaur. Soon, I was up and running.

It was a major concern to Winged Wolf to have been out of touch with her apprentices for several days during the move, and becoming established with an Internet Service Provider on Orcas Island took patience and perseverance. For the first two days she was unable to get the system set up. I watched with great interest as she prioritized the steps of this move. There were so many opportunities to become scattered with the overwhelming task of getting an operation like this up and running quickly and smoothly. It took tremendous focus of attention, energy and order.

My job was easy: to organize the kitchen and to unpack the books; I stuck with this because it was well-defined and I could see how to do it.

An Opportunity to Serve

The overall project itself was the Teacher's vision.

Winged Wolf told me, *"When you have too much to do, an overwhelming project such as this, you must prioritize, and then begin doing. Keep moving and don't allow any distractions, but don't become rigid in what you do or you will fail. You must be flexible enough to change priorities at a moment's notice, depending on what needs to be done. The energies present in any given moment will let you know what must be done. That is why it is so vital that you be present and awake every moment."*

It sounded simple when she said it, but it wasn't natural for my mind to see what the priorities were when there were so many of them, so it was easiest to stick to what she asked me to do and let her determine the priorities. For once, I was happy to be led.

For this week only, Winged Wolf declared that there would be a moratorium on apprenticeship, which meant that we would all function more as co-workers, and keep it low-key and relaxed. The change in her behavior gave us breathing room to get the work done without being overly self-conscious. Of course, there were some Teachings she couldn't resist zeroing in on. It just wasn't her nature to let too many things slide.

For instance, I had spent a good part of one whole day unpacking boxes of books and placing the books on the bookshelves built into the walls of the cabin. Without giving much thought to how I was placing them, I unpacked and loaded the shelves.

Late that afternoon Winged Wolf walked into the cabin ready to take a break from her work, and she sat in a chair across from the bookcase I had been working on. As she glanced at the bookcases that were now filled to capacity with books, her eyes immediately zeroed in on the encyclopedias that I had randomly placed together on two of the shelves. I could see her lips part as she looked at me with twinkling eyes. I had no idea what was amusing her, so I waited.

"Wings of Change," she said.

"Yes, Winged Wolf," I replied.

"Do you see anything out of the ordinary in the way you placed those encyclopedias?"

I studied them for a while, and then I saw it. *"They're not in alphabetical order, Winged Wolf."*

"That's right," she said. *"Can you put them in order?"*

"Certainly," I was now feeling a bit huffy. Did she think I didn't know how to alphabetize? *"I was just hurrying to get them all unpacked."*

"You have a glitch in your brain, Wings of Change, and it's important to get it corrected. You don't see that it's important to have things in order; that's why it's a glitch. Having things in their proper order is part of higher consciousness, and that's a piece you don't yet have."

She turned and went on to do something else, and I began replacing the encyclopedias in alphabetical order. While I alphabetized the encyclopedias I wondered, 'why did she find it so important to have them in order right away? 'What am I missing in the point she is trying to make here? I know I have a brain glitch in certain areas, but is this really a glitch?' Round and round the conversation went in my head. It didn't penetrate, and I knew it. I was feeling too defensive about it.

Later that evening I saw her studying the encyclopedias, and nodding, apparently satisfied that I had sorted them properly. But, no, that was not the end of the incident, not by a long shot. This business of unraveling brain glitches was crucial to spiritual evolvement. And it was years before I began to catch a glimmer of understanding about the significance of order to the divine consciousness. There is a divine plan, and there is order to it.

In the blink of an eye it was time for me to return to work, my real job, as I called it. In those days, I was confused as to what was real and what was illusion, so I thought my 'real life' was home, work, and family; and Winged Wolf and the lessons were my spiritual life, as if they were two separate compartments of equal value.

Just before I got in the rental car to head off for the ferry, Winged Wolf asked, *"When are you coming back for a visit? How about April? Why don't both you and Walter come together this next visit? We can see how that works out. Will you pass that request along to him? I'll e-mail him in a few days myself and invite him."*

"Do you think the cabins will be ready by then?" I asked, thinking about how cold it was going to be in those non-insulated cabins, and she had already told me there would be no heaters this year.

From what she had told me, they were literally storage sheds with a window and a door. They would be placed way down the lane by the creek that flowed into the pond, in a stand of trees. It was a beautiful setting, but the bathroom was a long way off, all the way up the hill by the office, not conducive to middle-of-the-night trips.

"I'm sure they will be," she said decisively. *"Just let me know when you're coming and I'll pick you up at the ferry."*

I reviewed in my mind all that I had learned during the week I was there. Even though it looked like we were doing physical labor, and we were, it was the spiritual consciousness of the Teacher that forged the opening for so much to be accomplished. And even with all that was done, there was still no kitchen, no cabins, no office for the apprentice coming to act as office manager, no fencing or barn for Spirit, Winged Wolf's Lipizzaner stallion, or Pepe, her burro.

I felt badly leaving Winged Wolf with so much to do and so little help, now that I realized she really did need the help. Skywolf had to leave for Arizona to pack up and bring his trailer out to Orcas, so even he would be gone. Basically, she would be alone there until he or Standing Turtle arrived.

Sitting on the ferry, looking out over the sparkling waters dotted with pristine islands, my perspective shifted and I knew without a doubt, Winged Wolf was giving her life for me (for all of us), and I wished there was more I could give in return, especially heartfelt giving. And I also knew that was all I was capable of at the time. But she had touched my heart with her openness and giving nature. She was unfathomable from my limited viewpoint. I just knew with certainty that she was big.

Over the next two months, I heard bits and pieces as to the progress being made on the property. The apprentice from Arizona had moved out to Orcas to be Winged Wolf's assistant, and Skywolf successfully moved his trailer onto the property. That meant two full-time staff persons were available to help with all the work. There were also rumors about unusual weather patterns, excessive rain and storms.

The weather patterns are of interest because there is more to it than the obvious. I had noticed that wherever Winged Wolf lived, the weather patterns shifted and became unpredictable; and whenever we had events with Winged Wolf, they were usually preceded by unusually high winds. As the event progressed, the winds would settle down, except when a lot of energy was stirred up, then they might blow gently or rage, seeming to clean the area of released energy. We always had sunshine during an event, but afterwards, there might be more winds and even some cleansing rain. Winged Wolf didn't speak much about it, so it took me a while to see there was a definite pattern.

When I heard about the unusual weather patterns on Orcas, I suspected they were due to the arrival of the divine consciousness and the impact of the energy that it carried. But I was still a skeptic, still taking notes and observing. My mind had difficulty accepting these occurrences as resulting from the attention and energy of the divine consciousness. It was challenging to my view of how life worked.

We heard that two cabins had been erected down the lane in the woods by the creek, and that would be where Walt and I would be staying. Winged Wolf said she had built the bed frames herself. There was no heat, electricity, or other amenities, but at least there were beds with mattresses for comfortable sleeping, single beds, of course.

The Dreamtime

During this time, I was working on a difficult Initiation Journey that had to do with recognizing life as the dreamtime (vestiges of my talk at the Sedona Empowerment), and myself as the dreamer. Winged Wolf had taught me, *"All life is the dreamtime, a dream being a succession of images passing through the mind."*

Those images are the pictures of the life that I am projecting outward. But most people are unaware they are dreaming. They are asleep to that fact. So even though all sentient life dreams their mind images into existence through the placement of their attention, they are not aware they are doing it. Waking up to the fact that we are dreaming our lives is akin to waking up in a sleep dream and realizing that our bodies are lying in a bed 'sleeping' while our consciousness is awake and dreaming.

She said, "*The difference between the ordinary consciousness and the awakened consciousness is that the awakened consciousness is aware they are dreaming and therefore, consciously chooses the images they wish to present as an environment in which to live. In this way, they are never a victim.*"

Intellectually or conceptually, this was so simple, yet it was difficult for me to grasp the full meaning of it. The idea of it was fascinating, but also conflicted with what I had previously learned about life. It made my head swim if I thought about it. How could my entire life be a dream? And if I wasn't awake when I thought I was awake, what was I? Who was directing my dream if I wasn't, and how could I think I was awake if I was not? At least in a sleep dream, there was a sense of 'now I'm asleep, now I'm awake.' There were clearly defined boundaries. But if it was *all* a dream, then there were no clearly defined boundaries, and what was the purpose of the dream anyway? My head ran in circles on this one, and the answers weren't there, only more and more questions leading me in circles.

Winged Wolf kept telling me, "*It isn't something you can mentalize about. You must keep your attention at the Third Eye to grasp it. We are moving from the conceptual to the ineffable in our work together; from the dual worlds to the non dual, and 'it can't be taught, it must be caught.'*" This nearly drove me to distraction as it brought me up against one of my strongest mind-sets called, '*I don't do well with abstractions. I can't do this.*' She told me, "*It is not abstract; it is ineffable.*"

In a letter to me responding to my Initiation Journey report in which I had described this mental dilemma, along with the feeling that I couldn't grasp it, Winged Wolf wrote, "*If you must have an imprint from the dual worlds, it is more useful to have 'I can' than 'I can't.'*"

For some reason, reading this, it struck me right between the eyes that she was right. If I was determined to hold on to duality, to see life from a little-self viewpoint with its belief in opposites: good versus bad, hot versus cold, 'I can' versus 'I can't,' at least I could recognize I was doing it, and make some shifts that would support my evolution rather than hold me back. I vowed in that moment that every time I heard my inner voice say '*I can't,*' I would intercept it and change it to 'I can.' And each time I did that, I saw her words to me in that letter and felt the energy of them backing me up, and that gave me the strength to follow through.

It wasn't that this was new information. Who as a child hasn't read about *'the little train that could?'* It was the timing of the assertion and the power of the divine consciousness that stood behind the words. They were the matches that ignited the flame of my awareness of my own power to bridge the gap between the worlds by taking a flying leap into the unknown. And the unknown meant shifting the way I perceived the world, being willing to trust that if I followed my Teacher's guidance, I would eventually reach my destiny, even though I couldn't see something clearly in the moment.

This was one of those pivotal Initiation Journeys in my apprenticeship, because, as the lessons became more difficult to grasp on a non-conceptual level, my knee-jerk response was to panic. I pulled up the memory of the imprint *'I can'* and felt the power of having someone who truly believed in me and knew I could take that *'one more step'* she kept encouraging me to take.

Chapter 12
Living in the Moment

By the time Walt and I arrived back on Orcas in April of 1995, the cabins were ready for us to stay in, and Winged Wolf had decided it was time to plan another Empowerment to celebrate the relocation of our spiritual home. She was excited to see us and tell us all about the plan.

The fact that she was even contemplating another event like the last one was surprising. She had already told us how sick she had been for a week following it: all the energy of people's karmic baggage directed at her in the form of strings of energy pulling, pulling, pulling, as people looked to her for healing and guidance and renewed faith in themselves.

But she insisted another Empowerment was vital to keep the momentum going if people were to continue their spiritual growth and personal healing. And once again, she was full of enthusiasm for the task at hand. So we set about to find a location on Orcas Island that fit her requirements. There were several potential locations but after exploring them all, it was Moran State Park that became first choice, and so Winged Wolf set the date and we reserved their group facility for a week.

Winged Wolf asked Walter to assume his same role as at the previous empowerment, so I assumed that I would be chief again, although she made no mention of it. Walt was confident I would be chief, but something told me she deliberately had not brought it up. I watched and waited to see what would happen.

A few days later, Winged Wolf casually mentioned she had decided on the perfect chief for this empowerment and asked me if I could guess who it was. *'Perhaps this is a trick of some sort,'* I thought to myself and decided to remain neutral. *"No image comes to mind, Winged Wolf."*

There was a pause. I waited. I had learned something during my apprenticeship. There was great value in waiting for a moment to ripen and unfold.

This pause, any pause, when I was with the Teacher, became an important part of my learning to be awake and mindful. In the beginning, whenever there was a pause, or silence, I became anxious and tried to fill in the space with conversation. Invariably, she would silence me, *"Shhush, quiet your mind."* I learned to be comfortable with the pause, not giving any interpretation to it whatsoever. Pauses opened the doorway for the next expression of the energy to occur. To interrupt it was to interrupt the natural flow.

"Don't you see Walks Tall in that role?" This was the same apprentice who had the rat fall on his Third Eye. With that familiar gleam in her eye she added, *"Won't he be perfect as chief?"*

Disappointed, but curious too, I asked, *"What makes someone perfect as chief?"* From the way she referred to him, the inflection, I sensed there was something not so flattering about 'being perfect for it.'

And then the light went on! *"It's because he has a big ego, isn't it?"*

"Something like that," she smiled.

So she hadn't asked me to be chief last year because I was so wonderful, but rather because *I thought I was so wonderful!* How embarrassing to my little-self vanity to be so naked in front of the Teacher's eyes!

Tuning in to my thoughts she commented, *"You wouldn't have come last year without that big job for your big ego, would you?"*

"No," I muttered, *"I had already decided not to attend when you flattered me by telling me I would be a perfect chief. It made me feel needed and important."*

Blinded by my ego, I completely missed the 'subtlety' of how she was feeding it and helping me destroy it simultaneously. She had outmaneuvered me. And now someone else needed the experience.

There was relief in knowing; but even in knowing, I was disheartened because I still wanted to be chief. It was the most visible position.

Since she had already said that Walter was to be the MC again, what was my role to be? I wondered why Walter was given the same role twice. Maybe he was so valuable she couldn't see anyone else in that job.

Winged Wolf said, *"Don't worry, there will be plenty for you to do. You will have an important role in the event."* Ah, this time I saw she was feeding my ego, but that was okay. My need to feel important was still strong. But underneath, I felt diminished. Better to work my way up to something than to start at the top and lose it.

That first night of the April visit to 'Between' was cold and rainy. I slept with my clothes on and two sleeping bags over me. It was an act of bravery to move from the bed to the suitcase to change into some clean clothes. When morning arrived I was grateful.

Dawn was barely breaking on the horizon as I headed up the hill, and the relentless rains had paused for the time being. There was a fine mist visible hanging low over the trees, and drops of rainwater clung to the leaves of the bushes. Spider webs were glistening everywhere, with droplets of water making them more visible and acting as prisms, breaking the dawn's light into rays of brilliant colors. It was a magical time; how wondrous nature was exposed here in this pristine environment.

The energy was dancing in front of my eyes as the negative ions from the rain bounced and twirled about, leaving the tiniest of trails behind them. Winged Wolf had shown me how to focus my attention peripherally on them, and by concentrating fully and intently on their pattern of movement, I could impact their patterns of movement with my focused energy, literally turning them from counter clockwise to clockwise. She assured me this concentrated focus of attention would be useful to master for many other purposes later in our work together. I took this time to do some practicing as I strolled down the wooded lane.

Without realizing what had happened, I slipped into another world, a world of magic and fairies and dancing atoms. No longer was I chilled or tired or grumpy because of the restless night. My attention was so focused on what I was doing that I didn't see the others as they headed toward our outdoor platform for morning lessons. I was startled out of my altered reality by the ringing of the bell, which was our signal that it was time to begin. I hurried back to join the others on the platform, where they had spread plastic raingear out to protect us from soaking up the water from the wet boards.

The first meeting at *Between the Wind* had officially begun. There were five of us: the two resident apprentices, Walt, one other apprentice, and the Teacher, plus myself.

We greeted the day with a long and beautiful singing of the HÜM, which ricocheted and echoed throughout the bowl-shaped valley we sat in. After sitting silently for some time, Winged Wolf began the Teaching. I listened in total absorption as she spoke of her vision for Between the Wind as a place for all apprentices to visit, to study first-hand with the Teacher and receive personal one-on-one guidance toward their goal of spiritual awakening, which she called awakening to our true nature as divine self.

She told us that when she first became Thunderbeing she had made a promise in front of her Teacher that she would guide a large number of apprentices to this level of self-awakening, called Enlightenment. She laughed as she did an imitation of her Teacher's reaction.

"Are you crazy?" Alana Spirit Changer had shouted at her when she made this proclamation. *"You've got to be crazy. What do you want to do that for?"*

And she responded, *"Because that number will make a difference in the mass consciousness, like the hundredth monkey principle. And besides, I know it's what I'm meant to do."* She said Alana just shook her head in amazement.

We apprentices always loved it whenever she told Alana stories and we sat in rapt attention hoping she would say more. But that was all she said this time. She told us that later in the week we would do a ceremony to consecrate the property and we should all find some special items to bring to the ceremony, whatever called to us to be brought.

There was an overwhelming amount of work to be done, one of the first projects being to convert the old chicken coop into a meditation room. When she first took us over to the chicken coop, and it really was a chicken coop, wire mesh on the floor, feathers everywhere, I thought sure she was joking. But as I looked at Winged Wolf quizzically, she pointed out to me that this chicken coop was newer and well constructed. It had the basic structure we needed and as Winged Wolf described her vision of it, once renovated, I could see that it would be a perfect area for meditation.

It was only about three feet high on the outer walls and maybe six feet high down the center beam. Her vision was to build a floor, paint the structure inside and out, install thick acrylic windows and use it as our temple. I would never have seen the potential had she not painted that picture for me.

Then there was a barn to be built and fencing installed for the horses. That was a top priority, too. I began to realize that everything with Winged Wolf needed to be done right away, because, when she had a vision, she saw the entire picture.

Also, we needed to prepare for the Empowerment. Even though it wouldn't be held until the summer, still three months away, I had learned that really wasn't much time for planning such a large event. There were so many details to be worked out. Finding cooks and getting a menu prepared and the food ordered took time. The fact that we could order food directly from a supplier was new to me. Hearing about all the work to be done made my head swim. And Winged Wolf also needed time to work with visiting apprentices, finish writing her latest book, be on the phones two nights a week for apprentices calling in, and get the Teachings, which she transmitted to us each morning, written down.

About the third morning we were there, Winged Wolf took me by surprise by saying, *"Wings, I noticed this morning that you were listening in such a way that you were directly absorbing what I said."*

What she said was true; there had been nothing in my mind except Winged Wolf's words. So I nodded my head in agreement.

"Beginning right now, on the days you are present here, I want you to record each talk directly from memory. Don't take any notes; just

absorb everything you hear exactly as it is said. Then immediately afterwards, write it down and give it to me for review.

From this point on, Winged Wolf said it was important that we make a record of all the Teachings, beginning that morning.

"Why are we doing this, Winged Wolf?" I asked, puzzled.

"I'm not sure yet," was the response. *"Maybe we'll bury them around the property one day. I don't know, but for some reason it's important we get them all recorded."*

The experience of this type of listening was similar to direct perception, in which the mind is so totally still that all things are perceived directly, without interpretation, without thought and without words. To listen in this way is to become selfless, that is without personal response, comment, assessment, analysis or any of those functions commonly associated with left-side brain function.

One absorbs what is said in its entirety and then regurgitates it on paper. It is an amazing experience and requires the listener to let go of any attempt to use the brain for dissection.

We hadn't thought of a tape recorder; but if we had, we would have used that and I would have missed the lesson. So this was a prime example of my Teacher's innovativeness in creating experiences for us out of the natural elements of any situation, keeping the momentum going, rather than waiting until we were officially set up with equipment to do something. We never lacked for something to do because we never stopped moving forward and there were always plenty of natural resources available.

This continuous moving forward was the most difficult of all for me to become accustomed to. It was not my typical way of doing things. I was accustomed to 'my time' and 'work time' or some such separation. This relationship with the divine consciousness my Teacher carried was like a massive snowball that was rolling down a never-ending hill, gathering speed and size as it went.

Contrary to my stop-and-go method, Winged Wolf's life expressed a continuity of movement such that she never let a moment pass that wasn't somehow consciously connected to the previous moment and to the moment upcoming. This continuous movement produced whatever she placed her attention on.

After running along with her for several days, I was ready to quit, take a break, disconnect. Winged Wolf took breaks, but to my knowledge, she never disconnected. She couldn't. It was too easy for energy to become chaotic.

She used to tell us, *"Everything I do is part of the spiritualized consciousness, even brushing my teeth or going to the post office. There is nothing I do that I don't love to do, even cleaning the horse paddock."*

I found it incomprehensible that someone could do only that which they enjoyed or loved to do, and enjoy everything they did. Even while on the property, I had categories of likes and dislikes, a list of them that covered every topic. I'd never much cared for gardening and I really didn't want anything to do with that burro Pepe that she found so mischievous and entertaining. He was scary to me, unpredictable, and mouthy. Cleaning the horse paddock was dangerous because it meant Pepe might chase me around or try to knock the wheelbarrow over. On and on it went in my mind, like a radio that's been turned on; and the program keeps on going. At the time, my list of 'likes' was short; it included listening to and recording the talks, and spending time with the Teacher.

There were other things that were enjoyable, like writing stories and articles related to the Teachings. I assumed everyone was like me, including Winged Wolf, and I watched her carefully looking for any sign of falsity in her speaking versus her actions. No one I knew was that happy with everything they were doing. She claimed to feel alive and happy all the time, which also made me suspicious. I thought of myself as a happy person, but certainly not all the time. If life was going well and things were going my way, I was happy, but if I'd had an argument with my kids or my husband, or my job was creating stress, I was definitely not happy. Wasn't that how everyone was?

After the morning talks, we apprentices usually headed up the hill to what we laughingly called the kitchen. It was a tiny room tacked on to the backside of the future offices. We had a propane two-burner portable stove, an ice chest, and some old dishes that had been picked up at a place called The Exchange. The Exchange was a place where everyone took their old junk and left it so that other people could come and purchase it. Island folks loved it. We managed to cook some wonderful breakfasts outside on the deck with that little two-burner stove, our ice chest doubled as a table; and we ate on the cracked and mismatched dishes, then washed them in the bathroom, since the kitchen was only a vision at that time.

During that visit, Winged Wolf started poking at some of my long-standing unconscious behavior patterns, and I realized just what a serious commitment she had to teaching me. One night there was a loud knock on my door. I was deeply asleep, and it must have taken me awhile to figure out what the noise was, because by the time I stumbled out of bed and got to the door, she was banging loudly on it and calling my name.

"Wings, wake up," she commanded.

"I am awake," I mumbled, opening the cabin door.

"No, you're not. You're asleep."

"Do you mean I should be awake even when I'm asleep?" I asked trying to understand what she meant.

"You should have your consciousness intact at all times," she said. *"Now go back to bed, but don't lose your awareness."* And with that she was gone. I could hear her feet trudging up the hill for a long time as I stood there, now fully awake and trembling inside.

It frightened me to have someone demand that I be a certain way, and she hadn't told me how to stay conscious in my sleep. I was having enough trouble being conscious during the day.

Wide awake now, I remembered the day and realized I had been going through the motions most of the time, wanting a break from all this wholeheartedness, wishing I were back home, in my own bed, reading a Hurcule Poiroit mystery. This mindfulness training was hard work, and I thought she was being unrealistic to ask so much of me.

After tossing and turning in bed for what seemed like hours, I must have fallen asleep, because I suddenly heard Walter tapping on the door. *"Wings, are you up yet? It's almost time to meet on the platform."*

Oh no, now I'd overslept. Everything was out of sync for me, and I knew it, but couldn't do anything but watch it happen. I was dressed and out of the cabin in two minutes, which only left me three minutes to get my teeth brushed and hair combed and make a dash for the platform. Once again, I forgot my notebook but remembered that with the memory recording, I wouldn't need it anyway until after the talk. It made me feel more secure, though, to have it with me. Walt gave me a couple sheets of paper and a pen so I could relax a bit.

Winged Wolf was all smiles and no mention was made of her midnight visit, but I noticed once we got rolling I was back to feeling alive and present again, so something must have gotten rearranged inside of me. After that, I was fine; and it was easier to stay in the flow of her energy.

We went to town to do some shopping. My assignment was still to *'be so tuned in to the Teacher that she never has to call me to get ready.'*

I took this assignment seriously, which was part of why I kept longing for a break; it was taxing to try to be tuned in to the Teacher every moment. But today my senses were alert and honed in on her. I could feel when it was time for us to be at the car and dashed up the hill to meet her. She had instructed me not to even use a clock or watch on this trip, just stay tuned in to the Teacher.

We piled into the car, including Siouxy and Yoda, and went to the Island Market to stock up on supplies. Going to town with Winged Wolf was always an adventure. We headed for the market. This was a large, bright, well-stocked store, and the food all looked fresh and appetizing. The vegetables and fruit were often organic, and there was a large vegetarian section.

After the market, we headed across the street to the health food store, followed by the post office, and for a treat, she rented a movie for us to watch with her later that evening. Of course, we had to have popcorn to go with the movie. Winged Wolf announced we were all invited up to her house that evening to watch the movie and eat popcorn. The movie had closed captions so Mark, who was deaf, would be more comfortable watching.

Watching a movie with Winged Wolf was no ordinary experience. It was an event. We usually made Ovaltine, popped popcorn and crammed into her tiny living room to watch the movie on her antiquated, also tiny, television. During the movie she might pause it at any point and turn the story into a Teaching. I never knew what to expect or who might be on the hot seat, so it kept me on the edge at all times.

We were all in a gay mood by the end of our shopping trip, and on the way back to 'Between' decided to drive out to Moran State Park, the site of the Empowerment, so everyone could have a look at it. There was no one to show us around since it was a weekend. In the kitchen they suggested we come back on a weekday when the office was staffed. At first glance, the setting was beautiful, all soft, and brilliant shades of green with the spring grass. There was a small apple orchard in the center of the area the cabins faced and several deer were nibbling the grass near the trees. They seemed unconcerned by our presence even as we walked within a few feet of them. A beautiful, fresh-water, inland lake adjoined the property on one side, with small mountains surrounding it and inviting-looking walking trails at the base of the mountains that appeared to encircle the lake. The cabins were rustic, nothing fancy, but there was indoor plumbing and showers!

Heading back to *Between the Wind* to unload the groceries, there was excitement in the air as we looked forward to a creative meal, and then a movie and popcorn with Winged Wolf. It was a wonderful, relaxing evening and Winged Wolf seemed really happy.

While I slept soundly that night, there was a definite shift in my consciousness. Even though I slept, a part of me was conscious of where I was and focused on the Teacher. That 'wake up' knock on my door had left a deep imprint, one that would not be forgotten.

The next day was dreary and damp; it rained incessantly, so we donned rain parkas and boots and headed out to muck the horse paddock and begin cleaning the grounds. There was the skeleton of a previous owner's vision all around the place. Whoever had created the original design for this place had envisioned great beauty and unusual flora. For some reason, it had fallen into neglect.

There were a variety of fruit trees and other exotic shrubbery planted everywhere in the central area of 'the bowl.' Each tree was enclosed by wire fencing and tagged. Most of the remnants of this once grand vision could be revived and promised to be well worth nurturing: plum trees, cherry, apple, and other exotic trees unfamiliar to me. The outdoor work served as a vehicle to shed the energy of the city life most of us had brought with us.

Not this trip, but later in my apprenticeship, I got to where I could tell when my energy was off-balance. Cleaning the horse paddock worked the fastest to restore my equilibrium. One particularly difficult visit, Winged Wolf took me out to the back of the property where the horse manure was dumped and told me she wanted me to rebuild the mountain of it so that it was more compact. At first I resented the assignment, but after that, I became so absorbed in designing and moving it that by the next day I didn't want to stop. It felt so cleansing and gave me such a sense of aliveness. Any concerns I came there with dissolved into the mountain of manure.

There was a moment during that visit when I saw with complete clarity what it would be like to live in the present moment, right now, with no mind chatter, no hidden agenda, no past, no future, with only this present moment awareness. I prayed it would last forever, because there was no struggle to it; it was completely without suffering of any kind, and my heart was so open there was loving energy pouring from it. The physical work was a great catalyst for that state of mental quiet.

But it was because Winged Wolf's consciousness permeated everything on the property, that I could achieve this state of balance and quiet. I learned this, because each time I went home and attempted to replicate the things I had done to move me through my stuck energy, the results were slightly different. Yes, I definitely felt better, just as I did after a vigorous workout or the distraction of going to a movie with a friend. But that didn't transmute the stuck energy into the joyous, heartfelt balance I experienced at *Between the Wind*.

So this trip ended on a positive note, even though I still held a bit of pique about not being chief of the next Empowerment. This jealousy thing and my competitiveness for rank with my husband, and even some other apprentices, were surfacing as patterns with me. I was too embarrassed to bring it up to Winged Wolf, but I'm quite sure she was aware of it.

Several times I told her I thought she favored the men and went easy on them, whereas she was tougher on the women. She only laughed when I said these things, and sometimes she would say, *"Is that really what you think, Wings of Change?"*

"Yes, it is," I asserted. And she would walk away shaking her head. I thought she had a blind spot and couldn't see what she was doing.

Becoming a Sage Apprentice

It wasn't long before the next lesson came in the mail. I arrived home from work one day in February and found Walter waiting eagerly for me. He had a letter in his hand from Winged Wolf and another envelope that he handed to me which bore her handwriting. He wouldn't tell me what his said, but urged me to see what was in mine.

Curious, I opened my letter. In it was an invitation to become a *'Sage apprentice.'* As I read further, there was a familiar sinking feeling that represented what I described as 'the squeeze.' It meant the rubber band was getting stretched a little tighter. It was a feeling of tension that occurred when the Teacher asked certain things of me that challenged my little-self to let go of some attachment that had been held dear in order to gain another step forward in spirituality.

Essentially, Winged Wolf was asking me to take a vow to become a Sage apprentice, *to serve as a protector or guardian of the Path* and the key words were *'now and forever more.'*

As I read this letter, first fear, then anger welled up within me and I could feel my face reddening. Walter stood at my side, expectantly grinning from ear to ear, and all I wanted to do was growl at him.

Taking a deep breath, I said through gritted teeth, *"I know this will make no sense to you, but this really ticks me off."*

He took a step backwards and the grin faded. He didn't even know what to say.

So I carried on. *"Don't you see, this is just a ploy to squeeze us into taking more and more responsibility?"* The irrationality of my words bounced off him, and again I could see confusion flash.

"But this is an honor," he tried to reason with me.

"Do you think I'm so stupid I can't see that?" I ranted. Uh, oh, my emotions were getting way out of control. In a minute I would be picking

a fight with him just to throw in a distraction.

"I better take a drive and let this settle in me," I told him, grabbing my things and taking the letter with me. My reaction was so bizarre, so opposite from what would be expected upon being offered such an opportunity. To become a Sage apprentice, to guard the Path and the Teacher, why did that make me feel so squeezed, so resentful? It made no sense. The letter said, *"Take a few days and think about this invitation, and if you decide to accept, sign it and send it back to me."* I knew for sure I was not ready to become a Sage apprentice. I was quite happy right where I was.

Once I cooled down and realized I wasn't required to agree to anything I wasn't ready for, I turned the car around and headed home. Walt was tentative in his approach. *"Are you okay?"*

"Yes, I'm better now, but I'm not signing it." I responded tersely, knowing I would. Then as an afterthought, *"How about you?"*

"I already signed mine and sent it back," he replied.

"That figures." Changing the subject slightly, I mused, *"How many letters do you suppose she sent out?"*

"I don't know," he answered. *"I don't know what her criteria was for sending them."*

This made for some interesting speculation. I was sure it would be revealed fairly soon, since, although Winged Wolf urged us not to make strong connections with each other, there was an informal grapevine among apprentices, as in any organization, that spread information like wildfire. It was inevitable. All we had to do was wait, and make a couple phone calls.

The next morning, my mood had softened and I was less resistant; the anger had dissipated, as I realized I was *had*. My commitment bound me to go forward no matter what, while my personality tried to sabotage my progress. It was a continual struggle with me, and so very tiring. But I couldn't seem to give it up. Consequently, I was forever eating crow. My outbursts of temper and rebellion were so much noise.

Rereading the letter from Winged Wolf several times, I was humbled by the intent of the words. It said that a Sage apprentice vowed to honor and protect the Teacher, the Teachings and the Path, and went on to describe some of the specifics of the vow, ending with the words that had gripped and angered me, *'for now and forever more.'* Forever was an indescribably long time. In fact, it was beyond conception. Oh well, Winged Wolf always tells us there is only *now*, so forever is right now anyway.'

The vow had to be signed from a "pure and open heart," and I knew my energy must be clean, the intention sincere. It took me three days to arrive at this point of cleanliness such that I could wholeheartedly take the vow and honor it. By the third day, I was ready. I signed and mailed it. There was a sense of acceptance that I was giving up my past and my present to step into a future that was unknown, and scary, and bigger than I had ever intended to be. My commitment was the single thread that carried me on, but I wished it felt more like solid rope.

Word leaked out; there were six of us who were asked to become Sage apprentices. All had accepted the invitation. None of the others had the reaction I did. I was still the oddball of the group.

Happier times were ahead for me after crossing the threshold to Sage apprentice, but it was several months before I began to grow comfortable in the promise I had made. For the first few months I was so self-conscious that I could barely speak. It was such an enormous commitment. I was willing to grow into it, but I didn't feel I had a good grasp of what 'it' was. The Teacher had given me a signpost to light the way toward my destination, and I had taken her direction. My relationship with Winged Wolf continued to deepen.

As a result of taking the Sage Vow, I noticed there was a slight shift in the way the Teacher related to me; she began sharing more of her vision for the Spiritual Order, explaining some things I hadn't been privy to before. There were some privileges, too, that went with the responsibility of this expanded commitment. Now, I could call her anytime, any day, instead of the two-hour block of time available to younger apprentices on Monday and Wednesday evenings. And, she wanted me to call often, to discuss anything. She was opening herself to me as I was opening myself to her. It was a reflection of my growth, and a reminder that for each step earned through responsibility and commitment to the Path, there was also freedom equally earned.

The Michigan Empowerment

At last, Winged Wolf had agreed to come to Michigan to give a talk followed by a weekend Empowerment on healing. We had committed to have two hundred or more guests present for the evening of the talk. This made for major excitement, and some anxiety too. Tremendous focus was needed to set the wheel turning for this event. Winged Wolf was in companion energy with us every moment, but her physical presence was on Orcas where there was also so much to be done. It was a dance with all of us working together to bring the event to fruition.

Since I was the senior apprentice in Michigan, the responsibility for spearheading the project was mine. It was the type of thing that at that time, I found enlivening, a real joy to be involved in. It was also overwhelming when looked at from a 'what do we need to do' perspective. The list of details was endless.

My way of coping with those feelings of overwhelm was to have meetings. I know it was irritating to some of the local apprentices to meet so frequently, but it helped me to stay calm and focused, and to have a sense of the pulse of things as they were unfolding. The local apprentices were all deeply committed to Winged Wolf and the success of the event, so they participated.

We had committees for every imaginable aspect of the event: there was the evening talk committee, the book table committee, the registration committee for the night of the talk and the one for the weekend itself. Then we had the committee for Winged Wolf's food, the committee for her care and well being, the committee for her tent, the flower committee, the parking lot committee, the greeter committee, and on and on it went.

The evening of Winged Wolf's public talk arrived. I picked her up at the airport and brought her to the hotel where the talk was to be held. There was a moment of great suspense as she entered the room and looked around. Her eyes never missed a thing, so if something was not correct, she would spot it immediately. After scanning the room thoroughly, she turned to the small group of us who were to be her personal attendants and smiled. *"It will be fine,"* she told us. *"Now, I want to have look around and speak to my apprentices."* And with that, she was on the move.

There were apprentices everywhere in stages of set up. The speaker system was one of the crucial items and so Winged Wolf talked with the apprentice who was setting that up. Then she looked over the flower arrangement and talked with the apprentices who were placing them. She pointed out, *"If you put that one here, and that one over there, it will give a better balance."* Then she moved on to the book table and registration desk, chatting a bit with each apprentice, acknowledging them for the work they were doing, gently suggesting a shift here and a little something there, until everything was in order.

Pausing in midstream at the registration table, she said, *"Let's all gather together for a few moment and chant the HÜM, bring the energy into balance."* We pulled our chairs into a semi-circle around the Teacher and began to chant the HÜM. After a short time, I could feel the energy of the room shift, a peacefulness smoothed out the wrinkles of bumpy energy that had been present in the form of people's mind chatter over their different concerns about the evening. After the chant, Winged Wolf spoke to us about containing our energy, keeping our attention focused on the Teacher, and always remembering to look out from our divine selves. After making that connection with the Teacher, everyone happily returned to his or her tasks.

The evening was a huge success. There were nearly three hundred attendees, and the talk was so well received that nearly all the people lined up afterwards to have a closer contact with the Teacher. She stayed until every last one of them had an opportunity to speak with her. By the time we left the hotel and headed for the campgrounds, it was quite late. Personally, I remember that evening well, because it was my responsibility to drive Winged Wolf to the campsite, and I became so disoriented upon departing from the hotel that I could not remember where I was going. She kindly suggested we stop at a restaurant somewhere, anywhere, but preferably Chinese, and eat something. That would help ground me. She told me it was probably a response to so much energy being transmuted that night, and that it would pass. We ate something light and unwound a bit; it worked wonders. To my great relief, I could now remember the way to the campground.

It was pitch black as we drove into the campground. Fortunately, a few others were driving in ahead of us and they had flashlights to guide us to Winged Wolf's tent. After showing her the tent location and saying goodnight, I headed over to my tent nearby and slept soundly until about 5:30 that morning when I heard Winged Wolf's voice in my head.

Leaping up, I grabbed my clothes and rushed over to her tent. The tone of her voice had been sharp.

When I arrived, she was standing outside of her tent. I asked, *"Is everything all right?"*

Looking at me, she responded, *"I'd like to have a meeting with the local apprentices right after breakfast. Please let everyone know that, about 7 o'clock should be fine."*

We sat in a circle around her expectantly waiting for her to begin. She began chanting the HÜM and the energy came into balance. She began talking to us in a kind and gentle voice. *"I didn't sleep last night. My tent was on a slant, and the mat I was lying on kept sliding down the side of the slope. Did everyone else sleep well?"*

There were some nods among the apprentices.

"When your Teacher comes to be with you and to Teach you, it is not a personality coming. It is someone who embodies the divine consciousness, so I don't want you to get the idea that I am talking to you now as a personality, because I am not. But I do occupy a physical body, and my body does not feel well this morning because no one cared enough about me to see to it that I had a comfortable place to sleep last night or a comfortable mat to sleep on."

Silence fell upon the group as the meaning of her words sank in.

She went on, *"It isn't only that I was uncomfortable, although there is that too, but the fact that none of you cared enough about me to see to it that I was properly attended to. While the rest of you slept comfortably in your tents on flat ground, with air mattresses, I slept on the hard, uneven ground. And not one of you noticed or even gave it a thought. Oh, I know you are happy to see me and to have me here, but that is because you expect me to give you something, not because you care about me."*

Everyone's heads were hanging, and mine especially. I was responsible for her care and well-being.

One of the apprentices spoke up. *"I had everything for your tent in my van, but when I got here last night to set up your tent, the chain was over the gate and I couldn't drive in. So I decided to wait until this morning to bring in your mattress and the other items for your tent."*

Winged Wolf ignored her and looked at me, *"Do you see my point? You didn't care enough to find a way to take care of me. And I hold you accountable because you are the senior apprentice here. It is your state of mind that is reflected in the actions of the others. Do you understand me?"*

"Yes, Winged Wolf, I do. But you told me you wanted something simple."

"Simple, yes, but comfortable. I was not comfortable," she said.

She turned to Walter. *"Two Eagles, I doubt you slept on the ground last night."*

He smiled, seeing her point, and responded by saying, *"No, I bought an air mattress to sleep on."*

"You saw what Wings was doing and let her walk right into it. From now on, I want your standard of comfort to be the measure for how my tent is set up. Is that clear?"

"Very clear," he replied.

"Enough said," she went on. *"You can turn this around right now by shifting your attention to the Third Eye and being wholeheartedly in service. There is a great deal to be done to prepare this campground for the Empowerment. It is filthy. We need garbage bags and people to walk the grounds cleaning it up. Don't bother asking the camp officials to do it, we'll do it ourselves."* And from that moment forward, in the presence of the Teacher's consciousness, everything evolved into a pristine readiness for the attendees to register.

A knot had formed in my stomach and I could feel my jaw tense. 'Wait a minute here,' I said silently, 'I've worked for weeks to make sure this event was perfectly coordinated, and the one thing I didn't personally supervise falls apart. Why can't we focus on everything that went right? I don't understand why I'm getting all the blame when it wasn't even my area.'

I could feel anger begin to rise in me, and I suppressed it quickly. Winged Wolf taught us early on that we could not be angry under any circumstances. I didn't want that oozing out into the environment. So I stuffed my embarrassment and resentment behind a cheerful acceptance of what was said, and we carried on. But I was upset. Never again would someone else be in charge of Winged Wolf's living arrangements if I were part of the project.

It was good that we had physical work to do in preparation for the event because I needed to work off some steam. Every time I began to relax, another thought rose up in me. *'Why did she tell me she wanted something simple? Why not just say, "I'd like to sleep in relative comfort?" I would have understood that. And why did she interpret it that we didn't care about her?'*

When I was able to quiet my mind, I saw from the Teacher's perspective that it was true she had not been taken care of and I was responsible. And, since she was not taken care of, then logically it followed that I hadn't cared enough to make sure it happened. I had been so focused on the event. Everything had gone into it; all the meetings and preparation, the wonderful evening prior, but that had all been about my ego making a grand presentation. That would explain why the lack of care for my Teacher had shown up, as a mirror for me to see my own ego reflected in it.

Winged Wolf had more to say to me about what had happened, but she waited until later, when there were no other apprentices around. *"That was the beginning of my teaching you about real love, unconditional love, which is divine love. What you know of love is only from your little-self, which is ego. And the way you can know that is to look at the results of your efforts. You wanted me here to make yourself look good, and after it was over, you didn't give another thought to me."*

What could I say to her? The reflection was undeniable. It wasn't the first time I had misunderstood the Teacher's words. Many years later I came to realize that when I misunderstood something the Teacher said to me, it was usually because my ego was distorting my perception, and always in a way that put my needs and interests first. At that time, while I felt badly for my Teacher's discomfort, mostly I was embarrassed at being exposed publicly.

As a result of this incident, however, our Teacher's temporary residence was transformed, so that by the second night, she slept in a warm, comfortable bed, on flat ground, with almost all the comforts of home; and forever since, this has been so.

Chapter 13
A Big Lesson

The group of us who were Winged Wolf's first apprentices had worked hard to move ahead quickly on our Initiation Journeys, and Winged Wolf had sanctioned this saying, *"I need you to open the door for others."* I didn't fully understand what she meant, but as far as I could see, the time I spent on each Journey was sufficient. Certainly I was having many awakenings and feeling alive and evolving. There was also that ever-present goal in the back of my mind of becoming a Thunderbeing and that kept me pressing forward in my Journey work.

Although competitive, there was a wonderful camaraderie among the group of us so-called "frontrunners," and a grapevine whereby news spread rapidly. I and a few other 'advanced' apprentices decided our next visit to *Between* was to be *"the Thunderbeing trip."* We considered ourselves primed. It was just a matter of which one of us would make it first.

"Great tension, excitement and anticipation was in the air as a result of these expectations," I wrote in my journal, *"and many phone calls back and forth."* Although Winged Wolf strongly discouraged communication among apprentices for many of these reasons, and especially regarding our Journey work, we communicated regularly anyway. We felt each other out as to how the other was perceiving our trek on the Path trying to gain tidbits from each other's perspectives. We all wanted each other to succeed, yet at the same time, we held back just a little, because each of us wanted to have the edge. Our egos displayed themselves in many ways.

Winged Wolf had taught us that it was okay to have "friendly desires," in particular, a friendly desire related to our goal of reaching the enlightened state of consciousness. So we decided that competing to be Thunderbeing was all right, but wanting to be first or being attached to becoming that was not. It smacked of ego and attachment and guaranteed we would fail. *"It is spiritual law,"* she told us. *You can't achieve spiritual awakening and be driven by competition."* In my mind, I played games with what she told me about this. It was kind of a fine-line distinction, but becoming a Thunderbeing was something I wanted, and I had a great deal of attention on it now that it seemed within reach.

One by one, each of us made our anticipated Thunderbeing trip, and one by one we failed to become Thunderbeings. Winged Wolf had described the process of becoming Thunderbeing as like trying to push an elephant through the eye of a needle, and we were the elephants; but how this actually occurred was not clear to me.

I thought I would instantly become a Thunderbeing once I could spontaneously double, as Winged Wolf had with Alana Spirit Changer. And from the way she had described doubling in her books, I took it to mean I would be able to both teleport my physical body from place to place at will, and literally be in two places simultaneously.

Every time I would ask her anything about doubling, she would get a faraway look in her eye and say something vague like, *"When you are ready."* She wasn't giving me any instructions on how to do this; it was all guesswork and fantasy on my part.

So I concentrated intensely on the Third Eye and tried to image myself doing these things. But mostly I got a headache, or gave one to the Teacher. Through feedback from Winged Wolf, I quickly learned that if I became too intense, she got a headache from my energy. This whole notion of being One with everything and everyone had such ramifications to it; it made me anxious for fear of hurting others with my energy, especially the Teacher

Also via the grapevine, I had heard a rumor that a couple of visiting apprentices were asked to leave the property at *Between* because their energy was so intense and they were *oozing* (spilling energy). Not only was the oozing hurting the Teacher, but the apprentices couldn't profit from their visit because they were blocked by their own intensity. After spending a couple days off the property to relax and loosen up a bit, they were allowed to return. I'd never been asked to leave, but it now became a real possibility in my mind since it had happened to others.

A Big Lesson

The full impact of energy oozing would be brought home to me months later, when the chicken coop would be successfully transformed into the Happy House meditation hall and we would all be gathered there for a Teaching. At that time Winged Wolf would say, *"Most of you have an intellectual understanding when I say one of you is oozing, but you aren't aware of it when you are actually doing it. That tells me you don't really understand what I mean by oozing energy.*

"It is not only that people come here and ooze. People walk around in their everyday lives leaking energy into the environment constantly. It is the way they live and sometimes die. Over time, if you are in close proximity to someone who is constantly leaking anger, it will make you ill and you may die from it."

"To illustrate this, I want to do a demonstration. Here we have a clear glass vase and a stick of incense. I'm going to light the incense and then drop it into the vase," which she would do. *"Now watch what happens."* We would watch the vase fill up with the smoke emitted by the incense, and soon the smoke would begin to spill out of the vase into the Happy House where it would spread throughout the room, touching each of us, both physically and through its odor. The air would become sweet smelling and thick, making some of us cough.

"This vase represents your physical vessel," she would tell us on that day, *"and the incense is your energy. Everyone has energy outflow all of the time; it's part of being alive, but if the energy flowing out of you is negative, intense or angry, it contaminates the environment and all that it touches. If you emit enough of this negative energy, it will make other people ill, especially those you are close to, those you are centering your thoughts upon. But it will affect anyone who comes in contact with it, just as the smoke from our incense here is touching all of you."*

What a graphic presentation she would show us on that morning of how we impact each other without ever realizing what is happening. The karmic consequences of causes made like this were sobering. We would gradually come to realize that it was an awesome responsibility just to walk, talk and breathe.

Seeing the Dream

But for this first week during my 'Thunderbeing' visit, there were no other apprentices present yet, and I had the Teacher all to myself. It was a glorious time for me. Each morning we met on the platform outside the cabins since the Happy House was still in the visionary stage. We intoned the HÜM and then had a talk or discussion depending on what was occurring at the moment.

Several mornings in a row there was a mist that enveloped us as we sat on the platform, a light mist, but easily apparent to my eyes. It caught my attention because it was out of context. That is to say, there was no mist visible any place else beyond the platform. At first, I wondered if it might be morning moisture that the sun had not yet burned off, but why wasn't it visible anywhere else? Then I thought it might be from our breath, but the morning temperature was far too warm to produce that thick smoky effect that occurred when speaking or breathing on a cold day.

Finally, about the third morning, I asked Winged Wolf about it. She said, *"The HÜM manifests the mist. The mist is one of the first manifestations of matter."*

She had my attention now. *"What do you mean?"*

"The mist is what you see when you go through the grid to the other side. But I don't want you focusing your attention on that now. Later, when you are ready, we will talk more about it."

As she was talking to me about this mysterious grid and mist, I was gazing intently at her, trying to absorb everything she was saying. As I continued gazing, her body began to shimmer. In my peripheral vision, I noted that everything around us was also shimmering with vertical waves, something like heat waves, giving the scene a transparent appearance. The platform we sat on was no longer located on the ground, but was somewhere in space, nowhere really, and we were nowhere too, just two light bodies somewhere in space, a listener and a speaker. It had such a familiar feel to it, as though we had done this many, many times before in many different places and yet no particular place.

Once she finished speaking, the scene returned to a more solid appearance; the platform sat on the ground, the Teacher and I in solid form, but still shimmering. I told her of my experience. *"You're seeing the dream,"* she told me. *"That shimmering is the filament that holds the dream together."*

A Big Lesson

After that, our talk ended and I hurried to my writing bench by the pond to capture everything I could remember of the experience just past, as it had a profound effect on me. Winged Wolf had been teaching about life as the dreamtime for the past three years, but this was my first time of knowing by experience the truth of that statement. I wanted to record the incident, even though the imprint was firmly implanted.

One morning toward the end of my three-week visit, sensing my anticipation, and no doubt wanting to soften the truth a little bit that I wasn't a Thunderbeing, Winged Wolf said, *"May the blessings be"* three times, then she said *"Namaste"* twice, bowing toward me as I bowed toward her.

It seemed she was inviting me to respond in kind, so I asked: *"Does your invitation to respond mean that I've arrived someplace or earned the right to say it?"*

"I thought if you could hear yourself say the words, they would have more meaning. Sometimes saying the words makes them more real. (Pause) It's all action, reaction. If you have to ask if you've arrived at a certain point, then you have an expectation. Do you see?"

"Yes, I heard it in my words."

"No, you are not a Thunderbeing," she said gently. *"Your trip here has been wonderful. You've done a wonderful job. Standing in your way is your desire. It holds you back. Your desire keeps you from being it. I wish you could be here for six months. Then you'd forget about "becoming something," so that, when you're ready, it could occur naturally. You would be there.*

"One day, someone will become a Thunderbeing, and then another will become a Thunderbeing, and pretty soon there will be a group of you. But you're not there yet. It's a big step. You still want it too much. Everybody in Michigan is expecting you to come home a Thunderbeing.

"It will be good for you to be able to go home and tell them what happened. Tell them you wanted it too much. Expose yourself. Share it with them. They can all learn from your experience."

"I can do that." I responded, subduing my disappointment. Now that it was out in the open, at least I would be free from the anticipation. I

wondered, too, what it felt like from the Teacher's side, to have all these apprentices pushing forward to become something we were not ready to become. It must have been hard on her.

"Let's talk today about fantasy," she said.

"When I don't understand something, I make something up about it." I commented.

"Fantasy is so dangerous," Winged Wolf replied. "You don't understand something, and instead of looking at it in the stillness of a quiet mind, you try to make sense of it by making up a story. It's nonsense. No Sense. It makes no sense. Remember the second rule of spirituality: You don't need to understand everything. This fantasy stuff has got to stop."

"Is there anything you can do to help me?" I inquired.

"Learn to 'look.' Use direct perception. There's no thought involved, just a quiet mind. And I will work with you. In the beginning we talked about the myth in general terms. There's so much to it. Now, you have to be fine-tuned to look at the fantasy that lives with your myth.

"Impatience lends itself to fantasy. For example, you think you have to be the first and the best, the center of attention. That's a fantasy.

"The important thing is that you move forward on the Path. As a Teacher, I can only give what someone can receive. I can't give more than they can accept. That's how I know if someone is ready; they understand and can do what I ask of them. You see I have to be very careful in working with each of you. Right now, many of you are Sages, but even within being Sage there are levels, even though each of you has achieved a certain quality to become Sage. I have to hold the reins very tightly. It would be wrong to make someone a Thunderbeing before they were ready.

"That is why I Teach you to contain your energy in the two-inch capsule around your body. Then you learn to reach out with a smooth, easy motion. There are no side effects; it's all one smooth motion."

At the time Winged Wolf spoke of it, I could see what she meant--how my competitiveness and need to be first were all fantasy, but it was only a glimmer. By the time I returned home, I had forgotten all about that part of our conversation. I had to face my friends with the news that I had not become a Thunderbeing.

Years later, I recognized the wisdom, integrity and kindness with which she withheld what could not be given at that time. A challenging time for a Teacher with a bunch of over-eager, over-inflated apprentices who would have done exactly what she suggested: wasted, misused and scattered power with vessels unprepared to handle it, yet we needed to be encouraged at the same time, so as not to lose momentum toward our goal.

Growing Pains

Winged Wolf had not been at *Between the Wind* for too long, perhaps six months, when it became apparent that Evelyn, her key person in the office, was not going to stay. Evelyn's gypsy nature didn't lend to permanent residence and she didn't have the strong desire to stick with it. She was getting restless.

It revealed itself during Walter's "Thunderbeing trip" later that same summer. We were both scheduled for a three-week visit, but I had to postpone my arrival because of my father's sudden need for dental surgery.

Someone had to be available to take my father to his dental appointments, and it fell to me to do that. Irrationally, I was miffed, feeling I might miss something crucial at *Between the Wind*, even wanting Walter to take care of it since he was the one who had scheduled the appointments. I called Winged Wolf, expecting some support, but her response was, *"It really is Walter's time to be here, and they are your parents. You need to stay home and take care of them until other arrangements can be made for them."* She didn't mince any words, and with the emotion removed from it, I saw she was right.

By the time I was able to make arrangements to reach *Between the Wind*, it was over a week after my visit was scheduled to begin. Walter and Evelyn had developed a kinship of relaxed camaraderie and were having a great time. I immediately chose to feel like an outsider and was really suffering because of it. What made it even worse was that I *knew* I was doing it to myself. I arrived carrying a fear that Walter would become a Thunderbeing ahead of me, and as a result, I was way off-balance, feeling competitive toward him. The inner turmoil made me irritable and out of sorts.

Winged Wolf pulled me aside on my second day there and blasted me. *"Leave him alone, Wings. He was doing really well, happy and relaxed. Now that you're here, he's looking over his shoulder. Stop criticizing him in your mind. Let him be. Don't stare at him."*

"All right," I agreed, embarrassed at being caught, yet relieved, too. *"I'll stop."* I knew I was making him feel guilty because I didn't feel included. And I was picking on him, belittling him in my mind. After that, things smoothed out a bit. I shoveled a ton of horse poop and that helped restore my balance.

Late one night, Walt came to my cabin all excited, and told me that Winged Wolf had come into the kitchen while he was writing an article for the newsletter. She had asked how he was doing. He said, *"I told her I felt completely free and without attachment of any kind. Then she said that she was going to give me a shot at it* (becoming a Thunderbeing)." She told him to prepare by finding certain (secret) items she requested and these items would go with him into the Happy House where he was to spend the night, fully awake, and mindful of whatever happened. More than that, she wouldn't say.

The opportunity was also offered to Evelyn. Walter told me he was amazed when she declined the offer. He said later that at that moment he realized she had gone as far as she would go. To my great disappointment, the offer was not extended to me, so Walt turned out to be the only apprentice to enter the Happy House that next evening.

Winged Wolf had taught us to *"Just keep opening to the moment and see how far you can go in this lifetime."* She had said, *"That is my commitment, to see how far I can go, with my impeccability intact."*

But in spite of her cautionary guidance, I was acutely aware that there were milestones. And Thunderbeing was the first level of enlightenment, a major milestone from my perspective. I was eager to become that and knew that Walter was too, even without having any clear idea of what that meant.

A Big Lesson

What happened with Walter belongs to him and is his story. Suffice it to say, he didn't make it through the eye of the needle that night; and afterwards, he seemed to back off in his wholeheartedness of being there. But it was magnificent to watch Winged Wolf zero in on him and give him her absolute concentrated attention, such that I felt the power of the divine force expressed through her energy as it built up to a crescendo that night. For the most part, I was so impacted by it, that it was impossible to sleep most of the night. The air was electrified. Never had I experienced anything like this power that she exuded. This was another demonstration to me, albeit uncontrived, of the power available to her to be manifested when she called it up.

Shortly after that trip, Winged Wolf announced that Evelyn, would be leaving her position, and another apprentice named Julie, who had been writing daily pleading to become a resident apprentice, would be moving to the property and taking on the position. The new office manager was quite different from the original, although they were good friends. Julie would never be called 'laid-back.'

I was saddened by Evelyn's departure. She was one of the original apprentices and a stalwart sort, likeable.

When Winged Wolf told me that she had decided to let Julie become a resident at *Between the Wind* because of Julie's insistence on having that position, I asked, *"But, do you always give apprentices what they demand? In my (unsolicited) opinion, Winged Wolf, that's like giving in to someone without them having earned whatever it is they are demanding."*

There was a long pause, as she considered how to respond to me in a way that would teach me something and penetrate my righteous attitude.

"There is a saying," she said, *"that I'm sure you are familiar with about 'the squeaky wheel gets the oil.' Well, that's true. When someone is so wholehearted in wanting something, they deserve a chance to go for it. If it turns out the wholeheartedness is ego-driven, that will show itself and then the individual will either leave the Path, or they will transcend the little-self and soar. Either way, that step won't be revealed unless the person is given the opportunity."*

She turned and began walking away, but paused and called me to her. *"When someone is willing to throw caution to the wind and move here to become a resident apprentice, I have great respect for that. It is not an easy thing to do. Those of you who come and go can take all the time in the world to integrate the Teachings. If you are upset with me, you can sit on that for a long time if you choose to. But when someone decides to become a resident apprentice, they are giving up all those 'rights.' They no longer have the luxury of working at their own pace. They give up all their attachments, all at once, or at least know they will be confronted on a moment-by-moment basis. That is because whatever happens here at* Between the Wind *is broadcast out into the apprentice body and affects everyone, even if they are unaware of it. So I have to keep things as smooth as possible here or there would be chaos in our order. Do you have a better understanding of this now?"*

"Yes, I do, Winged Wolf," I said, *"I appreciate your explaining it to me."*

She held me with her gaze and said, *"I will be so happy, Wings of Change, when the day arrives that I don't have to explain myself to you."* And then she walked away.

I watched her back as she walked over to talk with another apprentice who was visiting, and I reflected on what she had told me. I understood it, and it certainly made sense, but the part I didn't understand was why she didn't want to explain things to me. How could I learn if she didn't want to show me how her mind worked? Maybe I was supposed to learn in a different way than what was familiar to me. That idea brought up resistance to changing my accustomed way of learning new things. So I put it aside.

My train of thought had to do with how Evelyn's departure and Julie's arrival would affect me personally. Right now, things at *Between* were relaxed and easy because that was Evelyn's style. The office person was in a powerful position; they were closest to the Teacher because of the constant interaction and the responsibility the position entailed. My relationship with Evelyn was comfortable and I liked things as they had been. Julie was an unknown.

'Oh, yes,' I remembered. That was how I had received my name, because of my resistance to change. 'Let it go', I told myself. 'See this as an opportunity for growth, not an obstacle to comfort.'

A Big Lesson

Winged Wolf had told me repeatedly, *"Don't become attached to people or to situations. They are all impermanent, part of the dreamtime. Love divinely, but don't let your personality get involved. It only leads to distractions. Keep your eye on the bulls-eye of where you are going."*

Divine love was more of a concept to me than a realization at the time. If it didn't relate to me personally, it was difficult to feel more than a passing concern.

So, Evelyn left and Julie arrived within a day of each other. And they were opposite polarities from a personality point of view. Evelyn was laid-back, mellow and well-liked by all. She was a 'down home' kind of woman. Her replacement seemed flamboyant, volatile, talented, intellectually quick, and she was also intensely devoted to the Teacher. There would definitely be changes out of this transition.

Chapter 14
Expectations Uncovered

The new office manager was in her second month at Between the Wind when I first met her in this role. Otherwise, I had known her casually from the Empowerments.

The Teacher always cautioned us about not setting up expectations for our trips to *Between the Wind,* and since I was a seasoned visitor, I was confident that I had learned to arrive with no expectations. Was I ever in for a surprise!

I had a strong relationship with my Teacher; and by now, had overcome most of my anxiety about putting my foot in my mouth by saying the wrong thing.

Whenever I visited *Between the Wind*, Winged Wolf spent a great deal of time with me. She told me I demanded it, but that was okay with me. I learned so much from being in her presence. I had come to expect that special relationship, a little like the only child I had been in my family.

Well, the law of impermanence stepped in. Everything in my world was about to change in an instant. I hurried off the ferry dragging my bags and searching the crowd for Winged Wolf. Always before, she would either park at the end of the ferry exit and wait in the car, or she would walk down to the docks to meet me. It was a special time to reconnect with the Teacher, that moment of arrival.

As I headed up the long narrow walkway toward the road, I had just passed the first section of the little shops that lined the waterfront, when I heard my name, *"Wings, Wings."* I looked all around for Winged Wolf's Chevrolet Blazer, trying to follow the voice that called my name. Not seeing her car, I continued walking, and again I heard, *"Wings."*

Whose voice was that? It didn't sound like my Teacher. I looked around again and saw a large white van with someone's head poking out of the window, and my heart sank. It was not Winged Wolf; it was the new office manager Julie. Where was my Teacher?

My reaction wasn't personal toward Julie. It was just that this was the first sign of a shift in my relationship with Winged Wolf, and I didn't care for it. It took away that feeling of being special. Now, I was just one of Winged Wolf's many apprentices. *'Oh well, anyone can pick up Wings,'* I groused, but then I stuffed it. This wasn't a proper attitude, and besides, this wasn't a pattern. I decided to give Winged Wolf the benefit of the doubt. Perhaps she was detained somewhere and this was only a one-time thing. Adopting this story, immediately I felt better and greeted Julie warmly, casually asking, *"Where's Winged Wolf?"*

"Oh, she's back at Between. *She asked me to pick you up,"* came the equally casual response.

"I see," I said, hiding my disappointed feelings. *"She must be very busy."*

"Oh, the usual," came the reply.

'She's smart,' I thought, *'not giving me anything specific.'* And we chatted casually during the drive back.

Winged Wolf came out to greet me after we arrived and then, *"Why don't you take your bags down to the cabin and get settled in. We'll have plenty of opportunities to talk later. Julie will help you take your things down."*

The first week of this visit it happened once again that I was the only apprentice at *Between the Wind,* other than the residents Julie and Mark. Mark, too, had a special relationship with Winged Wolf, but he never affected me in the way this new person was affecting me. I felt jealous and competitive, odd man out. Even though I knew my perceptions were distorted, I couldn't stop myself.

Winged Wolf had been very busy training Julie as well as keeping up with all her own work. The mature part of me understood that she didn't have as much time available to spend with me as she had in previous visits, but another part of me felt disgruntled. I watched the struggle as these feelings rose and subsided, becoming absorbed in them. When I casually mentioned something to Winged Wolf about my feelings, she said, *"Wings, you sound jealous."*

"No, I'm not jealous, Winged Wolf," I lied, *"maybe feeling a little upstaged is all."*

She let the subject drop. Winged Wolf stayed out of my little petty games and concerns unless the energy was too disturbing or I insisted on bringing it to her for resolution. Sometimes the ridiculousness of these concerns was astounding.

But if I or any one of the apprentices couldn't take care of our differences, there had been occasions when Winged Wolf would gather us all (whoever might be present at the time) in the Happy House, sometimes in the middle of the night, and it would be settled right then. She would say, *"I am only going to miss one night's sleep over this, so let's take care of it now."*

One day, Winged Wolf called to me, *"Why don't you and Julie and I take a walk."*

Instantly, my hackles were up. I didn't want to walk as a threesome; I wanted the Teacher all to myself.

We headed toward the bay at a brisk pace. That old adage about two's company, three's a crowd seemed true this day. Julie engaged the Teacher in animated conversation. She had a strong, vital life force and could easily dominate a situation by her style of relating to the Teacher. I felt a little intimidated by her.

"Tell me more about my past lives," she had asked Winged Wolf, resuming a conversation they had apparently begun earlier.

"The only important part for you to know about is that you were a Judas to me," I recall Winged Wolf telling her. This was a surprise to hear, and I found myself listening attentively to what was said.

"And not just once; it has happened many times between us. I have been your Teacher many times and you have betrayed me. And you will probably do it again in this lifetime, but it doesn't have to be that way if you are willing to work it through. It is my hope that, by telling you this, it will help you avoid repeating the same karmic pattern."

This was intriguing. Winged Wolf had previously refused to discuss anything about past lives with me, so I was curious to hear anything at all about how they merged with the present. Here was a living example of one, and a pretty extreme one, a Judas. And the Teacher was trying to wake her up before the cycle was repeated.

Even though I was jealous, it was fascinating to be privy to this unfolding story. Julie kept pressing Winged Wolf for more details of her past life in the Judas role, but Winged Wolf firmly declined no matter how Julie pressed.

Winged Wolf told her, *"It won't serve you to know any more than what I have already said, so why keep pressuring me?"* Still, Julie kept pressing.

Winged Wolf was masterful at dancing in and out of Julie's questions, never once becoming annoyed or impatient. In fact, much of the time she was laughing so hard that we sometimes had to stop walking because she needed to catch her breath.

Her laughter was infectious, and I found my face streaming with tears from laughter that had no apparent cause. Finally, Winged Wolf said something about the 'bubbles' in Julie's mind being so bizarre that she couldn't help but laugh.

While I joined in the laughter, I also became angry. All these feelings were broiling around in me. My anger was at Winged Wolf because she gave Julie so much attention, not at Julie, who I found sort of charming in an outlandish way. I longed to return to the 'intimate relationship' I had with my Teacher prior to Julie's arrival.

One of the things I realized much later was that I was defining 'intimate relationship' by my own standards, as though the Teacher were my friend and companion. Even though I was completely clear she was my Teacher, still, I thought that she was the same as I, only more knowledgeable.

That she lived in a whole different world than I, viewing what was going on from a place of divine awareness and moving according to what that divine awareness told her, was at that time incomprehensible to me. Had I been able to comprehend that, all that followed would likely have shifted dramatically. As it was, I wanted her to be like me, wanted to believe that I had something to offer her, not just the other way around. This was a huge confrontation to my ego.

So here we were—Julie, an outgoing, aggressive woman who wanted the Teacher's full-time attention, and me, also aggressive and outgoing, and also wanting the Teacher's attention.

When the Teacher was not physically present with us, often Julie and I acted friendly toward each other. In fact, without the dynamic of vying for the Teacher's attention present, I enjoyed her company. She invited me to her room and taught me a bit about playing the flute spontaneously. She had an alto flute and a tenor flute, so we could play together and be in companion energy in that way. Those evenings were stimulating. She was also athletic and taught me how to play baseball—that is, how to catch and throw a baseball. She had a wonderful sense of humor at those times and was good company. The underlying jealousy was dormant when the Teacher was not present. I wanted Julie to like me and tried to behave in a way that was pleasing to her.

Pretty soon though, Winged Wolf nudged me. *"I think you'd better give Julie some space,"* she said gently.

"Why?" I asked, surprised by her intervention. I tried to press her as to what had happened, but she only repeated, *"It would be best if you not spend time in her room. That's the only private place she has."*

After that conversation, I kept a distance. The boundaries were set. There would be no more psuedo-friendly encounters. While at the time I hadn't seen myself as being hypocritical, it was splitting hairs. I had rationalized that since I liked Julie, we could be on friendly terms, and the jealousy could be confined to our relationship with the Teacher.

Having Winged Wolf expose my hypocrisy, albeit subtly, put me in a new place, unfamiliar territory. It made me quite uncomfortable. Winged Wolf was showing me something that I didn't want to see about myself.

I felt I was between a rock and a hard place. I couldn't express my anger toward the Teacher and didn't know how to release it. Looking back, I see that the reason I couldn't release it was because I was so filled with righteousness. That gave me the justification to hold on to the anger. As long as my Teacher wasn't going to do what I wanted her to, I would hold on to the anger. Righteousness made me feel stronger.

For the first time, I considered leaving the Path, but I was too invested in it; I didn't want to leave, and certainly not in anger. I knew my Teacher was a true Teacher, yet, I acted as though she were on my level; and thereby I could be critical and judgmental. It was a confusing time. I felt trapped and alone and had no idea where the light at the end of the tunnel was. It became an obsession with me.

There were some other subtle changes occurring that unsettled me as well. In the Happy House, suddenly there were prayer flags with images of Buddhist figures on them. And often, while we were in the Happy House, Julie would talk to the Teacher about a country called Udyianna, where centuries ago, many enlightened beings had lived; it was near Tibet. She had books with pictures of various monasteries; and my Teacher seemed quite interested in them. This was something I knew nothing about.

On the surface, I adjusted, behaved myself, and acted as though everything was fine. And, because I was in the presence of the Teacher, it really was fine. It wasn't possible for me to feel unhappy when I was with her. My little-self disappeared. Such is the power of the divine consciousness. The Teacher related to me as divinity and I related back from my divine self.

Outside of the Teacher's presence, though, it came right back at me. I stewed, and complained and cast stones. I didn't know how else to cope. I wanted the Teacher, and in order to have her, I had to accept the world as she presented it. But deep down, I couldn't accept the world as she presented it. Yet I couldn't let her see that or I feared she might ask me to leave until I could get my act together. In my blind righteousness, I genuinely thought I saw something she didn't see. I couldn't let go of my position, and I couldn't express it. I had to stuff it. The only thing to do was to keep my attention at the Third Eye as best I could, pray often, and keep going. Eventually, something would tilt the scales.

Chapter 15
Box Mentality

Back in Michigan, after a few weeks, the glow from being in the presence of my Teacher began to fade, and once again, I was caught up in the demands and seductions of worldly living.

Oftentimes when I was in the world, a subtle shift in my attitude toward Winged Wolf altered the way I viewed her. She became 'the enemy.' It took many forms, but generally boiled down to some belittlement of her, resuming a mental argument about something I disagreed with, jousting for position. This time, I had written her with a criticism of what I labeled as 'her inconsistency in policy.'

I was sitting in my favorite rocking chair upstairs in our bedroom reading a book when Walt brought in the mail and called to me. *"You've got a letter from Winged Wolf here. Do you want me to bring it up?"*

As always, when receiving a communication from her, my heartbeat accelerated and I felt both eager and anxious simultaneously. Anything she might say would alter my life in some way. It always did.

This letter was a response from Winged Wolf to that lengthy letter I had sent her. In addition to challenging her on policy issues, it was filled with my struggles to understand life from the perspective of the divine consciousness. There was something I wasn't seeing clearly, and I knew it because I was feeling angry and frustrated. In the letter, I had cited several instances that left me feeling confused and critical of her.

Her response sent me reeling. I read it over again. She began with a reference to my seeing everything dualistically, as either this or that, hot or cold, up or down. She used the example of a coin. *"On the one side there is 'this,' the other 'that' and yet they are both the whole. As*

Box Mentality

divine consciousness, while one is aware of the opposite sides of a coin, the sides exist only in relation to the whole."

She went on to say, *"One's consciousness has to win freedom from paradoxical natures, which are mental interpretations of the whole. Once this freedom is won, one relates to the rules of human life without restriction, and employs the natural ability of being here and there, omnipresent, at the same time.*

"This is why when you insist on putting life in a box and saying it is this or that—that I frustrate you so. You have an idea of how your Teacher should behave and end up stamping your feet when I do not conform. I do not behave in the same way for every apprentice because you each require individual treatment. I dare not be consistent with you lest your box mentality deepen. You fight me because the box makes you feel safe. In reality, it destroys you, makes you side-step where you are headed."

I paused in my reading, my reactive mind was already screaming, *'BOX MENTALITY, what is that? I can't have it, I've never even heard of it.'* My stomach began to churn. I began to pace as I continued reading:

"No one can speak words of living as divine consciousness and understand what they are suggesting without an adept as a Teacher to direct their actions into 'doing/living' their talk. TRUTH MAY BE KNOWN, BUT TRUTH IS SELDOM LIVED.

"People do not want to take responsibility for themselves. They need a God to do things for them and a God to curse when they don't get what they want, and finally, a God to make them feel guilty. This is what perpetuates box consciousness. And, I repeat, you have much of this. I do hear you cursing me from time to time. You say you are committed to becoming an awakened consciousness. When you stop taking swipes at your Teacher, you will truly begin."

'Oh, my gosh,' I shrank with embarrassment, *'how does she know I take swipes at her?'*

"The box controls your thinking about imaging to receive. I do not image to receive. When I image, I have received. The two are one. Until that point of fruition, there is merely a tiny seed in germination, and I

don't sit and stare at it any more than a mother stares at an embryo she carries in her womb."

And it was signed, *"With Great Love."* I could feel the love from her, that unconditional love that flowed despite anything I might say or do. I sat down holding the letter; it must have been a long time that I sat there, because when I came back to the moment, darkness had descended and I heard Walter calling my name. He must have wondered what had happened to me.

The impact of this letter was so devastating to my self-image that I couldn't bear for him to see how raw and exposed I felt. It was part of my crusty front to always appear together and composed no matter how I was hurting inside. Quickly folding the letter and stuffing it in my bedside drawer, I gathered myself up and put a smile on my face. I'd deal with it later.

It is difficult to describe the impact of certain Teachings because they are so personal to the individual. On the surface it may sound as though this was a gentle poke at a mental state I carried and should have been joyously received for the light it shed on some karmic baggage I carried and the freedom it would bring from releasing such a disturbed mental state.

But, without consciously understanding it, because this *'box mentality'* was so ingrained in my being, I had no separate identity from it, no identification of it as a way of perceiving something versus 'the way things are.' That was my identity. It's one thing to change a behavior or an attitude, but how do you change who (you think) you are?

When I read that letter, even though I had no precise idea of what box mentality referred to, it sent shock waves through me because of the energy that was encapsulated in her words. My reading of the words released the ball of energy, like a detonator, which charged directly through my defenses and into the heart of the matter. I felt punched, out of breath, and admittedly, awakened.

Then I shut down. That evening and most of the next day, I was automatic in my movements and interactions, on auto-pilot. The observer in me was amazed that no one seemed to notice that I wasn't really present. Could we really function in life as just a shell of a being and have no one see what was happening, especially those who were closest to us?

Perhaps I was hoping someone would sit me down and say, *"Sharon, tell me what's wrong with you?"* That's about all it would have taken for me gladly to unload my feelings of inadequacy and despair of ever finding this wonderful, natural being that my Teacher assured me lived underneath all my defensive coverings.

By the end of the next day, I found the courage to read the letter again. The part about taking swipes at my Teacher rang true and was starkly revealing of my inner nature, the one that I didn't want to face squarely at all. I was a people-pleaser, so I was generally kind to people in the way I related, unless they crossed me or made me cross. Then there were a variety of behaviors that appeared depending on the situation, none of which were noble, compassionate or loving. I could become viper-like, sarcastic, biting; or, in this case, with someone I felt less-than or wanted something from, I would swipe at them behind their backs.

This was a really uncomfortable, ugly reflection for me to look at, and every time I reread those words I felt the stab in my solar plexus. And it wasn't a stab of genuine regret, but rather the sense of raw exposure one feels upon having a flaw exposed when it was thought to be a well-kept secret. There was an intimacy to it in a way, the feeling of being known so deeply by someone, in ways you may never have wanted to be known, places where you didn't even want to know yourself.

I kept looking at what she said, and recognized this was the absolute truth about my modus operandi, and still, a part of me wondered how she knew. No matter how many times Winged Wolf said to me, *"I hear your thoughts, not because I want to but because it is one of the attributes of being a Spiritual Teacher,"* it didn't make sense to me and so I disregarded it. I knew it was possible to anticipate people's thoughts because I had my own experiences as a therapist, of knowing what someone might be thinking or what they may say next. But that was quite scientific. Once you learn how someone thinks about things, they become predictable as to how they will respond in a given situation. I didn't like the idea that someone read me in the same way. And that she might actually hear what I was thinking was spooky.

The fact that she knew I was secretly 'taking swipes' at her to make myself feel more important, oh, did I squirm. She wasn't playing by my rules.

I used to try to argue with my Teacher, *"Winged Wolf, why do you have to do it all at once? Why can't it be a more gentle, piece-by-piece uprooting?"*

"Because it doesn't work that way," she would respond. *"That is the way of more suffering, long term-suffering. When the handle sticks out far enough, I know that is the time it must be grabbed. It is ready to be grabbed, and the opportunity may not present itself again for a long time. So I reach out and take hold, and then it is exposed, so it can be transmuted."*

Her words rang in my ear as I attempted to face my hidden, devious ways of massaging my ego. Now, I understood what she was telling me, why it must be done quickly and completely. It was really a mercy killing, in a way, because it put to death an old habitual pattern that was killing me slowly.

After several days of obsessive review of her letter, I began relating to the actual communication. I looked at what I had written to her. One of my criticisms was that she made rules and then broke them. Specifically, she had said 'no children, no pets' at the Empowerment, and then made exceptions to allow certain people to bring their children and their pets. I remembered how righteous I felt writing her about this, as though I was proving my point to her.

She was showing me that this was part of my box mentality, and part of my taking swipes at her. The swipe was clear, but how was this a reflection of box mentality, I asked myself over and over. I sensed that the box mentality was the core trait and everything flowed out of that, but how could I identify it in myself?

Calling Winged Wolf the next week, I saw my hands shaking and felt that anxiety that came whenever I stepped into an unknown situation that I sensed might shift my life around permanently. I understood that if I waffled at all in my intent to reach her, I wouldn't get through, so I refused to allow myself the luxury of waffling. She picked up the phone.

"Hello," came the familiar voice. I tried to read her mood but could not.

"Hi, Winged Wolf," I said and plunged in. *"I read your letter."*

"Yes, I thought you would by now," she said neutrally. *"How did it strike you?"*

"It was very disturbing," I said honestly. *"I've been reeling with it for days."*

"It really struck home, I see."

Here came the defenses, and I watched helplessly as I felt my insides recoil from the truthful response of, *'Yes it did.'* Instead, I gave her a half-truth. *"Some of it did, but not all."* Ugh. *'Why can't you just be honest?'* I said inside my head, but the response was simply to add a dead bolt to the lock. It was a knee-jerk desire to protect my ego by refusing to admit she was totally on the bull's-eye, and I couldn't let it go.

Her voice registered a combination of amusement and compassion. *"Which part of it?"* she asked.

"Well, I felt terrible when I read your letter, but I don't really even understand what box mentality is, especially what it is in me. I mean I can see where society holds certain beliefs that keep the status quo and prevent people from rocking the boat by seeing through the illusion, but I don't see how that applies to me."

There was a long pause, and I wondered if she was going to respond at all.

Finally, *"It's so much a part of you, you can't even see it, and you want me to tell you all about it so you will feel better. But you have to discover it for yourself. I can tell you that when you question what I do, like you did at the empowerment, when you argue with me and criticize me in your mind, you do so because of your box mentality."*

"What do you mean 'like I did at the empowerment?' I don't remember arguing with you."

"You criticize me when I break my own rules," she said. *"When I gave you a rule about dogs and children not being allowed at the empowerment, and then I broke the rule by making some exceptions,*

do you not remember being critical of me? You even wrote me a letter about it."

"Oh, that," I responded, bristling. I thought I had worked through this one, but righteous feelings rose up in me again when she mentioned the incident. I should have stopped there but I didn't. *"Well, I don't understand why you make a rule, and then let certain people break it; you let some people bring children and dogs and others were told they could not. It seems to me a rule is a rule and being impeccable means to follow that."*

Another long pause. My heart was racing in anticipation of what she might say. I had stated my case, and from my viewpoint, proved to her she was not being impeccable breaking her own rules. I had forgotten completely that we were talking about my box mentality.

"That's exactly what I'm trying to show you, Sharon." When she referred to me as 'Sharon' rather than 'Wings of Change,' I understood she meant that I was operating from personality rather than from my divine self. It was a warning flag; I heard it, but at that moment I really didn't care.

"Your box mentality defines reality for you; it makes you feel comfortable because you know exactly what is expected. You feel righteous in upholding the rule, and you judge others when they break it, just as you judged me when I made an exception.

"One day, you will come to see that rules are only guidelines set to point the way; there will always be exceptions. We live in the dual worlds; we're not talking about spiritual law or universal truth here. When you begin to grasp what I'm telling you, your box mentality will be less important and you will be able to look at what a situation calls forth, rather than what the rule is for it."

Since I couldn't think of anything else to say, I waited for permission to disconnect. Usually, she diffused the potency of her words somewhat with humor or sometimes a redirection of the attention. She might talk about what was occurring in the environment or the weather, or an upcoming event.

But this time she left me with, *"This is an important part of your training, and one you must get a hold on if you are to progress on the Path. It is your assignment for now. Look for it, pay attention to how it exists in* society, individuals and, especially, in you. It may be easier to begin by seeing it in others, but always remember, you are doing this for yourself and not to put the focus of attention on others. Structured beliefs are for those who need them. You <u>don't</u> need them, Sharon. Already, you have experienced a degree of cosmic consciousness. How would structure fit into that? It doesn't! Cosmic consciousness is an experience whereby the heart chakra opens and you feel unconditional love, which is unity, for all life.

"As this experience deepens, new doors will open. The divinity in you will look in a mirror and say 'I am.' It will come into even greater power when It recognizes that It is a part of God/Great Spirit/Divine Energy/etc. You will experience God....for yourself. And, of course, one could not structure that."

There was a sense of relief in having an assignment. I thanked her and we hung up.

Then I took it into the silence and looked at it. *'Please help me see what 'box mentality' is and how it operates in me,'* I prayed. I caught a glimmer, then another glimmer; they were elusive. I could almost see it, then a curtain fell over my awareness and I would lose it. But I had seen enough to have a sense of it and to realize she was onto something important and real.

For many weeks after that, I did nothing further with this assignment. Christmas loomed ahead of us and we made the usual preparations to head for Florida. Ever since my folks migrated there after my father's retirement, the boys and I had headed there for all holidays, and Walter had entered into the tradition. My mother lived for her grandchildren and had found the perfect carrot to bring us all running at every opportunity. There was warm weather, sunshine, usually cute girls on the beach, and my mother insisted on doing all the cooking. What more could we want?

Once there, I was swept up in the holiday energy and busyness so the 'box mentality' assignment went on the back burner. Frankly, it was a relief to jump into the ordinary consciousness for a time and relax into the familiar comfort of home and family.

But it was only temporary relief. Always the imprint of my Teacher was with me; the question, *'What would Winged Wolf do in this situation,'* arose frequently. One time during this visit, I remember being so exasperated with something one of my sons did, I used one of Winged Wolf's recommended antidotes for anger. Rather than opening my mouth and spouting a stream of words I would later regret, I excused myself and dashed down to the beach. Finding a secluded spot, I scooped up some cool wet sand and buried my face in it. Within seconds relief flooded my body, the tension drained and I began to giggle. It was the most absurd thing I could ever have thought of to do, and yet it worked. *'Thank you, Winged Wolf,'* I said silently, with gratitude in my heart, *'you saved me from setting a nasty little karmic cycle in motion.'*

After the holidays, we returned home and I began working on my Initiation Journey again. It was time to start smashing those boxes and wending my way toward freedom, as Winged Wolf put it. But how was I to discover what was so hidden in me? As it turned out, life would provide plenty of experiences to assist me.

The first week home it began to come together for me. It was as if I had been crawling through a long, dark tunnel and there was no light anywhere to guide me, so I just kept moving forward, no idea where it would lead. The Teacher had told me there would be dark times when I couldn't see the light. *"And in those times,"* she said, *"all there is to do is keep taking one more step."* How often during my apprenticeship did I hang my life's decisions on those words!

Suddenly now, I saw the light, saw the end of the tunnel, and I understood what the Teacher meant when she accused me of *box mentality*. I had thought it was about impeccability, but it was really a rigidified, black-and-white way of defining life. There was no fluidity to it at all. It was all about rules: the correct or incorrect way of doing something as proscribed by the invisible rulebook. It took the anxiety out of unfamiliar situations. As I meditated, it was as if a light was shining brightly as one realization after another passed through my mind: how I had lived my life; how I had made decisions related to people and situations; how my ideas of things were formed. I made notes of my discoveries, and one day, I felt ready to write up my Journey and put it in the mail.

Two weeks later came the reply. I tore open the envelope, which was a large one, and saw that the salutation said *"Wings of Change"* and instantly, I knew I was back on top of the mountain. All it said was, *"Wings of Change has flown into a bright clear sky…..Go for it! It's all here, and yours. This moment. This present moment."* And in it was my next Initiation Journey. Oh, how good it felt to be able to see clearly once again. No matter that it wouldn't last; another karmic suitcase had begun to be dismantled. I was free and happy until the next unraveling began.

Chapter 16
The Teacher Begins to Reel Me In

There was a gentle breeze blowing, and the temperature was in the 90's as we arrived by boat at a Florida island home we had rented for a few weeks in February with our good friends Bill and Myrna. I was due to fly to Orcas for a three-week visit with the Teacher subsequent to this trip, so this was to be a time of relaxation and low-key fun in the sun.

The weather was unseasonably warm for February, ideal for relaxing and walking on the long, mostly uninhabited, beach. We spent hours searching for sharks' teeth that washed up aplenty on this particular stretch of sand. Several of the adult children were due for the weekend.

Friends, family, Florida at its finest, and a beautiful beach home. I was as happy and content as I'd been in a long time. This was heaven on earth. The guys were having a grand adventure because we were on an island accessible only by boat, so even a trip to the store meant a half-hour boat ride. There were no cars on the island and no facilities but for a tiny waterfront restaurant at the northern tip. Otherwise, it was just miles of white sandy beach, fronting on the Gulf of Mexico.

Several idyllic days had passed when Walter returned to the house one afternoon after a trip to the mainland. Happily he announced, *"I just spoke with Winged Wolf and she invited us to come to Orcas for an extended period."*

Immediately, I tensed. *"What do you mean an extended period?"*

"Well, she suggested three to six months," he responded.

The Teacher Begins to Reel Me In

My whole being went into fight or flight mode. It was all I could do not to voice my disturbance. But our friends were present, and I had enough presence of mind not to make a scene in front of them.

As casually as I could, I said, *"Well, let's talk about it later."*

But our friend Bill was intrigued. *"That sounds like quite an adventure."* He was animated and curious and knew me well enough to know I was peeved. He was going to have a little fun with me. *"What did you tell her?"* he asked.

Walter took a deep breath, glancing quickly at me. *"I told her I would be willing, but I'd have to talk to Sharon,"* he replied quietly.

"Wow," Bill said, really getting into it. *"How is that going to affect your life? What do you suppose will happen out of your being there that long? Do you think you might move there permanently?"*

That was all I could tolerate. *"Not if I have anything to say about it,"* I snapped.

The reason for my apparently out-of-context response to this conversation was clear to Walter, but not to our friends, and perhaps not even to my Teacher, although in my own way, I had expressed myself to her.

I was happy with my life the way it was. I enjoyed frequent visits with my Teacher and yet was able to maintain my home life pretty much the way it had always been; plenty of time for friends, family, vacations and such. It was my idea of a perfect balance. Walter and I had previously discussed the idea of longer stays at 'Between' and I voiced strong objections. The underlying feeling was fear that if I began extending my time with the Teacher, major change would occur in my life and I would feel out of control.

Bill looked at me, startled by the intensity of my response. *"Oh, I guess you two have a difference of opinion on this one."*

Our dear friend, a psychologist by profession, was tuned in to the conflicted energy in the space and was open to proceed in helping us talk this through, if we so indicated, and he was also perfectly willing to back off and leave us to work it through ourselves. He simply paused and waited to see what would come next.

The temporary answer presented itself in the form of his wife Myrna entering the room, having awakened from an afternoon nap. Oblivious to the tension in the room, or maybe not, she said, *"Hey, it's beautiful outside, let's go find some sharks' teeth."*

It was a relief to turn my attention toward something light. We grabbed our beach shoes and took off for the shores.

The subject of Orcas was shelved until the next day when Walt and I took a drive up to Sarasota to visit my parents. It was an hour on the road, and almost immediately upon Bill and Myrna dropping us at the dock, I began to chastise Walt.

"How could you make such a decision without asking me?" I demanded. *"You know I don't want to be away from the family for that length of time. I'm not going to do it, so if you're going, just plan on going without me!"*

There was a long silence as we drove to Sarasota. Walter said little, although he tried to reason a bit with me. *"I feel I need to spend time with the Teacher. I'm having a difficult time right now in my apprenticeship, I feel stuck. The only thing I can see to do about it is to be there with her for an extended period to see if things become clearer. Why do you feel so strongly about not going?"*

My answer was absurd and I knew it, but my emotions were riled up so there was not a chance I would respond coherently. The truth was that I was paralyzed with the fear that if we spent an extended time with Winged Wolf, my entire life as I knew it would change drastically. I couldn't say how, but I felt the threat and knew the possibility was that I would move there permanently; and the thought of leaving my (grown) children, my home and my friends, life as I had arranged it, was overwhelming. How could I possibly admit this to him? Yet I couldn't let go either, because the grip of my emotions was so strong.

Once again, we were distracted from further conversation by the visit with my parents. Mother was deeply concerned about my father's growing disorientation and constant clinging to her. She was beside herself with the stress of his constantly following her around, never giving her any time to relax and do the things she liked to do. Any break we could give her was only a drop in the bucket, but we did what we could.

The Teacher Begins to Reel Me In

This day, Walt took my father out to the barber, the bank, the store, and kept him occupied so mom could have a little time to relax. I tried to reason with her about options that would give her a little freedom, but each time I made a suggestion, she dug in her heels and told me why it wouldn't work.

"I can't hire someone to come in," she said, *"your father's feelings will be hurt."*

"How about a retirement home for both of you where there are structured activities?" This seemed the most practical solution to me.

"Over my dead body," she said with conviction. *"Your father would be miserable in a place like that. He loves looking out at the water."*

In a brief flash, I realized she was as stuck with her situation as I was with mine. What looked like some fairly simple solutions for her from my perspective, were so far out of her comfort zone, it didn't matter how reasonably I approached it. She feared change as much as I did and resented the fact that life was forcing it upon her. I was stuck because of my refusal to take the next step toward a goal I had set for myself. I wanted something and I feared the cost of it at the same time. Both my mother and I responded to our stuck energy by stalling, wanting to remain in a comfort zone as long as possible.

We made these mental traps for ourselves, these boxes we lived within, and then believed them to be real; and I could even see it and still be just as stuck as my mother was.

I cried as we left them standing there, both looking so little, lost and vulnerable, but I could think of nothing to offer short of having them come to live with me, and I wasn't sure that I could retain my sanity if they did. I was absolutely sure that Walter could not, nor would it be fair to ask it of him. But it broke my heart every time we visited to see how unhappy my mother had recently become with her life.

She couldn't accept that this was happening to her, and insisted dad could get his senses back if he would just try harder. The only way out that was acceptable to her was to die and leave him in our care, but every time she brought it up, I vehemently declined, not because I wouldn't take care of my father, but because I didn't want to let go of my mother. I was emotionally dependent on her. She was my security blanket in life, a part of my identity.

Then it came to me: If we were to buy a home in Florida near them, I could participate in the care-giving, and she could have a break. I mentioned it to Walter and he loved the idea of living in Florida, at least during the winter months. There was no further talk of moving to Orcas during that vacation. We both knew it wouldn't be resolved by our discussing it between us, and down deep, I hoped that the idea of moving to Florida would distract him from the desire to move to Orcas.

Days flew by, and suddenly we were driving to Tampa where I would catch a plane heading for Orcas Island and whatever awaited me with my Teacher. Originally, the trip was scheduled as one of my regular three-week visits to have some direct Teachings and experiences with Winged Wolf that would result in my seeing things more clearly and evolving on the Path. This trip, though, would be different, because we were getting down to my core issues, some of my deepest attachments.

Up until now, I was able to live in two worlds, keeping my ordinary life with family, friends and children intact, essentially unchanged. My spiritual life unfolded in another plane, times spent with local apprentices, studies of the Teachings and visits to *Between the Wind* to see Winged Wolf. Intuitively, I understood this was all about to change. She was going to challenge me on my 'position' regarding spending more time with her.

While on our pristine little Florida island, we had looked at several properties and discovered one that suited us just fine, but it seemed a pipe dream to me, way out of our financial reach. Before I departed, we tentatively agreed on a lowball price to offer on the house if Walt still felt inclined that way after thinking on it for a few days. The likelihood of the offer being accepted was so slim that I put it out of my mind as soon as I boarded the plane. It had been an enjoyable fantasy while staying on fantasy island; still, secretly, part of me hoped that Walter would take the idea seriously.

More Boxes Smashed

I was sitting in Winged Wolf's office, looking above her head at the Charles Frizzel painting that had been on the post card that originally

The Teacher Begins to Reel Me In

inspired me to send for her book *Woman Between the Wind*. There was a feeling of such serenity about the woman in the painting that it gave me a sense of great peacefulness whenever I looked at her. Right now, I desperately wanted to feel peaceful. Winged Wolf had called me up to the office for a chat, and after some pleasantries, she had confronted me.

"Wings of Change, Walter wants to come out here for an extended stay, but he tells me you are refusing to come. Why is that?"

Immediately, I began to cry. *"I don't want to leave my kids for that long,"* I wailed. *"They'll be very upset with me. They all think I'm in a cult as it is, and if I tell them I'm coming here for several months, it will be totally distressing to everyone. And besides that, I've got my mom and dad to worry about. Mom needs my help with him."*

There was a long silence as I stared at the painting, praying for help in resolving this conflict. It was so uncomfortable to be saying 'no' to my Teacher, especially when I understood this was the opportunity of a lifetime. An invitation to come and study with the Teacher for this extended period meant I could advance more rapidly on my Initiation Journeys, perhaps release some of these conflicts I carried around with me. They kept me habitually going in circles. And ironically, this was what I had said I wanted to have in my life, an opportunity to pursue enlightenment full out, all the while protesting when the opening was presented.

Winged Wolf began speaking, *"You know, I've told you that many years ago when I was invited to Japan to act as a translator for some Buddhist Teachings, my father had a heart attack the day before I was to leave.*

"I'm quite sure everyone expected I would cancel my trip and go to be with him, to assist my mother while he recovered. It was a crossroads for me. Should I be the good daughter and help my family, or should I pursue the Path that I had chosen for myself?

"As you know, I chose to go to Japan. I realize you were shocked when I first told you about this. But, when does the time come that you choose what is right for you? I promise you it will not be given to you. You will have to fight for it, because whenever you take a stand for something you know is right for you, all the forces of the universe rise up to test the

strength of your commitment. This is your time, Wings of Change, what do you choose?"

Resistance dissolved within me as I listened to her words. I remembered why I was here and what my spiritual quest was about. Something deep down inside of me longed for release from the prison I had constructed for myself, a large box to give the illusion of security.

When I could see from my divine self, I knew exactly what I wanted and why I wanted it. It was my path to freedom, the Path to unlock all the secrets of the universe that were available to me and every individual if we were only willing to cut through all the garbage and see the truth.

In those precious moments of awakened consciousness, I knew there could be nothing else for me, I could not settle for less than freedom to live my divinity, to know joy from just breathing in and breathing out, and wonder at all the divine manifestations of life. Having tasted a few morsels of this divine expression, I wanted the whole thing. I would go as far as I could go, stretch as wide as I could stretch, to claim whatever I could in this lifetime.

There was a gradual relaxing inside of me, a physical sensation of my chest opening up, and a release of tension from my body. My jaws unclenched and my stomach unknotted, and I found the courage to speak my truth. *"All right, Winged Wolf, I'll do it."*

"Good," she said. *"Now we need to find you a place to stay. I suggest you start with the local paper* The Island Sounder*. I can pick up a copy when I go into Eastsound today."*

As I walked down the stairs from Winged Wolf's office, I asked myself, *'How did this happen? How did I shift from a position of 'absolutely not' to an easy 'yes, of course?'* My entire life plan was rearranged in a few moments. So, I had fought a battle against what I really wanted in order to hold on to what I did not want.

It didn't make any sense. It was as if the house I built my identity on had a foundation of fluff, appearing solid and stable in form, yet blown away by the slightest touch. Was it really all an illusion? Was this what she had been trying to teach me by smashing my boxes as they became evident? Nothing I had believed in or held on to as important had any

The Teacher Begins to Reel Me In

substance to it if it could all be changed 360 degrees just by a shift in my perception. Was this what she meant by box mentality?

Later that day, Winged Wolf invited me over to her cabin for dinner. She was cooking. I was honored and excited. Private time with the Teacher was to be treasured.

She had cooked a delicious meal of Swiss chard, polenta, sliced and lightly pan-fried in butter, accompanied by spinach salad. Conversation was light; we laughed uproariously as Winged Wolf told me stories of her apprenticeship with Alana and imitated her Teacher for me. She was a wonderful mimic, and could capture and replicate the essence of a person by their walk, facial expressions, energy and voice. When she 'did' Alana, it always made me howl with laughter.

Tears ran down Winged Wolf's face as she recalled an incident where she had taken Alana Spirit Changer to a large mall in Colorado, and Alana insisted on going into every shoe store, where she proceeded to try on every pair of shoes in the store, leaving the open-mouthed salespeople with boxes of shoes strewn everywhere, as they became more and more desperate to find a pair that pleased this unusual woman. Then, without a word, she would get up and leave with Winged Wolf trailing along behind her.

After we had eaten, I brought up the subject of my rapid turnaround earlier. *"Let it go,"* she told me when I asked her what had happened. *"You have such an analytical mind, always wanting to separate things into their parts and dissect them. You won't get to enlightenment using an analytical mind. Do you remember what Alana Spirit Changer said?"*

"Yes, I do, Winged Wolf. She said, 'You don't need to understand everything.'"

"Do you know why she said it?"

"I'm guessing it was her way of saying to put the analytical mind aside and just be with what is, or maybe allow what is to be acceptable to you. Maybe, too, she meant that it takes away all the magic of life if we are forever analyzing how this works and how that works."

"That is correct," she answered, "and she also said 'the way to learn about something is to become one with it.' What does that tell you?"

"It tells me that if I wish to become an awakened consciousness myself, then I need to put aside desire and study you, imitate you, become totally one with you to the level that I am able of doing so. And by doing so wholeheartedly, my capacity to do that will grow and expand; but if all I can think about is myself, and how I want something to be or how I think something should be done, if it all has to be done my way, then I'll be spinning my wheels forever."

"Exactly," she said, pleased with my response. "So if I ask you to do something, there's no point in kicking and screaming about it, is there? Just know that I wouldn't ask it unless it was something you needed to learn for your continued growth on the Path. I don't get anything out of this; I've already got it. I do this for you. I'm just a servant of the Path, committed to do whatever it takes to bring others forward towards their own enlightenment."

I nodded thoughtfully, accepting what she said, *"I really would like to be more grateful and more gracious about receiving the gifts you give me. I'm so blessed to have you for my Teacher, and yet I still fight and resist you whenever the going gets a little tough. I don't understand it."* Then we both laughed and said simultaneously, *"You don't need to understand everything."*

"Well, what I do see without any analysis at all is that whatever I'm deeply afraid of losing, I cling to with all my might. It's what you said before about 'what you resist, persists.' And usually, what I am deeply afraid of losing is what I need and want to let go of when I admit the truth."

Right about then, the phone rang and Winged Wolf asked me to answer it. To my great surprise, Walter was on the other end. He was excited, and I didn't know whether he was actually calling to speak to Winged Wolf or to me, but he said, *"We got it."*

My heart sank. The Florida house came into my mind's eye, and I knew the forces of the universe were now rising up to test me in my commitment. Keeping my voice neutral, I downplayed it as much as possible, thinking, *'Surely he realizes this will be upsetting to the Teacher who is doing her best to guide us in this direction (meaning Orcas Island).'*

The Teacher Begins to Reel Me In

But he was oblivious, chatting on excitedly with the details of the purchase. I interrupted, *"Would you like to speak with Winged Wolf?"*

"Sure," he responded. And I could tell he was relaying the information to her because she responded, *"What did you do that for?"* After a few moments of listening, she said, *"Wings has agreed to spend at least three months here,"* and then after a pause, *"we'll work out the details when you arrive."*

After she hung up the phone, she looked at me, *"Did you know he was going to do that?"*

"Sort of, but not really," I replied uncomfortably. *"We saw this fabulous place there and decided to put in a really low offer. We also agreed not to budge from that offer unless we both agreed. I figured that would be a safe way to leave it, since I knew they wouldn't accept the offer. But Walt got caught up in the wanting of it and agreed to a higher price without consulting me."*

"He's going to have so many anchors set up to hold him in place, he will never be free enough to pursue enlightenment." I could hear the sadness in her voice and felt ashamed of myself for the mental game I had played. Deep down, I knew it would be difficult for him to let the house go if there was any way at all to have it. I should have discouraged any involvement at all and I knew it; but I got caught up in the fantasy of it and didn't take a firm stand. I hadn't expressed this piece to my Teacher, so my complicity in the purchase was obscured. By withholding this from Winged Wolf, I skewed the picture and it looked like Walter had done it on his own. I had understated my part in the scenario, because I was the real catalyst for the purchase.

"We can use it as a rental, or resell it, Winged Wolf," I told her. Now that I was there on Orcas, without the fear, my interest in Florida had waned and I was eager to focus on finding a place to stay. And I was convinced Walter would have the same response once he arrived.

Now that the decision was made to stay on Orcas, everything lined up for us. Walter arrived at *Between* a few days later. After calling on a few places we found advertised in the paper, one of the local apprentices told me, *"There is a place right down the road that is for sale. I was talking to the owner this past weekend and asked if they would consider renting it to some wonderful tenants while they were trying to sell it. I* couldn't help but smile as I imagined her, with her Southern charm, talking to this total stranger about the 'wonderful tenants' she knew.

"Brenda, the owner, told me she might consider it, and to have you come over next weekend when she will be back in town. Of course you would have to move if the house sold, but it's completely furnished, so you wouldn't need to bring anything but your clothes. And it seems likely you would have a minimum of three months there."

Immediately I fell in love with the place. It was warm and cheerful, with plenty of space on several acres; but best of all, it was only a ten-minute walk from *Between the Wind*. We took it on the spot and decided to move in at the beginning of April. Winged Wolf had taught us that it was never acceptable to manipulate for self gain, so I couldn't pray** that the house would not be sold, but I did make a silent request that we could have a few months in it, if that was for the good of the whole.

All that was needed now was to fly home, announce to everyone that we were leaving, pack up the car, pick up the dogs and drive back to Washington. Fortunately, we still had two grown children living at home so the house would be looked after. The Florida closing we could do by mail, and we decided to basically use it as an income-producing home that we might visit from time to time.

One day just prior to the return home to rearrange my life forever, I was talking to Winged Wolf about all of this. She cut me off, saying, *"Remember, whatever you place your attention on is what multiplies.*

"I suggest you keep your attention away from all this mulling things over, all this analysis that you love to get into, and turn your attention toward your goal of enlightenment. Don't let anything distract you from your goal. It will be easier for your family if you simply explain that you

---

*(**Footnote on prayer—My Teacher taught us that prayer, generally, "is an invocation to the divine energy to draw upon the higher energies within ourselves. It evokes higher energies, and it does this by linking us with higher energy." Further she taught that, "If we are not truly fused in our attention, we can draw the opposite to us." And the conditions that are acceptable for prayer are quite specific. She cited them as, "When we are looking for clarity and have been unable to find it; when we are feeling unbearable pressure from negative forces and we have no clarity for our difficulties; and when we have concern for others." Finally, the prayer must be totally open-ended. We can set no conditions on what we are praying for. In that way we are open to whatever the divine consciousness shows us.)*

The Teacher Begins to Reel Me In

are leaving to spend some time with your Spiritual Teacher because this is what you need to do for yourself, and let them know that doing this will make you a happier, healthier person for them to be around. Also, let them know it in no way affects your love for them or your relationship with them, other than you won't physically be present for a while.

She went on, *"Then do what you need to do quickly, smoothly and with complete confidence. This way you won't be sending out mixed messages to people. Don't say, 'Oh, I have to do this because my Teacher says it will be good for me.' That will only set up a conflict in their minds."* She held my gaze and said, *"I suggest you tell them you are choosing to do this because it is important to you, not because it is important to me. Otherwise, you will never gain their respect."*

In this she really showed how well she knew me, because I had already planned to tell them it was something the Teacher said I needed to do in order to grow. The verbiage was subtle but the implication was there—it wasn't really my choice, but something imposed upon me. Boy, was I slick! But my Teacher had my number because she *knew* me. I could feel my courage begin to crumble as I pictured myself telling my family that I was choosing to go to spend several months with my Teacher. In the picture, I was totally alone and felt weak and unprotected.

"Why don't we role-play a bit," she suggested, sensing my alarm. *"You be the family members and I'll be you."* That was an unusual twist.

"Okay, I'll start with Kevin, He'll be the most distressed." I paused to create the image of my son in my mind's eye and feel the surge of righteous indignation I knew he would express when he heard the news. And I also understood he thought he was protecting me from making an unwise decision.

I drew a deep breath and started, *"Mom, are you crazy? Don't you know this woman is just out to take your money? Why do you need someone to do your thinking for you anyway? Can't you think for yourself? You're acting just like a sheep."* As I spoke his words, the energy of this certainty he carried rose up in me, and I could feel how closed he was to anything other than the way he saw it and me.

"Well, Kevin," Winged Wolf responded as me, *"I can see you have made up your mind about me so it won't make much difference what I say to*

you. So, I'll just say this. My life is taking a turn that I didn't anticipate when I began this course of study, and I'm really happy about the direction I'm taking. I'm sure, underneath it all, you have my best interest at heart; so if you can give me some leeway and watch to see what happens, perhaps it will be different from what you expect."

This response took the wind out of my sails, and I had to work at recreating what Kevin might respond to it. If my mother had said this to me, I would have been cheering her on, but Kevin and I didn't have the same type of relationship as I had with my mother. He was already angry and critical of me for the way I had parented him.

Again I dug into my image of Kevin and responded, *"I'm not saying that you don't think what you are doing is right, mom. I just don't think you're seeing clearly on this one. I think you're being duped."*

"Well, son," she, as me, said, *"I disagree with your conclusion, but I don't want to argue with you. That wasn't my point in bringing it up. Mostly, I just wanted to let you know how happy I am for this opportunity, and I would have liked to have you in my cheering section."*

"It's difficult for me not to get caught up in all the guilt I feel for the mistakes I made as a parent," I told her. *"I always want to try to make up for what I didn't do then by being accommodating now."*

"That's why it is so important for you to spend time here, to break that attachment to guilt. It does your sons no good for you to live your life trying to please them. It will cause them to disrespect you even more than they already do. The only way out that may possibly result in the healing of these relationships is for you to respect yourself enough to follow your own impeccability, but you can't do it for that reason."

"What do you mean?" I asked.

"I mean, you can't do something just to gain someone's respect. You follow your own impeccability, and even if they don't come around in the relationship, at least they will respect you for it. Alana Spirit Changer used to tell me, 'Not everybody is going to like you, but at least they will respect you if you are always impeccable in what you do.'"

This conversation left me feeling relieved somehow, bolstered, as though by facing the situation from my son's point of view, acknowledging the

The Teacher Begins to Reel Me In

image he carried of me, I could now face him from my point of view. The others, I knew, might disapprove but they wouldn't lash out at me the way Kevin would. Somehow I would learn to live with their disapproval. I couldn't change it, and I couldn't live to please them.

Terry, my youngest, would say, *"It's your life, mom, whatever you want to do with it is fine with me. Of course, I'd rather have you stay around here, but it's your decision."*

So for me, this was the beginning of a series of lessons on learning to live impeccably, which means to live my truth, regardless of public opinion, which implies freedom to choose. Up to this point, my life was constricted by rules that boxed me into only a tiny area in which there was freedom to choose.

This desire to please and be accepted by others was such a dominant force in my life; it colored my beliefs about what was acceptable and my limiting ideas about what I was capable of expanding into. This combination of limitations kept me in a familiar, comfortable prison, a prison built out of my ego's drive to feel comfortable and fortified. It wasn't easy for me to accept that I was living in a prison, because I designed it in such a way that there appeared to be space to move around in. The walls were far enough apart that I could almost pretend they didn't exist.

But my Teacher saw the walls and knew they would eventually prevent me from moving forward beyond a certain point, not to mention that I thought they were real. And always, there was the option of stopping. Repeatedly, Winged Wolf urged us to *"Go as far as you can go in this lifetime, but don't be ashamed to stop when you have reached that point. I won't love you any less."* But something in me kept saying, *'just one more step.'*

The decision to shift my primary focus of attention to the Path by moving to Orcas for an extended period created such a trauma for me because I was confronting a major box. Actually I was confronting two boxes: my children's disapproval and my attachment to the world and all its glitter.

All the tacit agreements that were existent in my life were now being confronted. Everybody and everything in my environment supported my staying within the boundaries we had mutually created for relating. We had tacit agreements that I would not exceed these boundaries, and in this way, we could all operate without major discomfort. And one of the primary agreements we had was that I would always be there physically and emotionally for the family. This was the dream I had created to satisfy my need to be loved.

Changing the dream meant disrupting the dreams of all those who were close to me: my children, friends and parents. It meant leaving familiar patterns that were nurturing and supportive. But deeper than all this, it meant surrendering to the Teacher, allowing myself to try it her way. That was a huge step and there were many ripples.

This was my first true act of power; my first act of true impeccability and also trust. They all seemed to be aspects of the same whole, not standing separate, but literally inseparable. By acting out that role-playing situation with Winged Wolf, I realized there was a deep-seated issue of trust involved here, not trust of the Teacher so much as trust of myself to follow my heart and, further, trust of myself to make wise choices. Each time someone strongly disapproved of my choices, I usually began second-guessing myself and backing down or going undercover. This time I was putting myself on the line and going for it anyway. I was out in the open, exposed.

A favorite line from a Walt Whitman poem flashed in my mind. He said, *"Hitch your wagon to a star and if you fall you won't fall far."* It struck me that I didn't want to die without ever having really lived. I was taking another step toward my goal of awakening and it felt like I was jumping off the edge of a cliff, only now there was excitement and anticipation over what I might find there, rather than paralyzing fear. It was an act of trust. As my Teacher said, I was *'aligning my actions with my dreams.'*

Winged Wolf often said, *"Only the bold and adventuresome can achieve spiritual awakening. The price is high; you feel you have to give up everything, all your attachments; but in return, you receive everything, but by then, there is nothing you want."* I had never thought of myself as bold and adventuresome because I was so fearful inside; but now I was beginning to get a glimmer of what she meant when she said this. I felt bold and adventuresome, and it felt good.

Walking My Talk

It would be great to be able to report that my new stance resulted in new responses from those intimately involved in my life, but it didn't happen

The Teacher Begins to Reel Me In

that way. It actually happened pretty much as we had role-played. The big difference was that I was composed and didn't get involved in any drama about it.

The one most important aspect for me was this: that if I was going to do something without the approval of my loved ones, I was going to do it without guilt or ambivalence, as if I were entitled to it. It was still 'as if' because the core of my being hadn't integrated the understanding that I truly was entitled, but 'as if' seemed a good starting point.

Packing was a cinch. We wrapped up all our loose ends, visited with friends and local apprentices, said our farewells and struck out for the long drive across country.

"The environment is a reflection of your mental state, so if your life is filled with chaos and conflict, you know that there is a lack of clarity in your mind. Your actions are not aligned with your dreams," was one of Winged Wolf's favorite sayings; and this trip was a perfect demonstration of it. We intended to leave on a particular date since everything was packed and our business was in good shape. But, here's where there was a glitch in my focus of attention, a moment when I allowed my attention to slip and indulged a whim. We decided to stay home one more week, just to have some fun.

Since I was far enough along on the Path to be attuned to the flow of life relative to the energies around me, it was with awareness of disrupting the flow that I had made this suggestion. The only thing I can say is that I was arrogant enough to believe I could do this without consequence. Another lesson was about to be delivered to me.

We spent our week wrapping up loose ends, visiting old haunts, seeing friends again. My intuition told me we were running around the karmic wheel, doing everything 'one more time,' pointless behavior, but knowing that didn't change the behavior. I called Winged Wolf to let her know our departure would be delayed a week. The weather had been unusually warm, sunny and free from snow, so the trip began smoothly. By the second day on the road, however, it began to snow and weather reports talked of a blizzard heading east and hitting the area we would be in the next day. I paid little attention, figuring we had driven in plenty of snow before; it was no big deal. What I didn't know was that the snow I was used to driving through in Michigan was child's play in comparison to the blizzards of the Dakotas, Wyoming and Montana.

The next day, after eight hours of inching our way forward, we got to Fargo, North Dakota, and were routed off the freeway. The roads were being closed. I had never been in a place where roads were literally closed with barriers dropped to prevent access. We were fortunate to find a motel that allowed dogs and had a restaurant next door. It wasn't much later that people were being turned away or sometimes allowed to sleep on the lobby floor. There was no place to go and nothing to do but stop.

For three days and three nights, it snowed; winds blew the snow into giant drifts and shaped them into snow banks. The restaurant next door became everyone's haven; the staff became exhausted, many were in tears, having children at home they couldn't get to while they were forced to sleep on the floor of the restaurant. The food supply was getting low, and we ate whatever was left in the kitchen. What a heroic performance from both the staff and the patrons who donned aprons and helped out in any way they could.

As I watched this drama unfold, I knew with growing certainty that this delay was a reflection of my resistance in going to Orcas. The ignored intuition, the postponed travel date, seemingly so innocent, had put a cog in the wheel of the flow of energies and this was the reflection of my state of mind. And Walter was a part of it. We had allowed the focus of our attention to slip just long enough to derail the train from the tracks, and now we had to live through the karmic cycle set in motion by our actions. Maybe we could at least neutralize it from any further turmoil by focusing more solidly on the direction we were headed. We both agreed it was an important shift.

On the fourth day of the blizzard, after talking to several truckers who were so pressed for time they felt they must go on, we learned of a route through the back roads that would take us all the way beyond the storm. They had heard those roads were passable. We decided to go for it.

The roads were still treacherous, but by careful, slow driving we crawled our way forward all the way from Fargo, through Idaho, and over the pass into Washington, where the roads were plowed and easily passable, albeit still ice-covered. Whew!

Apparently Michigan is one of the few states that uses salt to remove ice from the roads; all the other states we passed through shoveled some ash or sand in places along the way, with minimal effectiveness.

The Teacher Begins to Reel Me In

I was beside myself. The trip that was intended to take us four-and-a-half days had stretched into ten! What a painful lesson this was to have rubbed in my face every day we didn't get there. It was such an embarrassment to know, and to know that everyone else knew the extent of our resistance.

Winged Wolf was kind. She never said a word about our delayed arrival and welcomed us warmly when we drove up. I so appreciated that.

She had told me frequently, *"Don't miss the window of opportunity once it is open; if you miss your moment, it may be a long time before it comes around again."*

To myself I would respond, *'Seems to me I should be able to create my own window when I need it.'* Now I saw this was egotistical thinking. There was a synergy between my intent and the opening that occurred to reflect it, and I had to be ready to walk through it in that moment, or it would pass. This was why my Teacher was always tuned in to everything that was going on within the environment around her, so she could move quickly in any direction when the timing was correct. And I knew there were other environments she was tuned in to that had not been revealed to me yet.

Here we were at last, moving into our new home. What a happy day that was. Now that we were here, it felt like beginning a new life, with the other life a distant memory. The four days of being stuck in the blizzard had served as a buffer between the old and the new, a time of shedding one skin and preparing for a new one. We had been forced to focus on the present moment because of the bizarre circumstances we had presented. It had been a new situation that demanded our total focus of attention to navigate. By the time we reached Orcas, I was so glad to get there not a thought of home entered my mind.

Chapter 17
The Value of Life

In the Happy House one morning, Winged Wolf turned to Julie and said, *"Why don't you tell them what you experienced in town with me yesterday?"*

There were several of us apprentices present that morning as Julie related her experience. It had me sitting on the edge of my seat along with everyone else; then in tears. Here is the story she told us.

"I was in town yesterday afternoon with Winged Wolf and Mark. Winged Wolf had just parked the car, and as we were crossing the street, I noticed Winged Wolf was headed toward a truck parked about twenty yards away. We followed Winged Wolf. Behind the truck was a man selling fresh crab, along with a couple people who were completing a crab purchase. In the bed of the truck were ice chests as well as a huge covered black pot of boiling water.

"Winged Wolf approached the man and asked how many live crabs he had. He answered with a quick 'Seven,' not really giving any eye-contact to Winged Wolf. There was a noticeable familiarity to the exchange of words, as though this conversation had happened before. Winged Wolf then asked how much he was selling the crab for and he said, '$5.50 a pound.' Again, there was a quickness to his words and no inflection to his speech.

"With that, Winged Wolf asked that he weigh one crab. The man handed me a white plastic bag, went to a white bucket, removed the lid, and grabbed the first crab on top. He tightly held the crab's legs and shoved the crab into the plastic bag I was holding. He put a scale hook through the bag and said, '2 1/2 pounds.' Winged Wolf said, 'I will take it.' At this point, I noticed people were beginning to gather around during this transaction.

The Value of Life

"Winged Wolf then said, 'How much is it if I buy all seven crabs?' The man said, 'the same — $5.50 a pound.' Winged Wolf then said, 'I will buy them all.' The people standing by were looking in amazement at the transaction. A few people looked puzzled as if, 'what is she going to do with all those crabs?'

"After weighing the crabs, the man told Winged Wolf they weighed 14 pounds. She asked, 'How much is that?' and he replied, 'I have to get my calculator.' I noticed his face was beet red. He had no emotion to his words but I could sense there was a communication going on between Winged Wolf and the man on another level. I sensed this wasn't the first time she had bought all his crabs and that he was feeling anger because a button was being pushed that said, 'she is judging the way I make my living.' But she was not judging him. As I looked into her eyes, I was struck with the feeling of unconditional love and compassion she showed for him. She understood his ignorance. A healing was taking place before my eyes. He was given the gift of clarity, and for a brief moment he saw it through the Teacher's eyes.

"The man walked to the driver's side of his truck and about twenty seconds later returned saying, '$77.00.' Winged Wolf handed him the money and we walked away with me carrying the bucket and the white bag, which contained the first crab.

"We walked across the street and straight down to the beach about 30 yards away. I followed Winged Wolf as she walked to the end of the beach area. I noticed that the people who had been watching the transaction actually crossed the street to see what we were going to do. I even saw two people pointing at us and heard their laughter.

"Once at the water line, Winged Wolf traversed to the left. We walked up some rock formations to a spot that was sheltered. Winged Wolf said, 'Please hand me the white bag,' which I did. She then opened the bag, picked up the crab, which had no resistance, and put the crab in the water.

"What a sight to see! I cannot put in words the joy I felt to see this little 21/2 pound crab start to walk on the ocean floor, then in a spurt, start to take off. I mean it just took off! It hit me – Winged Wolf saved its life!

"She then asked that I hand her the bucket. She placed the bucket into the water and the six crabs tried to escape. At first they were *intertwined, one with the other. In about a minute, they were free and they walked on the ocean floor, and then began to swim away. What a sight to see. I wish you all had been with us because the impact of actually being there and witnessing it is more than I can convey through words. It is a lesson I will remember for years to come."*

When she had finished her story, there wasn't a dry eye in the Happy House. My attention had been glued to her as she re-lived the experience through relating it to us. It became my experience too! None of us had realized that our Teacher had been going to town every week to buy the man's crabs; it was heart-warming and inspirational.

Winged Wolf told us, *"From now on, when any of you go into town on a Saturday, be watchful for the crab man. Do whatever you can to save the crabs from being boiled alive. Use whatever money you have in your pockets to buy as many as you can and set them free."*

For several weeks after that, Walter and I made a point of going to town on Saturday morning, but oddly, either the man wasn't there, or when he was, he told us there were no live crabs. The season ended and we never saw him again.

Loose Lips Sink Ships

There was a definite rhythm and cadence to life on Orcas that was defined as time between the wind, and time not between the wind. It kept life so simple for me, although not so simple perhaps for Walter who was juggling his time trying to run the business and to be wholeheartedly present at Between on the days he was there. It was a continuous struggle for him to balance his spiritual life with his worldly life; and it resulted in split attention, an untenable condition for a spiritual warrior.

My life was less complicated. Since I had terminated my employment with the school system, I was no longer bound to a time or place, so there was no outside pull on my attention; I could focus entirely on my spiritual evolvement. It was so easy at the time.

Now that we were living on Orcas full-time, there was a different level of participation. This was my life, not the place I often visited for spiritual lessons. Each day we met at 8:00am in the Happy House for meditation and Teachings.

Winged Wolf told us, *"When you find the silence, everything opens up for you, but until then, we practice, practice, practice. Right now you are trying to hold your bodies still in a meditative position, but your minds are chattering away. That is not sitting in the silence. What you are learning right now is beginner meditation."*

My body hurt during meditation, a half-hour seemed more like three. When Winged Wolf told us, *"This is only the beginning, I want you to be able to sit for at least an hour,"* I groaned inwardly. Some apprentices literally moaned aloud. We were such babies. And yet when Winged Wolf called us beginners, a feeling of protest rose in me, of not wanting to be a beginner.

Winged Wolf began to confront some of my unconscious habitual behavior. After a morning sitting, we were having a lively discussion about patience and I cleared my throat. *"When Wings has something to say,"* Winged Wolf commented, *"she announces it by clearing her throat and making a blustering guttural sound."*

Color rose in my cheeks, I could feel the flush.

"And now she's embarrassed," Winged Wolf went on.

As usual, I tried to pretend it didn't matter, but I could feel that familiar stirring that said she struck a blow to my ego, and I wanted to retort, only what could I say? I vowed never to clear my throat before speaking again. And while the resolve came from a place of reaction, it did have the effect of stimulating mindfulness.

But the ego is so creative. A week or so later, again during a discussion, Winged Wolf said, *"Wings has something to say. Can you feel it? She just puffed up and sent a burst of energy out into the room."*

'Darn it', I thought, *'she's right again, that's exactly what I did. I projected my energy toward her to announce my desire to speak and it was felt by everyone.'* It gave me a spooky feeling to see these subtle behaviors that reflected my ego's need for recognition. It's one thing to do something consciously and know you are doing it, but these were unconscious behaviors. I felt out of control. And this was only a small dose. From this point on, she didn't let anything pass by her.

After the 8 o'clock sitting in the morning, Winged Wolf often gave a talk that we tape-recorded. By now, we were more sophisticated and had developed a program called The Wisdom Traveler. This was a monthly Teaching mailed to apprentices culled from talks she gave in the Happy House.

If Winged Wolf received an e-mail from an apprentice that morning complaining about her spouse's disrespect of the apprentice, we might well have a talk on the companion energy of relationships. Or, if Winged Wolf saw one of us doing something off-balance, the talk might be on the power of equanimity in our lives. She could take any presentation and extract the nectar from it, then turn it into a potent talk. One example of this happened to me shortly after my arrival.

It was about this time that Winged Wolf began alluding to the fact that she was having memories of many past lives when she had been Buddhist.* At the time, I didn't give it the proper emphasis that it deserved. Since I wasn't too interested in Buddhism, I tended to discount these references and focus on my Initiation Journey work; but she did tell us that these memories and the Teachings she recalled from these past lives formed the core material of the course work she called The Wisdom Teachings.

One morning, not too many weeks after our arrival on Orcas, I arrived on the property at about 7:45, the time we assembled for the sitting, and found Winged Wolf already on her cushion, a distant expression on her face. When life was flowing smoothly, she usually arrived after the rest of us and came in smiling in a friendly greeting. When there was a serious issue, she often arrived early and it was apparent in the energy; we all waited to learn who would be the brunt of the lesson.

To my knowledge, I had done nothing reproachable and was unconcerned personally about the mood. After a short sitting, she began to talk.

"Because I moved here for privacy, to work quietly with my apprentices and write, I asked each of you to respect me enough to maintain

---

*See HÜMÜH website www.HUMUH.org.

silence about our work together here. In fact, I even sent you all a memo explaining this. It was titled, 'Loose lips sink ships.' This was a way of addressing our vulnerability to bringing attention our way, which could destroy the privacy of 'Between the Wind.' I explained that now was not the time to be assuaging your egos by talking to everyone you meet about what you are doing here. It simply is not the right time for us to go public.

"I think it was made clear in the memo and in my direct verbal communications with you all that it wouldn't take much at this point to destroy what we are building. Our foundation is not yet firmly established."

There were many intense looks from her in my direction, and my heart sank as an image flashed in my mind of the previous Saturday, our day off from *Between the Wind*. Walter and I had been chatting with our neighbor, a friendly fellow who just moved to the island from Idaho and was managing the repair shop of one of the local marinas. His soon-to-be-wife was visiting for the weekend and we had struck up a friendly conversation that eventually led into our purpose for being on the island. It had seemed quite innocent and natural at the time. I had completely forgotten Winged Wolf's request for respect of her privacy. We had even shown them one of Winged Wolf's books.

I hadn't thought further about the incident. How Winged Wolf had found out about it was a mystery but it was obvious she had.

Each time she emphasized a point about respect of her privacy and honoring the Teacher's requests regardless of our opinions of them, she turned those penetrating blue eyes directly on me and shot me a look that pierced to my core. And each time she did this, I felt a combination of dismay, pain, embarrassment, defensiveness, guilt, shame and even some anger. It was the anger of the child being caught in the cookie jar and wanting, but not being able, to point the finger elsewhere. And underneath all those emotions was the recognition that I had been disrespectful by disregarding her request for privacy. It didn't matter whether I thought it was an okay thing to do.

I had done exactly what she had asked me not to do; I had engaged in a superficial, meaningless conversation with disregard for the potential impact on the Teacher and the Teachings. If there were only a way to disappear right then, I would certainly have gladly done so. Never had anyone been able to reach into me this way and cause me to feel so ugly.

She looked straight at me and fixed me with her gaze, *"Do you understand me?"* she asked.

Silently I nodded, head hanging.

The remainder of that day was torturous; I felt like slime, and prayed for the day to end quickly so I could get out of there. And I wanted to ask Walter if he had been responsible for telling her.

When I got a moment alone with him, I asked, *"What happened? How did she find out about our talking with the neighbors?"*

"I told her," he replied. *"I was chatting with her yesterday afternoon, and somehow it came up that Vicki was interested in learning more about the Teachings. I guess I said we'd been talking to them about the Teachings. It never dawned on me she would take it in that direction. She didn't seem upset at the time."*

"Well that's how she gets information out of people, by disarming them until they feel comfortable saying whatever," I snapped, relieving some tension by barking at him. *"I'd appreciate it in the future if you would leave my name out of your conversations with her."*

I knew that Winged Wolf did not want to have public notice at that time. First, we were in a residential neighborhood and did not yet have proper zoning approval. And, then, there were many opinionated neighbors in the area immediately surrounding the property. They were disgruntled because of Winged Wolf's desire for privacy; whereas they wanted to be able to drive through the property as a short cut to the main road, she insisted they respect the boundaries and not use Between the Wind as a drive-thru.

My response to Walter was so immature; I could hardly stand myself, but somehow it made me feel a little less crummy to dump on him. It sure was a wake-up call about the dangers of idle chatter. Over and over again Winged Wolf had cautioned me about my need to socialize. *"Give it up,"* she would say, *"your superficialities are holding you back on the Path."*

The Value of Life

One of the consequences of being in the hot seat like that was the other apprentices sort of shied away from the one who was the primary target. It just took awhile for the stirred-up energy to dissipate and return to normal. During that time no one knew how to be with the one on the hot seat.

For the next few days, I was still so disturbed that I'm sure it added to everyone's discomfort, and I spent my time working hard and being quiet. I did a lot of work cleaning the horse paddock during that time. It was cathartic.

There was always plenty of work to do; one of my primary jobs was to transcribe the talks Winged Wolf gave. But the paddock was a healing place, and when I felt really bad as I did then, I spent extra time out there cleaning. To be graphic, shoveling horse manure allowed me to shed my stuff.

By the third day, Winged Wolf was able to look at me again, and we tentatively resumed our relationship. Occasionally she referred back to the subject and asked, *"Did you really get it? This is a major lesson for you. You must begin to see how you operate in the world; observe how your ego operates. You have an attachment to a particular way of being and it will not serve you on the Path. You've got to intercept it and let it go!"*

"I see it now, Winged Wolf, at least the part about superficial socializing," I said and it was becoming true. *"As I keep looking at what happened and how it happened, I'm starting to see how I slip into these old habitual ways that used to satisfy a need to be approved of and liked. And to influence people."*

"It's got to stop," she said. *"You will damage everything I'm trying to put in place here. Your assignment is to be mindful every moment, every moment, not just some moments, every moment."*

That sounded like an enormous task, but I heard myself say, *"Okay, I'll do my best."*

"Let's hope your best is good enough," came the reply.

After that, balance was restored, the Teaching had come full circle; I accepted the lesson, and we continued on. She treated me with the same loving kindness she always had. The incident was complete, unless it happened again. Then she would pull it up and add it to the next incident with double the force. I had seen her do this a number of times with others. Her memory was uncanny. She saw the overview of a situation, and stored it in memory to pull up if needed for some reason. Otherwise her brain was like a computer, data was stored there, available, but inactive until called forth. I had no intention of calling up that memory again, if at all possible.

The Cave

One day, a couple months after the 'loose lips incident,' I was working on a transcription in the small office, when she stopped by to 'chat' and looked at me in an unusual way. Tilting her head to the side, looking out of the corner of her eyes, she looked intently at me for a few seconds. Satisfied, she nodded, *"I think you're ready for an experience,"* she said.

My hands got clammy and my heart raced, I tried to appear calm and only moderately interested so she wouldn't withdraw the offer. *"Oh, what experience is that, Winged Wolf?"*

"I'll tell you about it later," she replied. *"I have some work to finish now."*

An experience usually meant she thought we were ready for some major advancement, and I wondered what that could be. After my failed attempt at becoming Thunderbeing, it had seemed wise to take all attention away from advancement in rank and just learn to be.

This took all the pressure off and helped me stay focused on the moment. This was the first mention of an experience since Cottonwood. There had been mention of building a cave, but nothing had been done about it. This indicated there was something more than the growth that came from just being in her presence.

Eager to hear more about this 'experience,' it was hard to stay focused and not let my mind wander to the *'what could it be'* as I waited for her to call me up to the office. Images kept popping up. Several times during the week she had reminisced about the time she spent in a cave writing *Shaman of Tibet*, a book she had written that described the Tibetan Saint Milarepa's transformation.

The Value of Life

She told us what a powerful experience it had been as she re-created, in short form, his time with his Teacher Marpa who had placed him in a cave and covered it with a large bolder, telling him to stay there until he understood the illusion of his mind. It had been weeks before Milarepa finally realized the illusion and was able to transport himself out of the cave. It seemed our Teacher had a similar experience. But we didn't have a cave at *Between the Wind*. Maybe she would put me in the Happy House as she had done with Walter several months ago.

Toward the end of the day, Winged Wolf sent a message down, asking me to come up to her office.

"Sit down," she said gazing intently at me. She seemed hesitant, looking at me with a curious sideways glance.

I waited, uneasy but silently excited.

Finally she continued, *"We don't have an actual cave on the property, although I'd like to create one eventually. But we can transform one of the cabins into a cave and that will do for now. The idea is to be in total darkness for a period of time."*

"For how long?" popped out of my mouth, imagining how I might survive a week in total darkness.

"Oh, maybe four days, maybe more, maybe less. You should go into it with the idea that you might be there indefinitely, because I really don't know how long it will take you."

I swallowed hard. *"What am I supposed to be doing while in there?"*

"If I tell you that, it won't be your experience. But I will know when you're ready to come out."

"Will I be allowed to eat?"

"You will have one meal each day, and you can bring some snacks. I will bring the meal, knock once on your door, open it and slip the tray in. I'll pick it up the next day when I bring your meal. You can take the porta-potty in with you. If at any time you feel you cannot go on, simply call out to me in your mind and I will come and open the door."

Initiation

It sounded pretty cushy to me: food, a bed, and a toilet, of sorts.

"I must tell you I did this with another apprentice and they only lasted forty-five minutes before they had to be let out."

I was curious, but knew not to ask the details.

"Why don't you plan on entering the cave the day after tomorrow, first thing, before the sitting? That will give you time to prepare a few things to bring, and give you a day to adjust to the idea."

During the next day, it became apparent Winged Wolf had not mentioned this upcoming experience to anyone else. I realized this when she appointed Julie to be the cave converter, and Julie began hammering large pieces of carpet over the window and all cracks in the cabin and around the door.

There were whispers among the other apprentices as they tried to casually walk down to the pond, passing by the cabin along the way, stopping to stare at the goings on. I tried my best to become invisible, and no one said anything directly to me. *'Guess I'm just going to disappear for a few days.'*

Winged Wolf had told me simply to let Walt know I would be staying on the property for a few days and nothing else, but it didn't take long for him to figure out what was going on. I was getting good at maintaining silence in the face of others' questioning glances and side comments.

"Are you ready?" she asked me the next morning, greeting me as I walked up the lane. She reached out to take hold of one of the bags I carried, full of goodies.

"I think so," I gulped. How could I possibly know until I was there?

"Let's go then. It's all set up for you." And she walked quickly down the lane in the direction of the cabin.

When we reached the cabin, she said, *"Remember, if you get to the point where you can't take any more, call out to me. Otherwise, I will be down sometime this evening with your meal. As I told you, you may write, in fact I strongly recommend you journal about your experiences, even though it will be dark; and you may eat snacks as you feel hungry.*

The Value of Life

There's enough water to last you several days. Take a look around the room so you can fix in your mind where things are. Once I latch the door, it will be pitch dark in here and you might have difficulty finding things."

I looked slowly around the room, placing each item as I did. There was a bed, a writing table in one corner, the porta-potty in the other corner, and my supplies next to that. Nothing else. Taking a deep breath, I said, *"Okay, I'm ready."*

There were tears in her eyes as she backed out of the room, and I realized this was hard for her; her compassion for me said this might be a painful experience and she didn't want to do it, but that feeling would never interfere with her doing what was needed. *"When I knock at the door, I'll ask you if you are all right, and if you are, then I will leave your meal and shut you in for the night."*

The door closed and I heard the latch being set in place; panic arose in me. It was an instinctual reaction, the hairs stood on the back of my neck; and for a few moments, irrationally, I felt overwhelming terror. I re-placed my attention at the Third Eye, then miraculously, my sanity returned. I sat down on the bed, breathing slowly and rhythmically to regulate my pulse and heart rate. *"That was close,"* I muttered to myself. It was reassuring to say something.

This experience reactivated some primitive response in me to being cooped up, and darkness was something I had feared since my earliest childhood memories. As a little girl, I was afraid to go to bed alone, saw things in doorways, peeking around corners. I didn't feel safe unless someone was with me.

When that latch clicked into place on the door, it was temporarily impossible for me to separate this moment from the original panic response that I had experienced being left alone in the dark.

The panic attack lasted about as long as it took me to sit down, focus my attention at the Third Eye and chant the HÜM for a few moments, maybe two minutes, but they seemed like longer. As the vibration of the HÜM penetrated my being, the panicky feeling began to dissipate. I felt the tension flowing out of me and I knew that I would be fine. Whatever happened, I had passed through the worst of it in those few moments. Relief flooded me.

For the remainder of that day, I occupied myself with walking in place meditations, singing the HÜM, quiet reflection and keeping a journal. Surprisingly, after the first hour or so, the room became filled with soft light. In my notes, I commented, *"The room begins to get light. That frightens me. Why, my writing pad, I can see it! It must be the light coming through the cracks. No, it must be nighttime by now. Why am I so afraid that it's light? What a strange response!"*

A loud knock on the door startled me out of my wonderings and I realized several hours must have passed for Winged Wolf to be bringing my evening meal. She asked, *"Are you ready?"*

"I just need a moment, Winged Wolf," I responded, fumbling around in the darkness, as I searched for the brown paper bag she had given me that morning. My hand touched upon the spot where I remembered placing it, and the bag made a crinkling sound under my fingers. Before opening the door, I placed the bag over my head so that I would not be flooded with light nor would the continuity of the continuous experience of darkness be interrupted when the door opened. "I'm ready," I called out to her and stood back from the door as she opened it. I heard the sound of the tray against the wood floor as she slid it inside the room.

And I heard the door shut and the latch click into place and listened to her footsteps as she moved along the path away from me. And I was alone in the silence eating in the semi-illuminated room, even though I knew it was pitch dark.

There were many other experiences compacted into that four days. I will mention two of them. On the second day I had an experience that also imprinted me heavily. My notes read,

I must have fallen into a light sleep when, suddenly, I found myself in the Happy House. It was empty, and I looked around to make sure it was the actual Happy House and not a dream-state. It was both, because I could feel a pulling at my Third Eye that reminded me that my physical body was sleeping, dreaming this. Yet it was an actual experience. I noted Winged Wolf's Eagle Stick her Teacher had made for her, and looked around at all the items on the shelves. They were all there, just as they should be. I decided to take something from a shelf back with me to my cabin to 'prove' to myself I had actually been there. I took a small object and placed it in my pocket.

The Value of Life

Then I left the Happy House and spotted Winged Wolf walking down the hill with another apprentice; they were deep in conversation. Excited to see my Teacher, I hurried up the hill. She didn't seem to notice me, so I began jumping up and down, and waving my arms to catch her attention. Only once, briefly, she glanced at me out of the corner of her eyes, and then continued her conversation with the apprentice.

The third day was rough, because my dark side surfaced and confronted me with a continuous series of images that were 'ugly' and unwanted, frightening to my sense of self, the image I wanted to portray. In my notes I even disassociated from it by referring to my dark side as 'the old hag in the cellar.' I said 'she is critical, petty and nasty and spews ugly thoughts and profanities,' as though 'she' was not me, but some stranger who had entered my body against my wishes. But, of course, I knew that was not so. This was my karmic make-up exposing itself with a vengeance. It had to be looked at. I didn't know what to do with it except to chant the HÜM and continue to sit in the silence.

I fell asleep chanting the HÜM and when I awoke my mind was clear and a general sense of well-being enveloped me. Something had shifted and the darkness had receded. In part, the shift was caused by a realization. What I wrote was, 'I never please myself. I adapt to please others; then I become angry at myself and them because I'm pulling against myself. I have to live true to myself or I cannot be wholehearted. If others cannot accept that, then that is their choice. If I don't live true to myself, then they pay the price of my resentment as do I. That is foolish, a wasted life. I won't do it anymore. I must take charge of my life.'

Another striking part of my experience in darkness was a series of past-life memories that seemed to project out of my Third Eye and that could be tuned in to by shifting my attention to that point. Several times I found myself in scenes, at one point a small boy. I lived at a temple or monastery of some sort in a forest, and it was my task to wash the feet of the visiting lamas and monks. I was proud of my job and did it wholeheartedly.

It was on the fourth day, though, that I had the most encouraging experience. An agitation was developing in me and I wanted out of there. I wrote, *"I'm like a caged animal today. I want out — I want to walk through the door. I begin walking, my mind is racing, my body is pacing back and forth, back and forth. I'm walking with my blanket over my* head. Suddenly I realize I am in an old woman's body; she is walking back and forth across her cell. From time to time, someone brings her tea. She must live here. It's like a monastery. When the door opens to receive the tea, I see many robed people sitting in meditation in a large hall just across from her room. As I look out from her eyes, I realize she has spent many days pacing like this looking for an answer she has been seeking.

"The room itself is spartan, a small cot occupies one wall, a writing desk the other. There is one tiny window at the back, no closet, nothing else.

"I can feel she has no concern for her body. Little-self desires are an ancient memory. She is vaguely aware of the dampness in her room. She stops walking and looks deeply into the dark hole of the Void, a great silence envelops her, total quiet. She gazes deeply and I too gaze deeply. There is nothing else, a silence so profound that there is no end to it. I feel completely alone, one with the darkness, totally independent in this body. There is no desire for anything, just looking into the fathomless depths. I realize she is preparing to make the great transition from the physical body into the formless realms. There is no fear, just a quiet peace. She is ready."

This experience lasted for some time, and when I left her and returned fully to the room, it was with this sense of completion and serenity such as I had never known before. I prayed it would last forever, but of course, in the trying to grasp onto it, the fading began. Yet the core experience was mine, a gift from the past brought forward, at least I assumed it was from the past.

Two Steps Forward, One Step Back

The next morning Winged Wolf came for me. It was early before the others arrived. She suggested I go shower and clean myself up, and asked me to give her my notes. I left them with her and headed up the hill. It felt odd to be out in the daylight again. Looking at myself in the bathroom mirror, I saw the reflection of someone different; my eyes were distant, complexion ashen.

A hot shower brought me back into the outer world; my body was pink from scrubbing, and my hair squeaky clean. What a great feeling to be

The Value of Life

clean and back in this world again! I grabbed some fruit from the kitchen and headed upstairs to Winged Wolf's office. My notes were still in her hands, and as she motioned me in, there was a pleased look on her face. I sat on the sofa facing her and waited.

"You did really well," she spoke slowly. *"In fact, I must say I'm surprised at how well you did. You even saw your own death."*

That took me aback. *"That was a past life, I said."* I felt a little defensive for some reason. *"I was wearing robes and living in a monastery. Certainly that couldn't be related to this life. We're not monastic."*

"Oh," she responded, *"I thought it was this lifetime."* It wasn't a contradiction exactly, but she wasn't shifting her viewpoint either. Her tone of voice implied it was I who was missing the point, not she.

She was gazing at me speculatively, as though watching for a sign. Then she did something totally unexpected. She took off her gold bracelet and handed it to me. *"This is for you to wear."*

My eyebrows raised as her words penetrated. She had given me many gifts in the past, but they were given in the spirit of a gift. As I looked at the bracelet, I recalled an incident that occurred some weeks ago; it was not something that I wanted to remember. Winged Wolf, in her great generosity and giving nature, had presented Walter and I with twin necklaces with gold and diamond pendants hanging from them. They were beautiful. It was a time when she was giving her collection of jewels away to various apprentices who were close to her.

To my great shame, rather than having deep appreciation for the loving gift from my Teacher, instead, I lusted after the opal ring she had given to another apprentice. It wasn't long before I lost the necklace. Then I felt terrible, searched everywhere for it for weeks afterward, retracing my every step. But deep down I knew that I had lost it because I didn't care enough about it to deserve it. And so it had disappeared. That awful memory was pretty fresh in my mind as I received this bracelet.

The bracelet was not a gift in the usual sense. There was a deeper significance. It was a bracelet that she had worn for many years. I believed she was testing to see if I could hold more power. I didn't know what to say, so I said nothing as I put it on my wrist. It felt so strange to wear this bracelet, yet so thrilling to be given it.

"Others will be looking at you and the bracelet, wondering about it. I'd prefer if you not mention anything about it. It will only stir them up."

"Well, what do I say when they ask me where I got it? Surely they will notice it is no longer on your wrist." I was feeling uncomfortable.

"You've seen me when I don't care to respond to someone's question, Wings of Change. Why, if I don't choose to respond to something, I turn the conversation in another direction, or I find a reason to leave, or I simply smile and say nothing. There is nothing you need respond to if you don't wish to. It's between you and me, nobody else's business."

That was all she had to say to me on the subject, and she returned my notes with a smile. *"I'd like you to try it again one day soon."*

Downstairs, not five minutes passed before Julie noticed my wrist and asked, *"Did Winged Wolf give you her bracelet?"*

Startled, I made some mumbling noises and continued toward the bathroom where I hung out until she was back in her office. My gosh, what amazing antennae she had. This would be a challenge for me, and already I felt uncomfortable. Now I had a sort of gift that meant something about power, as I saw it, but it was a secret gift, yet she had made it clear I should never take it off. That evening I did everything with my other arm so Walter wouldn't notice I was wearing Winged Wolf's bracelet. I even slept with long-sleeved pajamas so it wouldn't be obvious. Much later, I realized my Teacher had not meant that I shouldn't share it with Walter.

For the next three days, I was paranoid someone would question me about what happened and why I was wearing the Teacher's bracelet. I began to fantasize about going home, taking some time away from Orcas. All the while, I was watching myself have this intense reaction. Fear was lurking underneath and I could feel it trying to surface. Questions kept arising. *'What does this mean? Does she think I'm a Thunderbeing? Is this some kind of test to see if I can hold some of her spiritual power?'* The more time went by, the more I obsessed on it.

On the third day, Winged Wolf called me up to her office and extended her hand to me, palm up. I looked at her questioningly.

The Value of Life

"Give me the bracelet," she said softly, *"it's tormenting you. You've done nothing but think about leaving ever since I gave it to you."*

I was horrified and resistant. *"Maybe I just haven't had it long enough, Winged Wolf. I might just need more time to adjust."*

Still her hand remained outstretched. *"Give it back to me, Wings; I'll hold it for you until you're ready. It's your bracelet, but I'm going to keep it for you for now. You're not ready to wear it yet."*

Resignedly, I took the bracelet off. She was correct in what she said. I had wanted to leave ever since placing the bracelet on my wrist. The terrible tension I had been holding while carrying it on my wrist began to drain out of me the moment I relented and handed her back the bracelet.

It didn't make any sense to me, but there was such relief in transferring it back to her. It seemed my balance was restored. I felt like myself again. Sadly, I shook my head, wondering what had gone awry.

"I have to admit to myself that I am still afraid of power," I told her, hardly able to meet her eyes, *"and your bracelet is a symbol of great power, and tremendous responsibility. Your life isn't your own, it is given to service, and while it sounds romantic when reading about it, it looks like hard work to me."*

Without intending to speak aloud, the words had come tumbling out on their own.

She looked disturbed as I rattled on, then interrupted me, *"My life is how I choose it to be."*

Quickly she shifted gears and lifted my darkening mood. *"One day, maybe this lifetime, maybe another, but one day, you will see from the perspective of the divine consciousness. Until then, I'll hold the bracelet for you. Now, why don't you go home and spend the rest of today doing whatever you need to do. I'll see you in the morning."*

So within a matter of a few days I reached a pinnacle in my apprenticeship only to fall back to a low point. Rationally, I knew it wasn't a dark hole; I had merely stretched beyond my ability to hold the stretch, and then, with the Teacher's help, I returned to a more comfortable level. I was still well beyond where I had begun prior to the cave. But what a roller coaster ride this had turned out to be. I couldn't control my obsessive, circular thinking about that bracelet.

It started with *'If only she had given me a few more days to adjust'* and moved on to *'If only she hadn't said it had to be a secret. It wasn't fair to ask that of me. Surely she knew that was too much pressure for me. It must have been a test to see if I could handle it. Well, I blew that opportunity.'* Round and round I went for days, even weeks.

In my more rational moments, there was a little voice that said, *'Where were **you** in this matter? What responsibility are you taking for what happened?'* But I was too preoccupied with stewing and pointing a finger at my Teacher at that time to look at facts. Eventually, I could acknowledge the sequence of events was simply a reflection of where I was in my spiritual evolution and not really anyone's fault. There was no one to blame, not even myself. Acceptance of that came gradually; meanwhile, I suffered. My ego had taken a whack.

Two Steps Forward, Two Steps Back

My relationship with Julie was tenuous at best. Rumor had it that Julie was taking the drug Prozac on and off, both prior to her arrival on Orcas and while she was a resident at 'Between.' All of this was unbeknownst to the Teacher at the time. But the result of the drug interaction on her, and there may be other factors, too, was that her moods and behavior were erratic. At times she was calm and contained, kind and loving; then for no apparent reason, her mood would swing wildly and another person would emerge, one who was not kind and loving, quite unpredictable. There was a sense of always walking on eggshells around her, not knowing what the mood might be. And she was in a powerful position at 'Between,' working closely with the Teacher at all times, so everyone tread cautiously around her so as not to set her off. As much as possible, I kept my distance, but I came to resent the atmosphere that was developing at Between the Wind as a result of what I perceived as Julie's 'reign of terror.'

 I never fully understood what happened, but it wasn't too long after Winged Wolf had mentioned to me that I might be crowding Julie by visiting her room regularly, that I heard a loud knock on my door late one evening.

The Value of Life

It was not unusual to be approached by the Teacher at odd hours; Winged Wolf spoke to us as was needed. This meant if I was at home in Michigan, she might call in the middle of the night if it was deemed important; and if I was staying on Orcas, she might show up at my door any time of the day or night. NOW was the operant word.

This was an accepted and agreed upon aspect of apprenticeship. There is an agreement between apprentice and Teacher giving the Teacher permission to do whatever she deems necessary to awaken the apprentice in consciousness and move them forward.

The evening this happened I had been staying on the property for a few days giving Walter some time alone. I quickly opened the door to the cabin and saw Winged Wolf. She looked stern and I could tell she had been drawn from her sleep to come here. *"This jealousy between you two has to stop,"* was her opening statement.

It took me a minute to register what she referred to, because I wasn't in touch with any current jealousy toward anyone. *"Do you mean Julie?"* I asked, puzzled.

"Yes," she said. *"If she is feeling this much jealousy toward you, it must be coming from you as well."*

"I'm not aware of it if it is, Winged Wolf," I said innocently. *"I thought I put that down a while ago. What do you want me to do?"*

She fixed me with her eyes, *"I want you to be mindful every moment of what you are putting out, take total responsibility. Do nothing that has any feeling to it other than divine love and compassion.*

"I realize she may be the greater cause in this; she is full of judgment toward you. She doesn't trust you, doesn't believe you are wholehearted, and in this I must agree with her. I don't trust you either. I don't mean you aren't doing your best, but you're not always wholehearted."

Uh-oh, I was starting to sink as she made this proclamation about me that I could not be trusted. Now it wasn't about jealousy but about trust of the Teacher. And it sounded as though Julie had it and I did not. *'Julie must have much say to the Teacher about me,'* I thought, annoyed.

"I'm not saying this is all your fault, Wings of Change, only that you are further along the Path than she is, and this makes it your responsibility to see to it that she doesn't feel negatively toward you. If she feels jealousy, I'm holding you responsible." She paused letting the weight of those words penetrate. *"This doesn't mean I'm not talking to her, too, because I am, but I need your total cooperation on this. Do I have it?"*

I nodded, unable to speak.

Tears were now running down my cheeks and I felt the weight of the world on my shoulders. *'Now Winged Wolf is upset with me, because Julie is jealous. And even if I'm not jealous, I'm still responsible for how she feels about me. That's not fair.'* I wept to the universe. *'And worse, she's turning the Teacher against me.'*

When one thing happens to start a downward cycle, another and another and another seem to pile on top. For a short while before losing the bracelet, after the 'loose lips' incident, I had regained my Teacher's trust, only now to somehow demonstrate I was unworthy of it again by projecting jealous feelings that I was not even aware of having. My unconscious behaviors were forever undermining my progress, and it seemed I only became aware of them after the fact, once the damage was done.

In retrospect, this was a powerful lesson for me in staying focused at the Third Eye in the face of strong winds, and taking responsibility for myself, including my unconscious behaviors, but in living those moments, it was anguish. And I understood anguish of this sort came from my ego feeling threatened; I felt I was being misunderstood and therefore, mistreated. Never in my life had an experience such as this one presented itself, but then, previously I would never have subjected myself to such a situation. I would have left in a snit; but I didn't want to leave; this was my Path!

From that point on, a part of me felt hurt and unjustly chastised by the Teacher. I didn't understand why she gave this person so much credibility. So, privately, I suffered. When I was with the Teacher, not only was I well-behaved, but I was genuinely happy. In Winged Wolf's presence, it was easy to live in an elevated state of consciousness, because her consciousness was so pristine it pulled me right up to it. Those hours at *Between* I really was beyond jealousy, self-pity or suffering.

It didn't hold during those times we were apart though, even when she left the property to go into town for something. The feeling was literally that of rising up and sinking down, depending on where Winged Wolf's attention was directed. If the focus was on me, I was right up there with her; when it turned away, I fell back into my little-self pity pot. There wasn't the refinement to consistently live the Third Eye viewpoint on my own.

Too soon, our three months passed, and it was time to return to Michigan. A part of me was ready to be back on my own turf where things weren't so intense. That was a schizophrenic time by Winged Wolf's definition; but it seemed normal to me. When I was with her, I wanted only to stay forever and be in this elevated state of consciousness where everything was clear. Once I was away from her, I wanted the *freedom* of living my way. And what made it schizophrenic was that each state felt like freedom to me when I was there, as though I were precariously balanced at the 50-50 mark.

Back in Michigan, I descended quickly into a place I called hell. And it was all focused on the disturbance with Julie that continued to fester in me. There had been some other instances of Julie's 'reign of terror,' and I was caught up, not only in my own drama about her, but in other apprentices' feelings about her as well. I felt she was damaging the image of the Path by her behavior and there was nothing I could do but stay centered and keep myself out of it.

I received a letter from Julie during this time. She was experiencing the same torment I was. It was so brutally honest and insightful that I cried reading it. She said, *"You are like a mirror that can amplify my own stuff back to me. I refer to such qualities of my wanting to control, which I see in you; my wanting to be 'top dog,' which I see in you,' my vying for Winged Wolf's attention, which I see in you; my competitive nature, which I see in you, and my coming across as innocent and naïve (although I portray it differently), which I see in you.*

In closing she said, *"I do not want our movement and our growth on the Path to be hindered by negative feelings. Although in the future I may slip, I shall consciously remember that when my heart is steeped in compassion, there can be no dissension."*

And she hand wrote, *"This is my vow."*

For the next several days my heart was singing with the joy of having such an opening in our relationship. I called Winged Wolf and told her, *"I received a letter from Julie."*

"I know," she responded, *"I insisted that she write it."*

My heart sank. *"You mean it wasn't sincere?"*

"Oh, it was sincere in the moment she wrote it," she said, *"but it didn't last. She's right back where she was before writing it. There hasn't been any lasting change."*

"That devastates me, Winged Wolf. I was so happy to think we could put our differences aside."

"Well, not in this moment," she told me. Her voice sounded like she might mean 'not in this lifetime,' but maybe I was reading something into it.

For hours after that conversation, I sat on my cushion praying to the divine consciousness to guide me. Finally a decision came. While sitting in my meditation room one night, I knew I had to take some action.

So I gathered all my nerve and wrote the most painful letter of my apprenticeship. *"My beloved Teacher, I can no longer live with this anguish in my heart over the situation with Julie. While it might be the coward's way, I know that I cannot not come to Orcas again while Julie is there, at least until she is a Thunderbeing. Then she will no longer carry those hateful feelings toward me. I do not mean that I am terminating my apprenticeship, not at all. I am as devoted to you and the Path as ever. I am only backing off on my visitations until Julie achieves the irreversible way."* Now, I would leave the letter on my altar for a day or two before mailing it.

After writing that letter, I felt such relief and tranquility, tinged with some sadness that such an extreme measure was necessary. But I slept for the first time in many nights, feeling at peace that a resolution was reached that allowed me to continue my work with Winged Wolf but took the struggle out of it. If I didn't mail it, would the energy of my words still carry through? I wondered.

The comfort that letter gave me is probably indescribable, but it took the struggle out of me and I found peace of mind. The letter sat on my altar for the next few weeks; then, one evening during a meditation, I knew with certainty it was no longer an issue. I ripped the letter up and burned it. It didn't matter how Julie felt toward me; I accepted her totally and unconditionally. Somehow everything would be all right; I could feel it. We determined to return to Orcas in February for five months.

Unexpected Changes

Shortly after that, in mid-October, we left for Florida to spend time in our new home and visit with my parents, who were struggling. The house we had purchased was about an hour away and made it possible for me to give my mother some relief in her care-taking of my father.

We had only been there a few days when one of the local Orcas apprentices called to say Julie had left *Between the Wind* in a most disturbed manner.

Walter was on the extension and there was some shocked conversation between us all, because this had happened only the day before; it was new to them as well. Apparently, she had become more and more difficult, emotionally volatile, and finally the Teacher suggested she take a few days off. However, Julie argued and threatened to leave permanently if the Teacher insisted on her taking time off. Naturally, a student cannot challenge a Teacher in this manner; so Winged Wolf restated her insistence that Julie take some time off.

They reported that Julie then left in a rage saying this was it, she was leaving for good. Then apparently she returned, cooled down a bit, wanting to resume her duties, but the Teacher again told her she must take some time to herself first, and perhaps should continue her apprenticeship at a distance for a while. It seemed that Julie agreed, at least she was able to bid adieu to the other apprentices present with some aplomb, but the Teacher said after that, she began to rage again and had to be firmly told to leave.

It was an ugly scene and terribly hard on Winged Wolf's body, which was in great pain due to the emotions being flung at her. Of course, we were hearing all of this piecemeal and third-hand so I wasn't sure how accurate the description was, but the result was clear. Julie was gone.

Winged Wolf had long ago told us that a Teacher's commitment to her apprentices prevents her from blocking feelings thrown at her; if she were to block them, they would ricochet back to the apprentices and hurt them. So the Teacher allows those feelings to pass through her, which can be terribly painful depending on the intensity of the emotion thrown.

We used to beg her to find another way of doing this because, in those early days, she spent a lot of time in pain. We were all so immature and unrefined; our feelings oozed out and wrapped all around the Teacher. It was pretty awful to watch the impact, and most of us worked diligently to learn to contain our energy and transmute our feelings; at least we learned not to throw zingers at the Teacher.

In a way, it made most of us more responsible and mindful of our energy, but regarding anger, Winged Wolf said, *"People who are angry don't care whom they hurt. That is a characteristic of anger. It is the worst mind-passion, because of its destructiveness. Anger kills.*

"Always remember the three-second rule: you have one second to recognize it, the next second to intercept it; and the third to completely release it. And, if it lasts for more than fifteen seconds, it becomes solidified and set in motion. You will reap karmic repercussions."

One apprentice said, *"Sometimes when I'm angry, I can't let go of it. What do I do then?"*

"If you can't let it go, do something, anything, to shift your attention." She looked at the question for a moment and continued, *"Here's what you do. If possible, go outdoors, dig a hole in the ground, and stick your face right down in the dirt, and shout into the hole, releasing the anger that way. The earth will absorb your anger without being damaged.*

"If you are not in a position to do this, for instance if you are at work, carry a plastic bag of dirt with you, go into the bathroom and place your face in the dirt there. Stay that way until you feel the release. I'm telling you to do whatever it takes to let it go. You will reap the most devastating karmic repercussions from throwing anger. You might even de-evolve."

"What does that mean?" we had asked her.

The Value of Life

"It means, someone like Hitler who cannot even occupy a bug's body without being squashed instantly. It means that until the memory of that anger is destroyed in the mind of everyone involved, he will be living out the karmic cycle that was seeded by that expression. If there is enough anger, one may de-evolve into a more primitive form, primitive because they do not have the same brain capacity as a human. And to live with human consciousness in an animal's body is a terrible experience. I know this for a fact.

"There is nothing wrong with being an animal when you are evolving, but to be one when you are de-evolving is awful because you know, and yet you cannot express what you know."

Winged Wolf confirmed that she, herself, had an experience of this sort in a previous lifetime but she would not go further into it at that time. It didn't sound like something I ever wanted to experience if it could be helped, and she said it could if we lived the Teachings.

So, what would become of Julie as a result of her angry departure was an unknown. As much as Julie had been disturbing to me in many ways, I also understood she had to have been suffering terribly to behave in that manner. And I knew Winged Wolf would be in great pain, too, filled with compassion for the hasty decision of an apprentice in the heat of a mind passion. But I didn't learn how difficult it really was until my arrival on Orcas some weeks later.

Chapter 18
The Divine Consciousness Moves Quickly

There were many more conversations with local apprentices about their perceptions of the incidents leading up to and including Julie's departure.

It wasn't a total surprise, because there had been difficulties all along with her volatility, but she was so devoted to the Path, I assumed it would all somehow work out. It did work out, but not in the way I had assumed. Julie simply left, sending a friend to clean out her room and pick up her things.

Although Julie had only been gone a couple days when I talked to Winged Wolf, already everything was quickly being rearranged. As always, with the divine consciousness at work, even an apparent trauma opens a gateway for the next evolvement. One thing moved out of the way, and another moved in. It was fascinating to watch how this worked. Every single time I thought, *"Oh, boy, we're in trouble now,"* I was off-base. Always, an opening appeared to step into that evolved us further in the direction of the refinement of the enlightened consciousness.

A local apprentice, one who had been filling in as a volunteer, stepped up to the plate and requested Julie's position. Winged Wolf agreed. Also, an apprentice who was visiting at the time decided to move to the island. She was a serious student, sincere and devoted, and could work part-time to assist the full-time person, although it would take several weeks to finalize arrangements for her move.

All this happened within days of Julie's departure. And the office work resumed. Winged Wolf regained her physical strength gradually as Julie's attention shifted away from Between into whatever new circumstances she was presenting for herself. But the experience was an eye-opener in many ways. It was a terrible shock to learn that my Teacher was using a walking stick because her body was in such pain.

Winged Wolf declared there would be no more resident apprentices, other than Skywolf, who lived in a trailer on the far end of the property. People could work on the property, but they would go home at night.

By the time Walter and I arrived in February for our five-month visit, there was a gentle flow to life at Between the Wind. The apprentices there were relaxed and happy. It had created a terrible strain on everyone to try to keep a balance while working with someone who was so volatile, and now things were gentler. The new office person was even-tempered, well-liked and capable; and at least in the beginning, she seemed happy and appreciative of the opportunity.

My Teacher Has a Secret

There was an addition to Winged Wolf's life that she had hinted at prior to my departure from the previous visit, but I assumed it was a brief fantasy. We had been sitting on the side of the hill overlooking the pond, when Winged Wolf began talking about fantasies. Normally, she smote any fantasies of her apprentices before they had a chance to blossom. But this day, she was unwinding from a difficult and demanding group of visiting apprentices who had just departed. She relaxed, lying back on the earth, and began to talk about having a boat that would carry her out to sea where she could roam from port to port, teaching informally as she went.

We enjoyed her fantasy, as it helped to ease the tension of the past week; after a while she said, *"That was fun."* And we went about our business. Then, later in the week we were driving to the post office when she swung the car down a side street and paused in front of the marina there, pointing to a boat that was in dry dock. *"Isn't that a good-looking boat?"* she asked me. It was an Albin cruiser, about 25-feet long, probably also 25-years-old. *"It sure looks solid, Winged Wolf,"* I answered, wondering where this was leading. *"That's what I think, too,"* she said. *"I could see myself as captain of that boat. I love the sea, and I would enjoy spending some time exploring it."* After that, there was no further mention of the boat and I decided it was more of a fantasy.

Well, I guess it shouldn't have been unforeseen, but it was. When we arrived for the five-month stay, Winged Wolf said *"I have a surprise but it's a secret, so you can't say anything to anybody."*

Later, I learned several others were also guarding the 'secret' but that was down the road. The Teacher loved secrets, but she also loved to share them with us, so often we would discover months later that each of us knew the 'secret' and had been faithfully keeping it.

Curiosity piqued, I asked, *"What is it? What's the surprise?"*

"Do you remember that boat I showed you before you left the last time?" I nodded and she continued, *"I bought it."*

"You did? What are you going to do with a boat?" She never seemed to have any time to herself so I couldn't imagine when she would be able to learn about boating.

"I'm going to go out to sea in it. And it can be my getaway place. I'm going to fix it up and use it for an office and a private hideaway. I don't have any privacy here. Would you like to see it?" she asked.

"Sure," I replied gamely.

We headed for the marina where the aptly named 'Liberty' was moored, and I was given the grand tour. Winged Wolf had the same vision for the boat as she did for everything that came under her wings. It would be painted, seats redone, polished and washed until it sparkled, and best of all, we would be going to sea. Winged Wolf informed me she would teach me how to be one of her crew-members.

I gulped at the idea of crewing on this large boat. *"I'm not a natural boater, Winged Wolf,"* I informed her. *"I've helped out a little on a sail boat, and I've got a tiny Boston Whaler in Florida, but boating doesn't come naturally to me. I'm sure there are others who are better suited to crewing than I am."*

She looked directly at me. *"I don't want you to mention the boat to anyone right now. When it's time, I will tell them about it. Meanwhile, you'll be just fine. Just keep your attention focused at the Third Eye. All you have to do is listen carefully to my directions and do exactly as I tell you."*

The Divine Consciousness Moves Quickly

"Okay," I agreed, looking skeptically at the large hull and the tiny space it was moored in, wondering what sort of adventures this boat might represent for us and what lessons were in store for me. There turned out to be plenty of both.

But for a while, there was no need to crew on the boat and I relaxed, almost forgot about it. Winged Wolf was too busy with the work she was doing to have much time for boating. This was a period in my apprenticeship that I remember as a steady upward climb, although in retrospect, the signs for my next 'apprenticeship crisis' were already in place and obvious to see if one was looking from that perspective.

Eventually the day arrived when the Teacher needed a break. We went down to the dock and sat in the boat for a while, enjoying the gentle back-and-forth motion as the waves lapped up against the hull. This was my kind of boating. Then we walked around the boat checking the lines and talking about what is expected of a crew-member. Winged Wolf was serious and stern as she cautioned me about doing exactly as she directed without question or hesitation. There were to be no accidents with this boat. It sure looked big to me when I imagined trying to tie up the lines as we came cruising into the tiny dock space where another boat was moored right next to us, and the winds had a tendency to push toward that other boat.

We didn't take the Liberty out on that day, but it wasn't more than a week later that Winged Wolf spontaneously looked at the sky and said, *"Wings, let's take a ride."* That was my cue to know she was making a double entendre. We had to take a ride to the dock and we were taking the boat for a ride. My heart started pounding and my hands were sweaty. Somehow, I managed to release the lines and get my body in the boat as Winged Wolf backed it out. It was then she discovered that the boat didn't back up well, it was a lobster boat and turned differently than most.

We were being pushed by the wind directly toward the boat on our starboard side. *"Get the rod!"* She shouted at me, *"Don't let us hit that boat!"* I had just leaped on the boat from releasing the lines that held us, and was still holding them as I looked around frantically for the rod. Spotting it, I grabbed it and ran to the other side of the boat where I hung my body off the side and pushed us away from the other boat. It was quite a while before my heart stopped pounding and I could breathe normally and relax as Winged Wolf headed out to sea. I didn't want to think about how we would get back into that tiny slot without running into anyone. Life was anything but dull with my Teacher!

Over the next weeks and months, we made many such trips and, although experience went a long way in helping to smooth out our docking, I was always tense for the exits and entrances. This leads me to a highlight of my boating days with the Teacher. It happened quite unexpectedly. We had docked successfully and were standing alongside the boat, when Winged Wolf decided to redo the lines and move the boat forward a bit. She told me to release the stern line, which I did, forgetting that I needed to keep one loop around the mooring hook for leverage.

The day was quite windy and, as I released the line, suddenly the wind gusted and caught the stern, pushing it away from me and toward the port side of the boat along side of us. I was confident, holding the line waiting for further instructions, when the line suddenly became taut in my hands and began to pull me off the dock. Nonplussed, I held firmly to the line as the wind pushed us farther and farther away from the dock until I was just about horizontal to the water. This all happened in a matter of moments. At that pivotal moment when I was looking straight down into the surface of the water, I heard Winged Wolf's shout, **"Don't you dare fall into that ocean!!"** And miraculously, I obediently stood upright, no thought, nothing but motion. I simply stood up, still holding the line, pulling the boat with me as I stood.

Since it happened so quickly, there was no sense of anything extraordinary from my eyes until I saw it afterward from Winged Wolf's description. I hadn't realized my precarious position, so confident was I that I had things under control, until I was nearly in the water, and then she hollered so there was no time to have a reaction, only to respond to her command. Winged Wolf saw something in that scenario that I didn't really grasp for a long time, something about my ability to respond with an act of power to the commanding tone of her voice.

I was in shock, the type of shock when something extraordinary has happened so effortlessly that it almost seems ordinary because the mind can't quite grasp what happened.

It wasn't until we talked about it afterward that I gained a clear perspective. When I said to her that she seemed surprised that I stood up, Winged Wolf said, *"If I had been surprised, you would not have stood up. I was not surprised; I was pleased to see your ability to be in such total companion energy with me for a brief period. Because of that, you could form a link to the Transhistorical Consciousness, and thereby respond with an act of power."*

She went on to make an important, fine-line distinction about acts of power. *"If it had been an individual act of power on your part, you would have remembered it differently. You would have been in a state of mindfulness when it happened, and in that state of mindfulness you would have called forth the spiritual power to stand up on your own. There are no true acts of power without that linkage."*

"This is important for you to understand," she continued; *"it happened because you were able to link with me, and when you heard my voice command you not to fall, you did not fall."*

Then she asked me, *"Do you remember the woman standing on the dock who was so angry with you?"*

"Yes, but I don't recall why she was angry," I replied trying to pull up the scene in my mind. I remembered the woman who was standing on the dock saying something to us after we retied the boat.

"She was angry because you didn't let go of the lines and you could have fallen in the water. She followed us off the dock, bawling you out all the way. She didn't see what really happened; all she saw was that you could have fallen in. If you had performed an individual act of power, you would remember what happened after you stood up, do you see?" she asked focusing her gaze on me, and waiting to see if I got it.

"Now that you have broken it down for me and showed me the different aspects and how they all fit together, I see it," I told her, marveling at her clarity. *"I even remember the lady and her distress, but until you reminded me of her, I had completely forgotten that part.*

"So, two characteristics of acts of power that I see out of this experience are mindfulness and an intact memory. And in mindfulness, it follows that my memory would be intact not only for what occurred in the moment, but what occurred in the moments following. But, since I did not have that mindfulness, what I did have was a strong link to you, my Teacher, and you are mindful and capable of an act of power, and

through that linkage with you, I was able to perform an act of power, but it was not my act of power. That's an important part for me to see."

"You are missing the point," she replied. "You have discovered the personal power that is developed by being wholeheartedly in companion energy."

The Wish-Fulfilling Gem Mantra Enters Our Lives

During my first three-month period on Orcas Island, Winged Wolf had introduced a sacred mantra to us. I'll never forget the morning this was presented. Winged Wolf met me outside the Happy House.

"I had a most extraordinary evening," she said, eyes sparkling, and I noticed her entire being was aglow, radiating with a shining presence. As I looked at her fully, I realized something had dramatically shifted in my Teacher and wondered what might have happened during the previous evening.

She responded, *"It isn't something I can talk specifically about except to tell you I have the most amazing help available to me. There is nothing to be concerned about at all."* Her voice was filled with awe and her eyes had a faraway look as though she were drawn to another place, another time.

The image flashed in my mind that she had been visited by enlightened Teachers from the invisible realm and had been given their backing for the work she was doing. And perhaps received some information about how to teach us. It was not something she talked about with me any further.

In the Happy House that morning, Winged Wolf announced, *"I am going to introduce you to a sacred Teaching in the form of a Mantra. There are a total of sixty-six stanzas but we will only take the first six to begin with. This is a secret Teaching and must be held in absolute sacredness. It has the power to heal, to transform and enlighten. It contains all the highest Teachings and its power is astonishing so we will take it slowly."*

Stillness fell over the room as she began to chant the first stanzas of The Wish Fulfilling Gem Mantra. Her voice resonated with power in the

The Divine Consciousness Moves Quickly

tiny Happy House. This was the beginning of her releasing the sacred Teachings to us. It was a momentous occasion. I was awed as I imagined the kind of night she had spent receiving these Teachings. Sixty-six stanzas! What an amazing gift for the Teacher to be given, and for her to give to her students. She had committed herself totally in service to all sentient life. She said, *"I am a servant of the Transhistorical Consciousness. Everything I do is in service to THAT."*

Under her direction, we began to chant the first stanza. It was a strange, unfamiliar sound, haunting. The words were part Sanskrit, part Pali, and had no meaning to me, nor was there a melody to follow. There was no denying the power of it; Winged Wolf's whole demeanor had changed. It was clear this was a major opening; a privilege granted to us through her dedication and commitment to serve.

"The words have a rhythm and cadence that has the power to bring about change within each of you, regardless of your understanding them, although I will share that with you as well. It is the vibration of the words as they are intoned in this rhythm I am showing you that has the power to transform. This means it is important you learn them exactly as they sound and in the cadence I am chanting them."

We went over and over it, spending extra time with Skywolf, who is deaf. Winged Wolf assigned someone to work with him afterwards so he could get the pronunciation and vibration correctly set in his mind.

"One day, I will write a book in English defining each of the words in great detail, but for now it will suffice for you to know that by chanting these first six stanzas changes will occur within you and doors will be unlocked. Practice it every day as often as possible and pay attention to what you experience from it."

Afterwards, Winged Wolf had rescinded the Mantra for a time, because she felt it was too powerful for people; there was too much happening too quickly. I really didn't comprehend much at that time, not fully grasping the significance of the Mantra. The Mantra had not yet jelled within me to the extent that I felt a strong connection with it, and as I had no experience of the power Winged Wolf spoke of, I could only try to accept what she said without really understanding it.

Gradually she began to reinstate it, but only the first six stanzas. She hinted she might be going to release more of it as we showed a readiness to receive.

Peripherally, I wondered how this Mantra fit in with Winged Wolf's idea of Shamanism. I asked her the question.

She thought a moment and said, *"You know I have always taught my apprentices that my view of Shamanism is not the typical one of drums, rattles and soul retrievals, and for this reason I am always needing to define and redefine Shamanism for people. It is difficult to shake people loose from their preconceived notions as to what constitutes a Shaman.*

"Alana Spirit Changer used a drum, but she had a purpose for it, and she was clear with me that was not my Path as a western woman. That was her *way. Her job with me was to re-awaken me, to shake me up enough that I remembered who I really was. Do you recall what I told you that she said to me?"*

"She said that you already knew everything, so she was not there to teach you, she was there to help you re-awaken to who you were."

"Yes, and you know I began The Eagle Tribe (the original name for our order) in honor of my Teacher for all she had given me, but drums and rattles were never my direction. Alana was clear about that.

"It seems I spend a great deal of my time undoing people's fixed ideas and re-educating them to what it really means to hold the Shaman Consciousness, which is the Christ Consciousness and the Buddha Consciousness. Since Shamanism has become such a popular pursuit among western people, there are mass misconceptions as to what it really means."

What was she really saying here? To me, becoming Shaman was all I had thought about for the past five years. Winged Wolf was redefining my understanding of what this meant. And while she had always likened the Shaman Consciousness to Christ Consciousness or Buddha Consciousness, this had merely given it definition in my mind. Now it seemed so much bigger than my limited idea of what my goal was, as though now my whole understanding of where I was headed was limited by my *box mentality*.

Well, I was willing to expand my idea of what Shamanism really meant, but I came back and asked her, *"Does this mean I will have no contact* with others who are Shaman, because the way we define it is so unusual?"

"That may be true. In the beginning, I used to hear from other Native American Shaman from time to time, but it didn't feel like the direction we would take, and, again, Alana was clear that it was not my Path to become like a Native American Shaman."

There wasn't any question in my mind that we were expanding, but I hadn't put the pieces of the puzzle all together during that trip.

Something's Got to Give

One of the things I noticed about Winged Wolf as the weeks passed was that her body was in pain much of the time. The trauma around Julie's angry departure apparently affected her physically more than I had realized from our phone calls. I saw she was using a walking stick again to come down the hill from her office to the Happy House, and one morning she called to ask me to feed the horses because she couldn't get out of bed; her back was in terrific pain. This went on for several weeks, to a greater or lesser degree, and my concern heightened. Something was really wrong here, but exactly what it was and what to do about it were unclear.

This was a time when Winged Wolf was working seven days a week, full tilt. The cabins were filled with visiting apprentices and she was on the phones two nights a week working with apprentices. She had recently shifted her primary method of correspondence from 'snail mail' to e-mail and this meant more correspondence at a rapid pace. And, on top of this, she was scheduling anywhere from one to three Empowerments, annually.

We were taking a minimum of two months to prepare properly for an Empowerment, including interviewing and hiring cooks, planning menus for over a hundred people and ordering the food, meeting the trucks wherever we were and overseeing the meals.

As my visit progressed, I could see how this continuous, non-stop work schedule was draining her body, creating physical breakdown, especially since she had no real privacy. We finally began scheduling an hour each evening from 5-6pm where she could go to her house and be undisturbed. But this was only a band-aid.

Apprentices continued to arrive for varying lengths of time, and each time a new batch would come, we noticed a cycle begin. Usually they were bringing heavy karmic baggage with them, eager for the Shaman's magic to heal their wounds. Many people had lifetimes of stored-up anger, fear, resentment, and multiple attachments. The image was of carrying a sign in one hand saying, 'Please Help Me,' and in the other hand was a huge suitcase, with ball and chain attaching it to their body. Then the image of the Shaman holding out her hands to take the baggage away, and the apprentice refusing to hand over the key to unlock the ball and chain that held it in place.

Those of us staying on the island and working on the property each day were privy to a side of the work others could not see. We got to see the patterns, not only of ourselves, but also of so many others, and really they were all the same.

We all said we would do anything to achieve the Shaman Consciousness, which we were now expanding to call enlightenment. I pleaded with Winged Wolf to tell me what to do to release my baggage so that I could become a Thunderbeing. No matter how mellow and relaxed I was, it was always there, badgering me in the back of my mind. *'Would this be the trip?'* This time I had waited until the last week of our visit to bring it up. She said, *"Move and live here full-time."* I replied, *"Anything but that."*

Winged Wolf told us repeatedly, *"This Path is for the bold and adventurous. But I'm very patient. I can wait. Anyone who is bold and adventuresome enough to commit to going as far as they can go, I will work with; and if you run into road blocks, I will help you with those too. As long as you keep your eye on the bulls'-eye, and do as I tell you, it is inevitable that you will get there. But if you don't give it all, every bit of yourself, you won't make it past a certain point."*

'There must be another way,' I argued with her silently. *'Surely you don't expect everyone who wants to become Thunderbeing to live here full-time. I don't want to leave my family.'*

It was interesting to watch the effect being with the Teacher had on people. They would come to see her, and for the first three or four days, it looked like nothing was happening, then about that fourth day a major shift occurred in the energy, and the apprentice suddenly let go of whatever was blocking them and then, oh my, they would soar.

Usually by the end of their stay, they were glowing and looked ten years younger and lighter than when they arrived. Invariably, they would be planning their next visit prior to leaving.

But, this was taking such a toll on my Teacher's being! It was too much. She was becoming crippled from it. We could see it couldn't go on, yet she was so committed to her work; each time one of us approached her with a plea to slow down, take a break, all she could see was the people who were counting on her help. For a while, it looked like an impossible situation. We feared she would surely die if this continued, and in fact, Winged Wolf told me one day, *"I know it will shorten my life to go on like this. My body can't take the abuse."*

It was wrenching to watch as she came to the decision that the schedule must change, wrenching because it was that way for her. But there was no choice. There would have to be a structure placed on visits that allowed for recuperation time for the Teacher, and for the staff who worked along with her.

An awakened consciousness has boundless energy, so there was never a difficulty for Winged Wolf in maintaining this grueling schedule energetically, but it was the physical body that suffered. It needed to be rested.

She often told us, *"Be kind to your bodies, they house the consciousness. Feed them properly; rest them, and use them wisely. Don't put any garbage into them, and this includes the images you input via books you read, people you hang out with, and activities you engage in. Remember, the brain is a part of the body, and it takes a healthy brain to achieve enlightenment. It is the divine consciousness that uses the brain to produce the mental images you live in."*

Winged Wolf restructured the visiting apprentice program to support having a healthy body herself. The newly implemented Wisdom Traveler program was already set in place. The program included discourses on topics across the board: science, parenting, healing, the dreamtime and more. Each discourse was presented from the viewpoint of the enlightened consciousness, making it a rich addition to the existing program. Winged Wolf perceived that apprentices had holes in their understanding of the Teachings, and this new program would help to fill in the holes.

The new schedule was implemented, and balance was restored. There was still a rigorous schedule to follow, but with time built in for rest and recuperation, the energy was much lighter.

Once the schedule changes were in place, and there were always exceptions, a new cycle was set in motion, one that had more definition to it and provided some much-needed structure. **It was educational to watch an organization evolve from the demands or energies of the moment rather than to begin with a structure and have the energies fit into it.** Out of the disorder came the order; it was as if the energies found all our soft spots and pressed on them until Winged Wolf responded by shoring up in that area.

Visiting apprentices found it difficult at first because they had to adjust to the idea of being flexible as to what time slot they were assigned, since it was sometimes impossible to give people their first or even second choices. Sometimes there was no room at all. Winged Wolf now had apprentices all over the world. Some apprentices became resourceful and began seeking out local apprentices to stay with, or renting places as Walter and I had done. How fascinating to watch as those who really wanted it found a way to be near the Teacher.

Our five months came to a peaceful conclusion and once again we packed up and headed east. The extended stay had been a time of rapid growth and expansion for me. But it had been bumpy for Walter who seemed to be floundering, unable to pass through some difficult spots. I was concerned about him, but assured myself that in time he would be fine.

Chapter 19
Attachments Threaten My Apprenticeship

"There are always signs that tell us what will happen next from where we stand, but our likes and dislikes camouflage them."
(Winged Wolf)

Rumors that Winged Wolf was considering a move toward declaring us a formal organization, a religion, in fact, nearly unhinged me. There was no reason I should have been so surprised, as several times during my stay she had talked about the growing necessity to formalize our structure. She said it was inevitable this would happen as we evolved, and even though she had previously assured us we would not move in this direction, for legal reasons, she was now convinced it was the only direction for us to go.

She talked with others as well, testing the waters, exploring, backing off if the reaction was strong, moving in again when things settled down. At the time my five-month visit had concluded, she was quiet on the subject and I had put it out of mind. There was no appeal to me in the idea, so less said the better.

One apprentice friend came home from a visit to *Between* in an uproar. She called to let off steam and probably gain support for her opposition, saying that Winged Wolf had called a meeting to discuss possibilities for registering HÜMÜH as a religion! Also during her visit, the name HÜMÜH had become the official name for the Path. It was a composite of the Sanskrit word HÜM that we chanted every morning, and the letters ÜH which, when added to the ending of HÜM, gave a mirror image or reflective quality to it. The apprentice told me she had tried to convince Winged Wolf that an educational heading would be just as efficient and not so defining as calling us a religion. Then the question was, *"What religion?"*

"Buddhist," was the response.

"Buddhist," I exclaimed! *"What does that mean to our goal of becoming Shaman? I don't know anything about Buddhism, and I don't want to know anything about it."*

The apprentice replied, *"According to Winged Wolf, the Teachings are exactly the same; in fact, she said the Teachings have been Buddhist all along, only she didn't fully realize this until her memories of previous lives began to return. And there are Shaman Buddhists called Bön or Dzogchen, which is identical to the Teachings of HÜMÜH, although she said that HÜMÜH also encompasses aspects of Mahayana and Vajrayana Buddhism."*

Hanging up the phone, I quickly called Winged Wolf who happened to pick up on the other end. My emotions were running high and I could feel myself shaking with righteous indignation. *"Someone just called to tell me you are considering calling us a Buddhist religion."* It was an accusation.

There was a silence. I knew she was debating whether to engage in this conversation. *"Now, Wings of Change, nothing is finalized yet, but it is true that this seems to fit who we are and it takes away all the misconceptions in people's minds about Shamanism as taught by HÜMÜH.*

"I've been trying for all these years to clarify Shamanism to people, but it's a constant effort. There is so much misunderstanding in people's minds, because most Shaman practices involve native rituals that are confusing to the Western Mind, and I'm not sure it is possible to untangle it. And besides, there is absolutely no change in our Teachings. Nothing I have taught has changed an iota. **The Teachings are exactly the same!"**

I could feel the ring of truth in what she said, but no words came. After a pause, in which I'm sure she could feel my rigid opposition, she said, *"Don't get caught up in thinking form is important. It doesn't matter. We need a form that supports the work I am to do. The only thing that matters is that I can do my work, and I can't do it if I'm spending all my time correcting misconceptions."* And then she said, *"I need you to be with me on this, Wings of Change."*

Attachments Threaten My Apprenticeship

Of course, a part of me understood exactly what she was saying and knew that form was only a man-made structure that supported the expression of primordial truth. All great religions were that, houses for the Primordial Teachings, but most religions had no living master to perpetuate the Teachings in their pristine form. This was what our Teacher represented to us, a living master to point the way to our awakening.

Finally I responded, *"I'm not sure I can do that, Winged Wolf. My goal is to become Shaman, and I have no interest in religion. That's why I'm not involved with any church."*

"You can still become Shaman; I'm still Shaman, that hasn't changed, but there is more, and I will be able to take you even further if we go in this direction. Becoming a religion will actually give us the freedom we need to do the work. You remember I always told you that Alana never wanted me to do what she did. She said I already knew everything, but I just needed someone to wake me up to it. That was what she did. It wasn't her intention that I follow in her footsteps."

Then she reminded me of something. *"It isn't as if Buddhism has not been a part of my life since childhood. You know I was given a book on Milarepa as a young girl. And, when I worked as a translator for Buddhist sutras in Japan, I was ordained as a Monk."*

She had mentioned this to me previously but it had been such a casual conversation and I had been so judgmental about her leaving when her father was ill, that I hadn't paid much attention to the Buddhist aspect and how pivotal a point that had been in her life. Now I saw how the strands of continuity to Buddhism had been woven into her entire life.

For the next several weeks, the conversation raged among apprentices as the word spread. There were three issues involved here that were directly opposite of what our origins had been, what had drawn many of us to this Teacher. We were looking at moving into a formal organizational structure, complete with government registration, and we were including Buddhism with Shamanism; and lastly, we were moving from a non-formalized religion to a formalized religion.

If we didn't take issue with one aspect, there were others to embrace and as it happened, I took exception to all and I did so vigorously and righteously. After agonizing for weeks over these changes, I wrote Winged Wolf and said, *"I don't feel I can continue with my apprenticeship under these circumstances, even though I am able to understand your rationale for taking these steps. It doesn't feel like the Path I chose when I became your apprentice."*

What a bittersweet moment this was for me as I recalled the tremendous relief of finding this Teacher who would take me to my heart's desire, happiness and peace of mind. And I felt sorry for myself that my life was now taking such a turn.

Winged Wolf wrote back; *"Call me"* was all she said. Although it seemed hopeless, I also prayed she might find some way to help me adjust my perception of what was occurring so I did not have to leave the Path. It would be much worse than any divorce from a friendship or marriage. This was beyond any worldly relationship. This was my life.

While my personality was raging, my inner voice, the one I had always valued to guide me in a sane manner in a direction that uplifted, was saying, *'It is not the time to quit. You have to ride this out to its natural completion.'* And I would respond, *'I'm not going to do it.'* Then there would be silence, but in the silence between the sounds, I knew the voice of my own divinity was telling me to go on.

I called. Again Winged Wolf talked to me, slowly and patiently, as to a stubborn child. *"If you want to leave the Path, I understand,"* she said. *"I will be greatly saddened, but I will always love you unconditionally. I realize there will be losses due to the changes in our Spiritual Order, but I also know it is the right direction, and I cannot go against that no matter how I might want to. I can't stop the energies that are evolving and guiding us or we will be as a derailed train, we will come to a screeching halt. I am a servant of the divine consciousness; it is not a matter of what I as a personality choose, although there really isn't much difference anymore."*

She paused, then went on, *"I have to move in the direction that serves us best even if I lose you. But once again I say to you, 'Do not get caught up in form because the form really doesn't make a difference.' Whether we are called Buddhist or Shaman or both; whether we are a religion or not, that's all part of the dual worlds. We are talking about what is the most effective way of functioning in the dual worlds, always maintaining our impeccability."* After a few moments, *"Why don't you take a few days to consider what will really serve you best, take it into the silence and really look at it?"*

Attachments Threaten My Apprenticeship

There it was. She was not pressuring me or trying to convince me of anything, nor was she going to change her course to please me. The bottom line was, I could take it or leave it. Winged Wolf and her vision would carry on with me or without me. I knew it had to be this way; she could not be run by all the whims of her apprentices or we would run amuck. I agreed to spend some time in the silence before making a final decision.

A week passed. I cried and grumbled and complained and prayed and felt sorry for myself. It felt like I was between a rock and a hard place. I wanted my Teacher; I knew she was enlightened. And she fully intended to lead me to my own enlightenment, but I had to be willing to give up *my way* and accept her way, and I didn't want to do it. None of the choices were acceptable; yet doing nothing was not acceptable either.

She would challenge me if I were not wholehearted in accepting her direction. It wasn't a Path where you could fake something for long. It showed up as a disturbance of energy in the pristine environment. Oh, she wouldn't turn me away as an apprentice, but she wouldn't allow me to be part of the inner circle if I was half-hearted. And the inner circle was where rapid growth occurred. Anything other than wholeheartedness was unacceptable to me because it wasn't impeccable.

By the end of the week, I had heard enough of myself, was bored with the obsessive conversations in my head and with others. It was decision time. I asked myself, *'Are you willing to trust Winged Wolf to guide you to where you say you want to go? And, are you willing to trust yourself in choosing her as your guide?*

'Hmmm, seems better to trust the Teacher than myself, since my own decisions haven't produced the spiritual awakening I desire.' Once I realized I was afraid of trusting myself, afraid of being made a fool of, it simplified things. I couldn't trust Winged Wolf if I couldn't trust my own decisions. I had already tried to do it on my own and discovered it couldn't be done, at least not by me. If I asked myself the question, *'If you die now, do you have any regrets?'* the answer came back, *'Yes, I stopped short.'*

Interestingly, I had asked myself this question many times over the course of my lifetime; it always had the potency to bring me into full awareness of the moment, and usually provided a pivotal viewpoint as to my wholeheartedness. During my apprenticeship with Winged Wolf, the answer had always come back, *'If I die now, I have no regrets because I am living wholeheartedly. Even if I have not achieved full awakening, I am on the road to it.'*

When I looked at terminating my apprenticeship, there was an awareness of collapsing the dream and returning to ordinary existence, a life of settling for less than one-hundred-percent. It was a depressing thought, terrifying really. The inner guidance I had always relied on for direction urged me to continue with my Teacher.

So I e-mailed her. *"If I look at my choices, and I must say these choices are defined by you, I choose to follow you regardless of the form that following may take. I realize there is nothing holding me to you except my own choosing of that. Once I choose to follow you, I also surrender my vote as to how you lead me. I see I must learn to be a better follower, a less-resistant student. I will give it my best no matter what."* And, before I could change my mind, I hit the 'send' button.

From this point on, I attempted to speak to others who were in similar states of ambivalence and upset as Winged Wolf had spoken to me. The more I spoke, the easier it was to let go of my attachment to the form, and to recognize how this attachment to form was a subtle thread weaving throughout my life.

Always I had designed my life in the form that felt right to me; and now I was looking at a design that worked to evolve the whole but had no personal vibration for me. What a realization it was for me to see that I could surrender 'my way' for the good of the whole and discover the good of the whole included me! It produced a shift in perspective. The viewpoint was larger than any individual, yet it encompassed every individual. Now, it was evident that Winged Wolf was not necessarily operating out of what suited her as a personality, but what allowed the maximum service to others.

How fascinating it is to contemplate this idea that what we dislike or like is irrelevant to defining our choices when the commitment is to awakening the divine self and live for the good of the whole.

After she received my e-mail, my relationship with Winged Wolf picked up where I had left off prior to my crisis. That is to say, she got back to the business at hand, which was teaching me, as she continued to set up the structure that would evolve the whole into a Buddhist religion.

Attachments Threaten My Apprenticeship

After all, her goal had not changed. She was committed to awaken individuals, and this was the vehicle she saw that could best accomplish that.

The next time we talked, she said, *"I want you to give up having opinions, likes and dislikes."* I reflexively said, *"Okay,"* then thought about it for a moment. *"If I don't have opinions, what do I have?"*

"Direct perceptions," she replied. *"You must learn to look at the energy of a situation and directly perceive what is occurring, but you may not have an opinion about it. In other words, I'm saying you must stop interpreting things through your little-self, dual-world viewpoint, and simply observe what is. Have no opinion about it whatsoever. I want you to practice this and notice what occurs as a result. Will you do that?"*

"I'll give it my best shot," I agreed, although in my gut I could feel a tightening. The squeeze was on. She had reached for a handle and pulled hard. My personality was loaded with opinions, about everything. I was always judging other people and situations based on my attitudes and opinions. It was part of who I was, how I defined myself. *'I am this way, and you are that way; I approve of you or I don't.'* It gave definition to life. And how could one live without likes and dislikes? How would decisions be made? That was even more elusive to grasp. There was this strange sense of loss that immediately resulted as I agreed to give these up. Also, it particularly meant I had to stop judging the Teacher via my opinions. In other words, if she said, *'We'll be Buddhist,'* I was to have no opinion about that, nor should I like it or dislike it. How bizarre! Down the road there was great freedom that became apparent from this perspective.

Unconscious Habitual Behaviors

Although things were flowing pretty smoothly, Winged Wolf never let up on me about the impact of my unconscious behaviors. Each trip uprooted different aspects of my ego's attempts to feel important.

It was a cool day, overcast but not unusual for Orcas in the fall. Two visiting apprentices had taken the rowboat out onto the pond and were happily rowing. I could see them from where I stood sweeping the office deck. As I watched, one of the apprentices stood up in the boat, and I inhaled, holding my breath as the boat first rocked back and forth, and then capsized.

By the time I reached the pond, someone had helped them out of the water and pulled the boat to shore. No one looked injured, only dripping wet. But I heard one woman say, *"I don't know how to swim,"* and her voice was trembling. And again, *"I don't know how to swim, I could have drowned!"*

Walter was trying to reassure her, by saying, *"There's no way you would have drowned; the water where you went in was only three feet deep."*

Her voice was getting shrill and she began to blame the other apprentice who stood up in the boat for capsizing them. It looked like the situation was about to escalate, so I stepped over to her and suggested we walk up the hill and find some dry clothes for her.

She came along with me, now crying and repeating herself about not being able to swim. We sat on the side of the deck and I said, *"Tell me everything that happened."*

So she launched into her story, crying and sniffing, and getting more and more sympathy from me. I was patting her on the back, trying to be supportive and calm her down, when Winged Wolf arrived on the scene, got a brief summary and said to the apprentice, *"You're fine. You can't drown in that pond; it's three feet deep at the deepest point. Go get some dry clothes on and I'll see you in a little while."*

To my amazement, the woman got up, stopped crying, and said, *"All right,"* and headed off toward her cabin.

Then Winged Wolf turned her full force onto me. *"What did you think you were doing?"*

"I was trying to calm her down," I told her.

"You were sympathizing with her, patting her. Why the next thing you know she would have been hysterical. Don't ever patronize someone. You feed their little-selves. There was nothing wrong with her. She wasn't hurt. That's all you needed to know. You were making yourself feel important by patting her."

Attachments Threaten My Apprenticeship

Inside, I rose up to argue with her. *'I'm a trained therapist and here my Teacher is telling me I don't know how to handle an emotionally upset person. I can't believe she didn't even give her a kind word.'*

The second time it happened was only a few days later with a different apprentice. She had come down from Winged Wolf's office in tears, and I was the first person she saw. I listened sympathetically as she told me how the Teacher had upset her. And I put my arm around her shoulders at the precise moment Winged Wolf walked up.

"Don't you dare interfere with the work I am doing with other apprentices," she glared at me.

The apprentice hurried away down the path and Winged Wolf continued, "She doesn't need your sympathy; she needs to be strong enough to face some things in her life. To give her sympathy will only weaken her."

"It wasn't sympathy, Winged Wolf, it was empathy. I was letting her vent her feelings."

"That's your ego talking again, playing therapist, wanting to feel important. You will undermine my work if you don't get a handle on your unconscious habitual behavior and see it for what it is."

'That's twice in the same week,' I told myself. *'There is something for you to see here.'* One conclusion was obvious. That would be the last time I would offer a sympathetic ear to a visiting apprentice. But in my heart, I disagreed with Winged Wolf's treatment of these apprentices. I felt she was being too harsh.

In meditation the next morning, I had a flash; a light literally went on in my mind. I was treating other apprentices the way I wanted Winged Wolf to treat me, to patronize and sympathize with me, to see my point of view, to make me feel important.

Joshua Tree

During this visit, we were preparing for the next empowerment, which was to be held at Joshua Tree, California. This was a big one because Winged Wolf had privately let us locals know she intended to release *The Wish-Fulfilling Gem Mantra* in full.

Previously she had withheld it for several reasons; first and foremost, it contained the encapsulated energy of all the Primordial Teachings. In other words, it held enormous power. Then, to write it down and distribute it meant trusting that those receiving it would treat it in the sacred manner in which it was intended. Further, it would have an enormous impact on peoples' lives, and the Teacher would ultimately be responsible for all that occurred as a result.

Even though it was written primarily in Sanskrit, the chanting of the Mantra, regardless of direct understanding of its meaning, gave one the full impact of the energy behind the meaning. This meant if it were chanted regularly, peoples' lives would never be the same. Eventually, they would develop a spiritualized consciousness.

The sixty-six stanzas to the Mantra had taken Winged Wolf two years to bring out in their entirety. There were months of bringing out a few stanzas, taking them back, bringing them out again, all in oral form, prior to her final decision to put it into print. Then she wrote an *Illuminator* to define the terms used. Just presenting it to us for usage at *Between the Wind* was a huge step, and the decision to give it to those attending the empowerment at Joshua Tree was enormous. Thus, there was both excitement and tension as the event loomed nearer.

This was a time in my apprenticeship that certain lines were clearly drawn for me in my mind that defined who I was to the Path. I was a part-timer. There were those apprentices who had chosen to live on Orcas Island full-time and devote their entire existences to the pursuit of enlightenment. Other apprentices were long-distance, visiting on occasion, living in the world, integrating what they learned from the Teachings into their lives.

Neither of those categories quite fit my situation. What worked for me, now that I was over the hump of 'believing' I could not be away from home more than three weeks at a time, was to spend three to five months at a time on Orcas, during which time I was a local, then leave for several months, during which time I was living in the world. There was a comfortable flow to this lifestyle and I appreciated each more for having the other.

This balance appealed to me on all levels. It appeased my appetite for worldly existence and a closer relationship with my family, and it satisfied my longing for spiritual development. To me, it seemed the

Attachments Threaten My Apprenticeship

perfect plan, but Winged Wolf was not in agreement with this lifestyle I had designed. She repeatedly told me I had a weakness for worldly things that would eventually sabotage my spiritual growth on the Path. I was resistant to this viewpoint, as I felt I had given in as far as I was willing to give when I agreed to spend several months at a time on Orcas. That was surely my limit. I still couldn't grasp that there are no limitations to an awakened consciousness. My limitations were always protecting my little-self interests.

The Power of Laughter

One of the things that made my Teacher so effective and engaging was her ability to laugh and make me laugh. Others experienced this as well. No matter how serious the subject, how difficult the situation, she could always find laughter buried at the bottom of it. I don't mean she laughed inappropriately, although to an outsider hearing about it, it might seem that way. When my mother was dying, Winged Wolf was the height of compassion and loving support, but she could still find a way to lift my sadness and burden with some laughter. She showed me the illusion, time and time again. After all, life is impermanent and my mother was ninety-two. She was ready to leave.

During that heavy time for me, prior to the Joshua Tree Empowerment, I called her in a fit of despair. My mother, now ninety-two, was in the hospital after experiencing heart failure. My dad was refusing to leave her side, and her doctor had no privileges at Sarasota Memorial, the only hospital in town. We were at the mercy of whatever staff resident they assigned her. I was beside myself trying to get her a good doctor, and she kept telling me she was ready to die.

"No, you can't die," I pleaded with her, panic stricken, *"who will take care of dad?"* That had been my ploy with her for the past several years to keep her alive. She kept saying her body was worn out and she was ready to go, but who would take care of dad? Selfishly, I simply couldn't bear the thought of her dying. We were so close and I so adored her that, while some sane part of me knew she was entitled to die when she was ready, the irrational part did everything I could think of to manipulate her into sticking around.

I was just returning from getting a bite to eat in the cafeteria when Walter pulled me aside, *"I told her we'd take care of your dad if she wanted to go."*

"What?" I screamed at him. *"Why did you do that? I don't want her to die."* While I was yelling at him, I was also running to her room to try and take back what he had said.

As soon as she saw me she said, *"Walter said you and he will take care of your dad if I die, will you?"*

"No, mom, we can't do that. You have to take care of dad; he won't listen to me." I said this simultaneous to Walter's saying, *"Yes, Kate, we'll take care of him. Don't worry. If you want to go, it's okay."*

I was beside myself. Walter couldn't make promises for me. We took dad home and spent the night with him, planning to return to the hospital the next morning. After getting dad to bed, I called Winged Wolf, crying. She listened compassionately for a while. Then she said, *"Have you had a dream of your mother dying?"*

"No, why?" I asked.

"She'll come to you in a dream before she dies. That's when you will know she's ready. You know, Wings of Change," she said gently, *"we're all going to die. There's nothing wrong with that. It's part of the cycle of birth and death. Your mother's tired, and her body is worn out. Taking care of your dad has been hard on her these past few years. Let her go. Don't try to hold her here. It's time to let go. It's not like she's actually going anyplace. She's just shedding a physical body that no longer serves her."*

Each time I felt myself begin to relax, listening to her soothing words and laughing with her as she gently prodded me to see the ridiculousness of the position I was trying to maintain, suddenly as I saw the truth, my fear would rise and I would feel defensive again.

Sensing this, Winged Wolf took a new tactic and began to distract me with something that had occurred at *Between the Wind*. As she captured my attention and drew me away from the heaviness of my present experience, she told me a story that was really funny, about an apprentice who had to be carted around in the wheelbarrow by other apprentices because she had arrived at *Between* in such a run-down state. Winged Wolf refused to allow her to walk anywhere as a result, of

Attachments Threaten My Apprenticeship

course exaggerating the situation to the extreme, until the apprentice felt totally foolish and embarrassed. For sure, she would never arrive in such a state again.

And as I joined with Winged Wolf in laughter at the ridiculous image this created, I could feel all the tension drain completely out of my body and I relaxed. There was life beyond my own little drama. It was a life seen from the divine perspective, free from attachment, unbound by all the entanglements. Yet I understood she was not telling me to pretend not to feel any pain from the loss, only not to get carried away with trying to hang on to something that shouldn't be held on to, to realize life as the dreamtime and not get caught up in the illusion.

There was such healing in those few moments of deep laughter, with full awareness that nothing in my situation had changed; yet my suffering about it had been lifted. I could see where I had been caught in the drama. I still had to face tomorrow, but that night I felt stronger and more able to do that because she had used the laughter to adjust my distorted viewpoint. My poor mother wanted nothing more than to be released from her worn-out body, and I was now able to let her go. My attachment to her was so great; it completely threw me out of balance into a state of temporary insanity. Winged Wolf helped me shift my assemblage point, so I could let go. And that night I dreamed of a beautiful yellow bird in a gilded cage. The bird was pecking away on the metal posts that held the cage together, finally breaking one apart. The bird flew out of the cage to freedom. And the next day my mother died.

Other times Winged Wolf would laugh because of the absolute absurdity of a situation, or the mental imagery we carried in our minds, often in the most 'serious' situations. Sometimes she would laugh so hard tears streamed down her face as she caught an image that flashed through the mind of one of us. She said, *"There are bubbles of energy that are released with the images that flash through your minds, and they can appear so ridiculous that all I can do is laugh at them."*

"People take themselves so seriously," she used to tell me, *"to the point that they spend lifetimes staring at themselves. You can't release your karma while staring at yourself."*

Then she looked me straight in the eye and said, *"You stare at yourself too much, always worrying about whether you did the right thing, or said the right thing. You have to learn to look* out*; stop that analyzing."*

"Do you mean that if I'm trying to understand something I did, or I am admonishing myself for something, that is staring at myself? I don't think I really know what you mean by staring at myself!"

"Yes, all of that is staring at yourself, but there's more to it than that. It's all the attention you give yourself, all the 'what ifs,' and the 'why didn't I's,' and the 'why me's?' See, it's all about 'me, me, me,' and it shouldn't be. That's not the way to develop your consciousness. You do that by looking out of yourself, by being in service to others, keeping your attention at the Third Eye, which automatically places you in the viewpoint of 'looking out.'

"The more you stare at yourself, meaning analyze things, the bigger your problems become." She went on, *"It is spiritual law that 'much makes more,' so the more time you spend looking at your concerns, the more you magnify them. They can never be released as long as you are staring at them."*

"But, Winged Wolf," I argued, *"I don't understand how something can go away just by my not looking at it. Isn't that just hiding my head in the sand?"*

"Not at all," she replied, *"quite the opposite. It isn't that you are unaware of what situations are in your life, but you might be surprised to know that by looking at what you do want, instead of what you don't want, and keeping your attention focused on that, wholeheartedly, the baggage just naturally drops away. You've had some experiences that demonstrate this.*

Chapter 20
Endings and Beginnings

The time approaching the Joshua Tree Empowerment had been spent in Florida, including my mother's illness and finally, her death. Also, I had been finishing a book I began writing the year before, mostly as an exercise in self-discipline, but it turned out to be quite enjoyable. It was a big commitment for me and, once started, the book had taken on a life of its own. Every day when I sat down at my computer to write, it was as if I were beginning an adventure. It was a 'sit-and-write-no-matter-what' type of thing. Winged Wolf had told me that the only way to actually write a book was to discipline one's self by writing every day, preferably at the same time. She had said if I felt stuck, to simply write about feeling stuck and pretty soon the blockage would open up and it would flow again.

It had become another form of healing salve, as I was still deeply grieving the loss of my mother who had been so much a part of my everyday life and thoughts that I couldn't imagine not being able to pick up the phone to call her. Plus, every day had been partly spent taking care of my father who was failing rapidly since mom's death. He was totally lost. I had hired a live-in caretaker but still had tried to visit at least every other day. Writing a book had given me some relief from the painful reality of losing one parent and knowing it was just a matter of time before the other one would go.

Since I never knew where the plot of the book was going to head or what would happen as I followed it along, it had kept me on the edge of my seat. The story seemed to be pulled from my subconscious. I wanted to be a writer, and the only way I could do it was to sit and wait for the words to come out. Winged Wolf had encouraged me to write and talked to me of the power of writing as a tool for self-discovery (She had even written a book by that title).

"No matter what, discipline yourself to write at a certain time each day," had been her advice to me; I had taken her words seriously and had committed time each day to writing. The experience had been expanding me, and it commanded my attention. Even when I wasn't writing, a part of me was living inside the book, merged with all the characters. It had been difficult for me to turn my attention toward the upcoming empowerment at Joshua Tree. It seemed like another lifetime.

When I arrived at Joshua Tree, a day early as Winged Wolf had requested, part of me was still in Florida, immersed in the book, writing, taking care of dad, walking on the beach, and trying to survive emotionally. Winged Wolf was full-speed-ahead with plans for releasing *The Wish-Fulfilling Gem Mantra* and excited about the evolution of our Spiritual Order into its newly developing form. I was personally excited because two of our adult children, my son Terry and step-daughter Michelle, would be in attendance. It was a dream come true to have Terry there, and a brave stepping out for him in view of negative family opinions. I hoped he would see the opportunity presented and become an apprentice. Michelle already was.

Three of us apprentices arrived in time to pick up Winged Wolf at the airport in Palm Desert, and upon her arrival, the energy immediately changed. It became electrified as her consciousness took charge of the situation. We had been casually enjoying each other, a bit too relaxed for what the moment called for. Shortly thereafter, the environment began reflecting this. The apprentice driving was a delightful woman and had become a friend of mine; she lived in nearby Palm Desert and had helped coordinate the event. Also with us was the office manager from *Between the Wind*, a capable woman who usually was good at managing all the particles. The three of us would attend to Winged Wolf while Walter and some of the others managed all the logistics.

Now, driving out of the airport after picking up Winged Wolf, the apprentice driving the van began driving erratically. This was totally unlike her. I mean really erratically.

"What are you doing?" Winged Wolf said sharply to her.

"I'm driving," was the response.

"Well, be careful, you're all over the road," Winged Wolf said more sharply as we barely missed hitting a car coming from the other direction.

The driving became more erratic. For some reason, she couldn't seem to keep the vehicle on our side of the road, and she was chattering on and on effusively. There was a hysterical quality to her energy that hadn't been present until Winged Wolf arrived.

"Pull over there," Winged Wolf pointed to an open place across the road. And the apprentice turned quickly in front of several oncoming vehicles that honked wildly at her. My stomach was in knots. *'What is going on here?'* I asked silently.

"What is wrong with you?" Winged Wolf demanded, her voice carrying the intensity of the situation. *"You just turned in front of all those cars without even signaling. Please, get in the back. Wings, you drive."*

After experiencing this intense comedy, I felt a bit smug, knowing my driving would be fine. But it wasn't more than five minutes later that I made a wild right turn, throwing Winged Wolf across the seat, and Winged Wolf once again cried out, *"Stop the car. Laurie, you drive."*

Fortunately things settled down after this, although you could cut the tension in the air. There was total silence in the van until we pulled into the parking lot of the motel where we all were staying the night. I could feel Winged Wolf holding the energy tightly as she looked straight ahead, probably wondering what had happened that two of her advanced apprentices were falling apart. What I didn't know at that point was that Laurie had her own difficulties, but that came out later. At the time, she seemed the stable part of our threesome.

We were a quiet group getting out of the van and escorting Winged Wolf to her room. I'm sure each of us was speculating on the reflections produced in the environment by our wildly uncontained energy. It was uncomfortable to be confronted with something so glaring that I thought I had well hidden, and for me, it was my difficulty in shifting my attention to being there. Awareness certainly had its painful moments.

I wasn't too surprised later that evening when there was a knock on my door and Laurie said, *"Winged Wolf would like to see you in about five minutes."*

'Oh boy, I know she's going to confront me on my not being wholehearted,' I thought, and began pacing. There was always anxiety present when I was called to task for something; it was not something I ever got used to, even though it happened often enough.

Gently I rapped on her door. *"It's open,"* I heard her say quietly. *"Come in and sit down, Wings. There is something I want to propose to you and I want you to consider it deeply for at least three days before you respond."*

This wasn't what I had anticipated. Now I was curious. *"All right, Winged Wolf,"* I responded, *"What is it?"*

She stood and walked around the room for a bit, then went to her briefcase and pulled out a folder. She came back and sat next to me on the edge of the bed, slowly opening the folder and thumbing through some paperwork that was in it.

"This will be a turning point in your life if you agree to it, a major shifting of priorities. I'm telling you right now, it will set something in motion that, once begun, you will not be able to stop."

A phone conversation that had occurred a couple months prior and seemed innocent at the time, popped into my mind. She and I had been on the phone; I was in Florida, and she had been talking to me about the difficulties of making the leap from Lightbearer to Thunderbeing. A Lightbearer was really an advanced Sage, and Winged Wolf had said, *"This is the last of the merit badges. Up until this stage, you earn titles based on successful Initiation Journey completions; and they are similar to completing courses in college. But beyond this point, there is a shift in consciousness that can occur only by 'catching' it."* In other words, beyond the merit badges was an awakening that couldn't be taught to the intellectual mind; it had to be caught by an awakening of the divinity of the person.

She was telling me what a big leap this was for most people and she didn't see quite how we apprentices were going to make that leap. She said that perhaps an interim level or step was needed that would be an awakening of a lesser order than the leap to Thunderbeing. I had giggled to myself at that because sometime earlier I had joked to Walter, *"Watch, she's going to have so many interim levels that we'll never get to Thunderbeing. I'll be walking with a cane before I get there."*

That little semi-serious joke flashed through my mind as she said, *"The only way to achieve these higher levels of awareness is through service. You know, all I am is a servant to the Transhistorical Consciousness."*

At the time she said it, it struck me that I, too, was a servant to the Consciousness via my commitment to the Path and Winged Wolf, although to a lesser degree because my consciousness was not as evolved, and I said, *"It seems to me the natural next step is to become a servant."*

She laughed and replied, *"Everybody would run for the hills if I told them they were to become servants. Can you imagine the reaction?"*

"Oh, I don't think they would see it that way, Winged Wolf, I certainly don't. You've always said you are only a servant. I'd consider it an honor. It seems perfectly natural to me to be called a servant, especially since that's how you refer to yourself."

Now, as Winged Wolf pulled a piece of papyrus paper out of her folder, I realized where this conversation had led us. She handed it to me and said, *"Read this first, then we'll talk about it."* I noticed that while she was referring to it as Savant now, my vow was titled 'Servant.' I wondered about that, but didn't ask.

Being a servant of the Path had seemed fine to me as we talked about it, an honor, but as was often the case, Winged Wolf had seen deeply into the real meaning or intention of the role and written the vow accordingly. This meant there was a twist. As I scanned it, my heart stopped beating for a moment.

The part that caught my attention said, *"Your first and foremost consideration is to be of service and to live in service to the* **Three Jewels, with the Teachings, the Teacher and the Path** *dominating your entire field of attention. This means, even though you may be attending to some personal matter, all thoughts, words and actions will be integrated into the* **Three Jewels**.*"*

I felt weak and dizzy, my mind reeling with thoughts and fears about what was to be given up. What about my husband? What about my children and my yet-to-be born grandchildren? With a sinking feeling, I saw how this would play out. It was inevitable that I move to be nearer Winged Wolf, that service to her would become my life; all else would be background. How could I possibly agree to something this profound without losing myself? And how would my family respond?

"It is a big commitment, I know, but it will take you where you want to go. I've always told you the Path will take everything from you and it will, but, oh, what you get in return! If only I could show you the bliss that I feel in living my life as a servant to the Transhistorical Consciousness, the freedom that comes with crossing that irreversible line. It seems narrow as you are walking toward it, but after you cross over it, the whole world opens up to you, without limitations or restrictions. It is pure joy and bliss, but I can only tell you how it is, you must discover it for yourself by stepping forward."

As I left her, with written vow in hand, she gave instructions to *"Take three days before making a decision."* That would put us at the end of the empowerment. She had asked me to send Walter over, and as I watched him head down for her door, I wondered if he, too, was to become a Savant, as she had decided to title it.

There was relief to having the room to myself for a while because my brain was so scrambled I didn't think I could act normally, and I was under orders to mention this to no one. I read and re-read the vow. *"Giving yourself means that none other comes before the Three Jewels; that is, your first and foremost consideration is to be of service and to live in service to the Three Jewels, with The Teachings, The Teacher and the Path dominating your entire field of attention."*

This was a life-altering vow. Was I willing to put the Path first and foremost in my life ahead of all else? While my mind hollered 'no,' I laughed out loud as once again I found myself in the big squeeze that had become so familiar to my progress as an apprentice. Knowing full well I would sign it, still the agonizing process of coming to a wholehearted decision took place.

On the one hand, I wanted enlightenment more than anything and I said I was willing to do anything to realize it; on the other hand, this squeeze that accompanied my growth was so miserably uncomfortable. It was my own resistance that produced the tension that caused the feeling of being squeezed, but knowing it didn't help. It was just intellectual information. Living it hurt. Questions raced through my mind as I read and re-read this vow.

'What about Walter and my commitment to him? He now takes a second position. And I have a family. Aren't they supposed to be first in my life? Why must there be a decision about one being over the other?' This was really confronting all my learned values. *'I hate always having to make these difficult decisions. Why do I always have to give up something?'* I fumed.

Finally, I saw the humor of my self-imposed crisis, and laughed out loud, a real belly laugh, as I watched the comedy of my life re-enacting itself the same way over and over again. It felt so good to lighten up and laugh; my heart could open now and I could relax. Of course I would become a servant of the Three Jewels. What else was I intending to do with my life? Hadn't I already given myself to this? Winged Wolf had been teaching us for years that our spiritual life had to take the number one slot if we were to make it to enlightenment. What was the big surprise? By the time Walter returned, I had accepted my decision.

He didn't say anything about their conversation and I watched him to see if he was reacting as I had to being asked to become a Servant, but he seemed perfectly normal. In the morning, after he had gone to breakfast, I signed my pledge, two copies, one for me and one for the Teacher. No need to wait three days for this decision.

After signing my name, I felt different. Even though it wasn't spelled out what this meant to my life and how it would be enacted in my relationship with the Teacher and the Path, changes began to take place in me immediately.

My attention became riveted on the Teacher, and all else shifted to the periphery. I looked about me with new eyes. Whereas before there was a split in my attention between what was called 'my life' and 'my pursuit of the spiritual Path,' now there was the Path and my life merging as one. This position was not possible for me to maintain consistently. And, since Winged Wolf had sworn me to secrecy, now I was a secret Savant, so I couldn't share it with anyone. *'Everyone must see I'm not the same'* was the thought that arose. This was a different type of identity crisis; it was a leap in consciousness that took me into more of an identity-less realm.

The morning arrived quickly and it was soon time to head over to the empowerment site at Joshua Tree to prepare for those who would be arriving. Looking at my two apprentice buddies, I knew they had not been asked to become Savant. Winged Wolf told me the timing wasn't right for either of them. And, she had told me I would no longer be 'one of the gang.' So as I looked at them, there was a difference in our relationship already and they didn't even know about it. Soon enough, they would feel it even if nothing were said.

This commitment meant I was no longer one of them, which I had really enjoyed, but now I was a servant, a servant of the Path and attendant to the Teacher first and foremost. My focus of attention shifted. It was an awkward time, as transitions usually are, another step into the unknown. The new role had no formal definition, so I was baffled as to how it should be. *'Just wing it,'* I told myself, *'what else can you do? For sure, Winged Wolf will let you know if you aren't doing it!!'*

The empowerment was amazing. The setting was breathtaking in its rugged beauty, and after walking the grounds, Winged Wolf chose to sit upon a huge bolder with all of us gathered around her. It was very dramatic. There were well over a hundred people present, and the expansiveness of the desert with its pure, crisp air magnified the energy of the Teacher's consciousness. We all felt high on the energy; massive gusts of wind nearly knocked us off our feet the day prior to the event. This was a sure indicator of what was to come; and when *The Wish-Fulfilling Gem Mantra* was released to a hushed audience, there was a moment where life stood still.

It was a long moment—no sound, no movement, no air moved, perfect stillness. Much later, after the weekend, Winged Wolf told me that at that moment her heart stopped beating, and she wondered if it would begin again or if this would be the end of her life.

She sat motionless on the granite boulder, and as I gazed at her sitting there, a metamorphosis took place. She was transformed into an old, Asian-looking monk, completely robed, and we were not gathered in Joshua Tree National Forest, but suspended in space, like a memory.

I attempted to focus my attention on the image to bring forth more details of the scene, but right then, the encapsulated moment ended as Winged Wolf began to chant the Mantra. It was a riveting moment as we joined her, tentatively at first, then with gathering momentum; and for the first time, *The Wish-Fulfilling Gem Mantra* was released to the world.

Endings and Beginnings

Afterwards, people were offered an Initiation, called the Abundance Initiation. In effect, it was a vow to live the laws of abundance as spelled out in the Initiation to the best of our ability.

My role during the Initiation was to stand off to the side of Winged Wolf and remove strings of beads from their plastic wrappers, then hand them to the Teacher to present to initiates as they came forward. After doing this for more than a hundred times, the line finally ended; now it was my turn to take the vow and receive my beads.

As I knelt before her, she handed me the beads and said something about *"these sandalwood prayer beads."* 'What?' I was taken aback. I hadn't considered that the beads were prayer beads. What would I do with prayer beads? I was highly resistant to all the trappings of religions; the idea of having prayer beads set off quite a strong but silent reaction in me.

Years later, after teasing me about that incident on several occasions, Winged Wolf pointed out that there is a part of me that goes unconscious when I don't want to look at something. So I pretend I don't know what I'm doing, make up a story in my mind that explains it away, in this case, helping her pass out a hundred sets of prayer beads without realizing what they represented!

The Next Step

After the empowerment, during the return to the airport, Winged Wolf said to me, *"It's time for you to let go of your attachment to the world, Wings of Change. And I don't think you can do that without spending more time at Between the Wind."*

"I'm already there six months of the year," I responded defensively.

"That's not enough for you," came the reply. She leaned over toward me and said quietly, *"You really aren't very good as a servant, you know. And you're definitely not Savant material. Not yet, anyway.*

"I'm not suggesting you give up your family. Visit them whenever you like, but you need to live nearby.

Initiation

I realized she was telling the truth; I wasn't very good in my new role. I was clumsy and distractible, too much attention on self. *"All right,"* I sighed, *"I guess it's inevitable, given my commitment to going as far as I can go."*

It was very important to be clear about this in my self, as Winged Wolf challenged it every time I began to settle into complacency or slip off-track. With this Servant Vow, I had made a promise and the entire Transhistorical Consciousness embodied in my Teacher was my witness. *'Oh my, what a commitment!'*

Now, the Teacher was challenging me to remember my promise to myself, with her as my witness that I would continue on. It was the impeccable thing to do.

What could I resist? Myself? No, it was time to move to Orcas. I knew Walter would be willing because he, too, had made a commitment to go as far as he could in this lifetime, although he was definitely in a slump and had been for quite a while. I refused to consider that he wouldn't pull out of it one day. It was too important to him.

I turned to Winged Wolf as we pulled into the airport parking lot and said, *"I'll talk to Walter. I'm sure he'll be willing to move. We'll be there as soon as we can find a place to rent on Orcas and do something with ours."*

After she was on her plane, some of my certainty faded and a sense of dread filled me. In my mind's eye, I could see that nothing about my life would ever be the same, and there was a bittersweet feeling to it. I could no longer have my feet in both worlds; a decision had been made.

Also, I wasn't quite as certain as I sounded that my spouse would feel as I did about this move. Ironically, it was he who was the catalyst for my move to Orcas the first time, for those long three months, with me kicking and screaming in resistance. After that initial experience, I had become the driving force in the apprenticeship as the freedom from limitations Winged Wolf had promised began to become a reality; then he had begun to drag his feet.

There are so many layers to work through on the road to freedom; often I had no awareness that my freedom was impaired until the obstacle was removed and the impact of its removal felt. That's how accustomed

Endings and Beginnings

I had grown to suffering; I didn't even know it was there. This meant initially I had to trust the Teacher and do certain things at her suggestion even if they didn't always feel right to me. What an unusual sensation that is, but whenever I trusted her, things always worked out.

It isn't easy to surrender totally to another when you've always relied upon yourself for direction, even if the other is your Teacher and an enlightened master. The Teacher is always impeccable, whereas I was impeccable when not being pulled hither and yon by mind passions; and without her continuous influence, I could take little breaks from the intensity of the commitment as I chose. That phase of my life was about to end.

Chapter 21
Embracing My Destiny

During our plane flight back to Michigan, I broached the subject of a move to Orcas.

"Walter, I told Winged Wolf we would move to Orcas on a more permanent basis. She thinks it's really important at this point in my apprenticeship that I spend even more time with her."

He looked at me wide-eyed and speechless, no doubt wondering what had happened to the woman who threatened him with dire consequences if he insisted on moving to Orcas merely for three months. Such a complete about-face must have been confusing. Yet from my perspective, after the initial letting go of that karmic thing I had been fighting and resisting, that huge illusionary obstacle called 'I can't be away from my (grown) children for that long a period,' it was no longer a threat. It had dissolved because there was nothing there to hold it together. This freed up the energy that I had used to hold that illusion in place and lightened my karmic burdens quite a bit. It allowed me to be more agile and flexible in making shifts that would expand my consciousness and begin to refine my personality. The illusionary aspect of the blockages showed up quickly now, so I didn't need weeks or months of struggle before the shift in consciousness came. But he didn't know all of that, so I must have looked pretty flaky to him.

"What does 'a more permanent basis' mean?" he asked quietly.

'All right', I thought, *'tell it like it is.'* *"Here's what I see, but it's not written in stone, so I'll say it and then you tell me how it strikes you.*

"It looks to me like we need to sell the house, or maybe even rent it out, whichever is easiest, and rent a place on Orcas for at least a year. Then we can reassess our progress and decide what to do next."

He asked, *"Has something happened to change your mind about living part-time in Florida or Michigan and part-time on Orcas? I really liked that plan."*

This was his way of saying, *"Are you really going to give up your cushy lifestyle, and put yourself under Winged Wolf's eagle eye full-time?"*

Since I was still under the secrecy vow regarding my Servant/Savant role, I merely said, *"Winged Wolf has challenged me to stretch myself beyond where I am now, and to do so, she says I need to be near her most of the time. My little-self really doesn't want to do it; I like our lifestyle as it is, but when I put my attention at the Third Eye and ask the question, 'Is this the right thing to do?' the answer comes up a loud 'yes!' From the perspective of divine consciousness, it's a one-hundred-percent decision, but when my personality gets involved, oh boy. If only I could stay at the Third Eye all the time, or even sixty-percent of the time. That would help a lot."*

"Well," he said after a while, *"it's not something I feel drawn to do. As you know, I seem to have lost my momentum. I've been stuck for a long time and nothing I've done so far has gotten me unstuck. So maybe this move is the best thing for me, to help me get unstuck."*

"Are you questioning continuing as an apprentice?" I asked, alert to the energy of what he had said. While he spoke of getting unstuck, he sounded depressed. Irrationally, I leaped to my worst fear, rather than listening to the intent of his words.

"Not exactly," He replied soberly. *"I really don't want to quit my apprenticeship. It's just I don't know what to do. No matter what I try, it's still the same. I don't want to do anything about my apprenticeship. There isn't any drive toward or away from it."*

"I'll support you in whatever you want to do," he said. *"Regardless of what happens with me in the apprenticeship, I'm committed to your going all the way. I know you will do it, and I'm behind you all the way. If we need to move to Orcas for you to do that, then we'll move to Orcas. Besides,"* he added firmly, *"I'm committed to my apprenticeship, too, even if I am in a bit of a slump. Once we get to Orcas, I'm sure I'll be fine. Mostly, I need to be closer to the Teacher right now."*

The business of catastrophizing a situation and traumatizing myself as a result was a disturbing aspect of my way of perceiving energy, my ego fearing some fantasy loss. Reassured by the conversation, I relaxed and we both enjoyed the remainder of the trip.

The Teacher's Invisible Presence

During these years, empowerments were such a catalyst for growth spurts, I never knew where the next one would take me, but it was clear that whatever Winged Wolf saw as the next step, that was where I would be going. No sooner did she begin to put attention on the next step than experiences would begin popping into my awareness relative to that step. And, of course, it wasn't only me; it was all who were connected to her by strings of energy of their intention for spiritual growth.

During one of my evening meditations, I was startled to find myself atop an elephant, being jostled and jolted around as the huge animal made its way through a thick forest that looked to me like a jungle. The first time this image appeared, that was it; there was no flesh to it at all, just a moving picture of me, although this me was male and much younger. After the meditation, I made some notes in my journal about it and filed it away. Perhaps more would come later. From time to time during my daily activities, the image would pop up, accompanied by a strong sensation in my solar plexus.

Although our lifestyle change was still several months away, it was alive in me and occupied much of my attention. There was much to do, and so, after arriving at home from Joshua Tree, we launched a plan. The house would be both for sale and for rent simultaneously, and whichever occurred first, that would be the flow. We could have a major garage sale and pare down to bare essentials that we would take with us to Orcas. Because we had opted to buy a lovely home in a lousy school district, we knew it would take extra time to find the right occupants for it.

As to finding a rental on Orcas, not surprisingly, one of our previous landlords called and said they were planning on moving off the island for a year beginning late summer, probably August, after their son graduated from high school; and they wondered if we would be interested in renting their home? Would we be interested!! We had previously stayed in their guest home for a month after the house we were renting was sold, and we had been in the main house several times. What an ideal place. Oh, yes, we were interested!

It would be perfect for our needs; in fact, we had said to them at the time, *"If you ever want to rent this place, please call us."* The house had a spectacular view overlooking Deer Harbor and some of the San Juan Islands. It was breathtaking. We had stood on the deck with them looking out to sea, and I remembered the sensation of *'heaven on earth.'* It seemed too good to be true.

Since they would not be leaving until late summer, this gave us a few months to rearrange our life and bring some closure to the Michigan phase of it. It didn't take long to realize this move was going to be more difficult for Walt than he had let on, or perhaps he hadn't realized it himself. Suddenly, he was spending long hours in his basement office, seemingly so busy with the temporary help business we owned in Mississippi which he ran from afar, that he had no time to invest in mobilizing for the move. I watched with growing concern. Without his companion energy, it would be difficult to bring this together. His energy was powerful; after all, he had the male trait of dominance.

Winged Wolf had told us, *"The male energy is always dominant until a person becomes enlightened. Then it comes into balance."* In my reality, this meant if Walter was pulling against me, we'd stay in limbo for a long time unless I packed up and left; that would shift the balance of things. But I was confident he would rally when the moment arrived.

Meanwhile, as the weeks passed, I continued to have further images of myself on the elephant. I discovered that if I could relax my mind, rather than becoming excited by what I was seeing, the image would both enlarge and unfold or evolve. Over time, I could see it like a snippet of a motion picture except that I was often in that other body rather than watching.

The scenario was that there was a small procession of us, me in a male body on the elephant, with several people on the ground guiding the elephant and clearing the trail ahead, and sometimes several following on foot behind. We would reach a particular place in the forest, the elephant would be tapped on one knee by whoever was leading it and the elephant would lower so I could dismount. Then I would walk some distance to a cleared section of the forest where an esteemed person sat in deep meditation, usually surrounded by others. I wasn't clear what my relationship was to them. I was not garbed as they were. But I held this person in deep respect, as I bowed to the ground at his feet. We communicated briefly about something and I left. My intuitive senses produced the word 'messenger.' And I sensed my task was to carry messages to the forest dwellers from 'town.'

When I learned from Winged Wolf that the subject for the upcoming April empowerment was reincarnation, it brought clarity as to the impetus for my recent experiences. She was the broadcaster of spiritual direction and awakening. What she looked at while sitting at her desk at *Between the Wind*, or wherever else she might be, was broadcast through the ethers into the minds of those of us who, by our choice, were connected to her. She was guiding my spiritual unfolding, whether we were in direct conversation or not. My attention was directed to where she placed her attention. She is the higher consciousness, the Teacher and Spiritual Master; I am the student, the lesser consciousness because I am not yet spiritually awake.

After hearing about the subject of the empowerment, I shared my story with her, and without a second's hesitation, she said, *"You were a messenger for Sakyamuni Buddha."* I was so surprised I couldn't even ask a further question. And that was all she said about it.

That particular empowerment had an unusual impact on many people. For me it created an opening and memories continued to surface, clearly connecting me historically with this Teacher. But, some others, and this is my observation, not a fact, had a major fear response. Several apprentices dropped away after that empowerment, my sense being they became frightened of seeing themselves in the dreamtime on a continuum rather than with a set identity. The illusion of this life or this dream being reality was shattered as past-life memories surfaced, and the flight mechanism took hold. Oh, the bliss and the expanded awareness they have missed out on by making that choice to cave in to the fear and run!

One of the memories I had surface was a shared memory, making it doubly powerful because of the affirmation of its reality. I didn't learn of this fact until several weeks after the Empowerment when Winged Wolf asked me to draw a sketch of what I had seen and told me of another apprentice who had seen the same thing. Later, that apprentice and I talked and shared what we had seen. Apparently, we both had been students of the Teacher in that lifetime as well because the memories were identical as to place and visual description.

While sitting in a circle around the Teacher on the second evening of the empowerment, I noted that she no longer looked like herself, but had taken on the demeanor of an oriental-looking, sallow-skinned male of rather squat stature (since she was in meditation pose, this is conjecture). Her voice remained the same, yet I perceived it as male. In fact, the scene took on a surreal essence of one transparency laid upon another so that I began to see through the transparencies to who this person was.

While I was still gazing at the Teacher, the setting shifted to another outdoor scene, but the place was outside of what, at first, I thought was a castle, but it may have been a monastery. It was large, built of something similar to sandstone—heavy, thick stone with crude mortar holding the square grayish blocks together. In the center was the largest, thickest wooden door I had ever seen. I was with another group of people gathered around this Teacher who stood on something like a patio or porch surrounded by a knee-high stone wall. The crowd was mesmerized as they listened to this enlightened master's words, showing them the way to spiritual awakening.

After this Master's talk, a small group of us were invited inside the large structure. The doors opened from inside and we were led with lanterns down a damp, dark hallway, holding lighted candles interspersed along the walls.

At this point, something in my attention again shifted, and I was once again sitting in the campground in Vancouver watching my Teacher who was also now in her present body.

Later, upon hearing of my experience, Winged Wolf told me, *"That was Patrul, an eighteenth century Tibetan Teacher,"* (and part of Winged Wolf's lineage). At the time, I wondered why she had shapeshifted into Patrul's body. I concluded that it was to show others and myself, who had been studying with her/him at that former time, the continuity of our experience with this Teacher; and to trigger our memories of that important life together. It was probably what the energies of that moment called forth from the divine consciousness. At that point, I couldn't yet see who I was relative to that Teacher. I had projected myself with my current body into the experience of the past scene and was perceiving it from these eyes—it seemed normal at the time, but when I got looking at it, I realized I had not captured my identity in that time period.

The Environment Reflects

Our Michigan house was not moving either in the direction of a sale or a rental. This had never happened to us before. Over the years we had developed a knack for buying and selling property, and had acquired several rental houses in anticipation of retirement. I had extensive knowledge of the area and a sixth sense about good properties to invest in, while Walter was skilled in management and organization. We made a great team. This house was the exception. We purchased it because we loved it, but it was in a notoriously poor school district, a big no-no in the real estate game.

However none of this would have made a bit of difference if we were pulling together. In the worst market, in the worst neighborhood, I knew that if it was impeccably in pursuit of our highest good, it would come together. We were paying the price for a split in our energies. He didn't want to let go and I did. We lowered the price of the rental; then, reluctantly, I addressed the topic of resistance with Walter.

"It looks to me like we've got some resistance going here, Walt. In spite of the school district, this place should be renting at the price we're asking."

"Do you think so?" he asked. *"I don't feel resistant, although I see that I haven't done much toward the move."*

"I think we should ask Winged Wolf for her companion energy in this," I suggested.

"That's a good idea," he brightened. *"Why don't you call her?"*

And, I did; and she said she was always with us in companion energy. All we had to do was ask. It was a small opening on his part, but it was enough. A short while later, we had a nibble. It might prove to be a solid one-year rental, meaning the couple would pay us a year's rent up front if we would reduce the rent slightly. After a few days of negotiating, we settled on a price and a move-in date for them of June 1. That left us about six weeks to pack up and move.

We had to move quickly to schedule the garage sale and prepare for it. We had already decided to let most everything go, other than the bare necessities. We had purchased a 6' x 9' trailer and determined that anything we couldn't fit in the trailer was not going. It didn't look nearly as big as it had when we purchased it. As I considered what should be taken to Orcas, the trailer began to look downright small.

A feeling akin to panic set in. We had a 3000-square-foot house filled with furniture and our collection of junk and miscellaneous treasures. We had only lived there five years, but this house also held memories of wonderful times with parents and children, friends and family. It symbolized a successful time in our lives, a time of abundance in all areas. We had great neighbors, a lake to swim in, deer in the backyard. All the energy we had invested in developing this home was soon to become a memory, and it was painful to let go.

Once again, Walter took to the basement and the security of his desk. I watched with dawning awareness that for the first time since I had known him, he was paralyzed with fear of giving up anchors. He wasn't moving, couldn't move.

Our good friend and fellow apprentice Judy responded quickly to my plea for her help. She was such a wonderful, giving person that after my mother died and my dad went into a nursing home, she drove to Florida with me and helped pack up their condominium. I was deeply grateful for this act of kindness, and knew if I called her she would, once again, be of service.

What occurred when we spoke was an experience of the power of companion energy. Her response was instantaneous. *"Of course I'll help; I have plenty of experience with garage sales, and I am highly organized. Right now I'm even between volunteer jobs so I've got the time available to help."*

Her reassurance and companion energy pulled me out of my panic and helped focus my energy. She gave me directions to prepare for her arrival the next day: *"Put an ad in the local paper, identify everything you want to let go of. I'll bring the markers and labels for them."*

And she gave me some well-founded advice, *"Stop criticizing Walter,"* she said kindly, *"and realize he can't help his response. Be kind and stop worrying, we'll work it out."* I felt the tears rolling down my cheeks as I let my breath out. My whole body had been tense; without even realizing it, I had been holding on by a thread. I had been afraid it wasn't going to happen. Now, with her help, I knew it would.

The next day, Judy arrived with tape and labels and marking pens, everything we needed to organize a garage sale. We had picked a date for the sale just prior to our scheduled departure for Orcas which gave us about ten days to prepare. Then we got to work. It was unbelievable what was accomplished in the next few days, as Walter continued to work in the basement.

Every time I said anything critical, Judy said, *"Behave, leave him alone."* Then one day, she said, *"He's going to have to do the basement. It's full of his stuff. Go down and tell him he's got until Friday to sort through it and let me know what he wants to sell."*

So I stood in front of his massive desk, his empire in the basement, and interrupted his deep concentration. *"Walter, Judy and I can do everything but the basement. You're going to have to do this piece yourself, at least the decision-making part. We have to know what you want to sell, so we can tag it and get it ready for the sale this weekend."*

He sighed, *"I can't seem to get mobilized. It seems so overwhelming. I had no idea it would be so hard."*

"You can do it," I told him with more conviction than I felt. *"You just need to get started. I can help you. We'll do a little bit each day, but it must be ready by Friday. Is that understood?"*

"I'll start now," he responded, standing up. And, at last, he rolled into gear. By Friday we were exhausted, but ready. And at about 6:00am the next morning, two hours before the advertised time, the doorbell rang. It had begun.

That weekend was incredible. Many of our neighbors had added items to ours, and several of our friends joined us, as well as the grown 'kids' who came over to search our stuff for items they might want. We ended up selling things we hadn't even intended to sell. When it was over Sunday evening, we were down to a few items for the Good Will, and the few things we were planning to take with us. It was freedom, and it was shocking. We wandered about the empty house silently. A dream had been dismantled and the new dream had not yet begun. It was a twilight zone.

At a time when most of our old friends were looking at retirement, grandkids, cottages and golf, we were stepping into a life that had no particular form to it, an unknown outcome and no roadmap. The feeling was indescribable. For the past several months we had visited with everyone we knew, acting out our lives as if we would continue with them just as they would continue with theirs, normally. At the same time, we were saying good-bye. Each moment was precious because no one knew what the next moment would hold.

Of course, when one is living in the NOW, meaning the present moment, the next moment evolves naturally. And each moment holds the promise of freshness because it is new.

Our friends' lives were predictable and seductive in their predictability. We were choosing to break from the norm, and this made us oddballs, loveable oddballs, but oddballs just the same. Some of our friends were titillated by our adventures, others puzzled, some judged us as 'over the edge.' But none were interested in giving up their lifestyles to follow a Path such as ours.

Local apprentice friends were so supportive and cheered us on. We could do it even if they could not. But because they could not or would not, it also saddened them to have us leave, perceiving a loss or void would be left by our move. They liked having us around. We would be missed, and vice-versa, we would miss them. Some of us had been friends for over twenty years.

The nearby family, meaning my sons Kevin and Terry, and Tracy, my daughter-in-law, were baffled. They had perceived our spiritual interests as passing whims, and this move said, *'This is serious and it is real. It's not going away.'* Only our daughter Michelle was enthusiastic, as she, too, was pursuing the same Path, albeit with not such a singular focus.

It was time to load the trailer and be on our way. All the good-byes were said, and we were down to bare necessities: a couch, a couple chairs, our kitchen supplies, some clothes and Walt's office. There were some things we just couldn't bear to part with, so we packed them up and loaded up a corner in Kevin and Tracy's basement for the time being; a large corner as it turned out. Much of our furniture, including our wonderful Victorian bedroom set, we gave to them.

Here I was driving off into the sunset, literally, with everything I owned in a small trailer behind the car. If there was any way to tell you how this felt to me, I would. For many people this would be no big deal. But there is a culture in Michigan, the Midwest really, that if you are born and raised there, you are 'stable.' My family, my families' families, and so forth, lived in Michigan. They were successful people, predictable people and 'respectable' people. Everyone did what they were supposed to do, lived as they were supposed to live; if there were difficulties, they were kept behind closed doors. There were strong, unwritten codes of behavior. I had just violated all of them.

I carried the genetic make-up of a Michigander, born of generations of sameness. Even though my distant relatives were pioneers, migrating to Michigan from Ireland and England via Canada, the past three generations had acquired that crystallized stability that permeated Midwestern culture.

And so here I was driving across the country once again, moving to a state I had never ever considered living in, Washington. Walt and I were emotionally exhausted and physically depleted due to the ambivalence we felt about leaving, he more than I at that point, but his exhaustion was infectious.

The inner struggle took its toll and we barely drove a couple hours before fatigue demanded we stop for the night, but at least we were on the way. Of course, we could also feel the tugging from those we left behind. What power others' dreams have to impact our dreams, especially when those strings of energy are so strongly connected. It was startling.

People's faces flashed before me as we drove, and I realized these people were thinking about me and projecting their energy toward me, unaware or uncaring that they were doing that. And how many times had I done exactly the same towards others? Probably millions. And I realized that I was going because I had to, not because I wanted to, forcing myself to do something for my higher good, without full cooperation from all my fragmented parts.

Somewhere in North Dakota, the third day of our trip, the energy shifted and that which had been pulling my attention backward toward my ex-home eased; and the energy of where we were headed began to pull me forward. It was a moment in time, literally, when one let go and the other began. Once again, all of me was focused on where I was going. Did Walter feel the same way?

"My gosh," I remember saying to him, *"did you just feel the shift in energy that took place? I feel released from the past. Do you realize how subtle the energetic forces are in us? I didn't realize I was holding on to the past until I let go. And, the past was holding on to me, via our friends, family and anchor-points held in place by memory. Then I could see what I was doing. That kind of thing must happen all the time without our being aware of it."*

"Well, if that's what is making me so tired, I'll be just as glad when it lets go," he replied, tight-lipped.

The rest of the trip went smoothly. Our two dogs were great travelers and I enjoyed their companionship on the long haul across country. Arriving on Orcas was heart-warming; several of the local apprentices gathered at our new home to help unload the trailer and put things in order. They also brought food to share with us; so it was a wonderful feeling of acceptance and a smooth entry, nothing like the drudgery of releasing all the stuff we had let go of in Michigan. This was light and happy. I stood on the deck of our new home, looked out to sea, and, breathing the fresh sea air, relaxed totally.

Big barrels full of brightly colored flowers were sitting in all corners of the deck and they were in bloom; brilliant colors, sparkling in the sunlight. What a fortuitous beginning for this adventure into the unknown. I felt truly happy to be here. Still, I kept a part of me separate from the others, a part that said, *"I'm still a part-timer, so don't expect me to be like the rest of you."*

There was something about keeping a little separate part alive in me that provided a false sense of security. I understood it was false because the Teachings tell us that 'all life is one;' therefore there can be no separateness. But I hadn't really integrated the Teaching, otherwise it would have been impossible to maintain a feeling of separateness.

It soon became evident that those apprentices who lived full-time on Orcas had a particular attitude toward service that I respected greatly. They gave one-hundred-percent of themselves to the work they did for the Path. They were so devoted; it was inspirational to be around them. It was no accident they were referred to as 'full-timers.'

We took a few days to settle in before putting total attention on being at *Between the Wind*. The dogs needed some adjustment time to their new home as well. Then, it was full-swing as I plunged my energy into being with Winged Wolf and spending my days and many evenings on the property.

Surprisingly to me, my energy flowed pretty smoothly during this transition; and with mom gone, dad relatively safe, and the kids grown, I experienced a freedom I'd never had before. Always, a part of my attention had been on taking care of my parents or my children; no matter what I was doing, there was always that question whether they were all right, and a little guilt that I wasn't doing what would have pleased them most, living next door or down the block.

For the first time in my life, I had no obligations or responsibilities to vie for priority over my spiritual goals. While my adult children objected to the choices I had made, there was no obligation to please them. They were full-grown adults, living their lives. I had done the best I could to raise them. This was my time to go for it.

We had only been on the island for about three weeks when I received a call from my sister-in-law. *"You better get here fast. I don't think your dad's going to last much longer."*

By the time I arrived back in Michigan, he was unconscious, although he still was able to hold my hand for long periods of time. He lasted only two days after my arrival, sleeping peacefully away. He had lasted a little over eleven months after my mother's death, both deaths occurring in September, the month before my birthday. We gave him a wonderful send-off a few days later, in a manner he would have approved, and I returned to Orcas.

Maticintin

The first time I had noticed the word *'Maticintin,'* it had been on the program for our July Empowerment on Deities, where it had appeared in the tiniest font readable, centered under the name Winged Wolf. At that point, I had been so distracted and distraught that it barely penetrated. This had been within days of my making that grueling trip by ambulance, plane, and ambulance again to bring my father to the nursing home in Michigan where my sister-in-law had agreed to act in my stead.

Thus, it wasn't until after the move to Orcas that it finally penetrated my consciousness enough to ask someone what the word Maticintin was about. Our office manager looked at me wide-eyed, as if to say, *'Where have you been?'* and said, *"Why, that's Winged Wolf's Buddhist name. It was given to her long ago."* As usual, I was taken aback. *"I didn't know she was given another name."*

"I don't know all the details. Why don't you ask her about it, maybe she will tell you the story."

"Are we supposed to call her by that name?" I persisted, still wanting more details.

"Not unless we feel drawn to do so. She hasn't encouraged us to call her that, but she feels it is important to begin to share it with people, since it is her Buddhist name."

"I wonder what it means?" I queried.

"Virtuous Giver," she replied.

"Wow. That's powerful." This was something to be digested for a while. It made sense that she would have been given a name, and it probably came to her along with the return of her past-life memories. But it would take some getting used to because it was unfamiliar.

In a Teaching several months later, Winged Wolf shed further light for me on the acquisition of the name Maticintin. She told us of a vision she had some years ago in which an old man with an exceptionally long white beard came to her and bestowed upon her a staff. As his arm reached out to hand her the staff, he said, *"Go forth and lead the people."* At the time, she was taken aback because she didn't know which people she was to lead and where.

Then she became a Spiritual Teacher and found herself leading people toward their enlightenment. The vision returned in full this time. It showed her a time when, as a male disciple of Padmasambhava, he had sent her to a monastery in Bhutan. As she had rapped on the door, it was opened by the same man with the long white beard who had come to her in her vision years prior.

He took her to a room where there was a lectern on which was placed an enormous book that lay open at a certain page. She was told to go and read the book on the page where it was opened. There she read that in another lifetime she would become the Maticintin who would found a religion that would last for over 1000 years and she would lead thousands of people toward their enlightenment. It also told of Maticintin's birth date, which was her own birth date, and that Maticintin would be her birth name, which it was. This name also appears in *The Bradrakalpika Sutra*.

Chapter 22
The Bodhisattva Vow

Whispers were floating through the apprentice body about some thing called a Bodhisattva Vow. I first heard about it months before our move to Orcas Island. For some reason, there was quite a stir about it. At first, I paid little attention. *'What could I possibly vow beyond what I already have?'* I asked. *'I've already vowed to honor and serve the Teacher and the Path beyond anything else in my life. And I've vowed to do it forever. What else have I to give?'*

But as the rumors continued, my attention was finally drawn to them. *"What is all the fuss?"* I asked one of my apprentice friends.

"Don't you know what a Bodhisattva Vow means?" she asked.

"Well, it's a vow of service, isn't it?"

"It's a vow of service that lasts until every sentient being is enlightened. Do you see what that means? It means we have to come back forever and ever. We can't attain nirvana until then."

Put so directly, I had a realization of conflict. *"I'm not planning on coming back after this lifetime,"* I told her. *"This one is enough for me. I just want to become enlightened and fulfill my responsibility to bring someone else through."* This was an assumption drawn from reading Winged Wolf's experience with Alana where she was expected to bring at least one consciousness into enlightenment.

"Me, too," my friend agreed. *"This is the last one for me. I'm not going to take the vow."*

"Have you talked to the Teacher yet to find out if all this is true?"

"No, but I've researched it on the Internet and that's what it means to become a bodhisattva. Plus, it means we have to put off our own enlightenment until all other sentient beings have been enlightened."

"Well, I can't believe Winged Wolf would do that to us. I'm going to ask her directly." I said.

"Let me know what she says."

Winged Wolf responded quickly to my request for clarification on the Bodhisattva Vow, but first she confronted me about the comment I had made to my apprentice friend about this being my last lifetime in a physical body.

She said, *"Wings, you who are so attached to life, how can you possibly say you are not coming back again? And your friend, my apprentice, is in the same boat. Doesn't that seem paradoxical to you?"*

And while I was still reeling from her terse observation, she went on to clarify the Bodhisattva Vow for me.

"Don't alarm yourself with other people's mind chatter. They are speaking through fear and misunderstanding. I haven't even finished writing the Bodhisattva Vow as yet, but when I do, there will be time for you to look at it and make your decision then. Rest assured, you are not being asked to postpone your own enlightenment."

She went on to say, *"The Kentucky Empowerment will be when the Bodhisattva Vow is presented and you will be able to choose. It is the ultimate service and therefore opens the door to ultimate freedom."*

This was enough clarification to feel reassured that my ultimate goal of enlightenment was not being placed on the back burner, and I could still make the final decision after reading the vow. It was amazing how much reaction could be stirred up by listening to the interpretations of other people. And it seemed people fed on the frenzy of emotions that were stirred rather than attempting to discover the truth.

Upon hearing her explanation, I had regained my composure enough to tell her I could see her point about the paradoxical nature of my comments about not wanting to come back again. But at that moment in my life it still had a strong feeling component to it so I wasn't prepared to just drop it, but I was certainly prepared to take the Bodhisattva Vow as she had explained it to me. The other I would have to let percolate in me until its grip loosened. Fortunately it didn't take long to see that it was another illusionary obstacle that I had created out of a false sense that I knew about something that I really didn't know anything about.

Much of the work we did after settling into our new life on Orcas was geared toward preparation for the upcoming empowerment in Kentucky that October. Happily, we were not providing food for the attendees and we would be staying in tents. Everyone was to fend for themselves regarding meals. This took an enormous piece out of the workload of preparation.

Winged Wolf was sequestered in her office for long hours, and in between, she spent more hours in the Happy House in deep silence, preparing for the bodhisattva event. An unusual thing happened to her before Empowerments, and it might begin as early as two months prior and gradually intensify until the moment the event began.

Her physical body would begin to expand and she would take on the aura and physique of a pregnancy. Literally, she would grow larger and larger, and she shared with us that she felt 'pregnant.' As people sent in their registration forms and turned their attention toward the event, they naturally but unconsciously sent thought forms in the Teacher's direction. Her sleep would be disturbed with the weight and intensity of the energy, and astral presences increased. In addition to people projecting their own astral bodies in the Teacher's direction, since everyone tends to draw astral entities toward them during their lives, these entities would also be present in the space. Some mornings the Happy House took on a crowded feeling, as though we might explode with all the energy present. Everyone was impacted, but none so dramatically as the Teacher.

By the time empowerment day came around, Winged Wolf would usually be completely unable to eat or sleep. What she did while sitting in the silence was private to her, but there was the sense she was tuning in to the energies coming at her and aligning the Transhistorical Consciousness to meet and transmute these energies, so that people attending would receive benefits through the ethers long before the actual event. The Transhistorical Consciousness is the term Winged Wolf uses to describe the memory of the Primordial Teachings, Spiritual Teachings that have existed since the original dream of the Void. The

Primordial Wisdom or pure knowledge contained in these Teachings is accessible to an enlightened human being whose memory is ripe to remember the Teachings and carry them forward, and my Teacher is such a human being. She has referred to the Primordial Teachings as 'the treasure house of all memory.' It is called Transhistorical because the memory capsules that are accessed by the enlightened being are passed from one enlightened being to another, as one is prepared to receive them. Thus, the Transhistorical Consciousness exists, has always existed and the memory capsules are passed, usually through lineage, from enlightened being to enlightened being.

Once an event began, the pregnant appearance would dissipate and she could begin to sleep again. Winged Wolf said it puzzled her that she would be sleepless for weeks prior to an event, yet the moment we were under way, everyone gathered round, she had no difficulty at all sleeping, like being in the eye of a storm.

Whenever there was an empowerment scheduled away from home, Winged Wolf always arrived a day or two early; she said it was to prepare the site. Frequently she brought me with her. Invariably we started by walking the site, choosing a location where she would sit, and then consecrating the land. There were many disastrous beginnings. At the Michigan Empowerment, for example, the site, which we had checked out only a few weeks prior to the event, had turned out to be filthy with debris uncollected over the summer. We had spent one full day with eight apprentices, picking up everything from discarded car mufflers to children's bicycles. I didn't think anything could unsettle me by the time we got to the Kentucky Empowerment. Each site had its unique set of challenges, but traveling with the *Consciousness*, things always worked out.

"I'll be so happy when we have our own place," Winged Wolf always told us. *"We really need a large piece of land. But the time just isn't ripe for it yet."*

Unfortunately, while the property at Orcas was suitable for working with small groups of apprentices, it was unsuitable for working with large groups. The space itself was limited, not by acreage but by the structure of the acreage; and in particular there was not any place for parking cars. As noted previously, we were surrounded by unsupportive neighbors. In fact, our driveway was shared by one of the most antagonistic neighbors, so to have a hundred or so cars driving in and out would have caused a major upset.

Arriving at the site at Mammoth Cave, Kentucky, we were filled with high expectations based on all the feedback we had received. It was a gorgeous part of the country. But once we began walking the site, my stomach dropped. As we walked round and round, looking for the perfect site for the Teachings to be presented, no matter how many times we circled, nothing surfaced.

At one point, Winged Wolf pointed to an area and said, *"If we have to, we can make this work."* Immediately after she spoke, a motorcycle zoomed past, and we realized the area we were using had a road that passed through to another campground and was open to the public. There was no way to control the comings and goings of traffic.

"That's it," she said. *"We need to find the person in charge and tell them this is unacceptable."*

"What can they do for us?" I queried, thinking we were stuck. *"Maybe we could find another campground and get our money back."*

"It's too late for that now. They need to do something for us, so let's go." She had that determined look about her that said, *"Something's going to be done to accommodate us. They promised us privacy."*

So, off we went to the office. Another lesson for me in how the Transhistorical Consciousness works. The idea that they needed to 'do something for us' when there was nothing apparent they could do was interesting.

We stood at the office counter waiting. It was a while before the line ahead of us cleared, and Winged Wolf was face-to-face with a young woman who immediately took the attitude I had expected. *"What do you want us to do? We don't have anything else."*

"Well," she said, *"we were told this was to be a private space for us to have a spiritual event. Now we see there is no private space; there are motorcycles riding in and out right next to our site. It won't do for our needs."*

This conversation went back and forth in similar vein, Winged Wolf standing firm that we were promised a private space, and the woman insisting that was all they had.

Finally the woman said, *"Excuse me a moment,"* and went into the back room. I held my breath expectantly. It was several minutes. The energy seemed to shift.

Another woman came out from the back. Immediately the tone was different. *"How can I help you?"* she asked.

Winged Wolf again described our needs and the fact that our current site was unacceptable.

"There is some land adjacent to the area where you are camping. It isn't a part of the campground, but we do own it. There's a large red barn and acres of open land surrounding it. You are welcome to use it for your meetings. It will be totally private." She went on to describe how to access it.

"That sounds perfect," Winged Wolf nodded. *"We'll go take a look at it. Thank you for your service."*

The knot in my stomach began to unwind.

As we left, Winged Wolf said, *"The Transhistorical Consciousness will always provide for us, but we sometimes have to work for it."*

"Why do we have to work so hard for it, sometimes?" I wondered out loud.

"Because this is the physical plane. It takes more energy to manifest things, especially since we are operating outside of the box and having to work with the ordinary consciousness. We have to first break through their hardened mind sets. The first woman couldn't work with us, so she sent the other woman out. She wasn't as boxed in as the first."

"But how did you know they could help us?" I wanted to understand how she knew things, and of course it doesn't work like that.

"I didn't know they would help us. What I knew was the site was unacceptable and they were the ones who promised a private site. It

was their responsibility to make good on their promise. I don't ever try to conjure anything in the way of outcomes. For example, I didn't know they had that specific property available, all I knew was that there was an imbalance that needed to be corrected."

It turned out to be the pivotal point in this cycle of events. The newly discovered site was breathtaking, vast and open, brilliantly colorful with fall reds and golds, with the backdrop of an old red barn, a lone picturesque structure amidst the vast openness, exactly what was needed for the bodhisattva unveiling. We even discovered a secret cave on the property. Had it been a different type of empowerment, we might have used the cave, but this time Winged Wolf said we needed the openness.

The weather was crystal clear, crisp and downright cold at night, but the days were sunny and warm. And, best of all, there were real bathrooms, with running water, showers and heat. The weekend unfolded without further disturbance. Every talk was leading us to the crescendo of taking the Bodhisattva Vow of service to all sentient life.

On the final evening, we lit torches in front of the barn, which was the backdrop for Winged Wolf's platform and cushion. As dusk descended upon us, everyone gathered round the platform where the Teacher was seated. The atmosphere was charged with anticipation. A hundred people were gathered to learn what it meant to live life as a bodhisattva, and to decide whether to make the commitment. A hush fell over the group as Winged Wolf began leading us in *The Wish-Fulfilling Gem Mantra*. Afterwards, there was a long silence. Then she began to speak.

She told us that the life of a bodhisattva is a life committed to service to all sentient beings. I saw that Winged Wolf, herself, was a prime example of a living bodhisattva. She further explained that the beginning bodhisattva learns about service, learns what it is to live for others' sake. They still have attachments and little-self, or the unrefined personality is still operant at times; but even the beginning bodhisattva has placed themselves in the loving arms of the Transhistorical Consciousness. They are committed to serve even while they are learning what true service involves.

Winged Wolf also told us, *"For those of you who choose to take the Bodhisattva Vow, there is an accompanying guidebook titled* The Ten Levels of Bodhisattva, *that provides a blueprint for enlightenment."* We would know where we were on the road to awakening by the bodhisattva level we were on.

"At this point, there is no one who has arrived at Bodhisattva Level Two. You are all at some stage of Level One." So she clarified that. Lest any of us thought we were already farther along the road to enlightenment.

Winged Wolf went on to read to us from the Bodhisattva Guidebook what each level's road marks were, and how to recognize where we were individually. Immediately I could see why I was on Level One. It was all about trust and generosity. Then she read the Bodhisattva Vow to us.

It is as follows: *"I offer my existence to the pursuit of enlightenment for myself and all other sentient beings, to live in service for the upliftment of all sentient life…….. NOW AND FOREVERMORE."*

As I listened to her read the vow, I thought, *"There's nothing in that vow that I would disagree with. Of course I'll sign it. I want to become that."*

A long line of more than a hundred people stood patiently waiting to officially become bodhisattvas. I was standing in attendance to Winged Wolf, and while not listening in on her conversations, there was one point where she stated something to someone that I could not help but overhear. She said it twice, emphatically.

"Are you sure you want to sign this?" she asked the person. *"Once made, this vow is indelible, whether you stay on the Path or not."*

The reply was muffled, and she asked again. *"Be certain, because the further you are on the Path, the harder you fall."*

There was a sadness to her voice as she proclaimed this wisdom, as though her vision told her this person was signing under false pretenses. In a short time, this warning proved to be so true, as the person left the Path quite suddenly.

"It would have been easier on her if she had not taken the vow," Winged Wolf commented later sadly. *"People don't seem to realize these vows are not to be taken lightly. This vow is forever; it doesn't matter that you leave the Path. The vow follows you wherever you go for all the rest of your lives. There is no running away from such a vow."*

This was the only disturbing moment in an otherwise exhilarating evening. I couldn't wait to have some time to really study the Bodhisattva Guidebook and see what was involved in the climb, at least to Level 7, which was the level Winged Wolf had described as 'the irreversible way.' From that point on, one could never fall backward in consciousness. I wanted to see in writing what it would take to arrive at this level. A lot, I discovered later as I read and re-read the book.

For Winged Wolf and our Spiritual Order this was a high point in her Teaching, a time of 'counting coup' as she later described it, lovingly going through each signed vow. There were ninety-six of them as I recall, just short of her goal of one hundred, a magic number, based on the hundredth monkey theory. But she was not a tiny bit disappointed, knowing that it was only the beginning.

Living as a Bodhisattva

Shortly after we returned to Orcas from the empowerment, a group of us were sitting around the work table at *Between the Wind*. It was a quiet moment and I had wanted to take a closer look at my Bodhisattva Guidebook. It seemed like a propitious moment to dive in. The material on "The Six Perfections" could easily have been a book in itself. Then I went on to study Level 1, since Winged Wolf had declared none of us were yet on Level 2. I read it quietly to myself at first, then aloud, since the others present said they wanted to review it too. I could feel all the color drain from my face as I read what was said. This is a Level 1 Bodhisattva description:

1. *The Very Joyous – Having taken the Bodhisattva Vow, the bodhisattva is full of joy related to having entered the Path of Enlightenment. Such joy is an impetus that cultivates the virtue of generosity; which, when continually practiced, ultimately frees oneself from egotistical thought and the wishes for good karmic merit. Instead, the bodhisattva enjoys his or her daily movement of subtle refinement. Such refinement evolves into a peak level of conscious conviction of those truths that were already unconsciously known but never before validated in the bodhisattva's mind. It is from this place that trust is learned, and it is trust or conviction that gives one the vitality to ascend the first peak.*

As I read the description, one word leaped out at me— **Generosity**. Generosity was a trait that was high on my 'valuable traits' list, and an integral part of my self-image. *'Certainly generosity is not an issue with me;'* I thought. *'Everyone sees me as a giver.'* *'How come you're feeling so defensive about it then?'* I asked myself. Suddenly my self reflector said, *'maybe there is a hidden agenda to your generosity.'* A hidden agenda, for me, meant that I secretly expected to receive something in exchange for my giving something, even if it was merely a 'thank you' or an appreciative smile, still did I expect something? If so, then it was not true generosity. Perhaps that was why I felt uncomfortable with it.

Soon it was lunchtime, and the work table was quickly converted into our lunch table. Winged Wolf and her entourage of Sioux, Yoda and Ichinen arrived to take their places at and around the table. It happened Winged Wolf and I were side by side. On my plate was a large bunch of purple grapes, exceptionally sweet for the time of year. I was savoring each one, carefully chewing and swallowing, with great pleasure.

Winged Wolf commented on how good they looked and how much I was enjoying them. Immediately my insides began to churn. *'I should offer her some grapes,'* was the thought, but to my horror, I didn't want to share them. I wanted them all for myself. All the time the struggle went on, a few seconds or so, I was aware she was watching me.

"Here, Winged Wolf, please have some grapes," I finally said.

"That's all right, Wings, you don't have to share them," she answered, tuning into my struggle.

I could feel the blush as it moved up my face, no doubt turning it bright red. Just that suddenly my lack of generosity had been exposed, and in such a simple way. Over a bunch of grapes! I was mortified. Images began flashing through my mind, images of all the times I had ever withheld something from someone because I was feeling stingy and didn't want to share, and times I had made up for that by giving something that I didn't care so much about to balance the scales. With the images, came the sensation of black gook oozing out of my pores. I could see it.

This dark, oozing substance continued to pour out of my body for the remainder of that day and on into the next. If there were any way I could have discarded my body, I would have jumped at the opportunity, because it was so uncomfortable to be looking at myself in this way. I couldn't stand myself. It was that bad. By the end of the second day, the oozing sensation abated, the images began to fade and I felt purged. All the hundreds of scenes that went flashing through my mind, depicting my stinginess and withholding, ran their course and there was silence.

My self-image around the trait of generosity was completely shattered and left was the awareness that sometimes I was generous and other times I was not. Much depended on how good I felt about myself, how satisfied I was. It seemed I had more to give when there was no feeling of neediness, but the feeling of neediness wasn't based on actual need, it was based on perceived need. And then came the realization that this understanding of generosity was all coming from a personality interpretation, while true generosity was actually a trait of divine self, free from attachment or little-self perceptions. There were no strings attached to generosity when it was authentic, no expectations. The grip this struggle had on me began to lessen, and what surfaced were moments of genuine, open-hearted giving with no regard for acknowledgment of any kind, a real joy in giving and receiving.

The other major aspect in Bodhisattva Level 1 was called *trust*. I certainly couldn't trust myself to be consistently operating from a place of divine consciousness; there were too many slips and self-indulgences. Certain days I could be absolutely trusted to be impeccable; other days, one or another of the mind-passions dominated me; and even when it was in my awareness, it didn't always shift my perception into the oneness; it didn't always curtail the action driven by the mind passion. This was really sticky business, trying to measure myself by a standard of excellence that far outweighed my present abilities.

'If I can't trust myself to be impeccable at all times, then I will trust the Teacher,' I vowed. In those instances where the Teacher perceived I was off-base, then I would accept that and pray for the courage and strength to correct the imbalance. Whereas in the past, I might have argued with her in my mind, now I vowed to accept what she told me about myself as truth. And in that moment, I was completely sincere.

During these few months, each day was a roller coaster ride of self-discovery, one that could be so painful I would want to crawl off someplace and hide for a few years, and other times, such as in this breakthrough, I would feel supercharged, like I could glide through resistance as easily as a fish glides through the water.

There was an empowerment scheduled to be held on Orcas in February, and, as the time for it drew near, Walter began to express ambivalence about attending. This came as a shock; it would be the first time he had ever missed an empowerment should he decide not to attend. I could feel him agonizing over the decision, but there wasn't much he could say except that he was stuck and he knew it, but he couldn't mobilize his energy to work through it.

I didn't know what to do. As his wife and companion, I wanted to be supportive of him in deciding whatever he wanted to do, but as an apprentice, vowed to serve the Path above all else, I wanted to give him a boot in the buns and tell him to 'wake up.' Yet I could see he didn't know how to proceed. It was a difficult time, emotionally stressful, because of whatever he felt.

The only thing that made sense for me to do was keep my eye on the bull's-eye of my own awakening and pray that Walter would break through his stuck spot. I could see how troubled he was and had no idea how to help him.

About ten days before the event was scheduled to begin, I began to feel ill. My stomach and intestines were cramping terribly and I had a fever. It was all I could do to drag myself out of bed each day and carry on with my schedule. I thought it was a virus. The pains in my abdomen were terrible, sometimes causing me to double over in pain.

After several days passed and the 'virus' didn't improve, I became suspicious. Oddly, it never occurred to me to connect Walter and his crisis with my physical symptoms. My father had only been gone for a few months and I was executrix of the estate. I had been obsessively worrying about how to distribute the proceeds from the estate in a fair way, as my parents left everything to me and said, *'just do what you think is best.'*

I decided my virus was related to the stress I was experiencing due to the compounded impact of both mom and dad dying in less than a year's time, and the responsibility of distributing the remains of their estate fairly. It wasn't that there was so much, just that for some reason

I was obsessing over it. *"Please don't let me become a worrier like my mother,'* I prayed. It ate her up, literally.

"It must be a stress response to that loss," I told Walter one night as I was doubled over in the chair, in too much pain to get up, *"but I don't know what to do about it."* I should have talked to the Teacher, but I rationalized that with the empowerment a short time away, it would be too intrusive on her preparation time to talk about some personal concerns. If I had it to do over again, the decision would not be the same.

There was a viewpoint from the awakened consciousness, an awareness that all conditions are contained in the mind, meaning self-generated, habitual energy, often brought forth lifetime after lifetime. It was understandable to me in my head, but I was totally helpless to remain an observer to the situation; I couldn't separate my divine self from the pain and fear that illness represented, fear of not having control of my health.

The observer in me noted the pictures of my family that were placed all over the house; it looked like a shrine, and my therapist background told me this was my way of keeping them alive and present, rather than letting go and moving on. Even now, I think that was certainly a part of the trauma my body was responding to, but the other stress was created by Walter's difficulties. We had done everything together, our life together was focused on the Path and now that stability was threatened. But I missed that connection completely. And, because I didn't want the Teacher to know I was ill, I never mentioned it to her, so I lost the opportunity for her invaluable guidance.

Chapter 23
Being With the Nature of the Enlightened Mind

The empowerment was titled *GURU YOGA: Blending with the Nature of the Enlightened Mind.* This event was to be held on Orcas Island, so we were hosting it at the site of the local YMCA campground. It was complete with excellent vegetarian meals provided by their staff, so our physical needs were taken care of. Still, there was much work to be done in preparation for the 120 or so people who would be attending the event just a short week away. From the title, it was easy to see this would be one of the most impactful of all the empowerments thus far, because it defined the nature of the Teacher-student relationship as being like none other, and unimaginable to the ordinary mind.

Guru Yoga was the ultimate yoga, the ultimate surrender of student to Teacher, the complete merger of the student's consciousness with enlightened consciousness. What commitment could be greater than this and what commitment could be more threatening to the little-self or ego?

There was no choice but to carry on, in spite of the physical pain, so I did; but the pain was intense, coming over me in waves, doubling me up at times, especially after meals. During the empowerment, I tried to avoid eating but Winged Wolf insisted I needed to eat as a way of grounding. Since I was her personal attendant, we were constantly together and it was crucial that I be in companion energy with her at all times. The energy is so powerful at empowerments it can literally knock you down, so physical strength and grounding are essential.

During an empowerment, Winged Wolf's total focus is on the well-being of the whole, and she must keep it there at all times. So those of us in service to the Path would take care of all the physical and logistical needs of the Teacher and the participants. To those attending, it looked like one smooth move, and it was, but only because of Winged Wolf's power of attention and the support of local staff in companion energy with her. It is really quite amazing to be behind the scenes as an event such as this is put into motion, but it requires total, wholehearted participation, a willingness to do whatever is needed, whenever it is needed, even if that is in the middle of the night.

This was the most difficult empowerment, personally, I ever attended; the subject matter was such a stretch, taking us into uncharted territories and challenging our habitual, conceptual thinking, yet my body was in crisis, and I was still mourning the loss of my parents which made me hypersensitive and vulnerable. Tears came easily; for no apparent reason, waves of grief would pass through me.

While the subject of the empowerment was Guru Yoga, the ultimate merger of student's consciousness with the Teacher's consciousness, the theme or thread that wove it together was 'present moment awareness in conjunction with memory.' Memory is the link that connects the past, present and future for us, and memory is what makes it possible for us to merge consciousness with the Teacher, but real memory, not fabricated memory. Fabricated memory, Winged Wolf had taught us, is distorted memory; it could be a memory from our life experience that was distorted by becoming mixed up with our feelings about that experience or our attitudes and opinions.

It was not factual, or, it could be things we have seen, such as from watching a movie, and then added to our own memory about something we had experienced in our lives, and so the movie became a part of our memory and we remembered it as being ours. Winged Wolf told us that, for the average person, the ratio of real memory versus fabricated memory is about 60-40. *How sobering to realize that so much of what I remember is fabrication and much of what is told me by others is also fabrication, remembered as truth.*

This presentation and exploration of memory was a leap into the unknown for me and for the group, and Winged Wolf guided us into it in such a way that our brains were scrambled; and *by scrambling them in this way, an opening was created so we were able, as a whole, to spend a little time consciously awake in the present moment,* the place where an enlightened consciousness lives all the time. *We were getting glimmers into present moment awareness as it passed into memory* and tasting in those moments what it must be like to live life from the perspective of an awakened consciousness.

Winged Wolf was magnificent as she led us into her world of the present moment and showed us how memory overlays and parallel worlds are established through lifetimes, thereby giving us a distorted image of who we really are. As the divine consciousness awakens within us, these distorted memories are gradually untangled and the illusion is seen with clear vision, until only that which is the three-hundred-sixty-degree viewpoint of the awakened consciousness remains.

What became so clear to me as I began to integrate this information is how I had lived my life almost totally from unconscious memory, one lifetime to the next, doing the same things over and over again, living parallel existences, thinking I was psychic because I could predict the future, when all I really was doing was remembering from the past what was about to happen next. It was like the repetitive events in the movie 'Groundhog Day.'

In a sense, my physical and emotional misery forced me to become totally absorbed in the moment-to-moment progression of the weekend in order to live my vow as servant to the Teacher. It showed me the *power of attention* in a graphic manner. When I looked at myself, I suffered; when I looked at the Teacher and the Teachings, everything was fine. The pain was present but it was just background noise.

By the time I arrived home, the weekend complete and percolating within me, my stomach 'virus' was nearly over and I felt uplifted, flying on Garuda's wings*. We had taken all the apprentices who had not yet visited *Between the Wind* on a tour of the property. So many of them had been reading for years about our little Happy House, the chicken coop turned meditation center, but had no opportunity to visit. They were thrilled to at last have a look at the physical place from where the Teachings emanated, and to see the cushion their beloved Teacher occupied each morning. And, of course, the pond that had become infamous as a Teaching tool for those of us who didn't respond to gentler interventions.

---

*Garuda--a mythological bird, used as a symbol for the enlightened consciousness

There was so much to digest from the weekend, a part of me wanted to say, *'Let's stop right now, take a time-out, maybe for the next few years, to integrate all that the Teacher just gave us.'* But that isn't how it works living in the present moment. Life continues to unfold, moment to moment; it's best if we are present for it, and not on auto-pilot.

I had only what was left of that day, Sunday, to allow those Teachings to become a living part of me. But in a way, I was too full to do that. What I hadn't grasped yet was that if I left it alone and found that place of equanimity within myself, the Teachings would integrate naturally. But I was still using activity, motion, as a way to *zone out* and relax, so I was really stepping on my own feet. Not that there is anything wrong with activity when done from a place of awareness, but activity that is driven by the ego as a way of producing a certain feeling state is merely entertaining one's self. What all this means is that I went to Rosie's (a favorite local restaurant) and met my apprentice buddies for lunch!

Since I didn't know what to do about the situation at home, I basically ignored it and prayed it would resolve happily. Winged Wolf gave me some instructions that I tried to follow (at times, successfully) by saying, *"Just leave it alone. Don't talk about what goes on at 'Between.' Let him work it out."*

'Oh, boy,' I thought to myself. *'How am I to live with someone day in and day out, and not talk to them about what my life is about?'* I felt a big hole open inside of me as I could see our relationship split in two. The consequences were already beginning to take form.

Previously, Winged Wolf gave a talk in which she said, *"If your spouse or significant other is not on the Path but is supportive of you being on the Path, that is fine; but if your partner has been on the Path and then leaves, the relationship may be in serious trouble."*

That had struck a chord in me at the time she spoke it, because it said to me that if one of us left the Path, they may also eventually leave the relationship. I resisted accepting this idea and argued in my mind about it, probably because it rang true and I didn't want to accept it. I couldn't see the sense in it. Wouldn't a strong love bond take care of any differences people might have?

Now, here I was finding myself in exactly the situation she spoke about. I vowed it would not happen to me, at least not by my doing. And besides, he hadn't exactly left; he was going through a difficult time; that was all. He'd come around.

Days passed. A different type of rhythm developed in our lives. Monday through Friday, I went to *Between the Wind* and worked, meditated, and spent a great deal of time with Winged Wolf. Sometimes I attended the evening sittings as well. When I wasn't at *Between*, Walter and I carried on as usual, at least on the surface. We went to the movies, out to eat, took the dogs for long walks and took care of the business we owned jointly. The rest, we left alone. And I prayed for the best possible outcome for us both. Talk about leading a dual life! I knew it couldn't go on forever; something would have to give eventually.

When I asked the Teacher if there was anything I could do, she replied kindly, *"Nothing at all, just let it unfold. He will come around. All you can do is stay out of the way and let him work it out."*

A Glimpse from the Natural State

One day, not long after the Orcas Empowerment, Winged Wolf asked me if I would accompany her on a short foray into the rain forest. She hadn't taken any time for herself in several years and it seemed a good time for her to take a break from the day-to-day activities and give her body a rest. This would be a wonderful adventure into nature and a time for some quiet reflection, hikes in the forest and relaxation.

I accepted the invitation eagerly. Any opportunity to spend time with the Teacher was treasured. The day of our departure soon arrived and we headed off the island. I was eager in anticipation of the adventure ahead. As we were waiting in line for the ferry to arrive that would transport us to the mainland, a subtle vibration began in my body that was unsettling and distracting from the general mood of happy anticipation. I decided to ignore it.

After disembarking from the ferry, we headed west toward the rainforest. I had packed some snacks for us to munch on in our travels since I was usually hungry, and the Teacher rarely thought of food unless hunger arose in a particular moment. She told us that when she used to go hiking in the forest, she seldom brought food with her if she wasn't hungry at the time she left. Since I usually had plenty of attention on food, it became my unofficial job to be sure we had something to carry us through when we went hiking or on trips.

One of the most fun aspects of traveling with the Teacher was that we rarely chose a specific destination, or a particular place to stay; we just headed out, and at some point, it became clear to her we would go in this direction or stay at this place. I never knew what might happen during these adventures and it was a chance to let go and totally trust the Consciousness.

So, after a few hours of driving, we arrived at the rainforest and she pointed us in a direction. *"Let's see if we can find a place to stay that is rustic, quiet, unpopulated and in a beautiful setting."*

It wasn't long before just such a place appeared, a rustic lodge set facing a mountain, at the base of which was a crystal clear, deep blue lake that meandered for miles as far as the eye could see. And best of all, they had little rowboats.

Our rooms had little patios on the lakeside and were surrounded by huge pine trees, the scent of which wafted through the air making every intake of breath filled with the delicious scent of pine.

Winged Wolf convinced the owners we would be quite safe taking one of the boats out, even though it was off-season and they had concerns about weather, unexpected storms and such. Winged Wolf assured the owners we would be cautious and responsible, and off we went.

No sooner had we rowed out to the middle of this most spectacular lake, surrounded by the serenity of the mountains and forest, than I had another attack of the jitters. Waves of fear ripped through my body as I sat there in the total silence.

"What's going on with you?" she asked me.

"I don't know exactly, but I'm afraid, deeply afraid. This all seems so big."

She said, *"What is there for you to be afraid of here?"*

"I feel like I'm stepping into some place that is so vast I can't begin to comprehend it and it frightens me. And I don't want to ruin your vacation

by having my stuff come up in the space."

"Well it's up now, so we might as well deal with it. When did it begin?"

"We were coming back from Kentucky. On the plane I was reading Longchempa's book, Kindly Bent to Ease Us *and you asked me what I had learned about openness. Ever since we started talking about openness, something shifted in me."*

"Yes, go on," she replied.

"You explained to me that what he was saying is that true openness, which is the natural state, means to simply let go of all resistance, release all attachments and give freely in service to others. You told me that there are no limitations to openness and in this way there is a continuous flow of giving and receiving, meaning, you give to sentient life and you receive from the Transhistorical Consciousness, continuously. There is a never-ending wellspring of divine love flowing into and from you because you are that open."

"And what is there about that to frighten you?"

What could I say? There was no logic at all to the fear; it was instinctual, and by instinctual, I understood that meant my ego felt threatened, not that there was any real something to fear. I saw it but I couldn't live it.

"Nothing at all, really," I replied, feeling the tension fade. For a moment I could look out of myself and see and know that as the truth.

We finished our boat ride in relative quiet and brought the boat safely ashore. The rest of the evening passed peacefully as we sat and watched the sunset over the mountain, an unusual event, given we were staying in the rainforest.

But the demons weren't through with me yet. The next morning we awoke early planning a long hike into the forest. There were miles of trails surrounding our temporary home, all looking equally inviting.

As we hiked, Winged Wolf asked me, *"How did you sleep last night, Wings?"*

This set off an instant alarm that said, *'You disturbed the Teacher's sleep.'* I glanced quickly at her face and noted that she did not look her usual vibrant and colorful self (her complexion is hearty and rosy-cheeked normally). *"I tossed and turned but slept well in between,"* I said. *"How about you?"* During the night I had prayed that my restlessness and anxieties would not interfere with the Teacher's sleep.

She was silent as we continued our trek, the answer obvious. Coming around a bend, we stopped in our tracks as we heard a loud rumbling and felt the ground vibrating underneath us. The smell of the air was different.

"There's a waterfall up ahead," she announced, answering the unspoken question. *"It's a big one."*

We continued on for another eighth of a mile or so, the rumbling noise growing louder with each step. The air was crackling, filled with the scent of negative ions that usually accompanies the aftermath of a heavy rainfall.

"It's a beauty," I said in awe as we stood looking at thousands of gallons of water crashing down the side of the mountain into the swirling pool below.

After standing there silently together for some time, Winged Wolf said to me, *"I'm going to give you an experience of the natural state. Perhaps it will help you transmute this fear you are carrying around with you.*

"Look out over the waterfall and quiet your mind," she instructed me.

This was so unexpected; there was no time at all for my little-self to interfere. I stood and looked as I was told. It was subtle. At first, there seemed to be nothing happening, then I realized I was no longer looking at a waterfall crashing over a mountain, as a single event. What was being shown to me, in something like slow motion, was the individual droplets of water, each in their own unit, all flowing together as a whole, coming apart, then coming back together, forming peaks and waves, leaping out from the rock, pausing, holding in suspended animation for a moment, and then releasing and continuing down toward the pool of water below. During that time, I could see through the gushing water to the pieces of rock that formed the mountain behind it and I could see the crystal droplets of water as they bounced off the pool of water and leaped back into the air, only to fall back into the water again. Light refractions caught the individual droplets and shone in brilliant colors of red, turquoise, emerald green, orange and yellow.

And just as suddenly as the experience began, so it faded before my eyes and returned to its previous state of ordinary beauty. I could feel myself trying to pull it back, wanting more of the magical experience she had just given me.

"You were seeing from the natural state, Wings of Change. I showed it to you for a reason, so you would know there is nothing about the natural state of openness for you to fear. But it is not yet the place where you abide."

So my Teacher didn't get much of a vacation, and I didn't get what I prayed for (which was to be a good companion for her so she could get some rest), but it was more than I ever could have known to ask for; and that experience and the memory of it brought the Teachings alive in me in a new way, because through it, I glimpsed a tiny bit of what it was like to see through my Teacher's eyes. There was nothing to fear.

A Lesson in Giving

Winged Wolf made a trip nearly every week from Orcas to the mainland to visit her mother who lived in a town about two hours from the mainland ferry dock, and at times she would ask me to accompany her. There were usually errands to run in addition to the visit.

The first time I accompanied her, we were driving along, relaxed and talking about some cement statues of lions we had just driven past at a roadside market. She was interested in purchasing several for *Between the Wind*. She suddenly braked the car and drove slowly along toward the side of the road. *"Get my wallet out of the console,"* she commanded me.

Responding to the urgency in her voice, I fumbled with the latch on the console, until she finally assisted me by pulling the wallet out. She handed me some money. *"Give it to him,"* she said, pointing to a street person who was standing on the corner by the overpass to the freeway holding a sign that said, *Will work for food*. I looked at the money in my hand and it was a twenty-dollar bill and then I glanced at her questioningly. She nodded to me and said, *"Give it to him!"* then proceeded to drive slowly toward the beggar.

As we approached, I rolled down the window on my side of the car and reached my arm out to the man. There was a dull look about him as he reached for the money, eyes that looked flat and lifeless. I remember feeling a sense of hopelessness as I looked at him. He started to stuff the bill in his pocket without looking at it, but something caught his attention and he focused his eyes on the bill, and then quickly looked up at us. His eyes were shining, alive and excited. *"God bless you,"* he called to us as we pulled back out onto the road. *"God bless you,"* I could hear him call again as we drove away. There was total silence in the car as the energy of that experience filled me. *"It made a difference,"* I said in awe. *"The amount made a difference. It woke him up."*

She said, *"If you only have a dollar, then give at least half of it, but if you can, give more. Give enough that you penetrate a beggar's despair and destitution, so that, if only for a moment, that person wakes up. For a moment that man felt himself alive and aware. Sure, he'll go right back to sleep, but that doesn't matter. What matters is that his consciousness was ignited for a short period."*

All day, as we went to different places, she watched for beggars. Each time, it was the same. A man and his dog stood on one corner; I handed him the twenty and he casually glanced at, then looked again. The light went on and his eyes shone. *"Now I can buy food for my dog,"* he said with tears in his eyes as we drove off.

The next time we headed off the island, Winged Wolf cautioned me, *"Be sure and have some twenty-dollar bills with you."* And so I did.

The first time I pulled a twenty out of my wallet, there was a moment, a brief moment, when my brain felt like a wire had been pulled and I was discombobulated. All my life I had given to beggars in dribbles and drabs, a dollar here, a couple of dollars there, just enough to assuage my conscience and say I had done something. As I transferred that twenty from my hand into the beggar's, something was released, and it was released before he ever had an opportunity to see the denomination on the bill. I felt expanded: free, generous, not with him, but with myself. I was being generous with myself when I gave beyond my limitations, and it was exhilarating. I was eager to find the next beggar and give some more!

Many, many times we repeated this scene, until one day as we made our usual rounds, there were no more beggars. Winged Wolf was really pleased. It told a story, and the story was that there was no more poverty consciousness in her environment on that day. A good sign, the divine consciousness had reached out and touched those beggars so they no longer needed to beg.

Winged Wolf told me, *"Never refuse to give to a beggar. Give something, whatever you can, but give."* People who beg are at the bottom of the survival scale, living in such poverty consciousness they must beg to live. No one should be refused. And further, she said, *"Do not judge what they do with the money. If they spend it on alcohol, that is their business; you just give. Do not concern yourself with what someone does with what you give them. It doesn't matter."*

The idea of a non-judging attitude about what someone does with what they are given was, at first, challenging to my viewpoint. It seemed a waste of money to give to someone who was most likely going to 'squander' it (a judgment) anyway. But, after listening to the Teacher, and then experiencing the giving without expectation, I found great freedom released in me to give without concern for what the receiver might do with what was given. It wasn't my business. I wanted to run around giving for the sheer joy it gave me to free up that energy and to see that spark of awakening on the face of the beggar receiving the money, and to know that for a moment his/her consciousness was ignited. And, finally, to see the result of giving over a period of weeks and months, whereby there were no more beggars on the corners to give to. That part of the lesson was so powerful.

It seemed that the startling of their consciousness into awakening for that moment, by giving them more than they ever expected to receive, created an opening for something more than money to be given and received. It created an opening for them to receive the unconditional love of the divine consciousness; and in the receiving of that, their poverty consciousness was transformed. I saw that the divine consciousness has the power to uplift someone to complete a karmic cycle so that the possibility for the beggars to evolve spiritually out of poverty consciousness became a fact.

Being With the Nature of the Enlightened Mind

Transcendental Awareness

"Transcendental mind takes one's experience and uses it to leapfrog into the unknown. The unknown experience is a realization of self in relation to other selves. It takes all things and no thing together as the Oneness and operates in total companion energy with all existence." *(Master Maticintin)*

The morning was electric; we could feel it as we passed through the gate that set the boundary for *Between the Wind*. I felt a chill run up my spine and said to Walter, *"Something is in the wind today; can you feel it?"* He nodded in agreement. The energy was charged.

We hurried down to the Happy House and found Winged Wolf already seated, a sign that something was up. Once everyone was settled on their cushions, I thought sure she would say something, but she did not. We sat in meditation for a long time. Finally she spoke.

"I'm going to share a vision with you. It is premature for the entire vision to become a reality, but parts of it we can begin implementing right away. I need to prepare your minds first to receive it and then later we will develop it for the masses.

"For some time now I have been seeing that in the future we will have a school, and that school will be called The Transcendental Awareness Institute. It will be a place of higher learning, a place where people's minds are blown open by the process of transcendental learning. One day we will have schools all over the world where Transcendental Awareness is taught.

"In Buddhism, the word transcendental *refers to that quality of 'crossing to the other shore,' meaning to become enlightened. It is referred to as a Paramita. The transcendental mind is the enlightened mind, the mind that has transcended all little-self reactions.*

"This transcendental mind is mind-in-action and the only way you can learn about it is to actually experience it. So, I'm going to begin teaching the first part of it today after lunch, here in the Happy House. It will take place in the form of a debate."

She went on to describe a few details for us, but would not take any questions, saying, *"I don't want you to have any preset ideas about what will take place. All you need to bring with you is an open mind and a willing spirit."*

After we had all re-gathered in the Happy House, Winged Wolf divided us into 'teams.' We sat facing each other, sitting cross-legged on our meditation cushions.

She said, *"Is the essence of rose, a rose?"*

We all looked at her expectantly, wanting an answer. Instead, she said, "Team One," and she waved her arm to the right, *"you will take the position that the essence of rose is in fact the same as a rose, and you will debate it with Team Two, who will take the position that it is not the same."*

"Go!"

Silence. No one knew how to conduct such a debate. She pointed to someone on Team One and said, *"State your case. Why do you perceive the essence of a rose to be the same as a rose?"*

Pretty soon, we got in the flow of it and the discussion became lively, even heated. *"Whoa,"* she said, *"there is no place for emotion here. This is a debate, not a competition."*

This was mind expansion in action! I loved it, even though half the time I had no idea what I was saying, or how anything would end up; the transcendental quality of it brought a vigor and aliveness that was exhilarating.

For weeks, we gathered each afternoon and debated such questions, each one slightly different in twist. I learned there were no pat answers, nothing that could be memorized and recited; it was all spontaneously enacted in the moment. Each session was recorded, and after several weeks, our debates ended, and a new course had been born. Winged Wolf said this was a beginning whiff of the power of transcendental mind to awaken us, and when the time was ripe, we would take it up from there.

Chapter 24
Expansion

One morning, a week or so after our trip into the rainforest, I arrived at *Between the Wind*, and Winged Wolf was waiting for me. She pulled me aside and said, *"It is time to expand our Spiritual Order. I must have more space to accomplish the work I have set out to do."*

"How much space do you need?" I asked, puzzled. Already we had discontinued the visiting apprentice program, except under special circumstances. We all knew what a toll it took on her body to have apprentices stay on the property. Now she was talking about expansion; it didn't make any sense to me.

"I don't know exactly how much land we will need, but more than this, and different. The neighbors block us every time we make a move toward expansion. We can't expand in any direction here. And, we are moving into an expansive phase as we mature, so I must be able to work closely with my advanced apprentices."

Now I voiced a concern, *"How can you do that, when we can't even have a few of them here at 'Between' without injuring you?"*

"It will be different when we have more space around us. I can't tell you exactly how it will work, but it will; I know it. We need to have a Temple and a Stupa for the Teachings, and a more remote physical location."

"Does this mean you are ruling out the property next door?"

"Not necessarily, but so far, they have been unreceptive to all our advances about purchasing their property. We can no longer wait. I want the search to begin immediately, and we'll put the word out to others to search as well. At this point, we are totally open as to location. There are no limitations on our search."

Tuning In to the Present Moment by Tuning In to the Teacher

Thus began a year of intense searching for the property that would meet our needs for expanded service. It was probably the most intense year of my life with the Teacher thus far, because it was my role as Savant to be in companion energy at all times, as best I could. It was also an opportunity to observe on almost a moment-to-moment basis how the consciousness of the Teacher flowed with the energies as they were presented.

Winged Wolf called a meeting of the local apprentices to let them know about the need for expansion and to let them know we would be traveling as much as necessary to locate our new home.

When everyone was gathered, Winged Wolf said, *"Wings and I will be traveling later this month to begin a search for property that will serve our need to expand. Wherever it is, I can tell you it will be beautiful, and it will be our natural next step. It is very important that each of you is in companion energy with me on this. You must trust absolutely that everything will work out, and do not allow any of your little-self concerns to arise. If you do, it will interfere with our finding the right location.*

"Also, I ask each of you to carry on as though I were present while we are traveling. If you contain the energy here at 'Between,' the rest of our Spiritual Order will be fine, but if you allow your energy to spill over, and your mind to chatter on about all the 'what ifs,' that will spill out into the apprentice body and wreak havoc there. It will create chaos. Can I count on each of you to hold the fort while I am away?"

The local apprentices had been around during the time Winged Wolf's body began to suffer from the stress of the heavy karmic energy of so many visiting apprentices pulling on her at the same time. They voiced loud concerns as to what this meant in terms of visitors and pleaded with me to protect the Teacher.

"I'll do my best, you know I will," I tried to reassure them, but we all knew Winged Wolf would follow her vision, which came out of her commitment to serve, and whatever she saw as the impeccable way is the way it would be. *"We have to trust her when she says she is protected. We can't be second-guessing her. That will only cause more stress."*

One of the first lessons I received during this phase of my relationship with the Teacher is that once a decision is made, prompt action follows. Focused, contained attention is placed on the direction one wants to go, and it locks into place on that goal. From that point on, everything is directed toward that. I think I had a childlike fantasy that once a decision was made, a voice or such would suddenly come forth and say, *'Go there.'* But what I saw was a rational, deductive process that said, *'Where shall we begin?'* And then came a sorting of options.

Winged Wolf told us, *"There are no limitations to the divine consciousness. It is best to remain totally open to all opportunities so the divine forces can work without any interference from anyone's ideas about how something should look."*

Arizona became our first target, for many reasons. It was familiar; the climate was friendly; it certainly offered some wide-open spaces; and we needed to begin somewhere.

I was reminded of the time Winged Wolf talked to us about opportunities and used the analogy of looking for feathers. She said, *"If you pass up the first feather you see because it isn't good enough or pretty enough or whatever, it may be a long time before you find another. Always take what is offered as a beginning point. You have to begin somewhere."*

Saving Sentient Beings Takes Priority

So the search began back where we had started, Cottonwood, Arizona. It seemed to me to be the perfect location. After we checked in to a motel, it was time for dinner. One of our favorite gastronomical things to do, on the rare occasion we were in a position to do so, was to eat at a Chinese Restaurant. Winged Wolf had made up a dish that we often ordered, Kung Pao Tofu. The crucial factor was whether the tofu was sufficiently deep-fried so that it wasn't soft or squishy.

That night we headed for a local Chinese restaurant. It would be a special treat since there were no Chinese restaurants on Orcas. They seated us beneath a huge fish tank, and Winged Wolf commented that Chinese restaurants usually have fish tanks because fish are considered to be good luck.

As we looked up at the tank, we noted there were a number of enormous carp occupying it, such that the tank appeared greatly overcrowded. It was an uncomfortable feeling to see the fish fighting for space, and I looked away.

"That tank is overcrowded," Winged Wolf suddenly commented gazing at them. *"It's cruel to keep them in that condition."*

"I noticed it, too," I replied. *"Perhaps we should change tables."*

The waiter came to take our order and she said, *"That fish tank is very overcrowded. The fish are fighting for air."*

He looked up nonchalantly and nodded, waiting expectantly for our order.

"There are too many large fish in it," she persisted.

I geared myself for the inevitable tension that was to come. She wasn't going to let it go.

"The fish were small when we first had them, but they keep growing larger," he shook his head as though saying, *"What can we do?"*

We ordered and, when the food arrived, began eating, but there was now a concern in the space. I watched Winged Wolf, knowing she was considering how to assist the fish.

"I bet they could find a local pond owner who would take them," she told me.

When the waiter returned, she asked, *"Would you give them to someone who has a pond?"*

"We don't know anyone who has a pond," he replied.

After finishing our meal, we headed back to our motel. It was late and we had an early morning appointment with our real estate team. I knew Winged Wolf was still looking at what to do about the fish. It was a troublesome image.

"What can we do?" I asked her.

She brightened as an idea struck. *"What do you say we relocate them?"*

"How do we do that?" I asked.

"Let's go back to the restaurant and talk with the manager. I think he will be happy to have us help him. He just doesn't know what to do. Surely we can find someone with a pond who will take them. Or, I just remembered something. There is a park that has a large pond that flows into the Verde River. We can release them there."

We drove to the restaurant and asked to speak to the manager. I must say that at this point it felt surrealistic to me that we were actually asking this person if we could remove his fish from their tank and whisk them off to freedom. I wondered if he would be insulted.

Left to my own devices, I would have felt great compassion for the fish, but gone about my business and resolved never to eat at that restaurant again. The idea that we could intervene and actually DO something was revolutionary to me. It was only because of my Teacher that I was learning the DO of compassion and the responsibilities of serving all sentient life.

At first the manager was defensive, explaining to us how the fish were so little when they first got them and how no one realized they would grow so big; now he didn't know what to do with them.

Winged Wolf interrupted his diatribe, *"I understand what happened and we're not here to blame you; we simply want to take the fish to a place where they can breathe. The only thing we need from you is help in getting them into our container and then out to the car."* After a pause in which he looked as though he wanted to continue with his explanation, the manager said, *"If you can come tomorrow night after 9:00, we won't be so busy and we can help you load the fish."*

"Is that the earliest you can help us?" Winged Wolf asked. *"It's quite late at night for us to relocate them."*

"Yes, yes, that is the best time," he nodded firmly.

"All right then," she shrugged, *"we'll be here at 9:00 tomorrow night."*

As we drove away, I marveled aloud at how smoothly the arrangement was made. Since I had expected he would be insulted or feel we were intruding in his business, it was amazing how easily he became agreeable.

"If you will notice," Winged Wolf commented, *"a person can do or say almost anything as long as it is from a place of divine love. People recognize That, and they respond from their own divine self. He didn't feel insulted; he felt relieved."*

And she was right, I had watched it happen time and time again; I would be holding my breath waiting for an explosion, and situations would flatten out and flow smoothly, no matter what they looked like in the beginning.

The next day, the search for property began. Here, I learned another great lesson, and again it had to do with being open. Each time we arrived at a prospective property, I found myself making an instantaneous judgment. *'Oh, this doesn't look right,'* or *'we could never live here.'* Usually it was something negative that ruled the property out instantly.

However, to my amazement, Winged Wolf took an entirely different approach. She simply looked at what was being presented, quietly approaching each property. Occasionally, she pointed out something I hadn't seen, because, the door in my mind had already closed.

She might say, *'Well, we could put the office here,'* or *'that would be a good spot for the Temple'*. It wasn't until she had a complete overview of whatever property we looked at that she would make an assessment, such as, *'that one is a possibility,'* or *'that won't work, there isn't enough privacy,'* or whatever she saw that stood out. I could see what she was doing, but could not do that myself because of my strong reactions, triggered by my attachment to how I thought it should look.

As the real estate portion of that day ended, Winged Wolf turned her attention toward relocating the suffocating fish. She thought about it, *"I remember a large lake that is on the outskirts of town, and more difficult to reach. There's an old gravel road leading up to it. We'll start driving and see if I can locate the road. As I recall, it would be a perfect place for the fish and it's not privately owned."*

After a while, she spotted the turnoff. It was not marked; you had to know it was there. The road was in terrible condition, full of potholes, and traveling was slow. I imagined making the trip with a tank full of water and fish, trying not to jar them. It would be a long, slow journey.

Finally we saw the lake up ahead and as we approached it, we began looking for a good low spot to place the fish. After several exploratory stops, we found the perfect location: a gentle slope that led gradually down to the lake where the water was shallow and reedy, an excellent place for them to become acclimated to their new environment.

Satisfied we had found our drop-off place, we returned to Sedona, ate, and waited for 9 o'clock to arrive. We must have collapsed time on this day for so much to have been accomplished, because it was still only 7:30.

Precisely at 9pm we entered the restaurant, and, as predicted, it was quiet. The only people still eating were staff. The manager began speaking rapidly in Chinese to several younger men who were eating at one of the tables. He walked toward them, talking and waving his arm in the direction of the fish tank. They looked at him, uncomprehendingly. Apparently he had not mentioned our rescue mission prior to this, probably thinking we would not follow through. Most people wouldn't have.

Finally, after much talking and gesturing, two of the young men rose and headed over toward the tank. We handed them our temporary container and fish scooper; then began a painful process of capturing the now-frightened fish who were swimming frantically back and forth trying to avoid the net.

It was painful to watch this, and Winged Wolf was agonizing with the fish as, one by one, they were transported from the tank to our large plastic chest. We had asked the manager to fill it with water from the tank so the fish wouldn't go into shock and die before we could get them to the lake.

When the last fish was secure in the chest, the men carried it out to our car and placed it in the trunk. This done, we began the delicate process of driving to the lake as smoothly as possible.

I was the designated driver, while Winged Wolf navigated. I was so tense at first I could feel my neck muscles freezing up and my hands locked stiffly on the wheel of the car. After an eternity of driving and imagining what it was like for those poor fish crammed together in the chest being jostled about as we bumped slowly up the gravel road to the lake, we arrived at our spot.

We were almost there. Now it was a matter of lifting the heavy tank out of the trunk of the car without tipping it.

Inch by inch, we slid over to the water's edge and set the chest down, breathing a sigh of relief. No accidents thus far. Winged Wolf had a plan for releasing them. We had to take our shoes off and carry the chest into the water, where, ever so carefully, we turned it on its side and allowed the water from the lake to merge with the water in the chest. After a few moments, we lowered it further, and the fish were gently catapulted into their new lake home.

What happened next was a shock. Not one fish moved. I had anticipated they would swim off into the night, joyful at being free; instead, they did nothing. To a fish, they were absolutely still, hanging together in small clusters, as though unsure of what to do. They were free, but they didn't know it.

"They're paralyzed," I hissed to Winged Wolf. *"What do we do?"*

"Be patient," she whispered, *"let them adjust."*

"Are you sure this was the right thing to do?" I asked, wavering.

"Better they should have one moment of freedom, than to die from congested confinement," came the response. Hearing that made me feel better. She was right, of course.

After a few minutes they were still huddled together. *"I'm going to try using the light to guide them,"* she whispered, turning the flashlight on and shining it on one part of the group.

We watched silently as she played the light over them and out toward the center of the lake, as though guiding them in a direction. Finally, slowly, one of the fish began swimming toward the light. I almost jumped for joy. Pretty soon, another fish headed out in the same direction. After an hour or so of this guidance, we were down to the last two fish, the reluctant ones. We waited. Surely they would get their courage up and move on. It was after midnight now and I was tired, my legs ached from sitting on my haunches.

Another few minutes passed with Winged Wolf slowly rolling the flashlight first over the fish, then out toward the depths of the water. One of them began to move outward, and I let out a sigh of relief. It was inevitable the other would follow, and it did. We watched until we could see nothing in the water but blackness. Then we packed up our rescue gear and headed back to our motel. A job well done, and now I was exhilarated. Mission accomplished. The fish were free to live whatever life lay before them.

One thing every apprentice learns early on is the importance of quieting the mind, especially when it is time for the Teacher to rest. Many times Winged Wolf has said to me, *"Please, get to bed early so I can get some sleep!"*

Whenever we traveled together, I worried that my tendency to stay up late at night would keep her awake. But if I focused on it, my worry would only make matters worse and I'd begin obsessing on getting to sleep. Then I'd toss and turn for a long while, images of Winged Wolf sitting up in bed passing through my mind.

This night turned out well. By the time we arrived at our motel, I was wound down and exhausted. The adrenalin I had used to keep my energy strong during our adventure and immediately afterwards was used up, and I could barely hold my head up long enough to get my nightshirt on and fall into bed. The next thing I knew the phone was ringing and I was dazedly looking around the room trying to remember where I was.

I grabbed the phone and heard, *"Are you up?"* came her cheerful voice.

"Not exactly," I mumbled, trying to shake the fog out of my brain. *"What time is it?"*

"It's nearly 7," she said. *"I'm just getting up myself. How about breakfast at 8?"*

"Sounds good to me," I replied, grateful for the extra hour, and fell back on the bed. Usually when Winged Wolf is nearby, I am instantly awake when her consciousness awakens. It is such a powerful experience, I am pulled into instant alertness, but this morning I was really tired. The evening had taken me far out of my comfort zone, and I was riding in the wake of her consciousness, borrowing it, really.

Being a spiritual warrior was stressful mostly because I flip-flopped back and forth between living at the Third Eye and ordinary consciousness. I didn't have enough consistency to maintain the viewpoint all the time. If I had, I wouldn't have experienced stress and fatigue in the same way.

It showed up especially when I traveled with Winged Wolf and when we were together all day, because she was always operating from the divine viewpoint. With my Teacher, every moment was full and there was no break in the forward momentum.

At first I thought she never relaxed, but after observing her and being with her, I realized she was usually relaxed, but she was never unconscious. What I equated with relaxation was really being unconscious. When I was with her, I could live in her consciousness for a while, then feelings of needing to get away and relax into myself again arose; otherwise, I started to get tense and uncomfortable from being stretched too far, too long. It was a huge nuisance to have an active little-self, a major interruption.

The next day, we found what looked to be the perfect property, although it was priced at quite a bit more than we had intended to spend. At least seeing this property showed me something from the Teacher's viewpoint, gave me an overview of what it was that was needed for the expanded work she would be doing. There were some glitches that needed to be worked out, but this property was workable. We headed back to Orcas feeling encouraged.

Following the offer came a string of negotiations, based on the contingency clauses we had included, none of which seemed unsurpassable at the time, all part of working out the details. There was great enthusiasm among local apprentices who were eager for a land of sunshine and warmth. We figured service could be given just as easily in the sunshine of Arizona as in the rains of Orcas Island.

Weeks rolled by as we hammered away at the various stipulations to the contract, and one by one, they fell into place. A couple local apprentices made a trip to Arizona to view the area and scout out some places to live. They returned a little subdued by the lack of decent rentals they had seen, but surely it would all work out.
We had agreed on price and terms, except for a few conditions. Winged Wolf and I made a second trip to Arizona to re-look at the property and see if she could come to grips with one of her biggest concerns, and it was a big one: there was no written guarantee that the Forest Service would keep the road leading into the property open for us. That was the only entryway, and we would be the only property on the road.

Winged Wolf told me stories of the U.S. Forest Service arbitrarily closing roads. They could close the roads leading to someone's property, which would force the property owners to negotiate with the neighbors for an easement to access their property, which could be very costly, especially since we were a public organization.

"I assure you this could happen," she told me matter of factly, *"and given the future we intend for this property as our home for many lifetimes to come, the issue must be resolved satisfactorily for us to proceed. Our first step is to contact the Forest Service and see what can be negotiated with them."*

The present owners were nonchalant about the situation; they had always had rights of ingress and egress and couldn't see that it would ever change. It was understood, but nothing was in writing and the government had refused to put it into writing. Additionally, we were told that we would have to pay to have an archeological study on the existing forest service road to ascertain if Indian ruins were present, which was not only possible, but likely, since we were in Indian country along the river.

If this were confirmed, the access road would be closed to us and we would have to find another way into the property. The archeological study could not take place until the close of escrow and would be carried out entirely at our expense.

An Omen Is Received

Arriving once again at the prospective property, Winged Wolf walked down the curving road to the pond at the bottom of the hill. Large

numbers of Canada Geese waddled over to greet us. Others were swimming on the pond. We were enjoying watching them as the owner walked out to greet us. It was a pleasant meeting and we were chatting casually about the geese, when the owner began telling us a story.
"After the children were older and off at school," she told us, "I was so lonely and I wanted some companionship, so I began feeding the geese. The more I fed them, the more they came, but they all left for the winter, and I was lonely again, so the next season I clipped their wings."

She went on chatting with us, not noticing the absolute silence that had fallen on our side of the conversation. Winged Wolf said, "You mean their wings are clipped so they can't fly?"

"Why yes," the owner dropped her head and looked apologetic. "I know it was a terrible thing to do to them, but at the time, all I could think of was keeping them here for company."

Winged Wolf was deeply affected by this information, and I wondered where this conversation would lead. My stomach tightened. Our realtors hadn't yet grasped the disastrous significance of this seemingly casual conversation.

Winged Wolf continued, "So you mean that after you leave, we'll be responsible for taking care of them, since they can no longer take care of themselves?"

Awareness began to dawn on the others, and the owner began to squirm. "Maybe I can find a neighbor with a pond who is willing to care for them."

"I certainly hope so," replied Winged Wolf, "because we have enough responsibilities without taking on the care of all these geese. They would be dependent on us for their care and we will become responsible for them if we buy this property. And there is nothing we can do to correct their situation."

This couldn't be happening. How could a person have done this to the geese? And, on the other side, could a flock of geese be a big enough issue to block our purchase? And, besides, we had Ozzie and Harriet, our two Canada Geese back on the pond at Orcas that we always took loving care of. But then I remembered, they could fly; they could protect

Expansion

themselves if need be by flying away. They were with us by choice. These geese would be easy prey for coyotes and foxes; they were now dependent on humans for their survival. I said a prayer that things would work out.

Reluctantly, Winged Wolf left this conversation as the realtors urged us forward to walk the property again and ask any questions we might have of the husband who had taken the day off to show us about the irrigation system. But I could see her mind was still on the geese.

Now we had an additional issue to make peace with. The divine consciousness always drew these blemishes to the surface, the unseen blemishes. I had come to realize it, but was often still surprised by the many faces these blemishes could take, usually when they were least expected.

We got the name of the Forest Service agent from the owners so we could call to talk with him about the road, but he was away on vacation for a few days! This was not a good omen. It meant we would be leaving Arizona without having settled the road issue. And now we had the geese issue as an added responsibility. Once the realization of the damaged geese penetrated, the full impact of the action struck me, and I could see how we would be left with the responsibility of caring for something broken that could not be fixed, and feeling the pain of that every time we looked at them. At that moment, I knew deep down that we weren't going to be purchasing that property. I felt saddened. Only a few short days ago, it had seemed so perfect for us.

We returned to Orcas in a more somber mood. Perhaps we weren't moving to Arizona after all. The tides seemed to be turning away from it.

"I think we would be foolish to purchase this land without written permission from the Forest Service to use the access road indefinitely," Winged Wolf said on the plane trip back.

"What are you suggesting we do?" I asked. *"Are you sensing we should back out of the offer?"*

"It isn't time to withdraw from it," she responded. *"We have set a cycle in motion and we need to see it through."*

"What do you mean? Are you saying we can't withdraw the offer?"

Initiation

"No, I'm not ready yet," she responded. *"I like the property, but if we can't get some clarity on that road, I'm not going ahead. I say we should give them a deadline to provide us some valid reassurance about it."*

As we flew back to Washington, I completed my journal notes and started to pack up my notebook when suddenly a page flipped open, and I caught the words *'Secret Canyon.'* Immediately, my mind transported back to our first trip to Sedona to look for property. I flipped through my notes from that trip and looked over at Winged Wolf, who appeared to be asleep. She probably needed some private time and this was a polite way to have it. I continued reading, remembering as I read.

That trip had been loaded with Teaching stories, and upon our return, I had been asked to talk to the local apprentices at *Between the Wind* about all the lessons I had learned. There were pages and pages of notes on these adventures, but two of them stood out for me.

One part of the adventure had made a special impression on me, besides the poison ivy that showed up a few days later all over my body. We had been hiking into a place called Secret Canyon in the Sedona backcountry. The Teacher had said it was a really special place, a place of wonder. The day had been hot and dry, and it was a long hike, twelve miles round trip. Winged Wolf wouldn't say anything more than, *"Wait until you see it, then you will understand the secret."*

We had walked for a long time in the blistering heat, around and around the mountain, and down and down. The scenery was desert, dry and red, beautiful in a brittle way. After the first couple hours, there had been a subtle shift in the energy and the temperature. The descent had been gradual but continuous. I have no idea how far we had descended, but after a while, we were the only people still visibly hiking. A gentle breeze blew, drying the rivulets of perspiration from my forehead and eyes.

As we had approached the three-hour mark, I had been wondering, *'How much farther can this be?'* when we rounded a corner, and suddenly, *there it was*, the Secret Canyon. From the dusty, dry, red dirt and rocks, carved into the bottom of this long descent, a river rushed, surrounded by towering trees, cottonwood and pine; green grass grew on both sides of the river banks and the air was cool, probably 20 degrees cooler than just a few steps above on the red dirt.

Quickly descending the last few steps, we had rushed over to the river, taking off our shoes simultaneously and putting our hot, tired feet into the chilly clear waters of the rushing river.

"Oh, how sweet it is," Winged Wolf had crooned to the river as she dangled her toes in the icy water and rolled her eyes in pleasure. We had sat side by side on a log at the riverbank and breathed in the delicious pine-scented air. After some time had passed, she had asked me, *"Well, do you understand now why it is called the Secret Canyon?"*

"Oh, yes", I had replied, *"this is a magical place hidden in the desert."*

Suddenly the Teachers' voice shook me out of my reverie. *"Wings, where are you?"* she asked.

"Oh, I was just remembering the time we hiked into Secret Canyon and all the great stories we brought back to the others. It was such a magical hike."

"Yes, it was, wasn't it?"

The conversation distracted us a bit from the heaviness of our present trip and lifted our spirits for the moment. If it weren't that property, we would simply find another. Again and again, the urgency of living in the present moment was honed into me. What looked perfect on the surface, had perhaps some irreparable flaws, and the Teacher was unwilling to compromise on the one that could affect our well being as an evolving Spiritual Order. Each moment had to be lived in order for the next to ripen, and the moments could not be rushed.

Once we arrived back at Orcas, Winged Wolf cautioned us about the importance of remaining in a place of equanimity during this time of anticipation and waiting. *"I know it is difficult,"* she would say, *"but it is of utmost importance that each of you remain in a place of equanimity, where there is no push and no pull. If you are having conversations in your mind, pulling for something to happen or not to happen, you are interfering with the natural unfoldment of events, and making it more difficult for me. This is why I often keep things to myself until they have time to come to fruition."*

The day we were to return to Arizona for a tentative closing on the property, all planes leaving the island were cancelled due to severe weather conditions, and there was nothing flying even if we took a ferry to the mainland and somehow made it to Seattle.

We spent the afternoon driving around the island, walking the beaches to absorb this omen. Was it saying this was not the right property for us? Winged Wolf said, *"Do you remember the day we walked down toward the pond, just before we began talking to the owner, and all the geese appeared?"*

"Yes, I do, Winged Wolf."

"I had a premonition right before we began talking. It was fleeting, but it was a strong feeling that we would not be buying that property. Then when we began talking with her, she told us about clipping the wings of the geese. That was like the omen confirming the oracle, which was my premonition. I brushed it aside at the time because the property seemed perfect for us, and the geese were not on our contingency list, but a part of me knew it wasn't going to work. I think our plane (to sign the closing papers) being cancelled is a sign that it's over. We're going to have to call them and let them know we won't be purchasing the property. It isn't meant to be ours. We've come full circle with this cycle."

There was relief in having clarity once again and in having this intense cycle completed. What an incredible experience to be in companion energy with the Teacher in such a critical situation. I had learned so much about staying open and in a place of equanimity, with full attention on the Teacher. It was an 'edge-of-your-seat' type of experience. I developed enormous respect for the responsiveness of the Teacher to each situation as it presented and her commitment to the whole, that they be served in the best way possible, no matter what.

Some people were disappointed to learn we would not be moving to Arizona, land of warmth and sunshine; and so, for them it became an opportunity to examine the nature of their attachments, since it was that desire to be in a particular place that had become an attachment for them. We had to examine our responses, to see how agile and flexible we were in responding to change, not getting caught up in expectations of how something had to be a certain way. Everyone in the Spiritual Order was impacted. They had all been told we were probably moving and had seen pictures of the area on our website. It was a time of quick readjustment; something had become solid in people's minds and now that dream was being dissolved to begin another.

So, the word went out to begin looking for property again. There was a momentum going; it was important to keep the dream alive. And now, a subtle voice began making its appearance, a voice that said, *'How about Canada?'* Winged Wolf has a large Canadian following and, not surprisingly, as they learned that Arizona would not be our new spiritual home, they began to suggest that the Teacher consider Canada as a potential site for HÜMÜH's relocation.

Crossing a Bridge

One day, Winged Wolf came and got me out of the small, one-room Willow House, which had become my office, and said, *"Let's take a walk out on the bridge."*

No doubt she had picked up on my frustrated and tumultuous thoughts. The bridge over the pond was a place of equanimity, a place between the energies, between the worlds. Being on water had that effect, even if it was only a two-acre pond. We had learned from being out on Winged Wolf's boat, that once away from shore, all the stresses and strings of energy that pulled at her soon fell away, and relaxation followed. But a bridge had special symbolism.

We sat in the middle of the bridge over the water and just looked out for a while. The dragonflies were out in numbers. They were the most beautiful and varied I have ever seen. Looking at them, I understood why the ancient people were inspired to make jewelry and pottery in certain patterns. Some of these dragonflies were turquoise, and the tiny patterns they carried on their backs looked just like the necklaces I had seen Native American people selling. Others were brilliant red and bright green. How could these brilliantly colored little creatures not touch a spark of aliveness in all who viewed them?

"It's an in-between place out here," Winged Wolf said, *"a place of no push and no pull. Can you feel the struggle fall away?"*

"Yes, I can feel the natural peacefulness and serenity of being in a position of just looking out at life, without likes or dislikes, without attitudes and opinions pulling at me," I replied. *"Just being on this bridge gives me a sense of freedom, nonattachment."*

The inner turmoil I had been experiencing was pulled up to the surface and bubbled out of me. I knew I would speak that which I had not wanted to say. It was the way the awakened divine consciousness of the Teacher worked. The struggle was close enough to the surface that it could be sucked out. And there was another struggle beneath that one that I didn't want to come up at all. I really was feeling that I had come as far as I could in my apprenticeship. The feeling was completely irrational, but it was so insistent, I was at a loss to understand what was happening. In private moments, it tormented me.

Perhaps I anticipated the Teacher would be as upset as I was, but she was quite calm. *"Well, let's just let it play out,"* she responded, gazing at me with that sideways look that said to me, *'You're blinded to what is happening to you, but there's nothing I can say right now that will help you see it.'*

"I am not happy right now; it isn't rational or anything I can point to as a reason either. Every fiber of my being says this is where I belong, here with you on the Path, yet the inner guidance I have always relied on, that guidance that insisted I stay with you when you became Buddhist and I wanted to leave, tells me now it is time to leave. And I'm confused. It's always been this guidance that I rely on for making a correct choice. Now it's pushing me to leave you." I felt relieved having said this. It had been an undercurrent for the past few weeks, one I kept looking away from.

She was silent for a long time, looking out over the pond. I held my breath, hoping she could help me. She had never failed to help me before, no matter how bleak the outlook.

"It's because you've never been in this place before," she finally said, fixing her gaze on the pond. I perked up, listening attentively. This was not at all what I anticipated.

"Up until now, you've been operating out of memory. All of this you have done before, with me, at other times, but you've never moved beyond this point. Always before, you have allowed yourself to be dragged off the Path. You are distractible and restless; you allow others to pull you away from what you know to be true. Your infatuation with the world has always seduced you back into it.

"This time, once again, you are tempted to return to the world, but this time you are stronger and have more awareness than in previous lifetimes. This is new territory for you, a place in consciousness you've never previously been. The inner guidance you have always relied on is unable to guide you because this is a place of uncharted territory. Naturally, it feels strange because it is unfamiliar. You have moved beyond the place where you previously left off."

Relief flooded me as the truth of her words penetrated, and tears of gratitude streamed down my cheeks. I was not going to have to leave the Path. I could feel the truth of the words spoken, as that which I called my inner guidance shifted to embrace this realization. It made perfect sense. We were stepping into the unknown, and it was unknown because it was as far as I had come in previous lifetimes and in parallel lives. By refusing to be distracted from my Path, I was leaping into new space without recognizing it.

"Thank you," I whispered to her in the most profound gratitude. *"Now I can be at peace within myself. I am so grateful for your help."*

Often, in memory, I have returned to that day on the bridge, because it was the day **I shifted from relying on my own guidance as number one, to trusting the Teacher's viewpoint as taking precedence over my own.** Where I was blinded, she could see. And I didn't feel myself lessened by this, I felt expanded by it. It tasted of freedom.

The next few months were some of the most difficult I can remember spending with the Teacher, because the property simply would not manifest for us; and no matter how many avenues we pursued, we always ran into roadblocks. We almost purchased several different properties, but at the last minute, something would always interfere with the forward momentum. It was as though the property was waiting for us, but we just hadn't turned our attention in the right direction yet.

Up until this time, Winged Wolf had determined we should locate somewhere in the United States, even though she had declared we would have no limitations on our search. The Canadian apprentices were still sending listings of property they found in British Columbia, and she had put them off. Because the largest faction of the apprentice body was in the U. S., this was where our headquarters should be located.

One day, after another round of dead-end negotiations, Winged Wolf called me up to her office. *"Look at this,"* she said, handing me a listing on a large parcel in British Columbia. *"A Canadian apprentice has sent me this. She hasn't actually seen it, but look at the picture and what it's got."* I could feel her excitement as I read the listing.
"Oh my," I read over the listing, my own excitement growing. *"It sounds amazing. Look, it has thousands of feet of river frontage,"* I marveled, *"and a five-thousand-square-foot house. It looks perfect."*

"But it's in Canada," she lamented. *"Can you imagine the work that will be involved in moving to another country? It's hard enough to move this large an operation in our own country. Let's sit with it for a while until I get a feel for whether we should pursue Canada as an option."*

A Personal Farewell

I took a short break to spend some time with family, and Walt and I headed south to Florida. The Christmas holidays were coming up and all the adult children, plus my young grandson, planned on spending their time with us in Florida. It was the first holidays with both my parents gone and, in a way, I was dreading re-creating the holiday scene without them. Christmas had always seemed more for my parents' sake than my own thing. It had become such a commercial monster. But it was an opportunity for all of us to get together.

Our little island in Florida looked like paradise when I arrived. It felt good to unwind, spend time walking on the beach and enjoy the beautiful sunsets. Add to that, the bizarre experience of a northerner looking at Christmas lights twinkling over the sandy beaches of the Gulf of Mexico. One by one, the family arrived and were ferried over to the island. We had some great laughs as we met the ferry in our little golf cart and loaded everyone, plus luggage, onto it. Of course the boys got enormous chuckles over the idea of everyone driving around in golf carts, instead of cars. It had a kind of Disney World feel to it; fortunately, without any of the crowds.

Having my year-old grandson helped shift the focus of attention away from the absence of my parents, but everyone felt the underlying emptiness. Christmas wasn't the same. None of the rest of us really cared. It was also during that trip that we learned my daughter-in-law was pregnant with a second child, so even though she wasn't quite prepared for another one so soon, I was thrilled. This grandma thing was great fun.

Even with so much attention on family, my connection with Winged Wolf was strong and ever-present. We e-mailed regularly, and I continued to perform my duties as a part of the Spiritual Council and respond to any correspondence she directed my way. I also continued to pre-edit the Wisdom Eye discourses that were sent out monthly to apprentices. So, I didn't in any way dissolve my connection with the Teacher. I merely shifted my focus of attention to family, while keeping the Teacher in my awareness always. She was the guiding force of my life even when I was taking a break. I had even built a beautiful little meditation room just outside the house so there would be a place for spiritual practice in private. It was enjoyable to see everyone, but certainly not relaxing.

There was a high point for me on this trip. Before she died, my mother had asked me to scatter her ashes out into the ocean, and I had been waiting for the right opportunity to do so. It was New Year's Eve day, a beautiful sunshine-filled cloudless day, the first day really calm enough to take the boat out into the Gulf of Mexico, which was what my mother had meant when referring to 'the ocean.' This was her ocean. I awoke knowing that this was the day to give her a grand sendoff.

That afternoon we gathered everyone onto the boat; there were about ten of us, and we headed down the inter-coastal waterway for the channel that would lead us out to the gulf. It wasn't a somber trip but it was quiet, the awareness of our purpose put a respectful damper on the normal chitchat that went on among family members.

Once out of the channel, we headed out for a couple miles until the water quieted into gently rolling swells, and I signaled Walt that this was the place. He shut down the engine and the forward motion of the boat settled into a peaceful rocking, influenced only by the movement of wind and waves. I felt giddy, doing something so out of the norm for my traditional background. My mother was an adventurous spirit at the core.

"Bye, mom, I sure hope you're having a ball wherever you are," I said aloud, half-laughing, half-crying, and cast her ashes into the wind. And watched, and waited. Total silence. Nothing. I had anticipated something, what I did not know. I must have spent three minutes watching those ashes spread out over the water and slowly sink.

At the moment when I was about to turn and signal Walter to start the boat, the water erupted – everywhere, there were dolphins leaping out of the sea, leaping, diving, swimming all around us, under the boat, around it. Then a mother and baby swam right up to our boat and cruised along one side and then along the other, finally swimming off to join the others. The entire show lasted probably fifteen minutes, and then they were gone. The sea returned to its calm, gentle rolling as if it had never happened. But we all saw it. The boys were astonished. In fact, we all were.

"What an awesome sendoff," Kevin said in a hushed voice. *"Grandma would have loved that."*

"I'm sure she orchestrated it," I replied. *"It was her moment, and she wanted us to know how happy she is now, free from that old, worn-out body. She lived long and well; she was a loving, generous, feisty, Irish woman. No fear of death in that one; her only concern about leaving was that her husband be cared for. Otherwise, she was ready to go. Her message was for us really, to let us know there is nothing about death to fear. It is a joyous, freeing state of bliss."*

The joy and serenity that experience brought me will forever be locked in my heart, the visual image of the dance of the dolphins ever-available if ever I might need it. We had come full circle.

Chapter 25
Freedom from Limitations

The holidays were over in a moment, and we headed back to Orcas. Once back, the subject of Canada popped up again quickly. *"I may look at that property,"* Winged Wolf said, then she would lament about the difficulties of moving to another country.

We had many variations of this conversation. Winged Wolf was drawn to do this type of conversing, because as she talked, what she said was heard by all those who were connected to her via strings of energy. In other words, she was speaking to everyone as she spoke to me, opening minds and freeing people from limiting ideas. Since time and space are both illusions, it was as if she were speaking directly into their ears, although she told me that using an advanced apprentice as a buffer softened her words and made them more easily received by the listener. The more advanced the apprentice, the clearer the message was received.

Whenever there was something important to announce or to say to the group, she would often call one of us in and talk to us about it, the idea being that it would make it easier for the other person or persons to hear, and create less resistance than if she spoke to them directly. The more difficult the topic, meaning the more resistance it might produce, the more it was discussed aloud with one of us. So there was this multi-level effect occurring as we talked; and it was an incredibly powerful means of communication. All who were connected to the Teacher and the Path would hear it to the degree they were tuned in, and from whatever level their individual consciousness would allow.

One day the circle was complete and Winged Wolf said to me, *"I think I will go look at that property in British Columbia. And it should be as soon as possible. I'll ask an apprentice there to go with me since they discovered the property."*

While she was away, I dreamed of being on the Canadian property. At first, I was in the house with our cook and we were gazing at a picture hung on the living room wall by a famous artist. It was clear to me in the dream that we were living in this place, and the picture was the one Winged Wolf had hanging in her office over her desk.

Subsequently in the dream, I was outdoors at a bend in the river, admiring a beautiful rock cliff, when the spirit of the rock talked to me. It told me this was a sacred and protected area and it was waiting for us to live there. I awoke feeling certain the property would be purchased.

When Winged Wolf returned from viewing the property, we were all eagerly waiting for her. I could see by her face what had happened. *"I made an offer,"* she said. *"It's perfect in every way. I think we've finally found our new home."*

The Dream Manifests

A beautiful August sun shone overhead as we drove off the ferry in Anacortes on the way to inspect the property.

I rode with Winged Wolf and we chatted happily about the good fortune that was now shining upon us, the relief of finding a property that was perfect from her perspective for the work that needed to be done. There were 220 acres of land, approximately 3,000 feet of river frontage and the entire property was fenced, double-fenced really, since the orchard area was completely enclosed so the deer could not enter.

"The main house is huge," she told me, *"and we will convert the upper level into our Temple. It will be beautiful. We can have offices and a kitchen in the lower level for starters, until we are able to build a separate dining and office area. For now, we have everything we need to begin the next phase of the work."*

Driving into the heavily forested road that led to the property, I felt a sense of calm, mixed with anticipation. Although it was only 3 kilometers down the gravel road, each moment led us deeper and deeper into the rugged, mountainous area that was to be our new home. This was pristine land, and it called out to be spiritually enveloped. Already there was a familiarity to it.

It was, as Winged Wolf had described it, perfect. We spent several hours walking the land, inspecting the house, the irrigation system, talking with the current owners who were eager to show us how everything worked. They had built the home-soon-to-be-Temple themselves and were proud of the craftsmanship that had gone into it. The floors in the area where the Temple seating would be were made of larch, a dramatic, red-hued wood that is prevalent on the property, highly polished to a full shine. And there were large windows surrounding the room that let in the sun's light from the south, east and west.

We left after the inspection feeling completely satisfied that this would be the ideal place to build the monastery. And, while I was as confident as Winged Wolf that this was the correct move for the good of the order, I wasn't as comfortable with what might unfold for me, given my personal situation. That was the only dark cloud that hovered in the background of an otherwise elevating trip.

On the drive back to Orcas, my fear came forward enough that I was suddenly unusually pensive. It wasn't something I wanted to discuss with Winged Wolf because there was no place to go with the discussion. She was aware of my situation. I was praying continuously to the Transhistorical Consciousness that everything would work out for me to move along with the others; but it was not a hundred-percent certain that I could do it if Walter refused to move. And, for a fact, I would not be living on the property, so that would set up a slight distance between the Teacher and myself that I was not happy about. Somehow it would work out.

Chapter 26
Freedom Lives without Limitations

We arrived back on Orcas tired but happy. After so many hours in the car with Winged Wolf, the divine consciousness had worked its magic on me; I could see part of the vision through the Teacher's eyes and the divine energy that radiated from her had rained upon me and blessed me. It had penetrated my funk and uplifted me so I could be in companion energy with her upon our arrival home.

Everyone was waiting for us, anticipation on their faces. They all came out to the car as we pulled into the drive. *"Here we go,"* she said softly to me.

First, though, she greeted Sioux and Yoda who were happily dancing around her feet. Sioux had a special dance she did whenever she was exceptionally joyful. She kind of lifted up her front feet and twisted her body in a light and joyful expression of her happiness.

It brought a smile to my heart whenever Siouxy danced. Winged Wolf would use her special Sioux voice to greet her, and move her body in an imitative dance right along with Sioux. And Yoda's whole body was wagging along with his tail as he waited for Winged Wolf to greet him.

The way the relationship was with Sioux, she received the first greeting. She insisted on it. Yoda was willing to wait as long as he was included, and he always was; it was just that Sioux was different. Sioux and Winged Wolf were joined at the hip.

After all the dog greetings, came the people greetings; then we met briefly to let the locals who were present know that things had gone well. Winged Wolf promised a more thorough meeting in the morning if they could stand to wait until then, and they agreed. After the meeting, I left and headed into Deer Harbor and on up the hill toward home.

"How was it?" Walter asked when I came in.

"It looks like a go," I told him. *"Winged Wolf is convinced this is the future home of HÜMÜH. I think we're heading for a monastic setting."* Until the words were out of my mouth, it had not fully registered on me that we were about to turn in the direction of monasticism. Egads, what would that lifestyle be like? Different from anything I ever anticipated!

"That can't be a surprise to you, can it?" he asked. *"She's been moving in that direction for some time now."*

Suddenly we were heading in a direction I didn't want to go. Distraction seemed in order.

"Have you eaten?" I asked.

"No, I was waiting for you."

"How about pizza?" I asked, knowing his love for dough.

He volunteered to go pick up a pizza from town and that diffused the discussion until I could regroup. This was a tough one for me; because I had been so rigidly opposed to the concept of monastic living and so vocal about it, I was bound to pay a price for it. Now, I had to be on guard so as not to get hooked into a conversation that fueled my little-self objections. Maybe it was a previous life's bad experience or something, but even as a young child I recoiled from structure. Don't send me to camp, or to highly structured schools that require uniforms; it made me feel claustrophobic and confined. Of course, what is confinement is purely a matter of individual perception. There were many preconceived ideas running around in my head.

Now we were clearly moving toward a monastic, Buddhist life-style, including the wearing of robes. It was inevitable, and the purchase of this property would make it physically possible to develop the necessary structure to support this way of life. We'd just have to take it a step at a time. I knew I was going no matter what, and I prayed my husband would come, too.

The next morning, it became official. We met in the Happy House after our morning sitting, and Winged Wolf made the announcement to the local apprentices present. The HÜMÜH International Headquarters would be relocating to British Columbia, Canada.

"This property is perfect for us," she spoke animatedly, painting the picture as she described it. *"The house is 5,000 square feet; and the upstairs will make a beautiful Temple. The floors are all hardwood, made from the Tamarack tree, which has a slight reddish tone to it, quite stunning. Downstairs, for now, will be the dining area and offices. It's already set up roughly for offices.*

"And the property has 220 fenced acres with an orchard where we can grow our own apples. The climate is moderate and dry; not at all like Orcas. There's lots of sunshine, and there are four organic gardens on the property."

As Winged Wolf continued to tell us about how it would all work out, I watched the faces of those of us present. Their body language spoke more than any words could have. Those who were planning on moving became more and more enraptured in the vision being presented, their faces were absorbed and eyes were sparkling with the adventure and expansion of it, just as the Teacher's was.

Those who weren't sure or knew they were not moving wore plastic smiles and said little. One of my best buddies and heart loves had told me she would not be going to Canada; in fact, she planned to leave the Island in the near future. I could see the distancing in her face as she dove more and more into her resolve to leave. While she didn't say she was leaving the Path, I could feel it in the space and it saddened me greatly.

Another apprentice who was young and needed employment, had already told me she couldn't move to Canada, and she was distressed that Winged Wolf had chosen a place where she would not be allowed to work. Any place else in the United States and she could have found a job. This was all conjecture on her part, because, in fact, it is entirely possible for young people to qualify for work in Canada.

These people had been so committed to the Path only a few short weeks ago, it was puzzling to me they could have turned off in this way. *'And what about you?'* I asked myself. *'Aren't you being hypocritical? You've taken a vow as Savant to place the Path above all else, and yet you're balking again at following the Teacher's direction.'*

The conversation cast attention on a huge split in me and riled up the little-self to dig in its heels, so I quickly put it on the back burner and returned my attention to the current situation. There were many questions being asked and many of them could not be answered.

"I don't know the answers to those questions, yet," Winged Wolf finally told them. "I do know that it's right for us and we have the backing of the Transhistorical Consciousness, so everything will work out. As things become clearer, you can be sure I will communicate them to you.

"In the meantime, you can do a great service for the Path by staying in a place of equanimity and trusting that it will unfold in a way that serves you. I promise you we'll make it as smooth as possible for everyone, and those who are unable to move there will be welcome to visit anytime. It's really not that far to drive.

"First of all, we need to send a message to the apprentice body that we have located a property and sealed the deal. We need to get pictures on the website right away. Let them be a part of it now that it's a reality.

But we're a growing Spiritual Order, and we're young, so for now it has to be this way. You know, those Buddhist Temples in Tibet are so old; why, they've been established for hundreds of years. We're in our infancy. Once we're firmly established, and as far as I'm concerned, this location will be our home for hundreds of years, at some point surely I'll be able to drop back and do the work I'm intended to do. Do you realize I could do so much more sitting on my cushion than taking care of all these worldly matters?"

"I hadn't thought of it that way," I told her. "That you could be doing more for us if you didn't have to do everything yourself. I guess it's obvious now that you mention it. Yet, without you spearheading things, we wouldn't be able to evolve. There's nobody prepared to do what you do. I wish I could be of more help."

"You're not ready. That will change someday, but it can't be rushed," she said.

"It's all spiritual, but there are levels of impact, depending on where you put your attention. The more you can work through the ethers, the more we grow in awareness, and with so much of your attention being consumed on the physical plane, there aren't many hours left over for the other."

"Something like that," was the reply. "It's bound to happen eventually," she said, "and I'm betting on you to become a Thunderbeing one of these lifetimes."

We had had many a conversation over the years about what a difficult apprentice I am to work with because I have so many core issues. One of those core issues is what Winged Wolf called 'an aggressive mind.' Frequently, she would stop a conversation we were having because I was beginning to try to take control of it or push for something I wanted with my argumentativeness. My drive to become a Thunderbeing took a toll on her because it was so much on my mind. She didn't mention it often, but I knew I was exerting steady pressure on her to see if she thought I was ready.

"At least you can see that it's your little-self garbage. That's a beginning. It means you can look at yourself from a divine perspective and see what you are doing, even if you are unable to let it go right away. It sure would be easier though if you could just drop it. It would save you so much suffering, and me, too. Sometimes you frighten me with your obstinacy," she added quietly.

"I know I do, and it frightens me that you get frightened for me. I count on you to have faith in me even when I don't have faith in myself."

"Well, what will be will be. Let's move on to something more cheerful," she said, giving me some relief from this depressing conversation.

When would I ever learn to stay focused at the Third Eye and not get off into all the 'what ifs' and 'what about me,' and all that little-self garbage? "What a bizarre sensation to be able to see all my stuff and still hold on to it. It makes me feel crazy," I told her.

"You don't see all your stuff," she replied. "There is still a great deal of unconscious behavior that I see operating in you. What you see is only the tip of it. The only way to become aware of your unconscious behavior is to diligently practice mindfulness. Watch your mind, every moment. It takes tremendous discipline to develop mindfulness, but without it, you will not progress spiritually."

Building a Monastery

Winged Wolf decided we would spend two weeks each month at the Canadian property developing the Temple and all that went with it. This meant we needed first off to convert a home into a Temple. This alone was an enormous task. Then, and simultaneously really, we needed to build a guesthouse for visiting apprentices, five cabins for long-term retreatants who would live on the property, and offices. At least we had the space in the lower level for offices. The rest had to be built from scratch.

It was a pleasure to accompany the Teacher to Westbridge, BC, where the new property was located. From this point on, real movement, both spiritual and physical, occurred. There was much physical movement, in particular, but of course what went on with our physical movement was just the reflection of what was happening spiritually.

Winged Wolf wanted a May opening for the presentation of our monastery, via an empowerment. Everyone would be invited to come, bring their tents and experience the new HÜMÜH Monastery and Meditation Retreat Center. We were in high gear, and so much needed to happen before the May opening, it was mind-boggling. After I completed the list of priorities as Winged Wolf elucidated them, paralysis set in.

"It isn't possible," I told her.

"Of course it is," she replied cheerfully. *"It must be ready for the opening in May. I want all apprentices to come here and see their new spiritual home. It will be wonderful, and I know they will forgive us if it is a little rough in the beginning. They will be able to see where we're headed. It's important they know this is their home.*

"This year will be difficult on us; we will have no time to slack off, but I know we can do it if we all pull together."

And as I listened, I understood; it was going to happen.

"Okay, where do we begin?" The list looked totally overwhelming. *"How do we prioritize all this?"*

"Easy," she said. *"We start with what is most important,"* and then she laughed. *"I know, I always say it's all important. But for now, we start on the Temple and the guesthouse. Those are the two most urgent priorities. We must have places for visiting apprentices to stay and a Temple so people have a place to spiritually practice and to honor the Teachings. We need a Stupa too, but we'll begin with a prayer flagpole. Maybe the Stupa will come next year."*

As we stood in the orchard and talked, Winged Wolf pointed to the spot where the prayer flagpole would be erected, and I could envision it with all its brightly colored flags, filled with the Mantra, blowing in the breeze.

We were facing in a southwesterly direction, and as we looked across the land, Winged Wolf said almost rhetorically, *"What shall we name the Monastery?"* Facing southwest, the vastness of the land is magnified by the shape of the cliffs that surround it and a large V-shaped indentation where the cliffs fall away and expose a vast expanse of sky and distant mountains, giving the impression of 'forever expanding.' As she stood there looking out in that direction, she said, *"Skycliffe."* And now we had a name.

What an incredible adventure unfolded from here. Winter set in early in November so we were pressed right off to get the foundation for the guesthouse set before the big freeze. This meant first we had to find a contractor and settle on the type of structure, size and shape and so on. Winged Wolf's vision was of a log house. She said it would be beautiful, solid and warm. People would feel good staying inside of it because the logs are so pleasing to the sight as well as good insulators and a part of the natural environment.

Quickly, we learned that in a small town, word of mouth is the primary means of communication. So we put the word out that we needed trades people: carpenters, electricians, plumbers, cement layers, general laborers. Then there were interviews, bids, lengthy discussions on why this and not that, trying to convey the vision and not be run over by their ideas on things.

Winged Wolf was absolutely clear on how she wanted things to be, and it was fascinating to observe the interactions with trades people who kept trying to convince her why something couldn't be done the way she saw it. Every person who came in contact with her was, at some point,

Freedom Lives without Limitations

jolted out of a preconceived mind-set of how things should be done, stretched in some way beyond their limitations.

My Teacher could not be dominated, manipulated or condescended to; she knew what she wanted and intended to have it, always for the good of the whole. It didn't matter that it was someone else's area of expertise; she would still look at each situation and see what should be expressed, and insist on having it. Often there would be a lightening bolt of energy released when they finally got a glimmer of whom they were with. But it was grueling, because it was continuous. She had to be on top of things every second or they would revert quickly to old ways.

It wasn't unusual at all for her to stop in the middle of a sentence and say, *"Wings, go out there and talk to so-and-so."* Or, we would be out walking the grounds, and she would see some good wood left exposed to the elements and say, *"Wings, it's a terrible waste of good material to leave things out like this."* Meanwhile we would be covering the wood ourselves, or taking the tools left out in the ice and snow and placing them in a protected space.

Then there was the detritus left about. We hauled garbage cans out to the site thinking they might take a hint, but inevitably, something would have to be said. It was a matter of training people to show respect in the way the Teacher defined it. Don't just do things the way that you have always done them; do what is appropriate to the situation.

On paper, we had worked out a timeline for everything to unfold and it looked really good. There was time for everything to be completed by the May event. In reality, each project took longer than was estimated. Sometimes much longer.

A crew of apprentices had been working on Temple renovations for months. Winged Wolf designed the most elegant benches that would hold our meditation cushions, and each one fit into the Temple like a piece of a puzzle. One apprentice had a knack for capturing exactly what the Teacher wanted when it came to the projects that were his. His carpentry work was beautiful, and he expected the people on his team to do the same high quality work. At times, it could be a strain working such long hours on such a major project. There just wasn't any slack time.

The benches were different sizes and shapes, each one built from scratch, then sanded to a fine finish. Afterwards, they needed six to eight coats of stain, plus several finishing coats of lacquer. The team was working from early in the morning until eight or nine at night. Often we wouldn't do our evening meditation until nine or even ten o'clock because we couldn't stop working. During this period, we were all staying in the Temple on air mattresses. There was a large, effective wood-burning stove on each floor, and for the first few months, Winged Wolf and I took turns keeping the fire alive during the night. Every two or three hours we were up adding logs to the fire. During the day, it was so warm in the Temple we were in short sleeves and still sweating. The thermometer often read 30 Celsius inside while it was below zero on the outside!

Finally, Winged Wolf discovered the Temple would stay pleasantly comfortable if she built a fire just before bed and left it alone until morning. After that, we slept much better.

During this six-month period of Temple development, I learned more, in a condensed way, than during any other time in my apprenticeship. Spending two weeks of every month in constant companionship with the Teacher, undertaking such a massive project, going full-tilt without a break, stretched me more than I even knew at the time. There was no time we weren't together, except for the few hours we slept at night. I got to observe the Teacher on a moment to moment basis, to see how she related to each person who came across her path, to watch the vision unfold and to carry out her instructions in the moment.

Whereas the instructions were often opposite what I might have done on my own, by following what she said, I learned how things work; how putting a little pressure over here causes this to unfold, and withdrawing something over there causes something else to come forth, often just the opposite of what I would have predicted. By doing exactly as she told me, I began to see what she was seeing and to develop the intuition that often told me how she might be seeing a situation differently than I saw it. Gradually, I learned to read the energies and then test my readings against what the Teacher saw.

The discipline that she carried within her was even more apparent under these conditions; the nights we sat in meditation, when tired and worn out after working sixteen hours, most people would have simply dropped into bed. I saw compassion in all its expressions too: she could be soft and gentle, firm and exacting, and she could be fierce and unyielding, all depending on what the situation called for. I was stretched and stretched and stretched again, until I discovered there was no end to the stretching, and no end to my ability to stretch, as long as I was willing.

How the Teacher was able to accomplish what she did in the time allotted was nothing short of a miracle. There was no doubt in my mind that the Transhistorical Consciousness was totally behind her. When we needed a caretaker for the newly named Skycliffe, the perfect couple appeared; when we needed carpenters, it just happened that the two most respected local carpenters were available; when we needed the weather to behave in a particular way so the foundation could go in before the ground froze, the weather cooperated. When we had some major difficulties with building inspectors that should have slowed us down for months, the issues were quickly cleared up. That one was a miracle if ever I saw one. And it wasn't just one miracle, but a continuous string of them, that made it so clear that our Teacher was acting in the name of the divine consciousness and being supported all the way in getting the work done.

At times when I would become impatient with the way things were going, she used to tell me, *"Because this is the physical plane, there will always be mountains to move and obstacles to be removed. It takes longer on the physical plane to manifest something than it does on the astral. On the astral plane, manifestation is instantaneous, but here on the physical, matter is dense and takes longer to come together into a solid form."*

Even so, things 'came together' at an astounding rate, but to accomplish what we needed to accomplish required super-human effort on the part of those closest to the project. Mark worked tirelessly as did all those who helped him. He had so much of the physical work to do, everything that had to do with Temple renovation. Those beautiful benches we were to sit on took days for each individual one to come to the point it could be stained, and there were over twenty benches.

There was no way around the work that needed to be done, but through the Teacher's agility and lack of any limitations on the way she viewed situations, she was always able to guide us to the most expedient and often unconventional solution. Through this close proximity on a daily basis with the Teacher, **I came to truly and deeply appreciate that there really are no obstacles except those that we believe exist.** If this one point could forever penetrate my own and the reader's state of awareness, it would be worth the entire story of my apprenticeship.

Time and again, we faced situations that I *knew* in my own mind could not be navigated, especially in the time allotted to us, and sometimes not at all, and yet they were transmuted. Some obstacles appeared immutable. And each time I would say to myself, *'This is it; we've made a huge mistake trying to move here.'* Suddenly there would be an opening, a gateway, a tiny crack to slip through and we were sailing again. My mind repeatedly refused to believe what it was seeing! And each time, usually after the fact, I would see, through the Teacher's eyes, that what had appeared to be an obstacle was merely a mind-set carried by one or many that said, *"This cannot be done."* It was all an illusion! There was always a crack in the wall.

"People project their mind-sets out into the universal mind and they believe them so strongly that they become hardened facts," she told me one day. *"That's why there is always a crack in the wall, because the mind-sets aren't real."*

"Remember, there are only three realities."

"The Void, divine consciousness, and life," I piped in, reciting the three.

"But not situations in life; those are illusion," she added, *"but the ability to manifest life, the ability to dream, that is a reality."*

Even knowing this, there was a tendency to get sucked into mind-sets, especially if they were rules backed by a bureaucratic structure, but at times, even when just one person who believed strongly projected them. What I eventually came to understand and integrate is that **when one is divinely led to do a great act of service, there is no obstacle that cannot be overcome, because all the divine forces in the universe are backing them.**

Obstacles, which are illusions anyway, fall away, as the spiritual warrior's sword cuts them down. The enlightened consciousness sees through the nature of the illusionary obstacles and therefore knows which way to make the cut. This means **there are no limitations to what the enlightened consciousness can accomplish, none whatsoever.** It took months of being with this for the awareness to actually penetrate my density of consciousness; because there is a denseness to the ordinary mind that is covered in layers and layers of illusionary beliefs that must be cut away before the awareness can penetrate deeply.

This understanding in no way diminished the physical DO that was required for us to build a monastery. That was our side of the contract. The two, three really, were one. The spiritual, the mental and the physical all worked together. Everyone worked together.

"Spiritual practice is the key to evolving on all planes of existence," Winged Wolf told me one evening as I was grousing about her insisting we sit in the silence after a long, arduous day. It was about 9pm and I was ready for bed. *"Why do you suppose our work here is going so smoothly? And what keeps everything 'Between the Wind' in such balance while we are away? Don't you see the connection between spiritual practice and the easy flow we are maintaining? Oh, I know there's a great deal of work to be done, but it could never be accomplished in this manner without spiritual practice. If you and the other apprentices don't keep yourselves in balance, you could throw our move into chaos. Surely, you must see that. I couldn't do it all on my own, even though I am **awake**."*

"Well, I guess I wasn't looking at it from that overview perspective that you have. I was only considering myself and that my body is tired," I said. "Now that you lay it out for me, it's pretty obvious that regular spiritual practice is the anchor point."

It wasn't that I usually wanted to avoid meditation, because my silences of late had been ripe with realizations. All the Teachings Winged Wolf had given me over the years about the Oneness, and the everything-nothing essence of the Void, were becoming real to me, not just intellectual understanding as they once had been. In the silence I was learning so much, not by thinking or analyzing anything, but by perceiving reality.

They were still glimmers; I couldn't live from that place yet, but in meditation I saw that as divine beings we are all the same; there is only one divinity; no one is separate. I perceived the nothingness, and the something that came from nothing as impermanent. And I could see how this related to my life, that those things I was so attached to were all dream images, ephemeral, not much different than the sleep dreams I awoke from each morning. The only thing that would go with me at my death was the awakened consciousness I had acquired in this lifetime, and unfortunately, any unfinished karmic baggage.

I vowed to be more disciplined, like my Teacher, and not allow any laziness to creep in because of a tired body. Spiritual practice without excuses would be my stance from now on.

A Great Loss

During the months of our travel back and forth from Orcas to Skycliffe, we always took Yoda and Siouxy. Sioux especially loved the cold air, snow and wide-open spaces at Skycliffe, but her health was failing. She was quite elderly for a wolf and would never have known such longevity in the wild.

But Sioux was not a typical wolf. Winged Wolf had raised her from the time she was a young cub. Sioux had lived to a ripe old age and still had plenty of life force in her, but her body was failing. Looking into her yellow brown eyes, it was easy to see the consciousness of the being that lived there. This was no ordinary wolf. Sioux had near-human consciousness and all of it was focused on Winged Wolf. They were constant companions.

One day after a return from Skycliffe, Sioux's health went into a rapid decline, and Winged Wolf told us it was time for Sioux to translate. This was devastating news for everyone because we all loved her deeply; but the wonderful news Winged Wolf shared with us was that Sioux had achieved sufficient consciousness that she would not be reborn in an animal's body. Her next life would be as a human, and Winged Wolf said, *"She will not be a lowly human, not at all. Sioux will come back at least with the consciousness of someone midway on the Path."*

This was such wonderful news that it helped to ease the pain of losing Sioux just to know what an opportunity she had in store for her. Still, it was a terribly painful loss for Winged Wolf. After Sioux's death, she told us, *"The strings of energy between us were so strong, that there is a hole created from her leaving the physical plane. It actually hurts physically to have her gone."*

It was the first time in my life to witness the transition in consciousness of an animal to the consciousness of a human and to be able to identify those traits she possessed that were actually human as I watched her. Sioux had many higher consciousness traits, including the ability to think something through. She also was very attracted to *The Wish-Fulfilling Gem Mantra* and would sit at length outside the Happy House listening as we chanted it.

So we mourned the loss of our dear friend, and rejoiced at her accomplishment, achievement of a human body being no small thing, and wondered when we would meet her again in her new form. It was a profoundly moving time.

Meanwhile, Winged Wolf turned her attention toward Yoda and focused strongly on bringing him out of the lethargic mental state he had fallen into, as he was also in mourning for the loss of Sioux who had been his constant companion for all but one year of his life. And, because Sioux was such a dominant force and required constant attention, Yoda hadn't developed in consciousness the way Sioux had. Now it was his turn to benefit from Winged Wolf's full attention. He quickly blossomed and his life force became strong. He changed from an old dog to a spry young fellow in a few short months.

Satiety with the World

The first time Winged Wolf tackled me directly on the issue of *'lack of satiety with the world,'* was about six months prior to the current events. I had been in upstate New York attending a conference with Walter when I received, seemingly out of the blue, although such is never really the case, a communication from my beloved Teacher via e-mail.

This was a time of great personal stress for me. My spouse had just resigned his apprenticeship and was looking for a new Teacher, and I was doing my best to remain in a place of equanimity and basically keep my mouth shut and let him work it out. But when there is turmoil going on around you, it is bound to have an effect.

The Teacher was acutely aware of my conflict, and how it split my attention; I'm sure my continual beseeching her to help me, while done silently and in a state of prayer, must have caused her some sleepless nights, as it did me. Following is a portion of her communication to me:

Hello Wings of Change

I awoke this morning with a sense of peace about your predicament, which has been troubling both of us, and I feel I may have the solution.

In previous communications, you indicated wanting to have a HÜMÜH Temple in Michigan. If this still interests you, we can pursue this idea upon your return. You can travel back and forth for a while to work with me, and in the meantime continue to cultivate Michigan as a place for our Order to grow. Of course, I would travel to you, on occasion, as well, to assist in bringing this work to fruition, such as public talks, etc., perhaps speaking from town to town. We can concentrate on Michigan, build it up, establish a HÜMÜH Temple and you can be the head of it, once your training is complete or you have attained the 7th Level Bodhisattva.

If you'll study your 10 levels of Bodhisattva, you will see that you are now on the 2nd level, approaching the 3rd, and you can also see the key factor that keeps you from attaining the 3rd.

I will be waiting for you to drive to Canada on Monday the 16th (loaded with prayer flags).

With Divine Love

There were two aspects of this communication that had served to bring me out of the despair I had been experiencing. The first was her reference to a HÜMÜH Temple in Michigan. Winged Wolf has a large following of apprentices and friends of the Path in Michigan; it's my home state, and the place where my adult children and my grandson live, and there is a great spiritual hunger present there.

The second point that really had riveted my attention was the reference to my being on the 2nd Bodhisattva level, approaching the 3rd. It may not sound like much, but I hadn't realized I had moved beyond the first level; this was good news. Immediately after accepting this piece, I began to wonder what she meant by the phrase, *"key factor that keeps you from attaining the 3rd level."* Was the key to this held in Level 2 or

Level 3? I wasn't sure from the way the e-mail was written. I decided I'd better scrutinize them both.

'Darn it all, I don't have my Bodhisattva Guidebook with me,' I had thought ruefully. The idea of waiting one whole week to return to Orcas and locate the Guidebook was out of the question. Who could I call and ask to read the description of the levels to me?

Of course! My dear and long-term friend Pat, also an advanced apprentice, would read it to me and ask no questions. As her phone began ringing, I had drummed my fingers impatiently on the bedside table, hoping this would be one of the rare occasions she would be at home.

"Hello." It sounded like the answering machine so I had waited a moment to see if there was going to be a recorded message, and by the time I realized she was really on the other end of the line, for some reason the phone had disconnected.

Frustrated, I had redialed, and when I heard the familiar voice sounding a bit wary, I quickly said, *"Pat, don't hang up, it's me."*

"Oh, Sharon, I thought you were one of those computer marketing machines. They always take a few seconds to start the recording and I hang up before they can begin."

"I was so expecting you to be out, I waited to see if it was your answering machine," I had laughed, relieved. *"Next time, I'll remember to talk fast so you don't hang up on me.*

"Would you do me a huge kindness and read Bodhisattva Levels 2 and 3 for me?"

Without a moment's hesitation, she said, *"Wait a second, I'll get the Guidebook."*

If she read them both, perhaps the essence of where I was and where I was headed would penetrate more deeply, and I had hoped to figure out what the missing link for reaching Level 3 entailed.

"Okay, I'm back; you ready?"

"I've got pen in hand," I had told her.

She began, "Bodhisattva Level 2 **The Stainless**

> *"Stainless means purity, whereby the bodhisattva reaches a point of realization about the necessary fuel provided by his recitation of the Wish-Fulfilling Gem Mantra, Wisdom Eye Meditations, and practice of the presence of his Teacher/Wisdom Master, and thereby perfects the self-discipline of these spiritual practices. He does this, and is continuous, without lapses in the self-discipline that he has developed.*
>
> *"While the bodhisattva will achieve this second level by the above description, the attainment of self-discipline, because of the bodhisattva's inability to fully maintain a quiet mind while functioning in the world, which makes it possible to fully retain what is heard, cannot be attained by the second peak. Through striving to climb the third peak, however, the third level will also be attained."*

"Okay, I've got that one written down, now I'm ready for level 3."

Pat had read on:

"Bodhisattva Level 3 **The Luminous**

> *"At this level, the bodhisattva gains insight into the impermanent, transient nature of existence. He does this through observation and relationship with people, things and situations, and develops virtuous patience in enduring difficulties while assisting other sentient beings towards spiritual liberation. This is accomplished through his own self-refinement which has cut off the three roots of unwholesomeness: the roots of desire, hatred and delusion.*
>
> *"The attainment of this level is made possible through determination, satiety with worldly life, and passionlessness. As a result, the bodhisattva acquires the five supernatural powers: 1) the ability to shapeshift, 2) to hear divinely (to discern the energy within sounds), 3) to perceive the thoughts and energies of other human beings, 4) to recollect previous existences, 5) to see with the divine eye, which means he*

contains knowledge of the cycles of birth and death of all beings......"

Okay, I could see that I wasn't at Level 3, which had sounded to me light years away from where I then stood. But where on Level 2 was she pointing me?

Thanking my friend profusely, we said our good-byes and, as I had written down the words as she read them, now they could be studied, and perhaps I would glean what the Teacher was seeing about me that was holding me back. At first glance it had looked like there were several things. It took a while to zone in on the words that had struck a chord on an energetic level.

But I rationalized, *'My goodness, she can't mean satiety with worldly life. After all, I've left my home and family, my house and the majority of my belongings. I spend most of my days with the Teacher in service to the Path. What more could I possibly have to give up?*

"If that is it, I sure don't agree with it. But, at least now I know where I am in the bodhisattva levels, sort of.'

Between the reference to a HÜMÜH Temple in Michigan and the definitive statement of my progress, all the tension had flooded out of my being and I relaxed for the first time in weeks. She had responded to my need to know something and have something to look forward to, a future, and now I had a bit of definition as to where I was on the Path. It was still eons away from Level 7 (Thunderbeing) but there had been movement in that direction and that had made me happy. When I returned to Orcas, I could ask about the puzzling comment as to what was holding me back. How she knew these things about what I needed always amazed me, and gave such a feeling of comfort that if I didn't know who I was or what was to become of me, at least my Teacher did, and would show me the way.

The rest of our trip had flowed smoothly with my balance restored. After enjoying a few days with my adorable grandson and family, we had headed back home to Orcas. We arrived on a Sunday, and Winged Wolf and I left on Monday for Skycliffe. Talk about changing hats quickly. There was no slack time with Winged Wolf, especially with all the work yet to be done. She was equipped with sixteen-hundred prayer flags to be attached to wires, extending from a thirty-five foot pole on thirty-two strands. The conversation about bodhisattva levels had shifted to the back burner until a suitable moment arose to bring it up.

Right then, curiosity about the purpose and function of prayer flags had my attention. Both at *Between the Wind* and then at *Skycliffe*, Winged Wolf had expressed great urgency about having a prayer flagpole. I had never fully understood the significance of them. And, she had made a change in them. Whereas before we had filled them with images of the Buddhas in our lineage, this time they were all filled with *The Wish-Fulfilling Gem Mantra* in its entirety.

"Winged Wolf, I know you place great importance on prayer flags. What makes them so important to us?"

"They broadcast out into the ethers all that is contained in The Wish-Fulfilling Gem Mantra, all the Primordial Teachings of the Transhistorical Consciousness. The benefits are felt for great distances. They assist me in my work. "

"Are they a protection?" I had persisted, beginning to see the picture.

"There are all kinds of negative energies out there; the prayer flags help to transmute that negativity."

"No wonder you express such urgency about having the prayer flag pole up."

A few days later, the opportunity had arisen to discuss bodhisattva levels, and it occurred quite spontaneously. Two of the Vancouver apprentices had driven down for the weekend; they were advanced apprentices and therefore the conversation was open. In fact, one of them actually had asked Winged Wolf the question, *"What bodhisattva level do you see me on?"*

Winged Wolf had responded, *"Each of you is on Level 2, but in differing stages of it. Wings is nearing Level 3, except for one small piece, but until she masters it, she will be unable to move forward."*

She had looked at me and asked, *"Do you know what that piece is?"*

After hesitating, I shook my head, *"Not really, I can see several possibilities."*

She had taken out the booklet and begun clicking off the items on Level 3. *"You've got that....got that....got that......"*

When she reached the part about satiety with the world, she had paused and said, *"You're still attached to the world. The glitter and all its busyness still attract you."*

Oh, how I had wanted to argue with her, to point out all that had already been given up, but what was the point? She was right. I did crave the world; it was a fun playground to me. *'This must be a part of my consciousness that is asleep and I'm not sure how to awaken it,'* I mused.

"How do I get past it, Winged Wolf?" I asked.

"It isn't something that I can teach you," she had replied. *"You simply have to reach a place of satiety with worldly life, become bored with it. At some point, you will, this lifetime or another."*

The conversation had moved on to the others who also wanted to know where their Achilles heels were, and I made a mental note to work on this aspect of attachment with all that I could give it. The idea of waiting for another lifetime had no appeal at all.

There must be something that I wasn't seeing, something that would push me past the fascination with the world that I carried. Surely, as my personality became more refined, it would occur naturally, I had hoped. So I added it to my prayer list; praying had never let me down yet, although it took longer on some items than others.

"Please help me get past my attachment to the world so I can be free of the limitations it places on my freedom," I prayed fervently to the Transhistorical Consciousness. *"I can't seem to do it myself."* And since I wanted to be sure the prayer was heard, I had repeated it three times.

"And for my part, I promise to catch myself whenever it strikes my consciousness that I am turning my attention toward the world." Winged Wolf taught us to be diligent in intercepting thoughts, behaviors and mind-sets that fed attachments, so I had determined right then and there to be a vigilant sleuth when it came to undermining those insidious mind passions. The hardest part was to become aware of them; the next hardest part was to be willing to turn my attention away from what gave me pleasure. But it would be worth all the hard work and

effort to achieve the state of inherent wisdom and detachment Winged Wolf talked about as being the keys to finding our freedom from the illusion of the dream.

At the time, it hadn't struck me that I was pursuing enlightenment in much the same way I pursued other things I wanted in life, with an aggression toward having them. It was an, 'okay, what do I need to do to have that?' type of mentality. It was such a familiar way of operating, I didn't even know I was operating.

At *Skycliffe*, with the Teacher, I was a different person than at home without her. There, my single-pointed attention was on Winged Wolf and the Path. Because I was working so closely with her, night and day, I was naturally able to live my divinity most of the time.

On occasion, when I went into overload, there were tears and a plea for help. Always, she eased the pressure on me and joined me to help with whatever project had me bogged down. It gave me confidence that we were a team, even though she was the director. She lent me her strength and power of attention, and, even more importantly, she taught me to laugh when things looked overwhelming. And to take breaks; sometimes we put everything down, no matter how busy, and went for a walk or even went up to Rock Creek where we could now have a veggie burger. *"The work will be here when we return,"* she would say. We had laughed during those stressful times. *"Laughter heals,"* she always told me, *"you just have to remember to do it."*

A healing had occurred for me during one of our trips to *Skycliffe*. It involved my mother. Before her death, my mother was of the opinion that I had lost my mind or given it over to the Teacher, and throughout my apprenticeship, she had maintained a steady commentary about my 'foolishness.' One night, I had awakened from a sound sleep to discover her in the bedroom with me. She had come with one purpose in mind. She told me, *"I am learning so much where I am now. Most of what I taught you was wrong, even though I didn't know it at the time. It was. Don't make yourself miserable trying to please me or wishing you could have pleased me, because I was wrong. Learn for yourself. Live your life as you see fit, not as I told you to. Become the person you are meant to be. Follow your heart and learn everything you can. And don't worry about me, I am happy and growing."*

Her energy matched her words completely; the room had been filled with her joyous, happy energy. There was no mistaking it for anyone else's energy. Anyone who knew my mother knew when she was happy, her energy was infectious. And I had felt a sense of relief and freedom; a little pinched-off place of sadness that had been in my heart opened up, and I was filled with the joy of knowing she had given me in death what she had not been able to give me in life, her unconditional support.

Chapter 27
Everything All at Once

Personal moving day, preparing for the empowerment, moving the HÜMÜH office and operations from Orcas to *Skycliffe* and business as usual, all ran together in my mind. Somehow, the office was moved from *Between the Wind* to *Skycliffe*; I moved from Orcas to Westbridge; Winged Wolf moved into the Temple full-time because there was no structure built for her to live in yet, and several of the local apprentices moved into some barely acceptable housing nearby, because their housing on the property was incomplete. Our cook had also moved into the Temple (a side room) the first of May to take over the kitchen, set up the organic gardens and begin preparations for the Empowerment which was only three weeks away, and for which she was going to be providing meals. This was, in itself, an amazing act of service and commitment. She stepped in with both feet, full-speed-ahead, with minimal equipment, space and help. Meanwhile, there could be no work stoppage.

The guys were working non-stop to have both the Temple finished and the empowerment area in a forested area of the property, now named Empowerment Lane, ready for guests. This meant building several outhouses and using the tractor to haul them out there, and, of course, digging some deep holes for them to sit over. The campground showers weren't ready and we had no running water as yet, but we had to have outhouses.

There was a feeling of disorientation at having made so many shifts and adjustments in such a short time. My body and mind were willing, but it was a bit like jet lag; I felt as though part of me couldn't quite catch up with what was happening so quickly. We all worked up until the final few minutes before registration for the event was about to begin.

Then all of this type of movement came to a screeching halt. When the moment of the empowerment arrived, Winged Wolf told us to 'drop everything' and relax. There was nothing more to be done until the empowerment was complete. It was time to introduce *Skycliffe*, our new spiritual home, to all the wonderful people who would be arriving in a few hours from all over the world. Time to let go of all the stress of the past weeks and months and bathe in the loving energy of the great Transhistorical Consciousness, as embodied in our Teacher. It was a job well done, and we were all ecstatic to be there.

Now, it was time to greet the arriving students, apprentices and others who felt drawn to attend. And they came in droves…from everywhere…even across the continent, from New Zealand. Happy, smiling faces arriving to see their new spiritual home, eager to be with the Teacher once again, or for the first time.

Those who came knew they were meant to be here. They were drawn to the light. And the empowerment was aptly titled, *"Reincarnation: The Merger of Energies Between the Past and the Present."* Most of us knew, at least intuitively, that we had done this before, been with this Teacher for one or many lifetimes and we were doing it again now, this time in the hopes of going further, getting past those rough spots that drove us away previously; so that we might, perhaps, even go all the way to our enlightenment. At the very least, we wanted to reconnect our past memories with our present circumstances with this Teacher.

Watching the faces of different people as they arrived to view Skycliffe for the first time was heart-warming, especially as they first viewed the Temple. The Temple is elegant in its simplicity. First impression upon entering, one is viscerally struck with the peaceful, stillness of the energy and visually struck with the beauty of the design. The hardwood floors are highly polished tamarack* that has a slight reddish sheen. The deep purple of the cushions against the polished wood, along with the white-rose wall hanging behind the Teacher's cushion, invites stillness, peace and harmony from all who step inside.

One entire wall of windows, covered with soft, oyster-colored shades, faces south. The room is long, rectangular, with rows of benches made of wood polished to a high sheen, the same color as the floor, paralleling each other, with purple zafus and zabutons sitting atop of them. At the far end of the Temple is the Master's seat that faces out toward the

---

*Note: tamarack is a kind of larch

parallel rows of seating. At the back and sides are pews, facing her, for visitors and those who are unable to sit on cushions.

Flanking each side of the Teacher's seat are a statue of Sakyamuni Buddha and a picture of Padmasambhava, the lotus born, our Teacher's Teacher (in another lifetime).

Tears rolled down some cheeks as people entered the Temple for the first time. Hushed whispers could be heard, 'This is like a homecoming," and *"I feel like I've come home,"* or *"This is the place I dreamed about a long time ago."* They were beginning to remember the past, and it was a profound experience to be a part of this homecoming.

About this empowerment, Winged Wolf, now emerging strongly as Wisdom Master Maticintin, wrote, *"The merger of energies between the past and the present stand hidden from the ordinary mind like thin layers of film placed over a glass. You can see the glass, and yet the film remains invisible, because it appears to be part of the same.*

"Life is an extraordinary substance of energy; one thing reflects another. Who you are is who you have been, and who you are is also who you will be; but the past, present and future remain mysteries that only the spiritually awakened can clearly see.

"In this empowerment at 'Skycliffe,' HÜMÜH's new Meditation Healing Retreat Center, we will examine the fabric of life so that you will gain an increased awareness of the past and how it interacts with who you are today, and how that interaction brings about your future.

"As an empowerment, the event is meant to be experiential, your experience as related to the Primordial Teachings of HÜMÜH, which are clear-mind Teachings of all Buddhist wisdom."

These people, now arriving in droves, were awakening to the merger of past and present as they walked onto the property and then into the Temple. The recognition was present in their eyes. They had come full circle; they were home. Maybe this time they would move forward into their enlightenment, overcome whatever obstacles had blocked the way in their past. And, of course, as I whispered this prayer for others, I also whispered it for myself. *'Maybe this time………'*

The May weekend weather was hot; temperatures rose to 90 F (32 Celsius), and we sweated. The Temple was not air-conditioned, the weather was a fluke (so the locals told us later); it had jumped from the mid-sixties to ninety-plus overnight. We had been concerned that people would be too cold in the campground as nights had been down in the low thirties up until this weekend; but there were no chilly nights during this weekend. Some of us with a long history with this Teacher giggled because we understood the weather patterns were never predictable around her, except they always supported the work being accomplished. If we needed heat, we got heat; if we needed rain to wash away the energies being released, it rained.

Being in the Temple with our robes on was much like being in a sauna; everyone was dripping wet, and no one really cared. They were so happy to be there. And we forgot about the exhausting pace that led up to the presentation of the event. Winged Wolf was so happy to have a place where her large spiritual family could gather; her heart was singing and everyone else was singing along with her. It was a splendid time for all, a perfect homecoming.

When the weekend was over, people cried with the joy of being so loved and welcomed. Many people had profound experiences of memories of other times in similar situations with this Teacher. The day after the empowerment ended, the weather turned cold, really cold, even a bit of snow fell on us. That first year it didn't warm up until July, and local people told us this was also highly unusual. This was now the third move I had experienced with Winged Wolf, and each time brought highly unusual weather patterns.

The next four months were difficult for me personally on the home front, although my apprenticeship was going well and the Teacher was a great friend and compassionate guide during this stressful time.

Walter decided to pursue a course of studies in the eastern US and planned to be gone six months to a year. Naturally, it didn't make sense for him to live in this remote area of British Columbia if he wasn't part of the *Skycliffe* community. There was nothing for him here, other than a wife who would spend most of her time at the monastery. It hurt my heart to have him leave, especially since I knew deep down he really wanted to be with Winged Wolf and was too stubborn to admit it; so I helped him pack the car and sadly watched him drive off.

In some ways his move was a relief, because a burden lifted. He had felt burdened being with me and yet not being able to participate in my life. There was no joy in that, and so I felt what he felt, heavy. That part lifted, and, while I missed him, it freed me to spend my days happily at *Skycliffe* helping Winged Wolf oversee the ongoing development of the property. At last the resident apprentices could move into their dwellings and delve into Skycliffe living.

With Walter leaving, there was no reason for me not to live on the property with the others, except now, all the units were spoken for, so I continued to live down the road a few kilometers. For the time being, this was an enjoyable life style, a little distance between my two lives, that is, the daytime monastery life and the evenings in a more familiar setting, a country neighborhood.

Nights were so dramatic. The temperature dropped from ninety or a hundred degrees to a cool fifty degrees, and I would sit on the porch watching the twinkling stars pop out into visibility as darkness descended. Sometimes my dogs and I sat for hours watching the evening creeping in over the daylight. The mountains that rimmed the Kettle River shone white in the bright light of the moon, and the coyotes howled in the distance. It was starkly beautiful, and I began to feel at peace with my new life.

Lack of Satiety with the World Resurfaces

Now that some of the dust from our whirlwind of physical activity had settled, Winged Wolf began to hone in again on my 'major hole.'

"You still have one big thing that holds you back, Wings of Change. Do you know what it is?"

"My attachment to being busy." I was pretty sure this was it.

"No, although that is an aspect of it. It's lack of satiety with the world."

"Do you think I'm still attached to the world?" I asked, surprised. *"I thought I'd gotten through that one."*

"Oh, you're better than you were," she told me, *"but you haven't gotten through it, not yet."*

"Well, what do I do about that?" I was puzzled. "Isn't my move here a sign that I've given up worldly attachments?"

"It's a step, but that's not the end of it."

"What else can I do?" I asked, suddenly realizing I knew the answer to this one.

"I need you here on the property, full-time. It isn't the same for those who live off the property as it is for those who are here full-time. You can't see it because you're not here, but I see it clearly. The ones who live here full-time are so calm and peaceful. Why, they are growing in leaps and bounds."

"How long do you need me to be on the property?" I asked her, knowing that my husband was going to be away for six months or more.

"At least six months," she replied,

"I can do that."

Quickly, she added, "Really, I need you here for a year."

"Oh," I hesitated.

"I'm not your enemy, Wings of Change; I'm trying to get you through the eye of the needle. It would be helpful if you could see that and not pull against me."

Awareness flooded me. How could I have forgotten she was trying to help me? It was as though a dark cloud had shrouded my vision.

"I'm sorry, Winged Wolf, for a moment I forgot that. With Walter away, there's no reason I can't move onto the property for a year. Sure, I'll be happy for the opportunity. But how can I do it? All the housing is spoken for."

"You'll have to work that out, I don't have an answer for you. There is another apprentice who is ready to move onto the property. Perhaps you and she can work something out."

And so it evolved that the other apprentice and I found a place that built homes right in their factory and delivered them to the site in a few short weeks. I had to pinch myself to make sure this was really happening. What a relief to give up all that resistance and just allow things to unfold. It took tremendous energy to resist the flow of my life, and once I surrendered, all that blocked energy was released back into the natural flow.

An Unexpected Change

Not long after he left, and just after I agreed to move onto the property, early in September, while I was visiting the grandchildren (a new granddaughter had just been born) in Michigan, Walter called from Vermont and told me, *"Things aren't working out here the way I had anticipated. It isn't a comfortable experience for me. I'm seriously considering leaving and returning to British Columbia, and I'd like to resume my apprenticeship with Winged Wolf, if she'll have me."*

"Call her," I urged him. *"She said she is there for you if you ask for her help."* (She had told him that before he left.)

What transpired between them is not part of my story, but the result was that Walter called back to say, *"I'm leaving here. I'll be in Michigan in three days, and then I'm heading back to British Columbia."*

My heart was singing because his divine sense was returning, he was heading back to the Teacher he was meant to be with. I knew from what Winged Wolf had told me about our relationship that we had done this so many times before, and with certainty, I knew we had never passed this point in our previous lifetimes. This time I was going for it regardless, which was new for me, but as a couple, we had never made it past this obstacle. I could feel the tightness that had been squeezing my heart loosen its grip. Still, it was way too soon to feel confident of anything; this was only the beginning. There was no guarantee it would work out. But it was a good sign.

My sons were watching this strange drama of ours with concern and with the typical questions one might have about the strange behavior they were observing in their parents. *"What's wrong with Walt?"* they kept asking me. And, *"Why are you letting him do this?"* As if he could be stopped somehow. But it was alarming to them, especially the one who was married, because he was identifying his situation and his marriage with ours and feeling uncomfortable, already making comments about what he would do if his wife ever acted like me. The response to his fear was to try and take control of the situation. I understood, because I could see it from their viewpoint.

I told them, *"You can't control what another person does, even if it's your spouse. People have to make their own decisions, even when those decisions are painful to others involved. He's trying to find his way in life and having a difficult time of it right now. But he's coming around. He just needs a little space to work things out."*

It was an awkward time for us all. Walter arrived, but he was too preoccupied with his situation to relate much. He just needed to rest a bit and gather his strength for the long drive back across the country. It would take close to a week of steady driving. But he was back, and in communication with the Teacher, ready to resume his apprenticeship.

One thing that was becoming apparent to me by this trip was the pattern between my intestinal and other physical disturbances and certain types of life stresses. Walter's struggle created in me one of those trigger points. Perhaps seeing it clearly would help me unhook, but those strings of energy were pretty tightly knotted. And my sons were so angry with me, each for their own reasons. It wasn't their fault, they were just being themselves; it was my responsibility to learn how to stop internalizing that energy, how to turn my karma around. I kept repeating my Teacher's words, *"You can heal the past, but first, you must heal the present."* Was I too involved in what they thought and not centered enough in myself?

A journal entry dated September 21, reflects my split state of mind:

> *"Today, I am on a plane flying from Detroit to Spokane, WA, from where I will drive to Westbridge, British Columbia, Canada. There is a monastery there, which I have participated in building, at least helped in overseeing the building, along with the constant support and companion energy, vision and tireless efforts of Winged Wolf and many others. This part of my life, the spiritual part, is evolving and growing.*
>
> *"Meanwhile my personal life has been sadly stressful, but the good news is my husband has decided to move back to*

British Columbia and, hopefully, resume his apprenticeship. Who knows where this will lead. I am still trying to recover from the shock of all that has happened. My adult children are angry with me for moving farther and farther away from them and have denounced the spiritual work I am doing as crazy. My health has suffered. My whole system was thrown out of whack by an attack of thrush; and direr, my left eye is losing its clarity of vision, cause as yet unknown. Winged Wolf says this is happening because there are things I am refusing to see.

"How can there be such a split in me? I thought spiritual growth meant peace and love in all aspects of life. The Teacher has taught us that we can heal the past, but first we must heal ourselves. There is something I am not seeing and it's blocking me on all levels and in all relationships. I pray continuously for guidance. But do I listen when it is given?"

Working at *Skycliffe*, often long, hard hours, was stressful in a way, but it didn't trigger stomach problems. It was my attachments that triggered them. When I really looked at what was going on, I could trace the incidents of physical reaction to emotional responses because I refused to give up a particular way of being or doing things. Staying in the house of someone I loved when they were angry with me is a good example of that, an attachment that hurt my body as well as caused mental anguish. It was a form of insanity, and I knew better. And there were other attachments that were equally painful to break. Could I step away from them? Many of them were like old shoes, so familiar. But these cycles of physical suffering were getting old.

Flying back to *Skycliffe,* I had no idea what to expect and felt a little anxious. Walt would arrive a couple days after me in spite of the fact he had left several days prior to my leaving. I hadn't yet told him of my decision to live on the property. The timing didn't seem right, so we would have many things to deal with after he returned. I prayed things would go well with Winged Wolf, knowing it was completely out of my hands. And, we had another empowerment to prepare for only a few weeks away. It promised to be a doozy, and according to the Teacher, this would be the final empowerment. The bottom line was she was going to teach us about death as a transfiguration! What would this chapter of my life look like? I had no idea.

To his great joy, the conversation with Winged Wolf went well, and Walter told me, *"She officially accepted me back as her apprentice, but the stipulation is that I have to begin again, from the first Initiation Journey."*

"That's wonderful," I told him, gratitude flooding me. *"I'm so happy for you, and me, too. Maybe now we can rebuild our lives in a more spiritually evolved way, coming together in the companion energy of service to the Path."*

"Was it hard to have her tell you to start over?" I understood this meant he had given up his status as a Lightbearer (an extension of the Sage Vow).

"Not at all," he responded. *"I think it will mean much more to me this time."*

With the big issue settled, it was time for me to tackle the personal situation, that is to say, our future living arrangements. *There's something I need to tell you,"* my stomach was in knots. *"While you were gone, there seemed no reason for me not to live on the property, so I agreed to move to Skycliffe for at least a year."*

"Oh." He was surprised, but not shaken. *"I can see why you would want to do that. Maybe Winged Wolf will let me live there, too."*

"Would you want to live there?" Now I was surprised.

"Yes, I think so. I know it would be a major life-style change, but if I'm to be serious about this apprenticeship, it would be a good move to be as close to the Teacher as possible."

"Well, that's a relief to me, because I wondered how you would feel about my move. Now, I can relax knowing it's a direction you want to head, too."

"I wonder what Winged Wolf will say about it," he mused.

A few days later he pulled me aside and said, *"I spoke with Winged Wolf about moving onto the property. She told me even though she would like to say 'yes,' it's too soon for her to make a decision. I have to be patient until the time is right for her to decide. She said there are many factors involved."*

During this time, we were in the thick of preparing for the upcoming empowerment in October, so there was no slack time and no time to ponder the outcome of our personal situation, which was fortunate, since there was really nothing to ponder. What would be would be. Our attention was focused on preparations.

Winged Wolf had chosen an unbelievable site on the property to hold this empowerment. It was called Amitaba Vista, and when she first showed it to me, I shook my head in disbelief.

"There's no way people can get to this site, Winged Wolf; it's too difficult a climb. Many people attending have health issues and could never take such a hike."

At first she backed off, recognizing the physical difficulties involved in reaching the spot. We had walked the property for hours looking for another 'perfect' site. And certainly we found many beautiful settings, but, no matter how she tried, there was no place else that showed up as ultimately suitable for this particular empowerment.

For this empowerment, she needed vast, open space, because of the content; that is, she intended to teach us how to die and how to set the stage for a propitious rebirth. This was a big deal. How this topic would stir up all sorts of feelings and reactions from people was immediately apparent. We needed spaciousness and height for this one so that all the feelings and emotions this subject would inevitably stir up could be blown away. There could be nothing closed in or confining about the setting.

"There is no other suitable site for this empowerment," she finally declared. *"We'll simply have to build a stairway to reach the site."* A small group of us were walking with her up the first hill leading to the site, and it was long and steep.

"We'll need a handrail too." She was pointing to the general area where the steps would be; and we could see there would be many of them needed if someone was to climb this hill. We only had a couple weeks left before people arrived and this looked like a major job.

After a few days, the report came back, *"It's too steep an incline, Winged Wolf, some of our attendees won't be able to get up there."* The team had already spent several days and there were only a few steps built.

One might expect at this point a new, more accessible site would be chosen, but this was not our Teacher's way. She set out exploring for another path to access the site, and to everyone's amazement, two discoveries were made. First, there was a path that began at the foot of the east side of the orchard and went directly up to the site. Granted it was a steep climb, but about one quarter the distance of the previous path, and a handrail could easily be installed all the way up, with intermittent benches for people to pause and rest. Best of all, Winged Wolf found a small logging trail that was just wide enough for a compact car to drive through, so those who were unable to walk could ride up almost to the site and be dropped off, leaving only a short walk ahead.

So the Teacher had her site, and it truly was breathtaking, a panoramic view high on a hilltop, overlooking the winding Kettle River and green pasturelands below. Whatever was stirred up and released during the talks could be carried away on the winds that blew continuously across the open expanse and be absorbed harmlessly into nature.

"This will be our last empowerment for awhile," she told us. *"People get filled up at these events and leave thinking they know all there is to know, but they are unable to integrate the Teachings into their lives. From this point on, I want them to come here on retreat, spend time sitting in the silence, learning self-discipline, developing their spiritual practice. That way, they will really leave with something they can carry into their lives. Otherwise, they just want more, more, more, but it's information they are unable to use."*

She was right in this, but always before she had given them 'one more empowerment' because people had come to anticipate that every three-month cycle, and used it as their infusion of the divine consciousness. Many of the attendees rode on the heightened awareness they received from being in the presence of the Guru from one empowerment to the next. Unfortunately, they began to think they knew a lot because of all the Teachings she gave them, but they weren't integrating the Teachings into their lives. And, for some, it became a social thing, a time to connect with old friends. The Teacher definitely did not intend for our spiritual evolvement to be a social thing. That would be a distraction from the work of spiritual development and frivolous. This was a serious Path; that didn't mean we couldn't laugh and have fun and enjoy ourselves, but we could never forget that our sole purpose for being together was to move forward toward our enlightenment.

This was probably the most confronting of any of the empowerments in a personal way. Death is a very personal experience. This was reflected by the responses of those in attendance. We were startled into honestly looking at ourselves. We were even provided a sample letter to give to our families giving instructions as to how we should be treated if they were with us during our time of death; and it was a strong, clear, and explicit set of instructions.

While the intent was to teach us how to die, or shed these physical bodies at a time of our choosing, so that we transferred our consciousness to a Buddhafield on the invisible side, thus insuring a fortunate rebirth, the group bogged down after the Teacher tackled the subject of *'lies we tell ourselves'* or *'lies we are living.'* There was so much to be revealed on this issue, so much depth to it, that people needed the time and space to work it through, much more time than might have been anticipated. Winged Wolf told us that these experiences were necessary before any of us could move any further forward.

Winged Wolf said that in order to prepare for our death, we first had to confront our lies. We had to clean the slate by taking a long look in the mirror and acknowledging the lies that were present in our lives. While she may have intended this to be an afternoon workshop, the arrow struck a bull's-eye and brought up all sorts of karmic baggage for people.

It was so powerful to unravel these lies that we had been carrying with us for lifetimes; but it took longer than was expected, and because it did take so long, the actual lesson on death had to be postponed. For the most part, I don't think anyone noticed. They were so caught up in self-discovery, stunned really. Now it was time for people to do their work on an individual basis, via spiritual retreat, spiritual practice, and relationship with the Teacher. This time I think people really saw there was serious work to be done if they were genuine in their commitment to enlightenment in this lifetime.

Winged Wolf told us, *"I pray for enlightenment for each of you in this lifetime, but you have to do the work. And I'll be with you one-hundred-percent of the way."*

She had brought us all the way to this point. We had the property; the retreat center was in place; the residents had moved into their homes and were assuming their roles as support staff to maintain the physical operation. The deeper work could commence. This was a turning point, a shift in focus that would allow people to move forward in a way that wasn't previously available simply because the physical structure had not been in place. The Teacher's dream had finally taken shape, even though there was plenty of filling in yet to do.

Chapter 28
My Teacher Is a Buddha

Way back on Orcas Island, while we were still struggling to find our new home, I remember walking into the Happy House one afternoon to meet with Winged Wolf. It was often the place where we met to have conversations that had a special importance to them; ones that had called for a sacred atmosphere. Often Winged Wolf would go there and sit on her cushion in deep meditation when there was something of a potentially portentous nature afoot, or a situation of great urgency to one of her apprentices or to the Spiritual Order. This particular afternoon she had been sitting for a long time while I was working on a project at her request. Her sitting was to provide companion energy and spiritual support for the work I was doing.

As I had quietly opened the door to the Happy House and stepped over the threshold, I had glanced in her direction and been momentarily mesmerized. She was deeply into the silence, her body relaxed and comfortable. But what had drawn my attention was her face and the aura around her head. There was light everywhere around her and her face radiated with light that appeared to be pouring out of her very being. My breath caught as I stood staring at her. What had flashed through my mind at that moment of hesitation was, *'My Teacher is a Buddha.'* Quickly, I looked away from that thought. It was incomprehensible.

Now, almost a year later as I sat in our new Temple night after night, my attention was again drawn irresistibly to her. I would be sitting in meditative pose when suddenly my head would turn to gaze at my Teacher. What was I seeing? A metamorphosis was taking place with her. The stress lines that had been present on her face during our property search and early days of the move were gone, replaced by the most serene, blissful, radiant expression I had ever seen. She was literally aglow. And there was the feeling of divine presences around her, many of them.

My Teacher is a Buddha

The conclusion was obvious to me although still startling for some reason, *'My Teacher is a Buddha.'* And then, *'My Teacher is Buddha; there is only one.'* Such peaceful reassurance this realization brought with it. Step by step, She had walked that impeccable line, from the beginning of this Path that She started, never wavering in Her service, never faltering in the direction, continuously, consistently leading us toward spiritual awakening, for the entire ten years that I had been with Her, until one moment She had slipped over the line and She had become Buddha. Somewhere along the way, She had become That. And I was only now able to fully acknowledge who She was. It was almost incomprehensible, yet without a doubt, I knew it to be true. *'She is a Buddha.'*

When I first had the glimmer that day in the Happy House on Orcas that my Teacher was a Buddha, it had been too much for me to absorb. Mind chatter had taken over. *'How would you know what a Buddha is?'* I had asked myself, questioning the reality of the experience. The bottom line had been that my perceptions revolved around me; they centered on how I felt about something. Was I comfortable or uncomfortable with 'it.' So right after the glimpse into who she really had become, I had asked the question, *'How do I relate to a Buddha?'*

As my Teacher, I had become so comfortable with Her, thinking of Her as a highly revered friend; and She was a friend to me, the best friend, but this did not mean I was that to Her. I was not Her peer although I desired to be that; but She assured me that was not possible on my terms. I was not Her spiritual equal, although I wanted to be; this was understood. She was my Teacher, but that seemed more reachable than a Buddha. So I had veered away from acknowledging Her as That. Now, I felt the most profound respect, literally wanted to throw myself at Her feet and ask for Her blessing.

A miracle is said to be a changed consciousness, so this was a miracle of the first order. At last, I could see my Teacher for who She was and not shy away from the realization. From this point on, She became even more precious to me than She was before. No longer did I refer to Her as 'she;' it seemed disrespectful. In writing, I began to capitalize all references to Her, because She was no longer a person or a persona to me but an embodiment of the divine consciousness that I recognized as That. It set me free to view the things She did and said from a different perspective, something I was incapable of previously.

Vajra House

After that 'final' empowerment, my attention turned toward moving onto the property and securing a structure that could be on the property as quickly as possible. It was decided that a dwelling, pre-built in the factory and delivered to the property in move-in condition, would be the most efficient way to accomplish this. It would only take eight weeks, so our move-in date would be around the first of December. Things were going quickly now. What would life be like living full-time at a monastery? I had memories of other lifetimes when I had lived in this way, but they were in different eras and I had become attached to my modern lifestyle of coming and going, my split-shift. How hard would I find it to give up this so-called freedom? That remained to be seen, but I was committed to it now, and the building was going full-speed ahead. Immediately after my visit to Michigan for the holidays, I would become a resident at Skycliffe.

What an exciting adventure life is. My life was living proof of the never say never axiom. My prayer was to one day learn graciousness, so that rather than allowing my ego to kick and scream at every turn of the corner, I could accept and embrace change as it came along in the natural flow of living. There was no point in promising myself that *'next time I'll do better'* because, thus far, *next time* I always did the same thing. If I was ever to become a Thunderbeing, those ego displays would have to stop; they were not possible at that level.

The upside was that I seemed to always get unstuck; but it was taking a risk each time that I could get permanently stuck and fall backward. *"Intercept it before the resistance takes hold,"* She told me. *"Otherwise you're just letting go because you are too exhausted not to. That's more of the same."*

It would take some pressure off of the Teacher who received the bruises from my struggles. The answer was obvious, if only I could integrate it into my being. Old habitual ways of being do not die an easy death.

The house arrived late in November just before the first heavy snowfall. Driving up the forest service road that led to Skycliffe with two huge pieces of a house was a harrowing experience, even without the ice and snow. These drivers were really skilled at what they were doing, and smart enough to take a small truck in first to check out the road conditions.

It was an intense experience anyway. Winged Wolf is fiercely protective of the land, which suffered painfully when trenches were dug for electrical cable and water pipes. To bring the house in required taking out part of the outer and inner fences, which meant animals could get in if we didn't immediately replace the fences that were removed. It also meant leaving deep trenches in the land from the weight of the load. Also, the long winding driveway was flanked with prayer flags, so the trucks had to inch their way in pulling the two halves of the house so as not to hit one of the flagpoles. At times they needed to remove a pole to pass by, and to their credit, they were so respectful, that not a flag was damaged.

This was an all-day affair, and there was a huge sigh of relief when the two halves were set in place and all the fences were restored. After that, it was a matter of a few days to patch and paint the drywall, lay the carpet and hook up the utilities. How amazing to see two pieces of something become a whole, livable home in just a few days. I couldn't quite believe that my new home was so attractive and comfortable. What good fortune! Somehow I had expected that living in a monastery would be stark and bare bones. What a thrill it was going to be for me to move in when the holidays were over. The new residence was christened Vajra House, for that diamond quality that cuts through all illusion.

Before my decision to move onto the property, Winged Wolf one day had asked a group of resident apprentices to talk about their experience of living on the property.

I remember listening with fascination and puzzlement as they tried to explain how it was different living as a full-time resident on the property versus going home in the evening.

One apprentice said, *"It's a whole different energy living here; it's hard even to describe what is different but it's so much softer."*

And another, *"At first I wondered if I would feel confined, like I was giving up some of my freedom, but after the first few days, I could see it was more relaxing. The energy outside is harsh; I'm glad I no longer have to face that each evening."*

I felt insulted when one apprentice remarked, *"I can feel the difference in the energy of those of you who go home at night and return in the* morning. It's subtle but it's there. You pick up a bit of the energy of the world; it's a harsher vibration."

At the time, I could hear their comments, but there was no frame of reference to hold them in. There was a sense, or a glimmer, of what they were saying but no experience of it.

That discussion flashed in my memory the first night I spent on the property. Now I would have an opportunity to experience what they had been expressing to me. It didn't happen right away; there was an adjustment period in the beginning. This was my new life, seven days a week, four hours of meditation a day, ad infinitum. In itself, that was a truly unique experience. **There were no divisions; it was all spiritual life manifested in a variety of activities.** And therein lies the difference. I saw it clearly after about a month of living on the property.

Meanwhile, my relationship with the Teacher took a leap, because I had finally let go of my resistance to living on the property. Living off the property had been a difficult attachment for me to let go of, but now it seemed so foolish. At the moment, there were no other attachments that were blocking me spiritually. I was living in the moment. Life was peaceful, and while we were terribly busy, it was happy busy. A journal entry dated January 17, reflects this newfound joy.

> "Now, for the good part. We began the evening sitting and almost immediately I began to feel the energy of the divine consciousness permeate the room and rain down on me. The impact was almost indescribable, but I'm sure going to try. If you can imagine, a divine bath, that is, energy that is so light, so buoyant, effervescent, invigorating, simply raining down on you continuously for an hour, massaging your heart and giving you such a sense of elation, joy, almost swooning, pulling your consciousness up to meet it so that all there is, is this divine bath, this sublime oneness, and you know this is how it is and there is nothing you could want more than this. You might never leave the cushion or do anything but walk around grinning at people, seeing the cosmic joke, feeling the joy of life, loving all that cross your path, and those that don't too, blissed out. It feels like a continuous orgasm, but not in a genital or sexual way, more an all-body uplifting, up, up, up. The body doesn't hurt, or if it does, you don't really care."

> And a week later, *"Tonight, at first I thought it wasn't going to happen, but then I began to get whiffs of it, then steady. I was floating most of the time, noticed that now when I see pictures or images I rarely get into words about them, because I'm so caught in the blissful state that words don't come up. It was a gentle, steady upliftment of energy giving me a sense of dreamy bliss. I can see how it would be easy to become attached to this state. It's such a high."*

What made it so blissful was the feeling I had of being connected to the Teacher's heart, the heart of the divine consciousness. That connectedness put me in a place of sublime awareness of the oneness of all life and it made my heart sing.

All the years and all the hours of practicing spiritually, sitting on my cushion, were finally reaping bounty. I was experiencing the sweetness of life in all its many manifestations. And I was detached from my feelings enough to see many of the patterns that had controlled me. Being a bodhisattva took on new meaning as the awareness of oneness with all sentient life penetrated. I began to wonder if I was approaching the eye of the needle.

One day in February, Winged Wolf and I made a trip to Kelowna, the closest large town, where we were frequently purchasing an endless number of supplies for our spring opening of the Log House and the campground. As far as I could see, we were having a relaxed conversation, when out of the blue She said, *"Who would you want to invite to your ordination as Thunderbeing?"*

"What?" Her question startled me.

"Well, it isn't quite time for it right now, but you should be thinking about who you would want to invite when it is time. You need to decide if you want to invite your sons, and any other friends or relatives."

My heart was racing. This was a conversation I had both anticipated and tried not to anticipate since my earliest days as an apprentice.

"Do you think I should invite family, knowing how they feel about this part of my life?"

"Well, you give it some thought. We don't have to decide anything right now."

The rest of that day was odd. One part of me functioned as though nothing had happened, while the silent part was still carrying the conversation about my becoming a Thunderbeing. It was surreal; I had wanted it for so long, now it was too big to grasp that it was going to happen.

Not a word more was said for a few weeks and I relaxed. Then, one morning, I went into Her office after the morning sitting, a routine we had observed for some time, an opportunity to discuss the day's agenda, when She held up the calendar and said, *"What do you think about June for your ordination?"*

Again, She caught me by surprise.

"Or, we could move it up to May, that's a beautiful time here at Skycliffe. How about the weekend of the 26th? The apple trees should be in blossom then; what a sight that will be with all those white blossoms. It should be warm enough by then so people can stay in the campground."

"That sounds like a perfect time for it," I responded, imagining the trees in bloom all over the orchard.

"You should plan on spending most of the time until your ordination in the silence, preparing yourself." Winged Wolf told me.

"Do you have any suggestions as to how I might go about preparing?" I asked Her. *"I've never done this before."*

This was something I had worked toward, placed my total attention upon for so long that it was impossible yet to grasp that it was to come to fruition. May 26th was only three months away! I understood the idea of preparation, but not the actual *do* of it.

Winged Wolf was thoughtful for a few moments. *"You have to come to know yourself thoroughly, and this can only be done through the silence. There can be no attachments, no ego flashing. This is a big moment for our Spiritual Order; you must be squeaky clean for ordination. This is a time for you to look deeply within yourself, and from a detached viewpoint come to know who you are."*

"What are the guidelines for being in the silence? I asked.

"While you are in the silence, you are to keep your eyes averted so there is no eye contact with anyone, except me. I don't want you to communicate except with me. You can take your meals alone in Vajra House."

Shortly after this interaction, I went into the silence, my opportunity to prepare myself for a life of service. Being in the silence was difficult for me at times. It was difficult to stay centered while there was so much energy and activity in motion around me. The air was charged with the energy of the activities surrounding the event; preparations were underway. Whenever Master Maticintin placed Her attention on something, there was a strong forward momentum to it. My challenge was to have the self-discipline to be still, balanced and directed inward toward self-discovery, with all the activities going on about the place. I was drawn toward participating in the activities.

Usually, the Teacher would give me daily updates as to how plans were evolving, and take a look at me to see how I was doing. There were aspects of my personality that concerned Her because they were ego-driven and habitual. She wondered if I would be ready in time for the ordination. Over the years of my apprenticeship, She had often cautioned me about my displays of ego, especially my need to be the center of attention; also there had been my concern with rank, and my ambitious streak, incompatible with the spiritualized consciousness.

Soon, things began to stir in me. The silence acted like a pressure cooker, pressing down on my being and pushing up a barrage of uncompleted karma. The Teacher was noticing handles sticking out everywhere and She instantly honed in on them. They had to be corrected quickly. Again She warned me, *"There is no room for self-centeredness in spirituality; it does not exist in one who is free from attachments. There can be no trace of ego, or you will surely fall."*

She went on to say, *"Whenever there is an initiation, which is a crack in the consciousness, an opening to a new level of awareness, you are at your most vulnerable. With the other initiations you have had, such as Savant, there was some room to fall backwards; the two steps forward, one step back type of thing. But with this initiation, there is no room at all for falling backwards. You can only go forward. There is not even a moment to stop and gloat over what you have accomplished. If you do that, you will lose it. It is not the same as out in the world where people can pause and enjoy their achievements.*

"With spirituality, the only way you know there is movement is by looking out of yourself and seeing the reflections in the environment, seeing that people are evolving, animals are happy, the land is flourishing, situations are being resolved. This is important to your understanding because you will be totally exposed after the initiation. There will be no place to hide. You just keep moving forward. Never stop, and never look back or you will fall."

"You're scaring me, Winged Wolf." I told Her.

"Maybe that will help you remember," She replied.

I felt a cold chill run up my spine. As I looked back over my apprenticeship, I realized that what She said was true. Each time I had taken an initiation, there had been an adjustment period, a time when I felt awkward, uncertain of myself in this new place, cautious and vulnerable. But at those times, there had been plenty of room for me to fall back a bit, to feel my way along and evolve into the fullness of what that particular initiation represented, sometimes it had taken months. With Savant, it had been more than a year. She was forewarning me now that there would be no 'grace period' to relax into this new level of consciousness; it would be all forward movement.

This was the first time we had talked about it being possible for someone to fall from the irreversible way. I had never considered it possible; after all, it was called the 'irreversible way.' Now I was learning what that meant; there could be no pause in my momentum. There was a continuous DO involved. It wasn't a place to arrive at; it merely marked a crossing over, a freedom from attachments, but it was only a beginning point, not the end of something. From observing my Teacher I knew that She never paused to look at what had been accomplished; She just kept moving forward.

Ten days later, Winged Wolf brought me out of the silence for a while and watched to see how clean I was. Each day She would call me into Her office for a review; there were many handles (attachments, behaviors needing correction, uncontained energy) popping up; and each day the list of corrections grew longer. There was never a time in our past history together that so many items presented themselves to be cleared up in such a short time.

After our talks, I would dash home and make notes of what I needed to work on.

Despite these intense sessions with the Teacher (or perhaps because of them), the quality of my meditations was surprisingly filled with a sense of serenity and great joy.

One evening in April, I had an experience while meditating that was striking. I wrote, *"Suddenly, I found myself surrounded by monks. On my right were four of them, linear position, but only one was forefront, the other three were like transparencies, as though they were layered. On my left was only one, and this one was in white; the other main one was in a dark color. They were chanting what sounded like 'amagee' over and over in deep baritones. It was beautiful and I was totally immersed, as though it were completely natural until I realized what was happening, then I became separate in my awe as I looked at it; and as my awareness returned to the present, the scene faded."*

So, it was a puzzlement to me that my meditations were generally uplifting, peaceful and stable, yet my times in-between were filled with inconsistencies and disturbing energy. Beginning April 28, the entire monastery would be going into silent retreat for a week and I would begin another extended period of silence, after my brief interlude. Oh, how I prayed for equanimity to become my mantra.

As Ordination Day drew near, Winged Wolf brought me over a copy of the program, which contained the actual vow I would be taking. She left it with me to study. The vow was simple; that is, the words were simple; the vow was profound. Essentially it said, *"I vow to place others before myself."* The more I read it, the deeper it went in me. I was vowing to live for the sake of others. What did that really mean? I would live for the good of the whole, make decisions for the good of the whole. I knew from the Teachings and from my experience in meditation that the identification with a self was the root of all suffering. I had watched my Teacher long enough to know that She lived for other's sake, in service. Now I was going to live that as well. It was the way of the bodhisattva.

As long as I remained centered, looking out of myself, there wasn't even a question, because service is all there is. In those moments when I

Initiation

slipped off center, and I did, my little-self was full of questions, none of which could be answered because it is impossible to talk to a little-self.

What my days were like in the silence varied slightly but, for the most part, I was alone and wrestling with myself, my desire to be actively involved in what was going on, versus my assignment to be in the silence and release any attachments that arose. And there were many that did. On the one hand, I wanted to learn detachment and mindfulness through the silence; and on the other, I wanted to actively participate. The fact that there was a struggle was a red flag. I prayed for guidance. Was this a natural process of shedding baggage I was experiencing, a letting go, or was something else at work here?

Winged Wolf had made it known to me that I could not get through the eye of the needle with any shred of ego still in control, and this time of silence was meant to refine any of those tendencies that might remain. If there were any personality issues, any games, any self desires for attention or personal power, all this had to be transmuted before the ordination.

It would sabotage me if I couldn't transmute them. I wouldn't be able to be with my Teacher in companion energy with that in the way; I would be pulling against Her. They could not be allowed to have control over me. I couldn't resist them or I would bind them to me, so I must accept them and transcend their influence.

Feelings and thoughts accompanying those feelings produced mood swings in me on a moment-to-moment basis. How was I to understand this, was it mirroring my ego, showing me how I would be after the ordination or was it the Transhistorical Consciousness squeezing me clean of all my karmic clutter?

Winged Wolf talked to me about this and told me to *"look at it and let it go; don't hang on to anything."* She reminded me to keep my eye on the bulls-eye of enlightenment, not to let anything distract me.

A feeling of great joy and harmony were in the air as preparations escalated for the event. I read and re-read my vow, trembling a little each time I said it. Gradually, it became a part of me.

Saying it aloud brought forth images of how I had lived such a self-centered existence during my life. I hadn't seen it so clearly until now. It had often been about what I wanted, how I felt, how I was doing, and so on. Now I was taking a vow, saying there was no me to look at, there was only a self-less embodiment of the divine consciousness. Surely this was something I would grow into as I evolved.

Here I stood at a crossroad in my life like none other, trembling with the vibration that rippled through me each time I read the vow. How my life would unfold afterwards was unknown to me. There was no vision, or strong instinctual knowing of what was to come. When I tried to look, I saw nothing.

There was a line; on one side was detachment and unconditional love and on the other was the personality that was driven by ego. The vow represented that line. I was postulating to the Transhistorical Consciousness that my life was to be lived for other's sake, not for my own sake. A postulation to the Transhistorical Consciousness was something Winged Wolf had talked to me about. This was not like any other promise ever made. It was a spiritual commitment that would enhance and uplift all sentient life, and if it was taken lightly or broken, disrespected in any way, the consequences would be grave, because of all the power that came forth to assist the sentient being who made such a vow. I wanted that vow to permeate every cell in my body, to become a living part of me, to take me over.

One morning, Winged Wolf called me into Her office after the sitting. She looked at me for a long time, saying nothing, then began. "You have a weakness," and here She paused again before continuing, *"It is a zest for life in the world, and that zest is the result of your ego that thrives on the attention you can generate for yourself out there. That weakness could kill you. If you were to lose consciousness for even a moment, you could be killed."*

Her words hung in the space between us and I held my breath, waiting for Her to continue. Here it was again in all its starkness, my lack of satiety with the world, my ego-driven behavior.

"When you are in the world, other people's energy, their mind stuff, can stick to you. If you lose consciousness at that point, you could die. Then you would have to live lifetimes in other forms, still with the consciousness, until you work through that karma. I've been there, and if I can save you from having to do that, I will, but I don't know if I can."

This was a reference to Winged Wolf's incarnation as Mahamaudgalyarana who was a disciple of Sakyamuni Buddha, and who lived a number of ensuing lifetimes as a less highly evolved form of sentient life, while still carrying human consciousness. In the case of Mahamaudgalyarana, it was his passion for the Teachings, a zealousness that became arrogant, that cost him his life, and the sixty-seven following lifetimes that it took to complete the learning of the lesson. Winged Wolf was attempting to save me from following a similar pattern, although for much different reasons. My lessons had to do with learning loyalty to the Path and the Teacher when that loyalty conflicted with my little-self ego needs.

This was a somber and sobering communication. I didn't quite know how to integrate it into my awareness so as to correct my imbalance. *I said to Her, "Winged Wolf, this concerns me deeply, to have come this far, and now to see the potential dangers I carry in my karmic make up."*

She lightened the moment a bit saying, *"Bittersweet candy is my favorite. There is an edge; you get right up to it, and then you stay there. If you do that, you will live in joy and bliss. That edge is called mindfulness.*

"Perhaps it will help if I tell you about one of your past lives. It was about a thousand years ago; you were an elf, one of the elementals, and you had been one for a long time; but you always envied humans and their ability to create their world. You see, you had mastery of the elements of nature, the ability to live in nature, but not the ability to manifest your world. You may not have known that was what humans could do, but you saw they had something that you wanted. If you can see that people's mind stuff is only illusionary, you can learn to create your own world, different from theirs."

Hearing this struck a chord of optimism in me, the idea that I could create a world different from the mass consciousness, full of bliss, free of suffering. It made an overwhelming task seem do-able.

"How do I go about doing this?" I asked eagerly.

"You will feel it rising in you, that feeling of passion for the world, and when you do, you must catch it and bring it back under control. And it will take many forms, so you have to be always mindful to catch that feeling before it catches you. Then, when you do, reach out and pat it."

The words *'pat it'* struck me as unusual, and I raised my eyebrows in question.

She explained, *"Say to it, 'I know you, I accept you, but I cannot indulge you.' Don't be harsh; don't try to push it away, just pat it and pull it in."*

"Is it possible for me to do this in one lifetime?" I asked.

"Yes it is, but I cannot do it for you. If I could, I would. You must do it for yourself." And with that, our conversation ended. I had to digest quickly. And it was deeply stirring.

Later that evening, Winged Wolf stopped by Vajra House and returned to the subject of the potential of my future lives should I lose consciousness and die in that state. She said, *"You could return as a cow with full consciousness, eating grass; and imagine what it would be like to have full consciousness and have a bull mount you, knowing what was going on but not being able to stop it."* With that image, She got laughing so hard the tears rolled down Her cheeks.

I managed a chuckle as I saw the scene through her vivid picture, but it was so distasteful that I grimaced at the same time. The images were so outrageous that it was almost impossible to contemplate them, yet I knew without a doubt they were entirely possible under the aforementioned circumstances. That night I prayed fervently for help to stay awake at all times, not to slip for even a moment!

Journal Entry

"Today is the 6th day of the silent retreat and there are a total of twenty-one participants here at Skycliffe through tomorrow. After that, there is only me (on silent retreat).

"I have been looking at the Thunderbeing Vow frequently these past few days, and at first it seems quite simple, but as I continue to look, I realize the vastness of it. It is huge, the commitment that is, and I see that it is so big that had I been able to touch upon it earlier in my apprenticeship, I would have run for the hills. But since I could not and could only perceive it from my own limited viewpoint, it worked to my advantage in a way, because I was not frightened by it.

"Today, I slipped over a line and stood in a place of really grasping more than ever before what a commitment it is to live my life in service to others 'without reservation of any kind.' It means letting go of everything I've held as personal—every attachment, even the most subtle, and these words have been said so many times they have no real distinction to the listener except as the ability to perceive the meaning expands. Today my ability to perceive expanded and I saw myself letting go in a total way, no clinging to anyone, anything, any idea, to the best of my ability from where I now stood.

"Winged Wolf tells me she will teach/give me everything as I am ready to receive it. I am so honored. For Her, this is a continuation of a thread from one lifetime to the next, with consciousness. For me, I guess it's still a thread, but the course is being charted as I go, having no previous history to build from... I mean, She has been other enlightened beings in other times, and so is always the reincarnation of………, but I have not, so I am not the incarnation of anyone, but the culmination of lifetimes of becoming, and now, if this means I've stepped over a line in consciousness, in the future then I will be the reincarnation of ……. What I leave as a legacy will be passed on, even though I have no idea of what that might be.

"All I see in this moment is that if I can live my life in complete openness, meaning open heart, love flowing all the time, giving and receiving, in service to all sentient life, then I can be an example for others to learn openness themselves. I will have served well. It seems an enormous commitment at this time, but this is only a beginning. Winged Wolf pointed to the view of the mountains off in the distance and said, 'You can see the beautiful mountains from here, but there are many more behind what you can see. What you see now is only the tip of what there is to see.'"

Journal Entry

"Now that the group silence is over, there is so much energy flowing through me, it is hard to really settle back into the silence. It is so hard to describe this sense of uncharted *territory, no blueprint, the future not quite clear; there is a tendency to want to grab at the familiar, something to anchor myself, things are moving so quickly. But I must not grab or try to cling to some false sense of identity. I must continue to let it unfold, hold to nothing but the trust in my Teacher and the Path to guide me forward in the direction of my destiny."*

Winged Wolf had told the Savant apprentices and myself that my head would be shaved for the ordination, but now, for the first time, She made the announcement to all the resident and visiting apprentices that my head would be shaved. This sent some ripples through the apprentice body, as people had varying reactions and responses. Some people were strongly attached to their hair! Others wanted to jump right in and shave their heads, too. It was interesting to note how much conversation was aroused by this announcement. My response was mostly one of curiosity, wondering what it might be like to have a bald head. It was a one-time experience, and a bald head is truly impermanent, usually.

People were curious. They asked the Teacher, *"Does she have to keep it bald?"*

Winged Wolf responded, *"No, this is a one-time only."*

Many times as Winged Wolf came by to give me a progress report on the preparations, She cautioned me to be mindful, keep my energy contained, stay in the silence. There was a momentum building and to some extent, it was impossible for me not to be affected by it. My entire body vibrated with the charge of the energy.

The Teachings Winged Wolf gave in the Temple each morning during the month approaching my ordination, were particularly potent for me. Since I needed to make so many corrections at one time and absorb all that was given, I was grateful to be allowed to attend. Her viewpoint from the top of the mountain, which is Third Eye Vision, spoke to the divinity in me, showed me, through Her eyes, how to view a situation correctly.

One week prior to the ordination, Winged Wolf arrived with a Savant apprentice who was to do the actual shaving ceremony. She had her clippers and camera in hand. The head shaving was symbolic of letting go of all attachments and she carried it out with dignity. Winged Wolf was filled with compassion for me as though sensing it would be painful. I was grateful for Her presence and companion energy. This was more stirring than I had anticipated.

The Savant was gentle with my head as she began shaving my hair off. Winged Wolf took several pictures at different points along the way. When it was finished, we were all stunned. I hadn't seen myself yet, except through their eyes, but I could see the effect was quite startling.

"Go look at yourself in the mirror," Winged Wolf told me.

What I saw was uncanny, not because my head was shaved, but because it was a different person than the one with hair. After seeing myself this way, I felt altered, monk-like, and surprisingly, it felt familiar. I felt certain I had been a monk in some other lifetime.

Observing people's responses when they first saw me also gave me pause. Frequently, I was not recognized. People tended to bow spontaneously without knowing my identity, and then a look of recognition would come into their eyes as it registered. The overall impact of this head-shaving experience was much more dramatic than anyone might have predicted, especially me. It brought my vow into greater focus.

That week flew by quickly. There was an informal rehearsal to get a sense of how things would flow; and that relieved some of the tension that was building in me. One apprentice was in charge of the music for the program, and from the little I was allowed to hear, it was beautiful.

Skycliffe looked so fresh and sparkling, adorned with statues of figures seated in meditation here and there in the rock gardens; there were flowers everywhere, and the apple trees were in full blossom, their white petals shining in the sunlight, some blowing off the branches in the gentle breeze and floating to the ground. The property was spotless; the Temple deck had been freshly painted.

The day prior to the ordination, Winged Wolf had everyone out in the orchard picking up the petals from the apple trees, blessing them, saying, *"I pick this flower petal in the name of the divine consciousness."* The petals were for them to throw at the end of the ceremony.

> I wrote in my Journal that, *"My task at hand is to find that place of detachment, where the mind is not attached to anything, and hold my attention there – to be an observer, even while I am a participant – this is the state I must live in to take the Vow of service I am preparing to make."*

Chapter 29
Ordination Day

Journal Entry May 26, 2003

It's here; the day has arrived—a glorious, brilliant, blue-skied day with puffy white clouds passing overhead. People are gathering all over the property, walking about, admiring the Skycliffe grounds, and breathing in the pristine air. They have come here from all over the US and Canada to witness the installation of the first Thunderbeing in our Order. It is their installation too; they know they can do it, because if one can, everyone can. They're seeing themselves walking down the aisle, taking the vow.

The ceremony begins; spiritual music fills the Temple. Then, I am given my cue; there is total silence as I walk down the aisle on a white carpet that leads to the cushion where my Teacher sits. I prostrate to Her three times, each time holding out my begging bowl; and three times I repeat the vow, each time with more conviction.

"I stand in the presence of the Transhistorical Consciousness, my root Guru Maticintin, and all Buddhas past, present and future, to offer myself without reservation of any kind to live my life as a Transcendent Bodhisattva in service to others.

"I call upon the particular presences of Sakyamuni and Padmasambhava to bear witness to this vow...and I call upon the fearlessness of Amoghasiddhi to lead me into the boundless light of Amitabha, under the protection of Vajrasattva, the wisdom of Vairocana, and the all-powerful, transcendent Ratnasambhava."

My voice trembles as I feel the power of the initiation ignite within me. This is all I have to give; I am waiting to see if it is enough. The Teacher tells me to rise and opens Her arms to me; I have been accepted. Tears flow freely now. She has filled my empty bowl with gifts of amethyst prayer beads, a medal with the image of an eagle carrying a lighted torch in its talons, and the gold bracelet She had many years ago retrieved from me, to hold until such time as I might be ready to wear it. The bracelet has come to be a symbol of my preparedness to carry the power of the spiritualized consciousness. Now She is returning it to me.

As I stand there before my Teacher, She asks me, *"Why have you come?"* And I reply, *"To offer my life in service to all sentient beings."* She asks, *"Does this mean that you will put the needs of others before yourself?"* and I reply, *"It means that I live for the sake of others."*

Winged Wolf says, *"Arise, Wings of Change,"* and I stand while two of the savants place the white mantle of Thunderbeing over my head. I then kneel before my Teacher, still holding my begging bowl filled with the gifts She has given me in it. She takes the ribbon holding the medal of the Transcendental Bodhisattva and places it around my neck. She reaches out and takes my head in Her hands, bringing it forward until my forehead is touching Hers. She says, *"I love you,"* and I respond, *"I love you."* She releases Her hands and we part. I look into Her eyes and feel the power of Her love flowing into me, filling me and filling the entire room with its enormity. I have never felt such overwhelming love. Her being is pure light radiating outward and touching each of us.

I rise and take my seat, forever altered by choice and by vow. The Teacher gives a powerful Teaching about what it means for both the student and the Teacher when the student becomes a Transcendent Bodhisattva.

Then I speak from my experience about overcoming obstacles to enlightenment. Those present have an opportunity to ask questions, and they have many; everyone wants to become a

Ordination Day

Transcendent Bodhisattva. A hush then falls over us as everyone reflects on what has been said.

The initiation is complete; I have been ordained. The Teacher concludes the ceremony, *"May the Blessings Be."* As She rises from Her cushion, the rest of us rise with Her. We bow to honor the divinity in each of us. Then the Teacher begins to walk down the aisle. As She passes me, I step into the aisle and follow behind Her. There is absolute silence in the Temple. People's heads are bowed in deep reverence as the Teacher passes by them.

A shift occurs in the energy as I walk past. Everyone has been holding on to all the flower petals they collected earlier in the day. There is a moment when suddenly everyone is bursting with happiness, and they are ready to throw their petals.

In that subtle moment, my attention is drawn to the people who are queued along either side of us as we walk past. Now, on their faces they wear huge smiles, and they are looking at me as I walk by them. I am bursting with happiness as I feel their happiness. They begin to throw their petals. From everywhere, flower petals float on the energy currents filling the Temple, and fall on me, as I walk past; apprentices fling them joyously into the air, their part in the ceremony. There is deep reverence as my Teacher walks past, but as if on cue, as soon as She passes by, heads come up and arms are in motion as the petals are flung."

What Also Happened

A feeling of elation fills me as I savor the moments; each petal that falls on me adds to my joy of accomplishment, I am full of myself. There is a widening gap between my Teacher and me. I have been walking slowly, taking in the experience of receiving all this attention. She continues walking, steadily and humbly, head lowered in quiet dignity. I see Her and how She is, but I have been swept away in the glory of the moment and have placed myself in the forefront; already, I have forgotten my vow of service. I am being celebrated and I am on stage, dancing down the aisle like a happy bride. This is my moment; I feel I have earned it.

As my attention swerves from the selfless promise of the vow I had only moments prior given my entire being to, and resurfaces on the 'me' I had sworn to disallow, something happens. From deep within me, a feeling of pride rises: the pride of achievement, the pride of having arrived someplace. I have paused to enjoy a moment of silent triumph, to bask in the glow of celebration.

And there is a wonderment, about it, too. Can this really be happening to me? Have I truly become a Thunderbeing? All those years I worked toward it, it seemed such a distant mountain, and yet here I am walking down the aisle after having been ordained, so it must be real. My excitement builds with each step I take. More and more, my attention is turned inward toward the swell of emotion that floods my body. And in so doing, by turning inward to stare at myself and my accomplishment, I separate myself from my Teacher. Suddenly it becomes about me, a personal attainment.

In those moments of self-admiration and feelings of personal victory, my connection to the Initiation I had only moments ago received is diminished; my awareness of the oneness of the merger that had taken place with my Teacher quickly fades; more and more I am staring at myself. The result is inevitable. I fall backwards in consciousness. The moment I stopped to look inward at myself, the connection to the divine consciousness was severed. I am no longer united with my Teacher's consciousness. I have returned to my ordinary, dual world viewpoint. Only I don't recognize it when it happens. I am too caught up in the excitement of the moment. I fall without it ever registering in my conscious awareness.

Chapter 30
The Fall

In the days that followed my ordination, there was a wonderful feeling of afterglow and an incredible, sustained energy level that was charged. I felt comfortable and confident, pleasantly satisfied, and complete, loving and kind. It had all the characteristics of a grand honeymoon, the grandest imaginable, because it was a marriage of divinity; it was not dependent on another for completion.

Master Maticintin suggested that we begin to have some training sessions now that I was a Thunderbeing. She had this little elephant bag that was always by Her meditation cushion. It had been with Her for years. Back when we were at Between the Wind, some mornings She would carry a piece of paper into the Happy House and stuff it into that elephant bag saying, *"When you are Thunderbeings."* That bag was now stuffed with all the goodies She had been filling it with over the years for the time when She had a Thunderbeing.

The morning we began my first training session, I sat on my cushion, watching Her in eager anticipation as She rummaged through the bag, looking carefully at each scrap of paper with the secret words written on them.

"Hmm, this is where we should begin," She said, settling on a small scrap of pink paper

I looked at Her expectantly. *"What does it say?"*

"It says, 'extend your awareness'."

She looked over at me. I don't know what She saw in my face, but She continued, *"This may sound simple, but it is the key to unlocking all the* secrets. *This is the Teaching you must master, before you can acquire the Siddha powers. It is the first step.*

"So, what I want you to practice is this." And She went on to show me how to 'flatten my mind' as she referred to it, empty and extend it out ad infinitum into the universe, and the universes of universes. Although she told me in the beginning, just to *"flatten it out in all directions as far as you can, and with practice, it will expand further and further."*

She sat with me as I practiced flattening my mind until I had a sense of what the experience of it was like. *"Now, go and practice,"* She told me. *"We'll meet again tomorrow."*

As I left the Temple after the Teaching, I felt strangely let down. I asked myself what I had expected, and the answer came back, 'something more.' Off-and-on during the day I puzzled over my reaction to my assignment. Then it dawned on me. I had been anticipating some magic trick, like the day I watched Winged Wolf bring the little dead hummingbird back to life. The bird was clearly dead when someone picked it up from the ground and handed it to Her. Before my eyes, I saw that tiny bird 'wake up' from the dead and walk up Her arm until it was standing on Her shoulder looking into Her eyes. It stood there in relationship with Her for probably fifteen minutes before flying off to continue its life.

And then, there were countless times when I saw Her manifest something we needed. Maybe it was a small thing, like the time at the hardware store when they were out of the paint we needed. Suddenly, there was one can that appeared on the shelf before my eyes. And there were more private things that had to do with perhaps someone's health being miraculously restored, or for a dedicated apprentice, it often happened that abundance manifested unexpectedly. In my history with Winged Wolf, I had observed many 'miracles' as being the way life is with the Teacher. They were who She was. So I was almost insulted to have Her choose 'extending my awareness' rather than 'moving mountains!'

One day thereafter, Master Maticintin asked me, *"What do you want to do with yourself now, Wings of Change? How do you see yourself being of service to our Spiritual Order?"*

Her question puzzled me. I didn't know how to answer it. Was there something else I was supposed to be doing? *"I'm happy just as I am,*

Winged Wolf; I don't see myself doing anything different. What possibilities do you see?" I asked Her curiously.

"Well," She prodded, *"do you see yourself staying at Skycliffe? You can do anything you want to do. I can't make that choice for you."*

I felt uneasy and shied away from any answer that committed me to more than what I was already doing. *"I'm not sure what you are asking me,"* I told Her evasively. *"I'm forever a servant to you and the Path. I'll do whatever you ask me to do."*

"Or," She went on, *"might you want to go to Michigan and open up a satellite center there?"* This was more rhetorical than calling for a response, because She continued, *"Although you can do anything you choose to do, I really could use you to stand at my side here at Skycliffe as we continue to build a solid foundation."* Since I had been harboring the hope that I could do something that would put me in closer proximity to my family, there was a flicker of disappointment when I heard Her close the door to Michigan. I brushed it aside; I wasn't ready for that anyway.

A few days later, we were sitting up on the Teacher's porch at Samadhi House when she brought the subject up again. *"Have you been looking at the question I posed to you, Wings?"*

"Do you mean about what I want to do with my life?" I asked, stalling, knowing that was what She meant.

She waited, looking at me.

I began to feel uncomfortable; this wasn't going to go away. And I understood intuitively that She was really saying, *"Are you going to become my Ananda?"**

"Every time I look at what you said about my staying at Skycliffe, I feel myself pulling back from making that commitment." I hadn't wanted to say this, but it came out anyway. It hung in the space between us. I should have been filled with gratitude and humility even to be considered for such an intimate relationship with the Teacher, such an

---

*Footnote—Ananda was Sakyamuni Buddha's close personal attendant, and this reference to him was asking if I was willing to step into some large shoes, as Ananda was the prototype of impeccable service to the Master.

opportunity to serve. It pointed to quite a split in me. I worried that it might keep me from seeing my grandchildren. Worry had no place in the being of a true bodhisattva. But there it was.

"I figured that if I continue to do what I'm doing, eventually the clarity will come, and I will have an answer for you. Shouldn't I have a strong feeling inside of me about a direction before committing to something?"

She simply responded, *"You really should be thinking about what course you want to strike for yourself. Only you can make that decision."*

There was a stirring in me that felt like obstinacy. *"I didn't realize there was a decision to be made. Why can't I continue to do what I'm doing? I know there's so much more for me to learn."*

"You can, for a while," She replied kindly, *"but eventually, you still will have to make a choice as to what you want to do with your life."*

Shifting the attention, She asked, "How are you doing with the practice of extending your awareness"? Whenever She talked about extending my awareness, or flattening out my mind, She would take her hands and, like pulling toffee, pull outward from both sides of Her head, starting at the ears. Watching Her do that, I could feel my awareness stretching out, relaxing, and the tension that had been building during the first part of our conversation flowed out of me.

"It's not that I haven't been practicing it, Winged Wolf, but it is more difficult than it seemed when you first showed me. The first time it seemed natural to me, easy. But after that, my mind started resisting it; now it has become a struggle." And then I said something I fervently wished later I could take back; I said, *"Frankly, I find it rather boring."*

The expression on Her face when I said that is indescribable. She looked at me in total shock. "How could you possibly find extended awareness boring?! There's nothing boring about it at all. Boring is your ordinary way of viewing life, boring is samsara, boring is living with ignorant ideas and attitudes! Extended awareness is never boring. Does my life look boring to you? I am never bored. My life is filled with joy and bliss; every moment is an adventure, never boring!"

"I can't believe those words came out of my mouth Winged Wolf."

"Well, I can't either, Wings of Change."

And that was the end of that conversation. I left feeling totally ignorant on the one hand, because I could see myself as She saw me; yet what I had said reflected how I was feeling. What a dichotomy this was.

Our training sessions had basically come to a halt, since there was nothing further She could Teach me until I had some ability to be in extended awareness. And my resistance prevented me from learning.

An underlying tension developed as a result of this struggle I was caught up in, a tautness that was the result of the clash of opposing forces within me. Past experience taught me it would get more and more taut until something shook loose and brought clarity with it. I defined it as growing pains and told myself it would take at least a year to adjust to my ordination. *'She is trying to show you something'*, I told myself, *'but it isn't penetrating. Why is that?' 'Because you are being resistant.'* I answered myself. *'You think She is pressing you to make a decision you are not prepared to make.'*

I carried on inside myself, *'She thinks I should now be ready to face the world with inherent knowledge to guide and direct me. But I don't know anything yet.'* That was a startling realization. I always relied on Winged Wolf to show me things. I didn't have a real sense of who I was in terms of expressing the Teachings on my own. I saw a wide-open space with no definition, only vastness. It was overwhelming, nothing at all familiar, not like graduating from college and looking for a job. There was some definition to that. Underneath it all, I guess I was anticipating either the Teacher would have a strong sense of what I should do, or a strong vision would come to me that would give me clarity, but that wasn't happening.

> A journal entry dated June 5, 2002, gave a forewarning of things that were to come. In it, I commented, *"My ordination seems long past; it's back to work, as the Teacher focuses on our upcoming strawberry social to introduce Skycliffe to the community. I find myself irritable, uh-oh. What is this about? Was I so enjoying my solitude and time to explore that I'm reluctant to pick up the ball and start running with it? Or, have I achieved a goal that I had placed all my attention on for so long that now I'm not sure what I want next? The Teacher is moving forward while I'm waiting to see what is next. It makes*

a friction between us. Spiritual arrogance has also come to mind. Perhaps I'm full of myself. That's an ugly thought. Maybe by reaching this pinnacle, I don't have the natural drive to go farther, and the Teacher is ready for me to move forward. All seem possible, maybe all are true, but I'm guessing there is one underlying truth, if I can only see it. I pray for help from the Transhistorical Consciousness to clear my vision."

By now, Skycliffe's summer schedule was in full swing. There were many visiting apprentices, weekly classes, and, it was generally a busy time. But, there was one striking incident that stands out in my memory during that summer, because it was a shadow, a portent of what was to follow.

It happened one June morning prior to the morning meditation. I had stepped out of the shower and begun to towel-dry myself when the bracelet my Teacher had given to me at my ordination, the same one she had been safeguarding for me the past several years, suddenly snapped in two. As it snapped apart, I felt the energy of its breaking, and I stood staring at it, as though it had a life force of its own.

"*Oh, no,*" I said aloud, fear rising from my belly. "*This can't be happening.*" Paralyzed, I stood looking at my wrist where the two parts dangled, still held together on top by the clasp. My mind willed them to go back together. My mind raced as my anxiety increased. *'This is not a good sign.'*

And then, I thought, *'How is Winged Wolf going to look at this?'* I tried to picture my Teacher's face when I told Her the bracelet was broken. There was no way I could hide it from Her; She would see right away that the bracelet was not on my wrist.

I heard the gong sounding the twenty-minute alert for Temple meditation. It was time to get dressed and leave for the sitting. Hurrying, I put the bracelet in a bowl on my altar, finished dressing and dashed over to the Temple.

During the meditation, a memory came forward of a time I was with Winged Wolf on Orcas Island. She was holding out Her hand for me to return the bracelet to Her because I wasn't ready to wear it. *'No, it can't be that,'* I told myself firmly, brushing that thought aside.

The Fall

Back at Vajra House after the sitting, I took the two parts of the broken bracelet and gazed at them, wondering if they could somehow be soldered back together. That afternoon, the Teacher came over to the house to ask me something and I knew I had to tell Her. My stomach knotted. *"Winged Wolf, I have to tell you something. I don't know how it happened, but this morning the bracelet you gave me broke."*

She looked at me for a long moment, a puzzled expression on Her face. *"Let me see it,"* She said. I took it from the bowl and handed it to Her. She studied it for a few moments. Apprehensively, I watched to see how She would react, but She didn't show concern. *"My advice is that you take it to a jeweler and have it fixed,"* She said. Then She turned and walked away.

Without realizing it, I must have been holding my breath. A huge sigh relaxed the knot in my stomach. If She didn't say that it meant anything terrible, then I wouldn't worry about it. I put it out of my mind for a few days. It didn't seem so important to me now. In fact, Winged Wolf had to jar me into action by asking, *"What did the jeweler say about fixing your bracelet?"*

"I haven't gotten around to taking it in yet, Winged Wolf. I'll do it this week on my day off," which I did. I took it to a jeweler in a town nearby (about two hours drive). As I had anticipated, the jeweler looked it over skeptically and said, *"I doubt this can be soldered together. Why don't I melt it down and make a nice nugget for around your neck?"*

"Oh, no," I protested, *"this bracelet is a special gift and I've only had it a short while. It has to be restored as a bracelet. If you cannot fix it, I want the bracelet back."*

Again she said, *"I'll take it in the back and see what I can do, but I think you would like the nugget."*

This wasn't going well. Should I take it to another jeweler who might be more interested in doing what I asked? I tried again, *"I'm counting on your expertise. I'm sure you can fix it."*

"I'll do what I can," she told me. *"But I won't be able to get to it for a while. I'll call you when I know something."*

This conversation was bizarre; I could see how it was going to play out. Deep down, I knew I should have taken the bracelet to another jeweler, but I didn't feel like going through the hassle. So I left it with her, knowing she didn't want to do the work.

Several weeks passed and Master Maticintin asked me about the bracelet. *"Oh my gosh, the jeweler hasn't called me back about it. I've stopped by the shop twice on my days off, but it always has the 'closed' sign in the window. I'll call there right now."* This was like a bad dream. I didn't tell Winged Wolf this, but I was concerned that the jeweler had gone out of business. The shop had always been locked and dark when I went by there. Then it had slipped my mind.

The jeweler answered the phone on the first ring and immediately said, *"I have been wondering where you were. I left several messages."* That was odd because I hadn't received them, but I let that go, relieved to have reached her.

"What about my bracelet?" I asked. "Were you able to fix it."

"No, it was as I expected," she told me. "It cannot be repaired."

"Then I want it back as is," I told her. *"I will come by to pick it up"*. As I hung up the phone, I had the strangest sensation of déjà vu. It felt like this had happened before, and not just on Orcas Island. It was a familiar feeling. Nothing would quite come together; the dream images were out of synch. I could see part of it; how I had expected it couldn't be fixed and had then taken it to a jeweler who couldn't fix it, and now here I was back where I started, with a broken bracelet.

When I told Master Maticintin that it was beyond repair, She said, *"Give it to me. I'll get it fixed."* And She did, quickly and easily. When the bracelet was returned to Her a few weeks later, She showed it to me. It was fully restored and looked brand new. But She didn't give it back to me. *"You're not ready to wear it. For now, I'll keep it."* Then she looked me straight in the eye and said, *"I have the feeling you didn't care enough about it and so it broke; and then you didn't care enough about it to have it fixed."* Her words were tough as nails, but I saw sadness in Her eyes, and compassion too.

Silently, I protested at the harshness of Her words. Of course, I cared. But Her words ran around in my head and found their way to my heart where the truth lay bare for me to see. I hadn't cared, not enough anyway, or the bracelet wouldn't have snapped apart. And for sure, I could have moved heaven and earth to find someone to fix it. I lowered my eyes, unable to meet Her gaze. After that day, we didn't speak of the bracelet again, but the imprint was there, and I couldn't forget what She had seen in me, what I hadn't wanted Her to see.

Life went on. Summer was soon over and our missionary trip to Africa was in the forefront of everyone's attention. But underneath the surface of life's busy pace, something was stirred up.

> October 4, 2002, Journal entry, *"Life isn't quite the same anymore. I'm different. Still waiting for the big call to tell me what my life is to be about. Perhaps that's why I'm kind of flat right now; the enchantment of the ordination has faded and I'm in a holding pattern. Was thinking to myself, maybe I need to be stretched in some way that hasn't happened yet. I'm not bored, but not invigorated either, I don't have a strong sense of purpose. Where is my life headed? Would hate to think I've come all this way only to be starting over again with the same questions I began with.'* And then, *'May not write again until after October 27 when we return from Africa. I wonder who I'll be then and what I'll have to say."*

Unwanted feelings began to surface in me; I felt unsure of myself in this new place, and watched helplessly as I reverted to old, familiar behaviors. I felt comfortable in a counseling type role, and often I would talk with apprentices who had questions, problems or concerns. As we strolled around the grounds, occasionally I would see Master Maticintin passing by. In the past, out of respect for my Teacher, I would have paused in what I was doing, and in some way acknowledged Her presence, but now, rather than doing that, I continued what I was doing, without making any effort to greet my Teacher, treating Her almost as though She was a peer rather than my Teacher, one whose consciousness I depended on for guidance and direction.

Later, She reminded me of another incident when I exhibited this arrogant behavior even more blatantly. It occurred one morning after meditation, mid-summer. One of Winged Wolf's apprentices had asked to have a conference with me about a situation she wasn't sure how to handle. It was a simple, administrative type question, one that would normally fall to me to take care of. We found some space in one of the downstairs offices, and I pulled the curtain over the doorway to afford us a little privacy.

The apprentice had begun to give me the details of her question when the curtain was pulled back. I instinctively looked toward the doorway and was slightly surprised to see my Teacher's face, as She entered the room saying, *"Excuse me, I don't mean to interrupt you, I just need to get something."* I watched as She headed over to Her mailbox.

I paused in the conversation to wait while She found what She was looking for. *'Why is She interrupting us in the middle of this conversation?'* I wondered to myself as a feeling of resentment arose in me. Since I had become a Thunderbeing, my attitude toward the Teacher had changed, at first subtly, but now more dramatically. Even though I knew She was my Teacher, I was acting as though we were peers. Instead of rising as She entered the room and turning my attention fully upon Her, wondering how I could be of service to Her, now I felt that what I was doing was equally important; and so I failed to give Her the respect due Her as my Teacher.

In a few moments, She found what She needed and slipped out of the office, leaving me with a sensation of conflict. *'What just happened?'* I mused silently, feeling uncomfortable, yet not fully cognizant of the reason for it. I pushed my resentment into the background, knowing it was inappropriate, and returned my attention to the apprentice who had been sitting quietly during this brief encounter.

Looking back, I see a continuous pattern of competitiveness in situations and relationships, an aggressiveness toward having whatever I wanted in my life, a kind of dogged pursuit of it, and toward being center-stage. This pattern of pressing for what I wanted without concern for the impact it had on others was subdued prior to my becoming ordained, but it remained an undercurrent. There was that impetus to push toward a goal until achieving it; and in this case, to press the Teacher for an ordination, more because I insisted on it than because I earned it; so that, in the end I could have this experience of falling flat on my face.

Chapter 31
Satiety with Life - Leaving My Cravings for Life - The Teacher Drives a Stake in My Demon

The day of our departure for Africa arrived, nothing had been settled as far as my direction in life. That would all be suspended as we set forth on this exploratory mission at the beseeching of some Kenyan people who had pleaded with Master Maticintin to come to Teach them. I didn't know it then, but this trip was to become the pivotal point for what was to follow in my life, pivotal in that it brought my problems to a head.

International air travel was so different from the domestic flying I was familiar with. Winged Wolf had traveled extensively all over the world, so She was accustomed to it. The quality of service was much higher and a steady flow of food and drinks were provided. Each of us had our own movie screen with abundant choices of movies. For a while, it was entertaining and held my attention. The trip was long and arduous. I watched four movies on the first plane to Amsterdam.

During the second flight, to Nairobi, Master Maticintin began to talk with me about my lack of wholeheartedness since I had become Thunderbeing. She asked me, *"Why do you think that you are lacking wholeheartedness, Wings?"*

As I looked back over the scenario since May 26, I said to Her, *"It happened at about the three-month point, although stirrings were evident even earlier than that."*

"Anyone can sustain something for three months," She said pointedly.

"Winged Wolf, my heart isn't in what I do. I'm going through the motions, but I'm flat. Ever since the time you gave me that first Teaching on extending my awareness, I have failed to bring my mind into quietude and receptivity. My attitude is arrogant. I can see it but I

can't seem to control it, and I feel distant, far away. My heart is closed off, especially toward you, and I'm critical of other people and their situations. Instead of living in openness, with the divine love flowing through me, I have pulled back into myself. I don't know what is wrong with me."

"When you are not wholehearted in what you are doing, all the rest follows," She told me. "A part goes dead inside and there is no joy."

"What should I do?" I asked Her.

"Give yourself to whatever you do, wherever you decide to go," She said. *"How can you be wholehearted when you won't commit to anything?"*

There it was again, the commitment talk. *"How can I commit to something I am unable to see?"* Once again, I backed away from the conversation. And She didn't press it further.

I had assumed the seventh bodhisattva level meant that life would be a series of smooth, ever-spiraling upward growth experiences. But it hadn't been that way for me.

Africa was an experience unlike anything I had encountered before. When we finally arrived in the town of our destination, the chaos of sounds, smells, sights, which were unimaginable in contrast to our western culture, overwhelmed my senses. Three million people lived on the plateau where Kisii Town was located, and all of them were in the streets doing something, and with them, were all sorts of animals. Roads were little more than hard earth, and they were cluttered with vehicles, people, animals, bicycles, and goods for sale. Driving was hazardous, not only because of the myriad pedestrians and animals in the road, but the potholes were huge. When it rained, and it did everyday, the roads became slick and dangerous, running with red slippery mud.

From the first moment of putting our feet on the ground, several things became apparent: first, we were welcome, because we were perceived as having money; second, communication was difficult, because the Kenyans had their own agenda and any time we said 'no' to something, they took it to mean 'yes.'

Late the first night we spent in the Catholic Guest House, where we stayed for lack of better accommodations, Winged Wolf knocked on my door. I was in bed, not yet asleep, and jumped up when I heard the knock. *"Let's take a walk,"* She said tersely, looking grim. I threw on some clothes and we headed to the courtyard. We had been warned not to venture outside of our walled community after 6pm, so we walked back and forth on the driveway.

"I have a bad feeling about this," She told me. *"The people who greeted us had their own agenda, telling us how it will be. It's not the way a spiritual Teacher works. I can bend to meet their demands, but only so far. If the situation can't be turned around tomorrow, we're leaving."*

"What do you mean by 'turned around,' Winged Wolf?" I asked Her.

"They have to come to an understanding that I came here to Teach them. It is apparent that their reason for having us is not the reason we came. I came to Teach the hundreds they said were already studying the Teachings from the website. Now we are told there are only ten people, and they want us to give them money we don't have. There's chaos here, but there is plenty of food, etc."

After returning to our rooms, I tried to get a perspective on what was happening. I thought perhaps Winged Wolf was being hasty, after only one brief meeting, in drawing such a drastic conclusion that we would leave if things weren't turned around in a day! This was such a different culture from what we were used to. Perhaps what she was seeing in their behavior was an expression of an unconscious cultural attitude.

We ended up staying on for another ten days; some of those days were high points. There was a small core group of 'leaders' who expressed interest in becoming students and propagating the Teachings within their communities. But interspersed with the highs were late night walks, as Winged Wolf struggled with the underlying expectations they had that She would take care of all their needs, plus build a monastery for them and provide teachers to live in it and teach them; but first, they wanted the money. It seemed insincere to Her. And to a point, She was willing to do what they requested, but it all hinged on them being willing to give up their agenda and surrender to the Teacher's guidance. That theme persisted during our entire trip and was never resolved.

And my attitude made it doubly difficult for the Teacher, because She had to try to penetrate my wall of arrogance toward Her while trying to penetrate the Kenyan attitudes as well.

One afternoon after a particularly difficult day in which I had argued with Her about something, Winged Wolf came to my door. She stood outside in the hall, probably not wanting to step into my energy.

"What is wrong with you? Your attitude toward me is condescending. You act like you think you are above me. Are you jealous of me?"

I retreated into the room a step, *"I don't know, Winged Wolf. I certainly don't feel that I am better than you."* But secretly, I knew She had touched upon something that I couldn't explain, a feeling of superiority. I was observing Her, critiquing Her, and jealous of Her all the while I was trying to serve Her. And now I was uncomfortable knowing that she had 'caught' me in the act.

Each day, taxi cabs would arrive at the Guest House, either to bring the 'leaders' to meet with Winged Wolf, or to take us out into the villages. Either way, we were expected to pay for the cabs, the gas, the meals, the materials and so on, and we were not prepared. Before we left for Kenya, we had spoken to the leader there on the phone, sent many questions by e-mail, but received no information of this sort. In fact, they had made light of our questions, had been nonchalantly matter of fact.

Some of the people who attended the Teachings spoke no English, and others had a minimal understanding. The villages we traveled to were remote and getting there depended on the weather. If it rained, we could not go, and if it looked like rain after we got there, we had to leave quickly or we would be stranded there until the rain stopped and the roads dried.

The villagers seemed eager to see Westerners and gave us warm welcomes, sang to us, danced for us, but what they understood of the Teacher's message is questionable. Most places needed money, and it was easy to see that this was the underlying motivation for their friendly greeting.

The Teacher's message was simple and perfect for the situation She was observing. *"Be kind to all sentient life,"* She would tell them, *"they are divine just like you and I. And be kind to your animals, they are divine too."* Eyes opened wide as some of the people realized what She was telling them. This was not a message they had ever heard before.

Everywhere She taught about loving kindness to all sentient life. How much was understood is difficult to say, but that didn't stop Her from delivering the message. The hardest part was that Master Maticintin had rolled up Her sleeves and was ready to work, really work, but by the time we were rolling each day, there were barely a few hours available. Usually we were back at the Guest House by 3 in the afternoon, and that was frustrating for a Teacher who wanted to Teach, and had expected, based on what She was told, to teach great numbers of people, all day long and into the night.

It wore on Her, and there didn't seem any way to shift it. It was time for us to go. She made the decision one night as we walked in the courtyard. *"I can't do any more here this trip. They have to study the Teachings and get some foundation under them before I can do any more. They aren't going to like it, but tomorrow I'm going to tell them will be our last day."*

Several days later, sitting in the restaurant the evening prior to our departure from Masaii Mara, where we had spent our last few days in Africa, I decided the young man who had been our server deserved a large tip for his attentiveness. In fact, I had been showing off, using my personality to engage the young man to give us special service, trying to make myself feel important and to look important in the eyes of the other two apprentices who were with us. I knew deep down what I was doing and that it wouldn't serve the young man to over-tip him. Still, I argued, *'it's something I want to do.'* So as we were leaving, I slipped him some extra money and Master Maticintin saw me do it.

Afterwards, She confronted me; tuning into my thoughts She said, *"That was your ego showing itself. Using your money to make yourself feel like a big shot. That is incorrect behavior. You shouldn't be having displays of ego, not ever. And you knew it was wrong, and you did it anyway. That makes it even worse."*

And in Amsterdam, a similar incident occurred. We had been walking around looking for a restaurant that pleased everyone, and we walked for a long time. I was tired and crabby, and I longed to eat at a posh restaurant, but I saw that Winged Wolf was concerned about putting the others in a position of having to spend a large amount of money. So I said, *"I'm happy to...."* And I saw clearly where that was headed, and sucked it quickly back in. But She picked up on it.

"There you go again, using your money to try to throw a situation your way," She admonished me.

"But I pulled it back before I said anything, Winged Wolf. I saw it and I caught myself."

"Yes, but that is what you always do, try to get your way by throwing your money around, or throwing your personality around. You did that the whole time we were in Africa."

She was really disturbed with me. I didn't know what to say. I knew I had overstepped my boundaries with Her. I thought there were a few isolated incidents, nothing more than that. In Africa, I had felt my life force return, my wholeheartedness, except She told me later *"You felt more of a personality in Africa, that was not your divine self."*

After our return from Africa, it took almost two weeks to be fully rested and have our bodies restored to normal functioning. Then there was the excitement of presenting Africa to all the apprentices who had been holding things together until the Teacher's return. They were eager to see the video and hear every detail they could extract from us while the images were alive and vibrating in our minds. So it was a couple weeks before the Teacher turned Her full attention on me and began again to confront the demon.

The conversation began innocently enough with a talk during one of the morning sittings. In this manner, She could confront me without necessarily having the entire group know specifically what was happening. The sentence She chose to work with was from the bodhisattva prayer, and it said that to achieve bodhisattva level 2, we should have come to a point of *satiety with the world.* There it was again. This issue of non-satiety with the world had been an obstacle in my relationship to the Path since the near beginning of my apprenticeship.

Over the years, the Teacher had frequently told me it was the main area of my development that concerned Her. She used to comment to the group at times that *"Wings really desires the world."* For many years, I didn't even see why this was a concern. In fact, to me it seemed healthy. Further along, I became aware of the underlying issues of desire and attachment to sense pleasures and how they interfered with my spiritual development.

Satiety with Life

This particular morning when my Teacher began speaking about apprentices who lacked satiety with life, I foolishly wondered, *'Is She speaking to me now? Is it possible this is still an issue in some way that I don't see?'*

Quickly She put my question to rest by saying, *"There are even some advanced apprentices, bodhisattva levels 5, 6 and 7, who have not achieved complete attainment of satiety with the world."*

*'Bingo, there is only one level 7 bodhisattva in our Order; it **is** me she's speaking to. What is She intent on hammering home to me?'* I reasoned, *'Of course it is for the others, too, but I must be the primary target, since She chose to mention bodhisattva Level 7; I would be the one least expected to exhibit this flaw and, ironically, the one most strongly exhibiting it.'*

As always, I stopped by Her office after the sitting to see what was on the agenda, and She commented under her breath, *"I'm surprised you didn't run."*

"I thought about it," I said, recalling the image of packing up and driving away that had flashed through my mind during the talk, which had been scathing.

"You couldn't go off and live a solitary life," She said.

"Why not?" I inquired defensively, knowing She had plucked the image that was foremost in my mind at that moment.

"Because if you carry the seeds of lack of satiety with the world, you would soon be involved with life again; which, considering your vow, would be to your downfall. It may even cause your death."

"How can I correct myself?" I asked.

"It isn't something that can be taught," She told me. *"You have to be ready. It's a feeling, and you have to catch it when it first comes up. It isn't something I can do for you. You were arrogant when we were in Africa. I had seen glimmers of that in you previously, but never anything like that. And you aren't usually an arrogant person by nature."*

Images flashed rapidly across the screen of my mind, pictures connected with the words being spoken, and deep down inside, I knew She was telling the truth about me. Yet, even then, I could feel the resistance, the hard-core resistance to admitting anything from the heart. I made myself cold inside; I wouldn't let go. *"I don't know what to do,"* I told Her.

So I left and went about my day, alternating between righteousness and suffering. Finally, unable to stand myself any longer, I got down on my hands and knees and prayed to the Transhistorical Consciousness with all my heart. *"Please help me,"* I cried aloud. *"Please help me find the way out of this dark hole. I can't seem to control what is arising in me or the way I'm responding to it."*

For the next day or two, I felt a little better, quieter inside, but it didn't last long because nothing had changed inside of me. It was a couple mornings later when Winged Wolf picked up the theme again from another angle, and once again, She made a point of including 'advanced apprentices,' glaring at me.

In Her office after the talk, Winged Wolf tightened the screws. That tautness was about to be stretched beyond its limit, pressed into breaking apart. This time I could feel the ugly demon show itself. It's hard to describe what this is like, but it literally popped up to the forefront as She said something like, *"This time, I'm going to drive the stake into the demon."* And the next thing I knew, Her spiritual sword was out. I don't even remember Her words. Then I was walking out of Her office, dazed, feeling like there was no wind left in my sails at all. In fact, I nearly crawled home and promptly lay down on the bed, too tired to lift a finger. I was so listless, I wondered, *'Will I ever have the strength to get up?'*

How long I stayed there I do not remember. A knock on the door drew me out of bed. Someone had a simple question to ask, but it was enough to bring some life force back into me, and I managed to make the next sitting and carry on through the day. The following day, once again I dragged myself to the Temple and prayed for release from this misery. Later in the day, not surprisingly, because She is deeply compassionate, Winged Wolf arrived at my doorstep. I had known She would come eventually because She could see I was suffering and couldn't find the wherewithal to bring myself out of it.

"You've come to put some color back into my face," I smiled at Her, still feeling dead inside, but knowing from past experience that She would find a way to help me through this nightmare.

She saw the tears running down my cheeks. *"That means there's still life force. In fact, your life force is strong. I have no doubt you will be fine. You've always done this. First you look like death, white as a sheet, then after a few days of grappling with a problem, you come to grips and bounce back.*

"You have to kill the demon," She told me.

"It's dead now," I told Her, *"I can feel it shriveling up inside of me. I'm through fighting."*

Her eyes opened wide and She fixed me with them. *"That's not true and you know it. You don't really think this is over do you? It isn't anywhere near over yet. It has only just begun."*

"This is too painful to bear," I protested, feeling sorry for myself. *"I'd almost rather be dead than have to go through this."*

"Then you'd have to come back and do it all over again in your next life. Do you think you will be stronger then? You might as well deal with it in this lifetime. It gets harder each time you carry the karma with you into the next life."

Before leaving that day, She said, *"The demon is lack of satiety and it wears many faces that display many aspects of your ego."* Pausing to give that a chance to sink in, She continued, *"I stand next to you but seldom do you accept my presence. You are split. You must decide what you want and whether your two selves can merge."*

With that, She left me alone. For some reason, I felt at peace after that. There was no thought, nothing to mull over, just a feeling of being emptied out, a little tired, but otherwise intact. Whatever had just occurred pulled me round another corner. My heart was open and my arrogance was gone for the moment.

One of my fellow apprentices and a good friend confided in me, *"I didn't know who you were when you returned from Africa, and some others asked me about it, too. We decided maybe you were just tired."*

When I asked what she had noticed about me upon my return, she observed, *"You were curt in speaking to us, and your face had a hard look. Your face looked gray, and I couldn't feel your love. It was as if your heart was closed. Now, you seem to be yourself again; the color is back in your face and it is softer."*

It made me sad to hear this feedback and realize my demeanor had become so harsh and insensitive to my impact on others. I knew I was on edge, but somehow didn't realize the impact it was having on other apprentices. Whatever had arisen in me was pretty ugly to be around.

A few days later the Teacher said, *"I think you should leave and go to Michigan, soon, and plan on staying there. Take the dogs with you."* Her tone of voice told me in no uncertain terms, she was sending me away. What did that mean? She had never sent me away before. Part of me was happy to be going 'home' and another part was worried. Where was all this leading?

"All right, Winged Wolf, I'll do whatever you say." My head was spinning with the energy of what was not being said in this communication. I was eager to see my grandchildren for an extended period; still, there was a lingering uneasiness. My life was totally unsettled now. This interlude away from the Teacher was only a temporary break. What was going to happen afterward? I would have to carry the uncertainty with me.

Resolution

A Journal entry dated March 25, 2000, (just over three years earlier) — read:

> *"My next awareness is that I've avoided a level of maturity that is ultimate responsibility. It means totally looking at a situation and making your own decision. It means separating out, standing alone. It requires SOLITUDE, SOLITUDE, SOLITUDE, and SOLITUDE, with PURPOSE, PURPOSE, and PURPOSE in order to look at what's going on, what's next, what's there you aren't seeing."*

Sometime during that month of December, 2002, while I was in Michigan, Winged Wolf called and told me, *"I think I have found the solution to the suffering you have been experiencing. You require a time of solitude to release subtle and crude attachments. I recommend you spend anywhere from one to three years in seclusion to prepare yourself. There is no way to know in advance how much time you will need, which is why I have set the boundaries loosely.*

"You need some time to grow into those big shoes you've been stumbling about in. This solitude will give you that time. I'm calling such a retreatant 'The Jubilant,' because that is how you will feel once you have completed the journey into solitude. Take some time to think about it; I am sure there will be many questions."

At first, hearing Her words, my mind reeled in shock, and my response was to review all the reasons I either didn't need to or couldn't right now; but as moments and days passed, each of the obstacles that I had perceived was exposed for the illusion that it was, and I could see there was no reality to any of them. It was clearly the next step.

There were some details to be worked out, such as informing my husband and family that I was going to be gone for such a lengthy period. How would they react to this? *'Does it matter?'* I asked myself. *'Not really,'* came the reply. Naturally, I would prefer to have those closest to me, especially my husband, be supportive (and he was), but ultimately, this was my decision and something I needed to do regardless of anyone else's opinion. I told Winged Wolf that I was willing to go forward with the retreat. We set the date.

And at dawn on the morning of February 1, 2003, I entered the solitude.

EPILOGUE

The Pieces Fall into Place

It has been nearly two years since my ordination, and one year since entering the silence. Writing this book has been both a healing and an enlightening work-in-progress. Of all the experiences I have had during these two years, there is one that stands out as most pivotal to the understanding of my fall.

Journal Entry

I have just returned from being called to my Teacher. Over the long and painful months, She has helped me piece together the puzzle of my rise and fall, and today She has given me the final piece.

The feelings of pride and personal triumph that I experienced during those moments after my Initiation would no doubt be considered quite normal in the world at large where material gain, competition and personal accomplishment are all an accepted part of the modus operandi. But in the higher spiritual realms, such egoistic feelings and attitudes are non-existent. They are transmuted into the spiritualized consciousness, which knows only divine love and compassion. And that is not something that can be pretended.

A true Thunderbeing would have been aware of the thoughts and feelings of those around them only as an observer, not as a participant. They would have been untouched by them in any personal sense of accomplishment. Their mind would have been so calm and serene, so completely merged with the Teacher that there would be no ego self at all. If that had been the case, I would have walked as one with my Teacher down the aisle and out of the Temple, but I was not there with Her.

"Do you recall the photograph from your ordination?" She asked me. I nodded, seeing the image of it in my mind's eye.

"It always bothered me," She continued.

When I heard Her use the word 'bothered,' immediately my attention was on alert. That picture had been on Her wall for a long time after the Initiation, and for me, it had represented the expression of my great joy at becoming a Thunderbeing. Not long ago, She had taken it off the wall in Her office, a silent acknowledgment of its falsity.

"Oh, you were happy and joyous, yes, but it was a self-absorbed kind of happiness. It was not the joy of one who has merged with the Oneness. It was the joy of an individual who has accomplished something of great importance to them."

My heart sank, and I sucked in my breath as though struck. Concurrently, the memory of that moment flashed before me, and I saw it as She had already seen it. It was the joy of ego seeing itself in stardom. As often as I had gazed at the image in that picture, it had never once penetrated my awareness that my joy was personality-based. Yet it was so obvious to me now.

"I remember walking down the aisle," She told me, "and feeling like there was no one behind me, no one at my back. It's because you had already fallen. If there had been a Thunderbeing at my back, I would have felt the expandedness of our merger. But I did not."

Thoughts, feelings and images bombarded me as She painted the picture and I saw it from Her eyes. It was as though someone had exploded a bomb inside of me, and for a few moments, all was chaos, torn bits and pieces floating randomly in my mind. It literally exploded the image of my experience of the Initiation and destroyed it. It had been a false image. What a bittersweet realization. I had risen and fallen almost simultaneously with the Initiation. I had become the ego-driven star, the number one that I had always wanted to be, and in so doing, sealed my downward fall. I had left my Teacher and lost consciousness before we ever walked out of the Temple.

Her words, 'no one at my back,' reverberated in me, tore at me. I had left Her and let Her walk out of the Temple alone.

Seeing me shrink in the chair as I absorbed the impact of this realization, She spoke encouragingly. "Knowing this should be liberating to you. It is the missing piece, the one that puts everything into perspective. You took your vows with great sincerity; then you rose, turned around and looked out into the room, and you fell. All the rest that followed was the aftermath of your fall."

This realization brought my story full circle. The puzzle had been pieced together and was complete. Where the silence leads me from here is another story.

"One day, maybe this lifetime, maybe another, but one day, you will see from the perspective of the divine consciousness."

Wisdom Master Maticintin
-- from Chapter 17: *The Value of Life* p.231

HÜMÜH:
The Fourth School of Buddhism

Before the dawn of HÜMÜH in April of 1992, there were three schools of Buddhism, or three main systems of attaining the Buddha Consciousness, also referred to as the Awakened Consciousness. These are categorically named 1) Vipassana (India), 2) Zen (Japan), and 3) Tibetan. Each of these schools has its own set of Teachings, practices and rituals that are characteristic to the view of the Teachings propagated by the individual school. Viewing each school as a flower that contains a fundamental Buddha quality or attribute, HÜMÜH, the fourth school of Buddhism, or western world Buddhism, extracts the nectar or essential essence of the Teachings and practices from each school to combine the three with a fourth view, or fourth school that expounds life as a transcendental dreamtime, which opens the door to proliferate the fully enlightened consciousness and is under the protection of the Transhistorical Consciousness.

The essential Teachings of HÜMÜH encompass loving kindness and compassion toward all living beings, and they contain specific practices for opening the heart. The practitioner of HÜMÜH can become a Bodhisattva, a person who consciously acts for the benefit of others in his/her pursuit of his/her own enlightenment. Bodhisattva action and meditation are combined with shamanic healing and systems of alchemy through the transcendental transformations of energy, pure-vision, non-duality, equanimity, and spontaneity. Since it recognizes life as the dreamtime in which all situations can be transmuted, and since all knowledge is at hand, HÜMÜH employs the skillful and powerful creative practices, initiations and mantras that lead to transcendental awakenings.

Two additional essential instruments of HÜMÜH practitioners are: 1) *The Wish-Fulfilling Gem Mantra*, a sixty-six stanza mantra mostly in Sanskrit, which is chanted daily for the cultivation of the enlightened mind; and 2) TaiKar Chi, an ancient pre-martial art system of stillness movement that opens the heart and quiets the mind.

The Path of HÜMÜH has an extensive home-study course, comprised of Teaching instruction mailed monthly to students, as well as a 220-acre monastery, retreat and empowerment center located 42 miles across the United States border in Canada. There are HÜMÜH study groups throughout the Americas, Europe and Asia.

About the Author...

Since her youth in Detroit, Michigan, Sharon Shier has always had a curiosity about life, a penchant for journaling, and an interest in the dynamics at work in the evolution of human consciousness. Prior to obtaining her Masters Degree in social work, Sharon worked for the city's Department of Social Services. Post Masters Degree, she held a daytime position in one of Detroit's large inner-city public school systems as a social worker, while also maintaining an evening private practice as a psychotherapist.

In 1992, Sharon began her apprenticeship with Wisdom Master Maticintin, who is both a Buddhist Monk and a Shaman. Her more than a decade of studies and spiritual formation activities involved her in travels to various parts of the United States and North America, notably, Arizona, the San Juan Islands of Washington State, and finally, the woods of British Columbia.

Sharon was ordained in May of 2002. At the time of this writing, she is on silent retreat at the HÜMÜH Buddhist Monastery in Westbridge, B.C., Canada. She is sometimes seen shoveling the horse paddock or walking by the quiet beauty of the Kettle River with a golden retriever called Dallas and a small, white poodle named Minnie Pearl.

The Awakening Stone

The Awakening Stone is a profoundly stirring spiritual adventure story. It seizes the imagination of its readers and propels them into a daring, no-holds-barred journey of multi-dimensional exploration that eventually transcends every limitation of the conventional mind.

Written in a vivid and visual style, this is the compelling saga of a young woman, Deetra, who is invited to become one of the Askan, the legendary crystal bearers and seers of her people. Deetra's quest begins as a lyrical tale; however, it rapidly becomes an exploration of such mature depth and spiritual boldness that it challenges our very view of self and what we call the limits of the world we live in.

Poignantly accurate and humanly honest, there are moments in *Awakening Stone*, when, along with Deetra, we become absolutely transfixed with awe or frankly terrified at the sudden recognition of both our potential and our responsibility. We discover that we are beings whose consciousness actually creates the world around us. The author's clear and stunning grasp of the mechanics of spiritual law lead Deetra and the reader to see our amazing capacity for freedom. It is the freedom to choose a love vast enough to go beyond the illusions of warring dualities and realize our ultimate Oneness.

The Awakening Stone is itself a jewel—a crystalline viewing device, through whose facets the reader is empowered to perceive from the heightened awareness that is hidden treasure within each of us.

366 pages $24.95 US

website: www.HUMUH.org